Peter J. (Peter Joseph) Hamilton

Colonial Mobile

An Historical Study, Largely from Original Sources, of the Alabama-Tombigbee

Peter J. (Peter Joseph) Hamilton

Colonial Mobile

An Historical Study, Largely from Original Sources, of the Alabama-Tombigbee

ISBN/EAN: 9783337144401

Printed in Europe, USA, Canada, Australia, Japan

Cover: Foto ©ninafisch / pixelio.de

More available books at **www.hansebooks.com**

COLONIAL MOBILE

An Historical Study, largely from
Original Sources, of the Alabama-
Tombigbee Basin from the Discovery of Mobile Bay in 1519
until the Demolition of
Fort Charlotte
in 1821

BY

PETER J. HAMILTON, A. M.

LATE FELLOW OF PRINCETON; AUTHOR OF "RAMBLES IN HISTORIC LANDS," ETC.

ILLUSTRATED

BOSTON AND NEW YORK
HOUGHTON, MIFFLIN AND COMPANY
The Riverside Press, Cambridg.
1897

I.

PREFACE.

I HAVE endeavored in this book to paint the exploration, settlement, and early development of the section of our country which is tributary to the Alabama-Tombigbee river basin. The vast region draining to Mobile Bay shows much diversity of soil, elevation, and climate, and is not less rich historically than in natural features. For here Indians, Spaniards, French, and English have lived and ruled before the American republic was born.

And yet it is an unexhausted, in part an almost untrodden, literary field. Spain, France, and England lost the territory so long ago as to have lost likewise interest in its history. It has, too, so long been severed from the Mississippi valley, which was colonized from its shores, that the historians of modern Louisiana have known personally but little of this the original seat of that great empire, and have devoted their attention mainly to the later growth which centred on the lower Mississippi. And, on the other hand, the Americans, who made the basin and port of Mobile their own, approached from the north, where traces of earlier influence were slightest, and have now all but completely obliterated, even about Mobile, the Latin elements. An old-time local chronicler excused the meagreness of his earlier work with the remark that the French and Spanish times were hardly worthy of record, and that their land titles had only served to complicate and retard American enterprise.

Some day the archæologist will go yet farther back, and throw light on the southern mounds and canals and shell banks which, near Mobile as elsewhere, far antedate the white man, and make European epochs inappropriate, if not indeed too recent, to mark the divisions of American history. But the Mobile basin, from the Tennessee watershed to the Gulf, was the seat of an important history from the early part of the sixteenth century of even our era. Within these three centuries taken for our present theme came the discovery by the Spanish, exploration by the French, and the growth which we shall find under the French, English, Spanish, and Americans alike.

And during much of that time, too, this was not done in a corner. The Mobile basin and port were explored by Piñeda, Bazares, De Soto, and other Spaniards, both before and after the greater Mississippi was discovered, and the whole was repeatedly mapped and claimed for Charles V. and his successors.

When the curtain lifts, over a century later, Iberville of France is taking up the plans of murdered La Salle, and from the capitals on Mobile River the Le Moyne brothers direct the settlement of the Mississippi as well as of the Alabama-Tombigbee basin, and oversee the intercourse with the natives and commerce with Europe. Iberville, Bienville, Chateaugué, Penicaut, Davion, St. Denis, John Law, De Lusser, Grondel, and other famous men become familiar to us about Fort Louis, afterwards Fort Condé, and the outposts up the Tombigbee and Alabama rivers are not less centres of Indian trade than of French influence against the growing English colonies on the Atlantic coast.

This remained true even after Mobile sank from her proud preëminence as capital to be but the head of the eastern department, but at last those English became masters of half of Louisiana. And yet Mobile then, severed from her old country and associations, under Haldimand, Farmer, Durnford, and other Englishmen, largely recovered her touch with that eastern half of the Mississippi valley by communication through Bayou Manchac (or Iberville), until excesses of the soldiers brought the place into unnecessary discredit on the score of health.

Galvez drove out the English, and for some years Spain seemed about to reëstablish her vast American empire. But the rapid development of the United States was to make this period one of transition; and Panton, Espejo, Eslava, Price, Favre, and others are as memorable for the great land grants which were to become valuable under another government as for themselves and their own history.

Still, in one way Wilkinson's capture of Mobile, the Creek War, the defence of Fort Bowyer, the development of the city which led to destruction of its old Latin fort, are even more attractive. For Sam Dale, Jerry Austill, Sam Mims, and George S. Gaines are every way closer to us than Bienville, Farmer, or even Forbes. They open the American period, and are akin to us as well as interesting historically. But, because they do introduce a modern period, they close the colonial epoch of Mobile and its river system. They bring us to a time, within the memory of men now living, when this district lost its individuality by merger into the greater sisterhood of American States.

Others have partly studied the Latin past. The works of Monette and Pickett and Meek of Mississippi and Alabama before the Civil War were as valuable as those of Martin and Gayarré of Louisiana, and it is a public loss that the rich learning of W. T. Walthall, W. S. Wyman, and others has not thus far been put in a form accessible to historical students. To them I yield their full meed of praise, and this book on many pages refers to their work and adopts it.

But geographical research shows the full Spanish exploration of Mobile Bay under other names, and the Mobile church records from 1704, perhaps by myself first thoroughly studied, not less than the invaluable publications of Margry in France, make the French period almost a new thing. The papers of General Haldimand, only lately become accessible through Canadian enterprise, and the search made on my behalf by experts in the British colonial offices, throw undreamed-of light on the English times, and reveal that obscure epoch to us in a surprising manner. The land and court records, too, which survive at Mobile, enable us to restore Spanish Mobile as of yesterday: strange it is that they have so long escaped attention. The American State Papers, too, are valuable. Perhaps only men of my own, the legal profession, can appreciate the value of some of this material; and they will find valuable the summary of city land titles in the Appendix, even if much of it is not new to them. The American occupation is now first told from department reports, and the recently recovered corporation minutes of the town give us a picture of the change of Latin to Teutonic Mobile never yet in print. I have, at the apparent sacrifice of consistency and style, thought it best, in order to secure greater lifelikeness, to preserve the spelling of proper names as found in the authorities for the time under contribution. Family traditions have been used where probable, the old files of the "Register" examined, particularly the Reminiscences therein of George S. Gaines, and in fact aid has been levied from every source.

Among the illustrations are Biloxi Bay, Dauphine Island, and Mobile in 1711, which have been kindly furnished by the French Minister of the Marine, the map of 1760 unearthed at Washington, and Ellicott's stone photographed by myself. Neither these nor the pictures of old autographs and documents have been in print before. The other illustrations are rare, two being from Dr. Winsor's "Mississippi Basin," and of the map of 1824 now reproduced but three copies are known to exist.

It will not be the least reward of my years of labor if I show, what has been all forgotten, the important part played by my loved native place in the early history of the Gulf coast, if I can restore her statue to its rightful pedestal, and perhaps even write my own name in some humble spot upon its base.

The work has not been done in one place. At Waukesha was it first drafted, and the public libraries of Milwaukee and

Chicago were of great assistance. Later, valuable books from Harvard have filled out gaps in my own collection made during many years; but investigations and studies at Mobile, Bladon Springs, Wetumpka, on the bluffs of Mobile River, the eastern shore of the bay, Portersville, Dauphine Island, and other historic sites have aided me even more than books. The most of this volume has been written and revised, several times over, in the Mobile law office where my father so long worked, and especially in the pleasant study of his old home on Government Street, — to his children and friends a sanctuary. The enforced leisure of this fall (memorable for its panic rather than for fever) has enabled me the more carefully to revise the proofs, and even incorporate new material, particularly for the British and American periods.

And now my pleasant task is done. But I would not lay down the pen without recalling some to whom I am indebted for assistance. To the War Department of the United States and to the Minister of the Marine of France I am under special obligation for maps and information available nowhere else. The aid and interest of Justin Winsor have been gratifying. His death, but a few days ago, is a loss to historical study in America. Professor W. S. Wyman of Tuskaloosa, Erwin Craighead of the "Mobile Register," Thomas M. Owen of the Post-Office Department in researches at Washington, Gorham D. Williams of Boston, Douglas Brymner of the Canadian Archives, Louis de V. Chaudron of Mobile, with his well-selected books, E. S. Barnes, lately deceased, and Julius Eslava in examination of records, and J. J. Delchamps as to sites and traditions of the lower country, have, with others yet, aided me by suggestions and information; and Hannis Taylor of Mobile, while United States minister, at least found that there was nothing new accessible in Spain. The lamented Catholic bishop, Jeremiah O'Sullivan, greatly facilitated my examination of church records; and of the many who have contributed reminiscence, William R. Yancey, a survivor of the War of 1812, and who died but this year in Baldwin

County, should be specially named.   To J. B. Thornton, Esq.,
of Mobile, and Mr. W. G. Brown of the Harvard Library,
I am indebted for help in revision and proof-reading.   Most of
all, however, I thank that patient hearer and judicious critic,
Rachel Burgett Hamilton, my wife.

PETER J. HAMILTON.

Mobile, Ala., *November* 2, 1897.

CONTENTS.

PART I. EXPLORATION. (1519–1670.)

CHAPTER   PAGE

   I. The Country and the Natives 3
  II. The Discovery of Mobile Bay 9
 III. De Soto at Maubila 14
 IV. A Century of Obscurity 18

PART II. THE FRENCH CAPITAL. (1670, 1699–1722.)

     V. From La Salle to Iberville 25
    VI. Founding Fort Louis 36
   VII. Bienville 48
  VIII. After Iberville's Death 56
    IX. Life at the Old Fort 62
    X. The Great Change of Base . . 69
   XI. Crozat and Cadillac 77
  XII. In the Time of Law's Company . . 83
 XIII. Next-door Neighbors 90

PART III. THE DEPARTMENT OF MOBILE. (1722–1763.)

  XIV. Through the Chickasaw War . . 105
   XV. The Provincial Town 115
  XVI. Some Old Families 120
 XVII. From the Curé's Window . 126
XVIII. The City Map of 1760 . . 134
  XIX. In the Archive Office . . 139
   XX. Dauphine Island and the Coast . 140
  XXI. Fort Toulouse and Fort Tombecbé . 158
 XXII. The Seven Years' War . . 171

PART IV. THE BRITISH DOMINATION. (1763–1780.)

 XXIII. Briton and Indian 181
 XXIV. Major Robert Farmer . . . 191
  XXV. In the Time of Haldimand . 198

XXVI. Sickness 204
XXVII. The Tombigbee River in 1771 215
XXVIII. The Seventies 228
XXIX. What Bartram saw 237
XXX. Politics 244
XXXI. Galvez at Mobile . . . 250

PART V. UNDER THE SPANIARDS. (1780–1813.)

XXXII. Settling down again 261
XXXIII. Under Folch and Lanzos 273
XXXIV. Judicial Proceedings 280
XXXV. The Demarcation Line and the Louisiana Cession . . 291
XXXVI. Streets and People 304
XXXVII. In the Country 315
XXXVIII. Church of the Immaculate Conception . . 328
XXXIX. The Indian Trade 336
XL. Mississippi Territory 343
XLI. In the Balance 351
XLII. The Capture of Mobile 357

PART VI. AMERICANIZATION. (1813–1821.)

XLIII. The Creek War 367
XLIV. Fort Bowyer 374
XLV. Municipal Growth 386
XLVI. Maps and Titles 400
XLVII. The End of Fort Charlotte 406

APPENDIX.

(A) The Induction of De la Vente. (1704.) 417
(B) Description de la Ville et du Fort Louis. (1711.) . . 417
(C) The Ordinance of 1667 419
(D) The Spanish City Grants 420
(E) Marriages since the American Capture 431

INDEX 435

LIST OF ILLUSTRATIONS.

PAGE

BIENVILLE, AFTER MARGRY (Winsor's " The Mississippi Basin ") *Frontispiece*

BILOXY BAY (French Ministry of the Marine) 32

INDUCTION OF LA VENTE (Mobile Church Records) . 54

FORT LOUIS, 1711 (French Ministry of the Marine) . . 70

MOBILE BAY AND COAST, ABOUT 1732 (Danville) . 86

MOBILE IN 1760 (French Ministry of the Marine) . . 134

CADILLAC'S DAUPHINE ISLAND GRANT (Mobile Archives) . 140

VEUE DE L'ISLE DAUPHINE (Ministry of the Marine) . . 152

THE RIVER BASIN, ABOUT 1732 (Danville) . . 158

THE INDIAN NATIONS IN BRITISH TIMES (Bowen) 182

MOBILE ABOUT 1765 (Pittman) 192

BRITISH ADMIRALTY CHART, 1771 (U. S. War Department) . . 210

THE ELLICOTT STONE (from recent photograph) . . 295

SPANISH AUTOGRAPHS (Mobile Archives) . . . 304

MOBILE IN 1824 (Goodwin & Haire 410

PART 1.

EXPLORATION.

1519–1670.

COLONIAL MOBILE.

CHAPTER I.

THE COUNTRY AND THE NATIVES.

A TRAVELER, sailing along the north coast of the Gulf of Mexico in the sixteenth century, would then as now observe but two main features. The green shore is much indented by bays, some the estuaries of large rivers, while to the seaward it is protected from the main by a series of sand islands, forming from Mobile west to an outlet of the Mississippi a protecting chain. These low islands are thinly clad with pine and other growth; and the mainland beyond the Sound, sometimes swampy, and never rising into elevations exceeding a few feet, is itself sandy, but from near the beach inwards thickly covered with pines, oaks, and magnolias, often of splendid proportions, and loaded with majestic hanging-moss.

Of all the inlets from the Gulf none would attract more attention, if indeed as much, as that then as now called Mobile Bay. Its mouth is deep and narrow, easily defended, formed by a long point on the east side and an island on the other, while its sides extend in graceful curves from headland to headland far into the interior. To the right as you enter is a cove, a wider sweep of water, and the deep anchorage of the lower harbor invites the commerce of the world. The bay averages perhaps ten miles wide by thirty long, and from each side receives dark but pure streams, even rivers, which have their origin in pine-shaded springs of the inland hills. The eastern shore offers steep bluffs, sometimes bare and red, but often covered with oaks and pines. At the head of the bay come in between marsh islands what would seem to be a half dozen large rivers, but on exploration these resolve themselves into two main streams, the Tensaw on the east and the Mobile on the west, and their connections, — themselves, indeed, all one river forty miles above. The intervening delta is intersected by bayous, and may be considered one large island, as it was mapped by the British, or a series of islands in one bay or estuary, as by the French. The southern third of the delta is so subject to overflow as to be of little value, but much of the rest, especially on Mobile River, is covered only by very high water. Much of the western bank is also subject to overflow, but bluffs twenty-one miles, twenty-seven miles, and at other frequent intervals above the mouth, offer a safe residence. About fifty miles from the bay, this one river Mobile is found to be the union of two that flow in, the one from the northeast and the other from the northwest, the Alabama and Tombigbee of our day, both subject to the tide over a hundred miles up from the bay. With their large tributaries, these wide, tawny rivers drain the greater part of our Alabama, besides much of the present Georgia and Mississippi. Fringed with willows and reflecting the cottonwood, oak, and beech of the higher banks, which hide the upland forests of pines and oaks, they are navigable for hundreds of miles above the bay, and play a great part in the country's history, even before the white man developed the rich lands adjacent. The low land extends up the rivers for many miles beyond the fork, but bluffs are frequent along the upper half of the streams, while the Coosa and Tallapoosa run, often in falls and rapids, through romantic mountain scenery, before uniting to form the Alabama and Mobile.

The Bay, often brackish in its northern half, once abounded all over in oysters, as it still does in the lower parts, and also in clams and crabs, while trout, mackerel, sheephead, and other sea-fish raced its waters. Sharks and porpoises prowled almost up to the fresh-water tributaries, in which sported the sluggish alligator among trout, bream, catfish, perch, and their like, and on land the deer, bear, wolf, and small game roved the coast at will, while sea-fowl and land birds lived about the shore.

In this river basin and bay, indeed, consists the historical importance of what is now Alabama and much of Georgia and Mississippi. The great Apalachian range, that continental ridge thrown up parallel with the Atlantic Ocean in remote geologic times, extends under different names from New England southwestwardly to near the Gulf. It determined the location of the Atlantic colonies by limiting them on the west, even where, as in New York, a river partially pierced the mountains. To the west was the great Mississippi basin, almost unapproachable over the mountains, except by the passes to the headwaters of the Ohio, Tennessee, and Cumberland rivers. It was readily accessible from the east only by the St. Lawrence and Great Lakes on the north, or by turning the flank of the Apalachian range far to the south in these foothills where the waters flowing to Mobile take their origin.

This Alabama basin, therefore, had a double importance, — for its own sake, on account of its soil, products, and races, and then again as being a gateway from the east to the greater valley of the Mississippi. Other streams, it is true, seek the Gulf to the east and west; but they are not so large and do not drain so great a territory as the Alabama and Tombigbee, which unite to form the Mobile. Hence the importance, geographically speaking, of a city near that river and harbor, particularly before the modern invention of railroads could pierce mountains, and capital could divert trade into channels which have no necessary relation to natural advantages.

On the waters tributary to Mobile Bay were in the sixteenth century many inhabitants of the industrious Mobilian race, whose empire extended from the Gulf up through the rich lands which we now call the Cotton Belt, with capital at Maubila. This was probably in the present Clarke County, on the Alabama River.

This extensive race was a well-formed one, the men brave, the women often beautiful. Agriculture flourished, and peas, beans, squash, pumpkins, and corn grew profusely.[1] If the plates and descriptions of Jacob le Moyne, of 1567 (reproduced by Pickett), apply to our own natives as well as to those of eastern Florida, the Indians had attained considerable civilization. They lived in wooden houses at the foot of artificial mounds, on which were the dwellings of the chiefs. In the delta above Stockton there is still a large mound, fifty feet high, necessarily made of earth brought in canoes from the mainland, and near Blakeley has been found a burned clay head of much artistic merit.

[1] Pickett's *Alabama*, p. 68.

Arrowheads, pipes, stones for grinding, and other Indian relics occur lower than Mobile, but there have been discovered few evidences of permanent settlements on the Gulf itself, unless we except the shell banks near Portersville and elsewhere, containing human remains and utensils. Near the seashore in Indian times, therefore, the mockingbird's charm was unheeded, and the glories of sunrise and sunset lighted up the surface of the lower bay in vain; for Indian canoes were unsuited to rough water, and the savages have never been famous sailors. Hunting and fishing are more easily pursued in the interior than by the sea, and so the natives have ever readily yielded the coast, and fought only for the forests and the rivers. To the early white explorers, on the other hand, the sea was to be of the first importance. From harbors like Dauphine Island, they could carry on commerce with the natives and still keep in touch with their European homes. In the interior of Alabama, ditches about Indian wooden forts are not infrequent, and also the small mounds in which at certain intervals they collected the bones of the dead gathered from their temples. In all ages and among all races, graves, reverently guarded by the living, have been the most imperishable memorials of the past. Of these mounds few have survived lower than the latitude of Mobile, although they are frequent in modern Greene County, Alabama, and elsewhere in the interior of that State and Mississippi. Perhaps there are more east of what we now call the Tensaw River than on the western shore of the Mobile delta. It may be that the mounds and shell banks about Stockton and the neighboring waters mark the villages which Spanish explorers were to notice, although we know that in later times Mobile River and its upper tributaries were the main seat of Indian life.

The rough country between the Tennessee and the main streams of the Warrior, Coosa, and Tallapoosa, which now supplies the great mineral wealth of Alabama, was but sparsely inhabited by the aborigines, and was indeed to remain of secondary importance until the last third of our own century, while the beautiful valley of the Tennessee was not important in colonial times, and will not figure much in our story. Its western portion was within the range of the warlike Chickasaws, but most of this region was the seat of the Cherokees, who extended into Tennessee and Georgia as well as Alabama; while east, over the Carolina mountains from them, were the brave Catawbas. Creeks and Choctaws will concern us more, for they lived on or near the rivers that empty into Mobile Bay.

Patient linguistic research, applied to our aboriginal tongues, has produced as interesting and unexpected results as in the older field of the Indo-European races. While language is not infallible, for conquered or even conquering nations may adopt that of their opponents, it is in general an accurate test, and often reveals kinship and alienage not otherwise suspected.

Scholars like Grote in Greek and Gatschet in Indian investigation find it necessary to respell and recoin names according to their true sounds; but suffice it for us to reproduce their results in more familiar terms. For Cha'hta let us still have Choctaw, for Maskoki, Muscogee.

It seems that the Muscogee race, extending from the Mississippi to the Atlantic, from the Apalachian range to the Gulf, living in what we may call the Alabama Basin, broke anciently into an eastern and western branch, and each of these then separated into tribes. Of the eastern branch the Creeks were the most prominent, of the western the Choctaws, from whom in their turn the warlike Chickasaws seceded, and intermediate between the two branches came the Alibamons on their river. In the eastern group we find the Creeks and Seminoles, the Creeks being on the upper sources of the Alabama River and on the Chattahoochee, and in the western, close akin to the Choctaws, were the Biloxi, Ouma or Huma, Pascagoula, and other familiar tribes.[1] Despite the kinship, the Choctaws, themselves in Upper and Lower divisions, were almost always at war with the Creeks. Their disputed boundary was between our Alabama and Tombigbee rivers, near the Choctaw Corner of later days.

In customs they show a unity in their very diversity. All used the colors red and white, as indicative the one of war, the other of peace; they all had some kind of family distinction by totems; all used the ilex cassine for a black drink prior to war; all worshiped the sun in some form; and all deified the Master of Life. Flattening the heads of children and gathering the bones of the dead for reinterment were more characteristic

---

[1] Gatschet's *Creek Migration Legend*, p. 52.

of the Choctaw branch, public squares and the green corn dance
(*puskita*) of the Creeks; but in both the descent of children
followed the mother, both had the chunkey game, and, like all
Indians, they scalped the fallen foe.[1]

The Mobilian language was understood by all, but no certain
explanation of the word Mobile is given, unless Gatschet's
suggestion be right, that it is from the Choctaw word which
means "paddling." The site of Mobile was Choctaw, as,
strange to say, was that of the tribes on the Chickasawhay,
near which dwelled Choctaws incredibly said to be, with those
of Yoani, the only ones who could swim. The Choctaws were
tillers rather than hunters, and, while the northern division
were warlike, the southern were dirty, indolent, and sometimes
cowardly. The mythical origin of the Choctaws was from Nani
Waya, a mound fifty feet high near the head of Pearl River,
which lasted down to our own days.[2] The Alibamons had a
somewhat similar legend about springing from the ground between the Cahaba and Alabama rivers; and indeed the Creeks
also believed that they originated in caves on the Red River,
and that they wandered eastwardly in ceaseless conflict with the
Alibamons, whom they were to absorb.

[1] Gatschet's *Creek Migration Legend*, pp. 51, 91, 102, 153.
[2] *Ibid.*, pp. 95, 102–105, 109.

CHAPTER II.

THE union of Castile and Aragon, the fortunate marriages of the royal house, and the discovery of America combined to make Spain in the fifteenth and sixteenth centuries the foremost country of the civilized world.

The great age of Charles V. was as momentous in America as in Europe. It saw the Old World rent in twain by the wars of the Reformation. It beheld the greater part of both continents of the New World made provinces of Spain. The West Indies, the first fruits of Columbus's discoveries, barred off the inquisitive English, who from Cabot's time were thus driven further northward, and this made the Gulf of Mexico a Spanish lake. From it, according to the protection notions of that day, all other nations should be excluded.

Columbus himself always supposed that he had reached the Asiatic islands, and he never touched our North American continent, although he explored the shores of Brazil. The oxhide map of his follower Coza, in 1500, and that of Cantino, two years later, show Cuba and the West Indies in some detail; but even the Ruysch map of 1508, while exhibiting the islands and South America as Mundus Novus, has no northern continent between Europe and Asia.[1]

Hayti and then Cuba were at first the great objects of Spanish interest, but as their explorations progressed they found the mainland of North America, and it gradually develops on the rare old maps which time has spared. In 1513, Ponce de Leon, in a vain search for the fountain of youth, led the way from Cuba to the Spanish colonization of the Florida he named, and six years later, Cortez from the same island conquered the rich Aztec kingdom, Mexico, the seat, it may be, of the Mound-

[1] Maps in Scaife's *America*. For the Admiral's map, thought to be one of Columbus, see 2 Winsor's *Narrative and Critical History*, p. 112.

builders once in the Mississippi valley. This fired others to seek, on the shores of our Gulf, dominions which would enrich themselves and at the same time spread further the sway of His Catholic Majesty. The Mexican gulf and its islands became Spanish, well explored by their navigators, but unfortunately little is even yet known of their voyages. Their reports and papers may some day be unearthed from peninsular convents and libraries to enrich history, but for the present we have only meagre outlines and few maps. From them we learn at least, however, that Mexico (including also our Texas and the Northwest) was called New Spain, and that all east to the Atlantic was also claimed for Spain under the name of Florida.

Indeed, a Spanish governor of Jamaica named Garay sent out, in 1519, an exploring expedition to find a passage west of Florida, — still supposed to be an island. The commander, Piñeda, coasted along the northern shore of the Gulf from east to west. He explored westwardly until he came to Mexico, and there can be no doubt that he visited Mobile Bay. He could not well have missed it, and next year Garay sent home a map embracing his discoveries, and this shows it plainly. Piñeda or Garay probably can claim to have given to Mobile Bay and River the name of the Holy Spirit, although the Admiral's map of 1513 may be thought to show it also as Rio de la Palma. This is supposed to have been based on a map of Columbus.[1]

On this expedition, Piñeda reports that he discovered a river of great volume, and on it a considerable town. He remained there forty days trading with the natives and careening his vessels. He also ascended the river, and found its banks so thickly inhabited that in six leagues he counted forty Indian hamlets. The Mississippi has claimed this exploration, but it cannot be. The lower Mississippi was always marshy and uninhabitable, and the conditions all point to a site on Mobile Bay or the tributary rivers. From 1520, the time of Garay's report of his discoveries, the Bay and River of Spirito Sancto (or Espiritu Santo) is on most maps. Indeed, the indentations

---

[1] See maps accompanying Scaife's *America*, and the many shown in 2 Winsor's *Narrative and Critical History*, particularly on pp. 112, 218–221, etc. Cf. also, 2 *Narrative and Critical History*, pp. 113, 237.

of the coast and the eastern offset that mark Mobile Bay made up henceforth the most prominent landmark on the northern, as R. de Panuco (Tampico) does of the western Gulf coast. This seems to show it as well known and often visited.

The plans in Winsor's "Narrative and Critical History" (Spanish Explorations) are unmistakable from about 1520 forward. The pear-shaped bay within the coast line, the long eastern offset at the mouth, which we call Mobile Point, are plain. No other harbor corresponds, least of all the Mississippi, with its projecting passes. A recent laborious investigator was attracted by the discrepancy between the early maps and the modern histories which say the Mississippi was called by the Spaniards Rio del Espiritu Santo, River of the Holy Spirit, and Scaife's careful examination seems to leave no doubt that this was really the Mobile River. Dr. Winsor's maps seem to disprove Dr. Winsor's text, and in a later work he in part admits the Mobile claim.[1] The Mississippi is the greatest river on this continent, and very possibly the Spaniards would have named it for the Holy Spirit, if they had discovered it first; but they did not, unless the unnamed three mouths on the Admiral's map alone be it. It is not easily found from the sea. A century and a half later, La Salle, who had explored it thoroughly from above, missed the mouth while seeking it from the Gulf. On the other hand, Mobile Bay is easily seen from without.

There can be hardly any doubt, then, that the Bay of the Holy Spirit was Mobile Bay, the only one named on many maps. Its shape and location bear no other reasonable explanation. It might be that if the great Mississippi was known, it might have been erroneously supposed to empty into the great harbor we call Mobile Bay, and so marked, as was, in fact, later done on Franquelin's map of 1681.[2] But where is the evidence that the Mississippi was known in 1520? Who was its discoverer before De Soto? Mobile Bay has a large river flowing into it, — two, in fact, and it is not only begging the question, but making a very improbable assumption, to

---

[1] W. B. Scaife's *America, its Geographical History*, 1892 ; Winsor's *Mississippi Basin*, p. 76. Erwin Craighead, of Mobile, by independent investigation, reached the same conclusion, but his essay has not been published.

[2] Parkman's *Discovery of the Great West*, p. 410.

suppose that the river of the Holy Spirit was thought to be other than the Mobile River which does empty into the bay.

After they discovered the greater stream, the Spaniards really called the Mississippi "Rio Grande," a translation of its meaning; but they did not discover it until De Soto crossed in 1541, nor did they probably see its mouth until Moscoso and his three hundred survivors of that ill-fated expedition drifted down, in 1543, trying to find Mexico. Meantime a dozen maps had already outlined the familiar shape of Mobile Bay, and called it and the river for the Holy Spirit.

The first with the name seems to be that of 1520, sent to Spain by Garay, probably embodying, as we have seen, the results of Piñeda's expedition of the preceding year.[1] The Ferdinand Columbus map of 1527 gives the bay as if with a double head, but, as copied by Winsor, has no names.

Preserved at Weimar, perhaps brought there by Charles V., is a large map of the world as then known. It was by the Spanish Ribero, in 1527, and is one of the cartographical treasures of Europe. The coast of North America is shown up to New England, of South America past Brazil, in incorrect relations, perhaps, while the Gulf of Mexico appears in great detail, — evidently the part of the Mundus Novus then best known. No name is given the continents or the Gulf, but Mexico is called Nova Spaña, Yucatan, Cuba, and Florida all have their modern titles, and probably a hundred points bear names about their coasts.

On it "by far the most prominent body of water emptying into the Gulf of Mexico" is a double bay called "Mar Pequeña," Little Sea, which indicates that the water is salt. Flowing into this bay is the Rio del Spirito (our Mobile River),[2] and the bay is correctly represented as receiving its water through several streams. The Ribero map of 1529 is in effect the same, giving the name as R. d Espiritu Santo.[3]

Meantime, in 1528, Panfilo de Narvaez had made his adventurous exploration of the Gulf coast. Foiled in his attempt to oust Cortez from Mexico, he undertook, with the royal sanction, an expedition to Florida. Where he landed is uncertain, but

[1] 2 Winsor's *Narrative and Critical History*, p. 218, etc. ; p. 43.

[2] Scaife's *America*, pp. 154, 159.

[3] 2 Winsor's *Narrative and Critical History*, p. 221.

at all events, he found a poor country. After many hardships he reached the sea again among the Apalaches of St. Mark's Bay, and built rude boats to take his little army to Mexico. Coasting along to the west, it is thought he landed in Mobile Bay for water,[1] — possibly at the Bellefontaine which was to be so well known in French times. A tradition afterwards among the French was to be that the bones of his men were those found bleaching on Massacre (our Dauphine) Island. Narvaez's own boat was driven out to sea by the current of a large river, but some of his followers lived to make, under Cabeza de Vaca, that famous expedition which first revealed the country near the Rocky Mountains.[2]

The next visitor to Mobile Bay, of whom we have an account, was De Soto's admiral, Maldonado. Him we pass for the present, but to Spaniards generally the place was apparently well known. Although they kept their discoveries to themselves, as did each exploring nation, even the English Cabot, in 1544, had a map of the world that shows our bay with the river emptying into it, while the greater Mississippi was not known to him, and French maps of about that time, giving both the Mobile rivers, mark the western for St. Esprit. What appears to be a Spanish map, preserved in the Bodleian Library, similarly marks the western branch R. del Spirit. Santo, while Homem, in 1558, shows the name as applying more especially to the river from the junction to the bay. In 1570 came Ortelius's map, and on this Mobile Bay is Baia de Culata, Muddy Bay, doubtless from a visit when the river was high.[3]

Reasonably certain it is, therefore, that the river and bay of the Holy Spirit were those otherwise called Mobile, and that when Maldonado sought westwardly for a harbor for De Soto, his charts would point him to our bay as the one receiving a large river named Holy Spirit, coming from that vast interior into which we must now follow his daring master.

---

[1] Gatschet, *Creek Migration Legend*, p. 190.

[2] As to Narvaez, see, also, 2 Winsor's *Narrative and Critical History*, p. 242.

[3] See map in Scaife's *America ;* 2 Winsor's *Narrative and Critical History*, pp. 224, 225, 227, 229, 292.

CHAPTER III.

DE SOTO AT MAUBILA.

IN the fall of 1540 of our era, near a bluff on the Alabama River, stood the principal city of the Gulf Indians. Its name is given as Mavila or Maubila, and so that, too, of the yellow river below, on which canoes then plied back and forth. The place was surrounded by plastered log walls, pierced with port-holes. To the west of an open square in the middle was the dwelling of the "emperor," Tuskaloosa, Black Warrior, — emperor, for he ruled not only his immediate town, but also distant tribes from the Coosa and Bigbee to the Gulf. His residence was on an artificial mound, and overlooked the rest. About the square were large wooden buildings capable of holding in an emergency a thousand men each, and occupied by tried warriors, and beyond them were the wooden houses and bark wigwams of many others. Food and arms were stored up, and messengers mysteriously came and went between the capital and its ruler.

The emperor and his chosen men had gone towards the northeast to meet a pale face, who seemed one with the animal he rode, and who was traversing the country with six hundred men. One third of these were mounted, and all were clad in metal, and bore weapons that belched fire and smoke. Such people reminded Tuskaloosa of traditions of the gods, — traditions old among these Mobilians. But this De Soto was not a god, unless a god of war. Reports had come of his cruelty, and that he enslaved or killed at will. From Tampa, where he landed the year before, from Savannah's Silver Bluff to Chiaha, where Rome in Georgia stands, he had come, intent only on finding gold and pearls, and respecting nothing. He kept captive the chief of one tribe until he reached the next. With him were robed priests, too, who bore a cross and adored a mysterious box.

From the kingdom of Coosa on the Coosa and Tallapoosa rivers he was now advancing. Tuskaloosa's son had guided him through the canes and autumn forests, the emperor had received him in pomp, but with dignity and pride, the equal of his own, in our Montgomery County. And now they were at the gates, the gigantic emperor in Spanish scarlet, and himself mounted on one of those strange steeds.

Tuskaloosa felt himself a captive, but he showed no signs of hostility. He had the sacred relics and vestments of the priests, the pearls and treasures of the Spaniards stored, and their wondering van under De Soto marched with him into that public square surrounded by great wooden houses, such as they had not seen in their year's exploration. Music lulled them, and beautiful girls danced a welcome to them, and as the two were seated under a canopy of state Tuskaloosa requested that he be held no longer hostage. When De Soto hesitated, the chief arose and entered a house.[1] He could not be induced to return, and warned the Spaniards themselves to depart. An insulting Indian attendant was cut in two by the sword of the incensed Baltasar de Gallegos, and that brought on a conflict.

Swarming Indians drove the Spaniards out of the city with the loss of five killed and many wounded. Charge and sortie followed each other for nine long hours. It was a contest for superiority between numbers with bows on the one hand, and a disciplined few with armor and powder on the other. In bravery there was no choice. In this hand to hand conflict, the Indian fighting for his king and home was as brave as the European fighting for existence in a savage land.

De Soto led his men more than once even into the city, but as often was driven out, until the arrival of Moscoso with the rear gave fresh reinforcements and decided the day. Fire was applied, and by its light in the great square was the conclusion of the bloodiest conflict in our history. A few warriors and priests had held a house in the city from the start, and were now rescued. About were piles of dead, and burned in their homes were Indians who died rather than surrender. The spring without the gate was red with blood.

The Spaniards conquered; but eighty-two men were killed

---

[1] Pickett's *Alabama*, p. 28 ; *Gentleman of Elvas*, pp. 157–159 (French's *Historical Collection*) ; Biedma's *Narrative*, pp. 102, 113 (French's *Historical Collection*).

and forty-five of the horses, — an irreparable loss. Every one in the army was wounded, De Soto seriously in the thigh. They camped in the smoking square.

The brave ruler was never found, and doubtless died with his subjects. Six thousand or more Indians fell on this fatal 18th of October, and the Mobilian power was broken. The natives who survived abandoned their homes forever, and it is supposed settled nearer the mouth of the river.

It was many days before the victors could pursue their march. The wounded must rest. Stores and treasures of all kinds had been burned. There were now no sacred garments, no wheaten flour and grape wine for the mass, and thenceforward they celebrated only Dry Mass in deerskins. Even playing-cards were gone, but parchment was cut up and painted to supply that need of the army of gamesters.

It was a Pyrrhic victory. The soldiers talked of desertion. At Achusee, forty leagues below, at the mouth of the river, they now knew was Maldonado and his fleet awaiting them. But all their pearls and treasures were gone, and De Soto determined to winter inland.[1] The adelantado took counsel only with himself, and on Sunday, November 18, broke up camp and marched northward. It was a thunderbolt to the army, but they obeyed.

Where Maubila was is not certain. Several sites, particularly two, are suggested. The Delisle map of 1707, drawn at a time when there may have been Indian traditions still available to the French, locates it on the Mobile River, where we shall later find the Mobilians settled.[2] This cannot be disproved, but the consensus of opinion, from the time of A. B. Meek's article of 1839 in the Southron, has been that it was more probably on the Alabama River, in what is now Clarke County. Probabilities point to what is called Choctaw Bluff, where a spring and Indian remains are found.[3]

The whole of his route is uncertain, although there is a general acceptance of the views of Judge Meek and Pickett, who make him enter northeast Alabama from Georgia, descend the Coosa and Alabama to Maubila, thence strike northwest towards the falls of Tuskaloosa, and march onward into Mississippi.

[1] Biedma's *Narrative*, p. 104 (French's *Historical Collection*).
[2] See 2 Winsor's *Narrative and Critical History*, pp. 294, 295.
[3] See Ball's *Clarke County*.

But Spanish descriptions are vague and stilted, and the daring expedition cannot in all details be tracked.

How he fought Choctaws at Cabusto on the Warrior River near our Eutaw, passed west out of the Alabama-Tombigbee basin and found the Alibamos then living upon the Yazoo, discovered the great Mississippi in May, 1541, near Memphis, wandered west in search for gold, and finally returned a year later only to be buried in its flood; how Moscoso led the survivors, and in July, 1543, floated down its bosom with his three hundred and twenty men and discovered the mouth, and at last landed in Mexico, — all of this cannot be detailed here. Mobile was not yet to be connected with the discovery of the Mississippi.

For us is rather the story of Maldonado. At De Soto's command this admiral had sailed west from Apalache and reached a convenient harbor at Chusee, where he traded with the natives in the villages for two months. This he reported to the adelantado at Apalache again in 1540, and was directed to take back to Havana Doña Isabella, De Soto's wife, obtain supplies from Cuba, and in October meet the army at this port, by the river Holy Spirit.[1] He obeyed, and was in Mobile Bay at the right time.[2]

As we have seen, the news reached the general at Maubila, but no message came back. The fleet waited, but the army never arrived. Why, Maldonado did not know, as we do. He stayed awhile, watching the shores, and then sadly sought other ports. He explored and left signals everywhere, but in vain, and finally returned to Cuba, with no news for the distracted Doña Isabella de Bobadilla.

Other voyages yet he made to find the army. After two years he touched at Vera Cruz, and learned the fatal truth, — the army a wreck, the general buried in the mighty stream which he had discovered. The search was over now. But not Maldonado alone was grieved; the faithful Isabel learned it, too, and at Havana, broken-hearted, died.

[1] Biedma's *Narrative*, p. 99 (2 French's *Historical Collection*).

[2] Pickett, Meek, and others seem to think that the Chusee of Maldonado (Ochus in their books) was Pensacola; but the recent examination of W. B. Scaife leaves little doubt that it was Mobile Bay. (*America*, p. 153.) Biedma says that they believed the river they crossed just before nearing Maubila emptied into the bay called Chusee. (Biedma, p. 102; H. Ternaux-Compans, *Recueil sur la Floride*, p. 72.)

CHAPTER IV.

THE fate of Narvaez and De Soto seems to have deterred Spaniards from exploring the interior. For it was clear that there were no precious metals easily accessible, and Mexico, the West Indies, and South America received such colonists as Spain could spare. Peninsular Florida was partly settled, but the Mobile basin was left to the aborigines. The bay, however, was well known to the Spaniards.

By the year 1558, New Spain, Mexico, had become as thoroughly Spanish as it was ever to be. Cortez, it is true, was dead, but the succeeding viceroys were even better rulers. One of the best, Velasco, like Garay of Jamaica, sent out an explorer towards the north, this time to examine for purposes of colonization, and thus in that year Guido de las Bazares sailed on this mission. Piñeda had explored from the east, and now Bazares explored the Gulf coast from the west towards peninsular Florida.

Bazares accordingly, on September 3, 1558, left San Juan de Lua (Vera Cruz) with sixty seamen and soldiers in a large bark, a galley, and a shallop. In 29½° north latitude, he discovered an island, perhaps four leagues from the mainland. He passed within it and the mainland and other islands, and, as he explored all the coast, he observed that it was bordered by marshy ground and not in favorable position to begin a colony; nevertheless, he took possession, and gave it the name of Bas Fonde.

Now offhand, without prepossessions, this reminds one of Pascagoula Bay, with its low coast and several protecting islands.

Ten leagues further east, he passed an island and discovered a bay which he named Filipina, — for King Philip II., no doubt, it being the largest and most commodious bay on the coast. The bottom was mud, and the bay four or five fathoms deep, the channel three or four. There he found fish and oysters. On the shore were pine forests, oak, cypress, ash, palmetto, laurel, cedar, etc., and there appeared to be the mouth of a great river. In an eastwardly direction were high red hills. Game abounded, and he found a large number of canoes and huts, also maize, beans, and pumpkins. Bazares afterwards renamed this bay Velasco. He was compelled to stop his explorations here, and hence returned to Mexico.[1]

It is not certain whether Filipina Bay is that of Mobile or Pensacola. The depth within Mobile Bay and other characteristics suit Mobile at least as well, however, and the only difficulty is the entrance channel, given as three to four fathoms, while Iberville in 1699, a century and a half later, was to report that he found the bar only thirteen feet deep, although within, the bay had eight fathoms.[2]

The fact seems to be that there are two channels into Mobile Bay, an eastern and western. This led President Monroe, on the report of the United States Engineer Department in 1822, to recommend · the fortifying of Dauphine Island as well as Mobile Point.[3] At that time the water on the outer bar, from which both led inward to the bay, was eighteen feet. The western channel along the north bank of Pelican and Sand islands (which are but parts of one breakwater) was from eight to eighteen feet deep and a half mile wide, against twenty to forty-two feet depth in the eastern channel, which was about a mile wide by Mobile Point. The two passages were and are separated by a shallow space called Middle Ground, but beyond the west channel and in the angle between Dauphine and Pelican islands was an anchorage eighteen to twenty-two feet deep.

The west channel in French and earlier times, however, seems to have passed between these two islands from the Gulf into this Pelican Bay, and thence on into Mobile Bay, and did not come over the Sand Island bar at all. We shall see this Pelican Bay closed by a storm in 1717, and only since that time do we find the main entrance to be over to the east near

---

[1] 7 French's *Historical Collection*, pp. 237, 238 ; H. Ternaux-Compans, *Recueil sur la Floride*, p. 145.

[2] 6 French's *Historical Collection*, p. 20. See 4 Margry, *Découvertes*, p. 232.

[3] *Message and Documents*, March 26, 1822.

Mobile Point. In 1558, the Pelican channel may well have had four fathoms. In fact, it must have been deep, for the same volume of water had to discharge from Mobile Bay as now. If it sought the west channel, it must have scoured that out as it now does the eastern.

All the other features agree with Mobile, — the island passed as he came from the west, red cliffs, fish, oysters, game, and the forest, while the mouth of a great river not only is true of Mobile, but is distinctly not true of Pensacola. So, too, of the distance from the last bay, ten leagues. This is about the distance of Mobile from Pascagoula Bay, while that of Pensacola from Mobile Bay, if this is to be Bas Fonde, is almost double ten leagues. Besides, Iberville was to report Mobile Bay "very beautiful for habitation,"[1] while Bazares says his Bas Fonde was not favorable for colonization. It would seem, therefore, probable that Filipina or Velasco was Mobile Bay.

The expedition of Bazares had the definite object of selecting the site for a colony, and was thus very different from the exploration of Piñeda thirty-nine years before. A settlement was actually made in the summer of 1559 by Tristan de Luna y Arellano on the Bay of Ichuse, with 1500 settlers and soldiers. Where this was is as uncertain as much else in Spanish colonial enterprises. Shea makes Ichuse to have been Santa Rosa Bay, but it would seem more likely Mobile, if we are right in regard to Maldonado. The report of Velasco to the king in one place identifies Fort "Ychuse" with the bay of Filipina de Santa Maria, and in another place says the port of "Ychuse" is twenty leagues from this bay, and that soldiers and horses were landed at this bay and marched across. Wherever it was, the colonists suffered from a hurricane and loss of supplies. They undertook expeditions into the interior to Nanipacna, a large river town, and again to Cosa, where they were aided by the natives.[2]

Tristan tried to maintain himself at Ichuse, but his men had suffered so severely that they all but mutinied, and in 1561 so many left on the vessels of Villafañe, which called in the port, that the settlement was practically abandoned.

Ichuse is sometimes spelled Chusee, sometimes Ochus, and

---

[1] G French's *Historical Collection*, p. 20.

[2] Gatschet's *Creek Migration Legend*, p. 190 ; H. Ternaux-Compans, *Recueil sur la Floride*, pp. 157, 158, 161.

it is at least significant that as late as 1786, when the Mobile
district was in Spanish hands again, we have a grant of land
near Portersville on the Mobile County coast bounded east by
Ocas Island.

After the Spanish Armada of 1588, the naval supremacy of
Spain was in question, and her power declined. The English
in the next century settled New England, Virginia, and Carolina, while the French colonized the banks of the St. Lawrence, and either race was ready to dispute with the Spaniards
the Gulf coast. For the Spanish claim was nominal between
Mexico and peninsular Florida.

During this time there is little history for the Mobile district. The Indian traditions are more interesting than reliable.

De Soto's expedition, according to these legends, played
havoc with the natives. Like the invasion by the Heraclidæ
in the early times of Greece, there resulted a legendary rearrangement of nations. These now discredited traditions say
that the disruption of the Mexican empire by Cortez a few
years earlier drove northwardly races that were not equal to
conflict with civilized arms, but were too brave to yield.
Themselves warring as they moved, the Alibamos and Muscogees followed the Mississippi, the former to settle on the
Yazoo, the latter on the Ohio.[1] The Alibamos, after their
conflict with De Soto, moved eastwardly to the river since
known by their name, and, on the extinction of the political
power of Maubila, the Muscogees came southwardly and settled
on the Coosa and Chattahoochee. They were themselves later
to be named, from the many water courses, *Creek* Indians.
The Creeks and Alibamos resumed their hereditary war in the
new seats, and the Alibamos also carried devastation down the
river. The fair Mobilian country as far south as the Gulf was
indeed the scene of invasion and ruin never to be repaired.[2]
But, as we have seen, the actual rearrangement of nations
was within much narrower bounds. The Mobilians, Alibamos,
and Muscogees were of the same race.

The Natchez, with their sun-worship and ever-burning
sacred fire, are said to have emigrated from Mexico and settled
on the bluffs where a city perpetuates their name, while the
Cherokees had reached the headwaters of the Tennessee River

---

[1] Pickett's *Alabama*, pp. 22, n., 78.   [2] King's *Bienville*, p. 122.

from the east. They alone of southern Indians claim to have come from the north.

Between these the Chickasaws, unconquered and unconquerable, held the land from the upper Bigbee to the Mississippi River, and the more timid Choctaws, in four thousand families, lived as before on the lower Bigbee, extending southwardly to near the Gulf. The Naniabas ("Fish-eaters"), of Choctaw origin, were near the junction of the Alabama and Tombigbee rivers, and lower down on the Mobile were the Choctaw Thomez, or Tohomes. Coxe tells us that Maubila, shorn of its old grandeur, existed even after 1715, but he must refer to the surviving Mobilians who lived near the Thomes, in all three hundred and fifty families.[1] For while the name "Holy Spirit" was on Spanish maps and copied on foreign ones, the natives persisted in calling the river and bay Mobile. Indeed, it is said to have been the native name in De Soto's time,[2] the explorer La Salle, in 1685, recognizes and adopts it,[3] and it was called Movila, also, by the Spaniards.

On the whole, however, there is, despite tradition and romance, no reason to suppose that the conquest of Mexico by Cortez had any appreciable effect on the Indians of the north Gulf region, and none that the subsequent expedition of De Soto found or left these Indians in any materially different location or condition from that in which we find them in later times. To this there may be some exceptions, as in the migration of the Alibamos eastwardly, if they be indeed the later Alibamons, and certainly in the destruction of Maubila and the removal of the remaining Mobilians southwardly to their later home on the Mobile River below the forks of the Tombigbee and Alabama.

But the Choctaws, Chickasaws, Muscogees, Cherokees, Catawbas, and other prominent tribes seem to be too settled and agricultural to have had in De Soto's time any different seats from those where history finds them at the end of this period of obscurity.[4] If we do not always recognize them in the stilted Spanish narratives, it probably is due less to change of races than to inadequacy in the description.

---

[1] King's *Bienville*, p. 129 ; Coxe's *Carolana*, p. 235 (2 French's *Historical Collection*).

[2] Meek's *Southwest*, p. 227, n.

[3] Quoted in Scaife's *America*, p. 169 ; 4 Margry, *Découvertes*, pp. 233, 111.

[4] Gatschet's *Creek Migration Legend*, p. 49 ; Pickett's *Alabama*, p. 134.

PART II.
THE FRENCH CAPITAL.

1670, 1699–1722.

CHAPTER V.

THE history of the Gulf in the latter part of the seventeenth century becomes closely connected with that of Canada. It was from that French possession that the Mississippi River was explored to the sea, and it was from Mobile that Canadians under royal commission colonized the great valley and built forts reaching up to portages to the Great Lakes. For explorers and colonists we are indebted to that dominion, and particularly to Montreal.

The seventeenth century was the epoch of French and English colonization in North America, as the sixteenth had been that of the Spanish in Central and South America. Virginia, in 1607, preceded Canada by but one year, and the Mayflower brought her famous cargo while French explorers and missionaries were pushing up the Great Lakes and the country behind was becoming the seat of French civilization. Quebec was much like a town in France, and Montreal, though near the frontier, was as Ville Marie becoming a settled place under the priests of St. Sulpice.

The discovery by De Soto had been forgotten even in Spain, and no maps pointed out the Mississippi River, although Mobile Bay remained well known. And yet, as the French explored the lakes and came in contact with the Sioux and other Indians near the sources of the Mississippi, they could not but learn rumors of the great river. Possibly the earliest to report it was Claude Allouez, first missionary to that tribe,[1] and from time to time others added information. Where it emptied no one knew, — possibly into the Atlantic, near Virginia, possibly into the Gulf of Mexico, or perhaps even into the Pacific about California.

[1] Scaife's *America*, p. 156. For life of La Salle, see Parkman's *Discovery of the Great West.*

One thing was certain, — the way was long and dangerous. Even hardy wood rangers like Duluth were not ambitious to make the exploration. The journey might be made by canoe, for the interlocking of the sources of western rivers with those emptying into the Great Lakes had not escaped the quick eyes of the French. This knowledge was to develop into a well-ascertained system of portages, by which canoes were carried with little trouble over the few miles of divide between the sources of rivers and launched on other streams. But the hostility of savages and difficulty of long subsistence in a wild country were serious obstacles.

Robert Cavelier, of Rouen, more commonly known as La Salle, passed over a portage from the lakes into the upper Ohio about 1670, and descended at least to the site of Louisville. He seems then to have gone no further. The same adventurous spirit nerved the trader, Louis Joliet, but the higher inspiration of religious enthusiasm impelled the Jesuit, Père Marquette, in their voyage of 1673. Going down the Illinois, they found the mighty Mississippi and rowed on it to the Arkansas Indians, not without dangers from man and nature both. Marquette, from his adoration of Mary, named the stream for the Immaculate Conception.

But these efforts were tentative. La Salle was to be the true explorer. He inspired the French court not less than the new governor, Frontenac, and in Henry de Tonty, a French soldier whom he brought to America on the recommendation of his patron, Prince de Conti, he had an assistant who was to do more for him than court and governor together. La Salle spent years in preparation; for he was to take a force along to awe the natives, and money and merchandise to trade with them. He built Fort Frontenac on Lake Ontario, constructed a boat on Lake Erie, crossed the portage from Lake Michigan to the Kankakee, and, after losses and discouragement, founded in 1680 his Fort Crèvecœur on the Illinois River, not far from the modern Peoria.

The brilliant pages of Parkman tell not only of the overwhelming misfortunes of La Salle, but also of a silent determination which overcame them all. In the early spring of 1682, the voyagers were floating on the Mississippi, which he renamed for Colbert, the great French minister, and they gradually descended to its mouths. The Mexican Gulf at last spread before them. La Salle had made his name immortal. With fitting ceremonies, April 2, 1682, on a dry place near the sea, he took possession of the valley of the Mississippi and its tributaries and named it Louisiana for Louis XIV., king of France and Navarre. A notary recorded the facts, and among the witnesses we find Tonty and Nicolas de la Salle, the explorer's nephew.

La Salle proposed to make French possession sure by a colony on the sea and one or more forts on the river, but had to defer this until he could obtain aid and authority from France. So they laboriously reascended the river.

La Salle left Tonty as his deputy in America, and returned to France. He was the hero of the day, and secured all that he asked, for his Gulf colony would not merely give the French a foothold, but gradually make this great river as much an artery of New France as was the Canadian St. Lawrence. All France, from court to peasantry, followed the movements of this resolute man.

Beaujeu commanded the little fleet upon which La Salle and his colonists, in 1685, sailed for the Gulf. They missed the mouths of the Mississippi, and landed near Matagorda Bay in the present Texas. There Beaujeu abandoned him, and apparently sailed back to discover and himself map the Mississippi passes. This is a serious charge, but Parkman seems borne out by the facts, and the whole history of the French in America is unfortunately marred by such quarrels of leaders. We see it in Canada; we shall find it on the Gulf.

The colony was rendered helpless by loss of vessels and stores, and La Salle saw nothing to do but go overland to Canada. Could he even reach Tonty in his Fort St. Louis, on Starved Rock, among the Illinois, all might be well. But some of his followers were desperate characters, and he died near Trinity River by the assassin's bullet. His brother and Joutel finally escaped to Tonty, and it is at least a satisfaction to record that his murderers perished.

His colony perished, too, and his plans died with him. Tonty had descended the river to meet him, and left a letter with some Indians, but, learning of La Salle's death, Tonty confined himself to the Illinois region. There, in 1690, he was by the government granted an interest in that rock fort, and he engaged in trade with the upper Mississippi. De Soto, Moscoso, La Salle himself, had suffered in exploring the river. It seemed as if the legends that evil spirits guarded the stream were true.

Times changed also. While the settlements in Mexico and east Florida, on which haughty Spain relied to prove her claim to all the Gulf, were more vulnerable because the mother country had sunk from her proud preëminence, the English colonies on the Atlantic coast were growing fast. Englishmen were to be heard of on the Mississippi, and even the fiction of an English discovery was broached.[1] It was still the great age of Louis XIV., who recognized no rights which hindered the grandeur of France; but it was the age, too, of William III. of England. France could not in Europe undo the work of the English Revolution of 1688, and in America did not go forward, excepting only the annexation of San Domingo.

We followed La Salle from Canada, and at the time of that explorer's death in Texas several of the Montreal family of Lemoyne, who should carry on his work, were winning laurels from the English in Hudson's Bay. Charles Lemoyne had emigrated from Dieppe in 1641, and in Canada gradually climbed the ladder of fame and fortune. He was soldier, interpreter, *garde magasin*, *procureur général*, and, as proprietor of that estate, died Sieur de Longueuil.[2] Of his twelve children, three sons died in the wars with England and all became well known. The oldest, Charles, succeeded to the title, and was as a father to the youngest, Jean Baptiste, to be Sieur de Bienville. Of the others, Iberville, Chateauguay (also spelled Chasteaugué and Chateaugué), Serigny, and St. Helene will often meet us, and the sister who married Noyan, or Noyant, became mother of men whom we will know.

Iberville was perhaps the most noted of these sailor brothers, and, besides his conquest of Newfoundland, is famous for a combat near Fort Nelson, where his vessel, the Pelican, contended with three English ones. The result was that Iberville captured one and put the other two to flight. In this battle

---

[1] Adair (*American Indians*, p. 308) says Wood discovered it in 1654, followed by Bolton in 1670, and that Cox's two ships entered the mouth in 1698.

[2] 4 Margry, *Découvertes*, p. xxii.

Bienville commanded a battery. Such exploits marked Iberville out for great enterprises, and, after the Peace of Ryswick of 1697, he was to be selected by the minister of the marine for service in another part of the world.

A map of 1699, dedicated to William III. of Great Britain, was made by the Recollect Hennepin, a missionary, and shows the knowledge of the day. The Great River, Meschasypy, is there first depicted, and east, entirely distinct from that stream, is the large harbor of Spirito Sancto, with Chicagua as the name of the Mobile River.[1] Virginia, New Netherlands, and New England fill up the coast until we reach New France or Canada, while in the other direction we find on the Gulf of Mexico the province of New Spain. No tribes are shown near the Chicagua River, except Cosa far to the northeast near some mountains, while many are placed on the Mississippi, — lyingly, as Bienville had later to declare on trying to find them.[2] The father clearly had not explored the interior near the bay of the Holy Spirit.

But the curiosity of the French was now thoroughly directed to the Mississippi region. Remonville visited America, and in 1697 wrote a full memorial, urging colonization of the region about the Great River, despite La Salle's failure. The idea grew that the Mississippi valley was to be a part of New France, which as Canada should front the Atlantic on the north, as Louisiana front the Gulf of Mexico on the south, and constitute an empire worthy even of the Grand Monarque.[3] French forts along the great lakes and rivers would protect the trading-posts, serve as strategic and diplomatic centres for French influence among the Indian tribes, and thus hem in the English colonies between the mountains and the sea. Mayhap these would be driven into the ocean whence they came, and the Latin races of France and Spain under their family compact catholicize and dominate the whole northern continent. For the French, like the Spaniards, wished to convert, as well as rule, the natives. Besides Jesuits among the northern Indians, those missionaries of the Seminary of Quebec, Father Montigny at the Natchez and Antoine Davion on his bluff

---

[1] Scaife's *America*, map 9.

[2] King's *Bienville*, p. 60.

[3] See recitals in Crozat's charter of 1712, 1 Martin's *Louisiana*, p. 178.

lower among the Tonicas, were the advance guard in the great valley for the lilies and the cross.

The minister of the marine and colonies had been Louis de Phelypeaux, Comte de Pontchartrain. In 1699, he was succeeded by his son Jerome, at first called Maurepas, but also known as Pontchartrain, who had for some years been co-minister with the father. His zeal for Louisiana was quickened by learning that the renegade Recollect, Father Hennepin, had interested William in the Mississippi, and that an English company was organizing under the patronage of that king. France must take possession first.

The minister selected Iberville to carry on the work dropped by La Salle. After the necessary preparations, the frigates Badine under that commander, and Marin under the Comte de Surgères, sailed from Brest October 24, 1698, to discover the mouth of the Mississippi and colonize the country.[1] There were also two transports, originally Norman fishing-boats, and at San Domingo they were joined by the corvette François under Châteaumorant, nephew of the great Tourville. Bienville was midshipman under his brother.

Sighting land off the coast of Florida, in the last days of January, 1699, they found Pensacola just occupied by the Spaniards, and proceeded westward, exploring as they went. They cast anchor January 31 off Mobile Point, and carefully examined what was later to be the chief seat of their colony.

One of the transports stranded in bad weather while sounding, but came off with the tide. Iberville soon determined to explore for himself, and was rowed with Bienville to the point. Despite a storm that night, next day they sounded the channel, but then had to run before the wind and make the long western island. This they named Massacre, from the heap of skulls and bones found with Indian utensils at the southwestern extremity. There they were weather-bound for three days, and hunted bustards (*outardes*).

Iberville made his way over to the mainland, and noted the flowers, and the oak, pine, walnut, chestnut, and other unknown trees of the forest. From a white oak top, four leagues up the bay, he took in the outline of the shore of the bay, and even noticed yellow water from the rivers. He saw signs of

---

[1] 4 Margry's *Découvertes*, pp. liii, 98, 213, 232.

recent Indians, and fired his gun and cut on a tree a sign of his peaceful visit.

Such was the French discovery and exploration of Mobile Point, Dauphine Island, and the land of Mon Louis Island. But their present objective was further west. The sounding of the channel was completed in good weather, a good harbor found off Massacre Island by Surgères, and, after taking on wood and grass for the livestock, the fleet sailed on to find the Mississippi.[1]

On the way they visited and named the islands of the sound, and had friendly intercourse with the Indians of Biloxi. The mouth of the great river they found on March 2, after much trouble and no little danger, for it was hidden in sandbanks, reeds, and logs like a palisade. Unfortunate La Salle could not see it from the sea, but Iberville was as fortunate here as in everything else he undertook.

The details of the subsequent exploration are not germane here. Suffice it, Iberville went upstream in boats as far as the Oumas, and returned to his ships by Bayou Manchac, to be named for himself. Bienville returned by the main stream, and, promising a hatchet, induced Indians to produce the letter which Tonty had written fourteen years before. This left no doubt that the river was the Mississippi, and further explorations were to convince them that Hennepin had never been on it below the Ohio.

The result of the exploration was that, while Bienville was to maintain a fort at a comparatively dry place some leagues above the mouth, Iberville decided that the swift, tortuous stream did not admit of sail navigation nor its marshy banks of habitation. A site for his colonial enterprise must be found on the seashore further east.

Mr. Green begins his great history of the English people by a study of their condition in the forests of Germany before the migration to Great Britain. Somewhat similarly can Fort de Maurepas, now built by Iberville on the Back Bay of Biloxi, be claimed as original Mobile. On that bluff behind the Louisville and Nashville railroad bridge Mr. Portevant, under his beautiful oaks, commanding so peaceful a prospect over the water, still digs up hatchets, cannon-balls, and even iron shoes

---

[1] King's *Bienville*, p. 21 ; 4 Margry, *Découvertes*, pp. 98, 99.

of tent or flag poles.   There, beyond doubt, seems to have been
Fort de Maurepas, and the little glade to the south, in whose
shelter grow so many kinds of trees, was once commanded by
French cannon.   Iberville slept on the spot which he selected,
and supervised the erection of his fort.   Like the later Fort
Louis, it had four bastions, of which two were of stockade and
two of logs.   It was guarded by twelve cannon, and seems to
have been surrounded by a palisade besides.   There was no
town laid out, however, and in fact this was intended only as
a temporary settlement.   There the Pascagoulas, Capinans,
Chicachas, Passacolas, and Biloxi came to smoke the calumet
with Iberville.[1]

The map drawn by F. Joussette for this occasion, still preserved in the Archives of the Marine at Paris, shows a channel
of seven feet out past Deer Island (Isle au Chevreuil), on
which were Indian cabins.   From there on, the water rapidly deepened to twenty feet at Ship Island (Isle Françoise
then), where on the north side was the anchorage for vessels.
On this island were large ponds where they watered.   This
interesting chart also shows the coast from "Pascaboula"
River on the east, facing Horn Island (Isle au Aigle), out beyond Isle Ronde, and extends as far west as opposite curiously
shaped Isle Bourbon, now Cat Island.   Between Ship and Cat
islands, but nearer the former, was the Pass Jordy, having
twenty-three feet depth.

At the entrance of Biloxi Bay, perhaps not far from the
present railroad cut, it was proposed to build a battery to
defend the entrance, but only in case the court fixed the colony
at Biloxi.   It is doubtful, therefore, whether this fortification
was erected.

The first commandant at Biloxi was Sauvole, hardly a brother of Iberville as claimed by Gayarré, the major was Levas-
seur Russonelle, and the garrison consisted of eighty men.[2]
Bienville on the Mississippi devoted much time to exploring
that river and its tributaries, as did Sauvole to examination and
sounding of the coast.   The latter thus discovered a harbor at
the east end of Dauphine Island, and from the Mobile Indians
learned the fertility of their river country.

    [1] Penicaut in 5 Margry, *Découvertes*, p. 378.
    [2] 4 Margry, *Découvertes*, pp. xxxii, xxxiii.

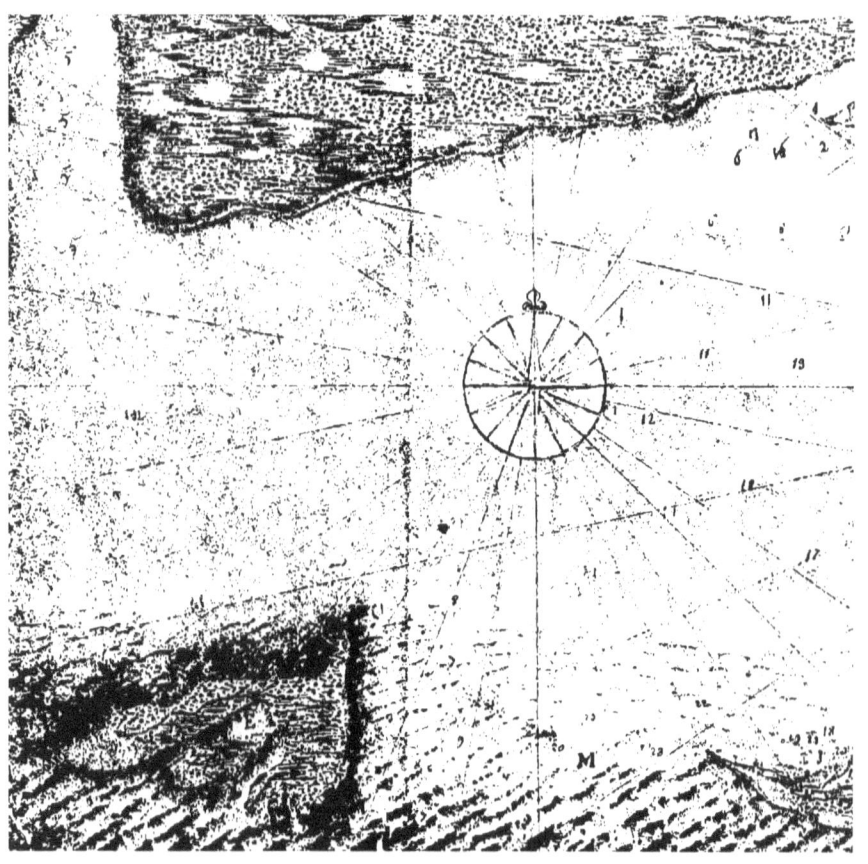

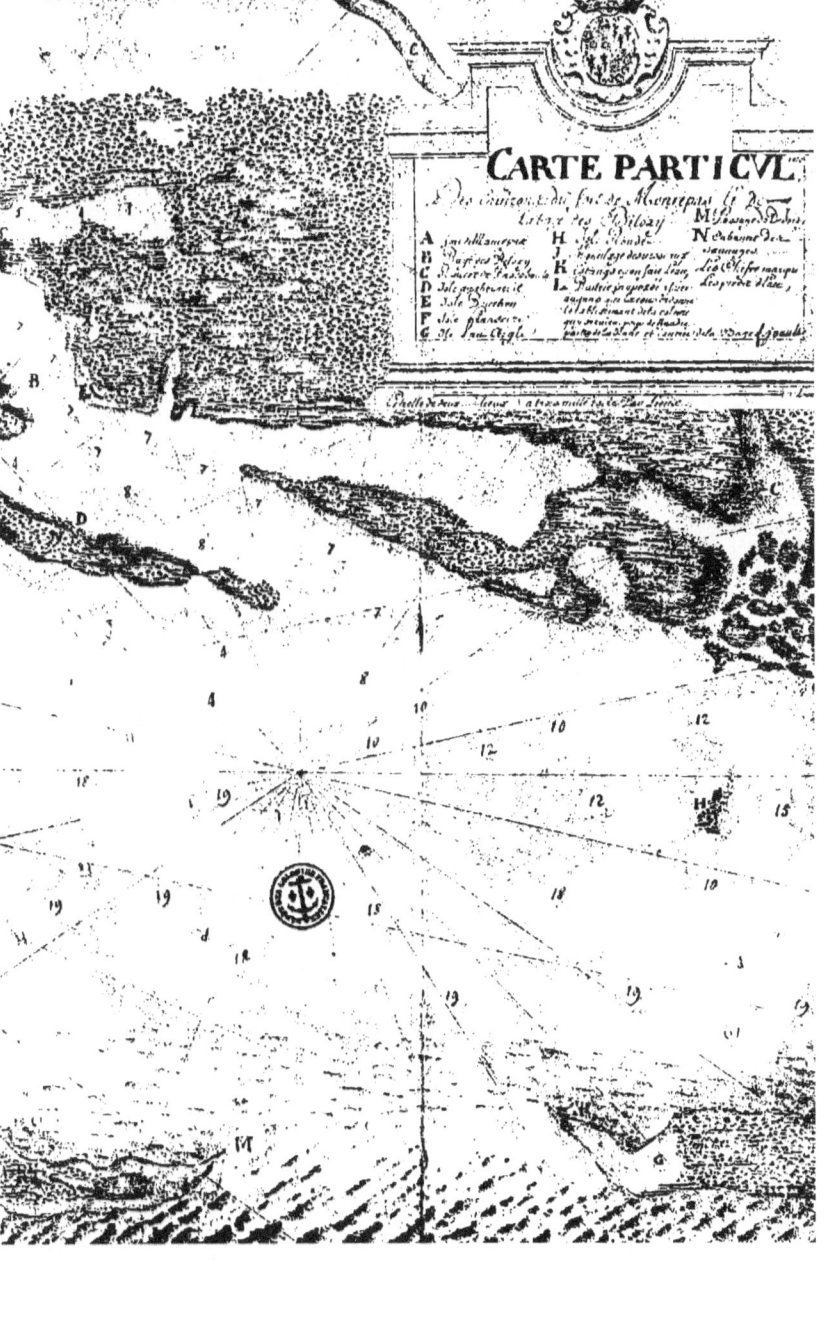

CARTE PARTICUL

macy, and in it he read the future as an unsealed book. The claim of Spain to monopoly, he showed, was without basis, and, worse than that, would soon be disputed by that Protestant country whose rulers recognized no papal gifts, whose pioneers on the American seaboard were increasing at a rate that would soon take them across the mountains to contend for the valleys of the Mississippi and its tributaries. In less than a hundred years,[1] said this prophet, the English, unless opposed by growth and persistence like their own, would occupy the whole of America. And so they did. One hundred and one years later, this people, as a new nation, were actually to buy from France that Louisiana which Iberville was now founding!

[1] 4 Margry, *Découvertes*, p. xli.

CHAPTER VI.

FOUNDING FORT LOUIS.

On one or more of his exploring expeditions from Biloxi, Iberville traversed the Mobile country, and seems to have selected it as the seat of his colony. Penicaut accompanied him, and to him we are indebted for perhaps the first detailed description of the bay and river that has come down to us.[1]

Our Bayou La Batré they named Rivière D'Erbane for a Frenchman lost there; Cedar Point, Pointe aux Huistres from the great abundance of oysters. Penicaut's dates may not always be correct, although he says he made his entries at the time of the events, but he is a good measurer. The mainland, he says, was two leagues from Massacre Island, and then it was nine leagues to the river. Two leagues below this Mobile River, which name he here uses, is Dog River, and two further, Fowl River. He gives no reason for any of the names. Dogs and deer they might have seen, but the only Indians known to have had domestic fowls were the Arkansas, for there La Salle found chickens and geese in 1682, and the Bayogoulas, whose stock came from a shipwreck.[2] Could Maldonado or other Spaniards have introduced fowls on the shores of Mobile Bay, or was not this river, and its Isle aux Oies, named from the wild-fowl even not yet extinct?

The bay was five leagues wide, and a league above the mouth of the river they found a confluent which they named St. Martin. It must be the later Bayou Marmotte, or the one afterwards renamed for Chateauguay, — One and Three Mile creeks respectively. A league further was the Rivière à Boutin, and this was probably our Chickasabogue.

On the upper bay and river they discovered a fine country.

[1] Penicaut in 5 Margry, *Découvertes*, pp. 383, 422.
[2] Parkman's *Great West*, p. 275 ; 1 Martin's *Louisiana*, p. 143.

The woods contained all the timber needed for the French navy, and Iberville had a dim vision of sawmills and of a great timber port. Twelve leagues up, on both sides of the river, they found the Mobile Indians (probably about Mt. Vernon Landing), already known to them at Biloxi. All the many Indians were friendly, and the Mobilian dialect was an important one, as it was the inter-tribal language of the Gulf races, the trade jargon from the Mississippi to the ocean.

Some point near the mouth of this river would serve Iberville's purpose very well, even better than the Natchez site first thought of by him. It would be near enough Pensacola to keep an eye on the Spaniards, near enough the Mississippi to be the port for the valley trade, which could come through Bayou Manchac, the lakes, and the sound, behind sheltering islands, to Mobile Bay, and with a fort on the Mississippi delta could guard the great river. Then also, with its easy communication by the Tombigbee River to the northwest and the Alabama to the northeast, it gave means of influence among the strong Choctaw, Chickasaw, and Alibamon Indians, and even access over the mountains, in case of war, to the English colonies of Carolina and Virginia.

It appears that Iberville selected the new site before returning to Europe, and when he sailed back towards the end of 1701, his plans were all made and ready for execution. They were sanctioned by Pontchartrain, but the selection of the site was Iberville's own work.

In the fall of 1701, Pontchartrain sent Iberville out in the Renommée, with the Palmier and *traversier*, for the express purpose of settling the Mobile region.[1] The daring fighter was transformed into a practical colonizer. We find him insisting on Spanish sheep for the colony instead of French, which he deemed inferior, a stallion to improve the American breed (which, if native, must have been of Spanish extraction, for the Indians originally had no horses), and taking only such things and people as were essential to the development of the country. No one realized better than he the sturdiness necessary for pioneers, and that the strength of the English colonies was in the kind of men sent out. He wanted no dependents,

[1] 4 Margry, *Découvertes*, pp. lix, 501–504, 512, 530. See 1 Martin's *Louisiana*, p. 152.

for the weakness of French colonies, he said, lay in sending out the poor and giving them no start.[1]

He called at San Domingo, and there refitted his vessels, and took on horses, cattle, and swine for the new colony. Ignorant of Sauvole's death, he sent word to him to remove to Mobile River. When he reported, November 24, to Pontchartrain from Pensacola, Iberville seems still not to know Sauvole's fate. There the governor was himself to be seriously ill with an abscess in the side, but finally, on December 17, 1701, despite the protest of the Spanish, he gave orders to abandon Biloxi and move everything to Massacre Island for greater convenience in making the new settlement.

During the days of transition to the new year, Biloxi and Massacre Island were scenes of activity. On January 3, Iberville sent a *lanche* or *felouque*, loaned him by the Spanish governor, Martinez, from Pensacola to the island with Serigny and Chasteaugué to join their brother Bienville, who, with forty men, arrived two days later in the *traversier* from Biloxi. Nicholas de la Salle (whom we have seen with his greater kinsman in 1682) came from Pensacola with his family in the *caiche* chartered by Iberville with the *lanche* to carry eighty workmen and the king's stores. On January 10, Bienville, Serigny, and Le Vasseur in the *lanche* and two *felouques* left Massacre Island by order of Iberville to occupy Mobile, "sixteen leagues off, at the second bluff."

We can be sure that the unfinished magazines on Dauphine Island, left for completion in charge of Chasteaugué and La Salle, were at the eastern end, where it is widest and accessible from both bay and gulf, for there was the harbor of twenty-one feet depth shown Iberville by a Spanish pilot. But where was this fort on the river, the original site of Mobile?

The direction and the journal of Iberville, the account of Penicaut, tradition, and physical remains all unite to fix the location. Sixteen leagues from Massacre Island at the second bluff is at Twenty-seven Mile Bluff. Near there Creoles still fondly point out the site of "Vieux Fort," and there French maps, as early as 1744, place a "vieux fort, detruit." A well under a hickory-tree still marks the spot, and bullets, canister, crockery, large-headed spike, and a brass ornament were picked

[1] 4 Margry, *Découvertes*, pp. 586, 604, 626.

up by the present writer near the river edge of the level bluff as late as the summer of 1897.

There, then, on a wooded spot, twenty feet above the river, hardly deserving the name of bluff, safe above ordinary high water, was Fort Louis de la Louisiane, commanding the wide, turbid river. It was not one of the many Forts *St.* Louis. Like Louisiana, it was named from Louis XIV. rather than for the sainted Louis IX.

Nowadays, when we lay a corner-stone, we have imposing ceremonies to commemorate the occasion, but when and how the first spadeful of Mobile earth was dug and post driven we do not know. Pontchartrain had, in the preceding summer, already ordered the occupation of the post, and Penicaut puts the beginning of work in 1701, and says Boisbriant arrived before Bienville; but the carpenter must be wrong. The journal must be correct. We can hardly suppose that ground was broken much before the middle of January, 1702. We can see the young Bienville — he was but twenty-two — carefully select the spot and superintend felling the virgin forest for room and material for Fort Louis. The woods found were white and red oak, bay, sassafras, cottonwood (*bois blanc*), walnut, and especially tall pines.[1]

The fort was of logs, "piece upon piece," sixty toises or fathoms square, with four bastions thirty feet long, having six guns at each corner advanced in semicircle. Within were four buildings, — chapel, *gouvernement* and officers' quarters, *magasins* and guard (*corps de garde*), and in the centre a parade of forty-five toises square. The barracks, however, for the privates and Canadians were outside, one hundred and fifty paces to the left, upstream, on the bank of the river. Such is the description of Iberville and of Penicaut. La Salle adds that there was by the river a powder magazine twenty-four feet square by ten deep. This, we learn, got filled for a time by the heavy rains.[2]

---

[1] See 4 Margry, *Découvertes*, pp. lx, 503, 512, 514, 531. For Penicaut's account, 5 *Ibid.*, p. 423. The error of Pickett and others in placing the settlement on Dog River could not be made now with the contemporary maps and documents before us. At best it rests on a misreading of Bartram. There was a *magasin* at the mouth of Dog River, but nothing more.

[2] 4 Margry, *Découvertes*, pp. lix, 512, 515, 530 ; 5 *Ibid.*, pp. 423, 424.

Iberville found difficulty getting his *traversier* even into the port at Dauphine Island during a northwest wind, and so directed Bienville to build a lighter or ferry-boat (with flat bottom, but pointed at the ends) to carry fifty-five tons and draw four and a half feet only.

Iberville never forgot that Mobile was to be the centre of French influence; the only place which, as he expressed it, could protect America against the English. While still sick at Pensacola, he sent two Canadians to Mobile (for Iberville gives the place this name from the start), with directions for Bienville to let Tonty have ten picked men to go to the Choctaws and Chickasaws. Tonty was to make peace between them, and by presents bring them to the new establishment to conclude treaties with the French.[1]

By the middle of February, Iberville had so far recovered as to sail on his ship Palmier for Massacre Island, but it was not until the 18th that the unfavorable northwest wind permitted him to enter over the bar, which was an eighth of a league from land, and had twenty-one feet. The harbor itself, between Massacre and a little (Pelican) island, showed thirty feet of water. It pleased him much by its easy defense and its protection from the wind on the north, northwest, and southwest, due to these islands, and on the northeast and east by the "east point of Mobile" two leagues away. He could not but fear, however, that a south gale might change the bar, — a fear which we shall have occasion to remember.

In this port he found Marigny, his *traversier* beached by a south wind as she was discharging what she had brought from Havana and Biloxi. Digging away sand and tying on empty casks did no good, and she lay there until a high tide on the 23d took her off. Meantime Iberville had to charter Pillet's *caiche* for five hundred livres to take provisions to the Mississippi fort. On it returned thither Gravier, superior of the Jesuit missions of the Illinois, and some *voyageurs*, come to discuss religion and trade. The beaver (*castor*) question was a troublesome one on account of Canadian jealousy, but Iberville promised provisions next year, and present transportation of their skins to France. The English were trying to attract them to trade with Carolina over the Ohio River (Ouabache).

[1] 4 Margry, *Découvertes*, pp. 507, 581.

Another important question was faced by Iberville at Massacre Island. Even during the brief Biloxi experiment, the secretary (*escrivain*), who had charge of the stores, claimed to have the right to direct everything. Iberville writes laconically that this man (Crassé) is going back to France. La Salle was acting as commissary (*faisant fonction de commissaire*) and applies to the minister of the marine for full appointment as such. His zeal had already led him to meddle, and Iberville thought best to establish a *garde magasin*, or keeper of the royal stores, in the person of Girard. He was to deliver goods, e. g., as presents to the savages, upon the order of La Salle, but La Salle was simply to carry out the instructions of the commandant.[1]

Iberville had been detained at the island by contrary winds, and on February 29 he sailed for Mobile, apparently with the two *pinasses* and a *chaloupe*, leaving one *chaloupe*, however, for La Salle to come on with his family. The governor kept his eyes open as he proceeded, and describes the lands very fully. He slept at a little river, elsewhere called Dog River, which had four or five feet at the mouth, and was bordered by high land, growing oak, pine, bay, beech, and elm. The next day he made three leagues, seeing mainly the swampy islands, for the river (Mobile) was high. March 2 he made six leagues, noting the fine cypress and some good land, and next day at a league and a half he found the establishment (*établissement*). His figures add up about twenty-eight miles from the river mouth. The lands above the fort he pronounces "perfectly beautiful," and he was especially struck with the fine pines. One he had cut to supply a mast lost by the Palmier in a West Indian storm, and in three days it was ready, and sent to Massacre Island.

He seemed satisfied with the progress made on fort and boat, and sent Bienville to explore the country. Bienville found on the banks and many adjacent islands places abandoned by the savages on account of war with Conchaques and Alibamons. An important discovery was that of five clay figures worshiped by the Mobilians. They were of a man, woman, child, bear, and owl, — the work, Iberville thought, of some follower of De Soto. They were shown Bienville by an Indian only when he

---

[1] 4 Margry, *Découvertes*, pp. 510, 529.

bribed him with the present of a gun, and were in the canes on a little hill near an ancient, destroyed village. The savage would not approach the heaven-descended gods nearer than ten paces, and then only backwards. When they were carried off, the Indians could not understand why the gods to whom the Mobilians sacrificed did not strike dead the impious white men.

The most natural location for this sanctuary would be that great mound to the northeast on what is now Bottle Creek, if "petit costeau" can be applied to a hill about fifty feet high; but any of the many shell banks will fairly suit the description. From about Twenty-one Mile Bluff upwards, the west shores of the river are habitable, and above as well as even lower down the opposite islands between the Mobile and Tensaw can and have been used. The figures were ultimately taken to France by the governor.

On February 6, Iberville himself began exploring by trying to find on these islands a waterfall for a sawmill and for a tannery. He was unsuccessful, but shortly afterwards took a *felouque* to visit the upper Indians. Three leagues up, he noted the end of the delta, and found the river a mile and a half wide, with a depth of five or six fathoms. On both banks he saw deserted habitations, but also on banks and islands, from four to a dozen cabins together, the two tribes of Mobilians and Tohomes who will become so well known to us. The Mobilians were six leagues above the fort, and therefore about the present Mt. Vernon (or Fort Stoddert) landing. The Tohomes, he says, were eight leagues above the establishment, which would be about Nanna Hubba Bluff. Their true seat was higher, at McIntosh's Bluff, but, as Iberville does not mention the Naniabes, he may have considered them all Tohomes. He must have had his sextant along, for he locates the main Tohome village of eight or ten cabins at 31° 22′, which answers very fairly for McIntosh's. The villages of both nations were near the river, connected by good horse-paths. He found the inhabitants industrious agriculturists. Their language was the same as the Bayogoula.

Iberville returned to the fort in a few days, but sent back to buy corn (*bled d'Inde*), of which he got three *chaloupes* full. He had to supply Pensacola with provisions also, — fifty barrels of flour already, to grow to a hundred quintals.

He now set about laying out his city, despite the incessant rain, and spent March 20–23 in aligning the streets and locating the inhabitants. This we may suppose was along the lower slope north of the fort, to secure easier access to the river. Besides the officials, he had four families of colonists. He had brought from San Domingo for his colony a horse, three mares, twenty cows, besides numerous pigs. He says the people called the place Mobile, — "que nous nommons la Mobile," although we know the official name was Fort Louis. No plan has survived, nor do our authorities give street names, but there is every reason to believe that Royal, Conti, and Dauphin were known there as well as at the later settlement.

One of the settlers, a master tanner, was lost in the woods, and went twelve days without food. He was preparing for death when found by some hunters under a tree on a hill, by a grave which he had dug. At its foot he had planted a cross, bearing an account of his mishap.

On Sunday, March 25, Tonty returned with seven chiefs and principal men of the Chickasaws (Chicachas) and four Choctaw chiefs. Iberville made them presents of considerable powder, ball, and lead, twelve guns, besides hatchets, knives, kettles (*chaudières*), beads, gun flints, and other small things (*clinquaillerie*). Next day he addressed them in due form, Bienville acting as interpreter, exhorting the two nations to conclude peace and abandon the English, who only aimed at making slaves of them. He cited the death of over eighteen hundred Choctaws, and capture of over five hundred prisoners sold away, and the loss of over eight hundred Chickasaws during this war of eight or ten years. If they would drive out the English, he would make the Illinois cease war upon them, and would establish a trading station, where they could obtain all kinds of goods in exchange for skins of beef, deer, and bear.

The talk was satisfactory, and general peace was arranged. Word was sent to the Illinois, to "Davyon" among the Tonicas, Foucaut among the Akansas, St. Cosme at the Nadeches (Natchez), and the governor wrote also to the grand vicar of Quebec, at the Tamaroas, to send missionaries among the Chickasaws and Choctaws as soon as possible. With the returning Chickasaws was sent back a little St. Michel child to learn the language. Iberville heard much that he would find useful as to numbers and location of the several tribes. The promised trading-post was to be established on the upper Mobile River between the two tribes, three or four leagues from the Chaquechoumas and twelve or fifteen from the Chickasaws.

Having founded his colony, Iberville, leaving six months' stores, set out on his return to the Palmier at Massacre Island. In the river, on his way, he took soundings, and found at least five and one half to six feet of water. He slept at Dog River, where he had established a *magasin*, which Chasteangué in the *traversier* and Grandville in the *chaloupe* had been busy filling. Bécancourt, who had been quite useful, was taken from the Renommée, of which he was *enseigne*, and put in charge of the *traversier*.

On March 31, the Renommée, towing the Palmier, went over the bar in twenty-one to twenty-two feet of water, and made for Pensacola. There they took on beaver-skins and minor peltries, brought by the *caiche* from the Mississippi, and sailed for Havana and France.[1]

Thus Fort Louis, the first Mobile, was founded. It was to guard the Mississippi entrance, be the capital of vast Louisiana, the meeting-place for the Indian tribes south of the Great Lakes, and the point from which English influence, not only in the Alabama regions, but in all the Mississippi and Ohio valleys, was to be overthrown. Iberville had personally, and through priests and traders, mastered the Indian problem, and he proposed to win the savage to the French side, and keep the English to the Atlantic seaboard. His plans we learn in full from a memorial of his.

The Indians were to be attracted to the French by means of river trade. The English could bring their wares only by painful overland journeys, crossing the Alleghanies, while the French would command the Gulf rivers, in particular the Mississippi, with its many tributaries. He would have about four grand posts on the Mississippi River, besides the capital at Mobile, and would distribute them judiciously. One he founded low on the Mississippi, another should be among the Arkansas Indians, a third on the Ouabache (our Ohio), and

[1] Iberville's journal in 4 Margry, *Découvertes*, pp. 503–523.

the fourth on the Missouri. Perhaps we may say that he thus foresaw the necessity for New Orleans, Memphis, Louisville, and St. Louis, if he did not select their sites. A lake city like Chicago would, in his division of territory, belong to the St. Lawrence rather than the Mississippi basin, and therefore not enter his plans. Mobile was the key, without which, however, the other posts were worthless. From Mobile there could be communication by horse with even the furthest in fifteen days. At each should be a sergeant and corporal with at least ten soldiers as a nucleus for a French colony, and the principal industry would be tanning buffalo hides and deerskins for shipment to France via Mobile.[1]

His plans contemplated resettlement of some Indian tribes, so as to put them nearer this river commerce and influence. We shall see smaller changes made, but none such as this daring mind conceived. The total Indian population that should be tributary to the French was, as he figured it, 23,850 families. Of these the most populous were the Sioux of four thousand, the Panis (Pawnees) of two thousand, the Chaetas of four thousand, the Chicachas of two thousand, and the Conchaques (Apalachicolas) of two thousand families. The well-known Mobilians and Tohomes he put at only three hundred and fifty families, the Tonicas and neighbors at three hundred. The Illinois and Tamaroua he estimates at eight hundred, the Missouri at fifteen hundred, the Quicapou and Maskouten at four hundred and fifty, and the Miamis at five hundred families. Except the Maha and Canses (Kansas), the other tribes named are small and now less recognizable.

The first tribal change he contemplated was inducing the Indians in the mountains west of Maryland, Carolina, and Virginia to settle nearer Mobile, doubtless on the waters we now call the Tennessee and Coosa, so as to substitute French for English influence. Next was to make the Ouabache (Ohio) of use to France. More than one hundred and twenty leagues long, it had not an Indian on its banks. There he would settle the Illinois, and have them bring to this river highway the buffalo-skins of their chase. With the Illinois, the French would have one thousand armed men in case of need, and their old grounds would then be occupied by the more distant Mas-

[1] 4 Margry, *Découvertes*, pp. 594, 601–603.

koutens and Kikapous, who were heretofore given to beaver
hunting. These would be four hundred and fifty friendly
warriors more. There were as many Miamis, who sold beavers at Chicagou. In their giving up that trade for buffalo and
deer hunting about the Illinois, there would be saved, too, the
expense of a fort among them. Iberville knew of the Miamis
from Gravier, superior of their missions. He admits that it
will injure the beaver trade of Canada, but this will only be in
order to give it an easier outlet down the Mississippi to Mobile.[1]

The Sioux, also devoted to beavers, were useless where they
were, as were the Mahas and other populous tribes between
the Missouri and the Mississippi. He knew of them through
Le Sueur, who understood them perfectly. They should be
placed on the Monigona (Des Moines) River. The Akansas
Indians were then extinct, and their place on their river he
would fill with the Kansés, Missouris, and Crevas. Like the
Mahas, they did not use firearms, nor had they heretofore
traded with Europeans. Up that river were the Manton, and
among them he would settle the Panis. All these hunted the
buffalo, and were often at war with the Spaniards of New
Mexico and their Indian allies.

Le Sueur was returning to France, and Iberville recommended him as suitable to superintend this readjustment of
nationalities so as to make them more useful to the king. The
expense, says Iberville, would not exceed twelve thousand livres
for moving all these twelve thousand Indians. Part could even
be met with knickknacks. In four or five years there could be
built up a trade of sixty to eighty thousand buffalo hides and
more than one hundred and fifty thousand deer and other skins,
which would bring in France more than 2,500,000 livres per
annum. Each skin would yield four or five pounds of good wool,
he says, which brings twenty sous, and two pounds of hair at
ten sous. Besides this, one would get each year more than two
hundred thousand livres of other peltry, such as bears, wolves,
wildcats, foxes, martins, etc., whose customs duties would
bring the king annually more than two hundred and fifty thousand livres. There would also be the products of numerous
lead mines, while silver could be found near New Mexico, and
copper mines were abundant, too.[2]

---

[1] 5 Margry, *Découvertes*, pp. 587, 595–597.   [2] *Ibid.*, pp. 587, 600, 601.

But no doubt Iberville dwelt even more fondly on another result of these proposed changes. Not to mention tribes further west, he could count on twelve thousand good warriors to invade Maryland, Virginia, and Carolina as a part of his plan to check, if not annihilate, the English colonies. In this way there would be no need of many French soldiers except as officers.

The Canadian company and officials of course looked with jealousy on the new colony, and at first claimed control over it. That beaver-skins should be taken down the Mississippi instead of the St. Lawrence injured their trade and infringed what they deemed their rights. Iberville, however, justly replied that all territory watered by branches of the Mississippi River belonged to Louisiana as a part of his commercial territory.[1] A century later, this doctrine was in other hands and another tongue to be stated as the right of the West to control the mouths of its rivers. Instead of Louisiana's controlling the West by its rivers, the West was ultimately, in order to secure their navigation, to annex Louisiana. But in the period now under review his claim was right, and it received the sanction of the king. Governor Callières of Canada was, in 1701, curtly notified that the new province could be better governed directly from France than by way of Quebec, and Iberville was made its commander-in-chief.[2]

[1] 4 Margry, *Découvertes*, pp. 591, 606.
[2] *Ibid.*, pp. 585, 622.

CHAPTER VII.

BIENVILLE.

LONELY enough those Frenchmen must have felt in their river fort, far from the sea, and thousands of miles from France. Their only neighbors were treacherous savages, their hope of subsistence in supplies from home. For these were no hardy pioneers, such as the English settling the Atlantic coast. Brave enough they were, but many were here for pay or adventure, and even those Canadians who thought of America as their country were rangers (*coureurs de bois*), and more at home in the forest than in the fort. Gentlemen were there, but few artisans in the little town overlooking the turbid Mobile.

Yet Bienville, the governor, began his administration under not unfavorable circumstances, for he could rely upon Iberville's influence in France. But the problems before him were serious. The Indians immediately tributary to Mobile waters must in some way be detached from British as well as Spanish interests, the vast Mississippi region explored and gradually colonized, and all by means of the rather heterogeneous population under his command.

Of his lieutenants, St. Denis, Boisbriant, and others we have met at Biloxi, and Henri de Tonty we have seen at Iberville's Indian conference.

The last, the best and most active of French pioneers, was of Italian extraction. His father, for political reasons, had moved to France, and there had invented the Tontine system, now so familiar in life insurance. The son, Henri, had lost a hand in the Sicilian wars of France by the explosion of a grenade, but the iron substitute was found perhaps equally useful after he came to America with La Salle and gained him among the savages the name of the Iron Hand. We have seen him at the discovery of the Mississippi, and cannot but admire his faithfulness during the long years at Fort St. Louis, the rock of the Illinois. We know his descents of the great river, his letter, his entertainment of Cavelier and Joutel, — always waiting and watching for the La Salle who was dead in a Texan forest. When granted an interest in Fort St. Louis and the fur trade, he still watched the river he had helped discover, and as soon as he heard of Iberville's expedition, descended to meet La Salle's successor. He visited Bienville at the fort near the Mississippi mouth, came also to Biloxi to see Iberville, as we have seen, induced Indian chiefs to go to the first congress held by that Frenchman at Mobile, and now, on the abolishment of the Illinois post, he moved to Mobile himself. He had hoped to find Iberville again, but, missing him, took up his abode at the new fort in order to aid the younger brother.[1]

And there was need of colonists of high and low degree, although the proposition of the freebooters of Carthagena to move their headquarters to Mobile was declined. The total population, probably including even slaves and soldiers, was about one hundred and thirty persons,[2] and, if Penicaut's date is correct, this year inaugurated warfare with the Indians. Those immediately near were friendly, but the Alibamons, high up on the river named for them, had to be conquered into friendship. Boisbriant went up the river with forty men in five canoes against the Alibamons. He succeeded in killing some warriors, and brought back to the fort women and children as slaves. The French, however, were generous enough to give the captives to the Mobilian Indians, who begged for them.[3]

In this same year, 1702, and possibly while "petit St. Michel" was learning Chickasaw, occurred, according to Shea, the murder of the aged Seminary priest Foucaut, as he was descending the Mississippi to Mobile from his station on the Arkansas. His Coroa guides saw his valuables, and killed him and his two companions as they slept on the river bank. Davion found and buried their bodies. Penicaut puts it three years later, and has it that Foucaut' was descending from Canada to visit Davion at the Yazoos.[4] The French may not

---

[1] 5 Margry, *Découvertes*, p. 427.   [2] 4 *Ibid.*, p. 536.   [3] 5 *Ibid.*, p. 432.
[4] 5 Margry, *Découvertes*, p. 458 ; Shea's *Catholic Church in the Colonies*, p. 545.

have been well settled enough in 1702 to avenge his death, and we hear nothing of any attempt to do so. But a similar assassination at the beginning of the next year, which Shea does not mention, although Penicaut does, was promptly punished. It was necessary, in order to keep open the river route.

St. Cosme, a missionary from Canada, was descending the river with three companions to visit St. Denis, then in command of the fort near the mouth. He reached the Natchez safely, but unfortunately spent the night ashore lower down, where had been a village of the Bayogoulas. These Indians were then at war with the Chetimachas, a tribe dwelling on what is now called Bayou la Fourche. These Chetimachas, happening to come, were so enraged at missing their foe that they massacred the priest and all his company, except a little slave.

St. Denis reported the crime, and Bienville authorized an expedition to punish it. This, composed of ten French and two hundred savages, Oumas, Ouachas, and Bayogoulas alike, St. Denis successfully led up their river. He killed fifteen Chetimachas and wounded and captured more, and among the prisoners was one of the murderers of St. Cosme. When they arrived at Mobile, Bienville had the murderer attached to a wooden horse and his head broken (*casser la teste*), after which his scalp was taken, and his body thrown into the river. Not content with this, Bienville offered ten *escus* per scalp or prisoner of Chetimacha or Alibamon race brought to him.[1] To this war and its results, we probably owe the Chetimacha slaves which abound in the church records a year or so later.

The main reliance of the settlement for soldiers was at first the Canadian wood rangers, who were so hateful to the clergy. And yet Iberville had no great love for the Canadian *coureurs de bois*. Their peltries were bought at Mobile and shipped from there, but no one realized better than he the inconstancy of such men.[2] They spoke French, but they were half savages, and had almost as lief trade with the English as with their countrymen. Lawless and irreligious, they counteracted the efforts of the missionaries among the Indians, and often by intrigue and crime injured the French name. His plan, how-

---

[1] Penicaut in 5 Margry, *Découvertes*, pp. 433, 460, etc.

[2] 4 Margry, *Découvertes*, p. 586.

ever, was to anchor even them by bringing over French wives to take the place of Indian mistresses.

There was a "Polastron company" of soldiers at the Mississippi fort in 1702, and Iberville was early solicitous to raise in France at least two companies of regulars for Mobile to take the place of the adventurous Canadians. We learn that in 1703 Volezard and Chasteaugué were each recruiting a company in France under royal sanction for this purpose. These companies in the baptismal registers are named for their captains. Blondel was to be *enseigne* of the latter.[1] In August, Chasteaugué actually arrived in the Loire, with seventeen passengers, sixty thousand livres, and goods and provisions. This was the first of those relief ships which Iberville's influence sent, and right welcome she was. Iberville did not come himself until next year.

The supplies ran low after a while, however, and in 1704, the flour gave out. Bienville sent his boat (*traversier*) under Bécancourt to Havana for more, and permitted fifty of his men to hunt for a living in the territory of friendly Indians, while he sought to obtain provisions for the rest by purchase. When he sent five of his men with some Indians to buy provisions from the Alibamons, they were all ambushed and killed except one, a Canadian, who, although wounded, swam the river, and succeeded in bringing the news to the fort. This attack, of course, must be punished.

Bienville at once organized an expedition to seek revenge. Mobilians, Tohomes, and Choctaws came to a grand campfire at the fort. The French feasted them there by the river, and they devoted several days to medicine, to the black drink from the youpon leaves, which Indians always took before war. They then started in pirogues, Boisbriant and St. Denis sharing the command with Bienville. But the new allies were treacherous. The Mobilians delayed, even notified their old enemies, the Alibamons, and finally deserted in a body with the Choctaws.[2] Bienville then played the ruse of returning, and quietly setting out again with white men only. He found the Alibamon village up the river and destroyed it. Although all but four of the hostile warriors escaped unhurt, the blow

---

[1] 4 Margry, *Découvertes,* pp. 586, 616, 620, 624.

[2] King's *Bienville,* p. 132.

served its purpose, and afterwards Bienville paid for other scalps.

Such was the opening of Bienville's troubled government. We have seen him in a naval battle on the waters of Hudson's Bay, then sounding Mobile channel and exploring the Mississippi, and later as commandant at the fort near the Mississippi mouth, and succeeding Sauvole at Biloxi. He was always active and clear-sighted, and this younger Lemoyne looks out of the portrait in Margry with a kinder face than the intrepid Iberville. And yet the brothers were much alike, and during his long life in Louisiana we do not find Bienville lacking in any quality necessary to a pioneer governor. He was patient even amid faction, and, if foiled in one plan, immediately prepared another. Successful always he could not be, but the best tribute to him is to compare Louisiana as he found it and as he left it, and consider not less the inadequate help given him in France than the love he inspired in his followers and the respect and fear he created in the savages who knew him.

He was a Canadian, early on the seas, and like many other Canadians, devoted to the Jesuits and expert in handling savages. He cajoled the Indians with presents, but punished with barbarity equal to their own when occasion required. One of his most politic acts was at this time, receiving and settling on Mobile River a band of fugitive Apalaches, who were driven from their Florida home by the neighboring English colonists, and he was to have occasion later so to colonize other Indians.

Iberville was to have come by the Pelican, but the vessel was delayed until midsummer, 1704, and then came without him, for he was sick.[1] But this second and famous relief ship brought out what he had provided. Livestock, food, and merchandise there were, beside a curé, missionaries, artisans, seventy-five soldiers, and, best of all, twenty-three virtuous maidens under charge of two gray nuns. The girls were all well married within a month, except one unusually "coy and hard to please," who would take no man in the colony. It is said that later all of them rebelled at corn, and perhaps corn bread, and that for a while the Petticoat Insurrection taxed Bienville's patience and ingenuity.

In July of the preceding year, St. Vallier, Bishop of Quebec,

[1] King's *Bienville*, p. 137.

had recognized Louisiana as a settled colony and made Fort
Louis a separate parish in his vast diocese, and now the Pelican
brought over the first curé, La Vente. Before that there had
been no regular pastor, although Dougé and Davion were there.

Davion's history is interesting. The bishop, through the
Seminary at Quebec, had established St. Cosme at the Ta-
marois, near modern St. Louis, Montigny among the Natchez,
and Davion among the Tunicas on the lower Mississippi.
Davion kept his sacred relics in the trunk of a tree, and the
chapel which he built long remained there at the foot of a cross
on a rock. He was influential among the Indians, and is said
to have once fearlessly destroyed the idols of the Yasous, when
his life was saved only by the exertions of the grand chief. In
1700, the Jesuit Gravier found Davion dangerously ill at his
post, and St. Cosme came to nurse him. Davion we know
visited Biloxi, and by 1704 was ministering regularly at Mobile.
He lived amicably with the Jesuit Dougé in an unfinished
house on the river, built with Dougé's means, and when La
Vente arrived, a church was building also.

Davion was a typical missionary, and was much beloved at
Fort Louis. We can imagine him, like Father Felician in
"Evangeline," going on his sacred errands, reverently welcomed
everywhere. It was fit that he should induct the first regular
pastor, but better still, as it proved, would it have been for
him to have occupied that position himself.

La Vente was duly put in office in September, 1704, with
ceremonies set out in the interesting entry on the first page of
the venerable baptismal register still preserved at Mobile.[1] It
is attested by Davion, Bienville, and De la Salle, and reads
as follows: —

I, the undersigned priest and missionary apostolic, declare
to all whom it may concern, that, the 28th of September in the
year of Salvation 1704, in virtue of letters of provision and collation granted and sealed July 20 of last year, by which Monseigneur, the most illustrious and reverend bishop of Quebec,
erects a parochial church in the place called Fort Louis of
Louisiane, and of which he gives the cure and care to M. Henri
Roulleaux De la Vente, missionary apostolic of the diocese of

[1] For original French text, see Appendix.

Bayeux, I have placed the said priest in actual and corporal possession of the said parochial church and of all the rights belonging to it, after having observed the usual and requisite ceremonies, to wit, by entrance into the church, sprinkling of holy water, kissing the high altar, touching the mass book, visiting the most sacred sacrament of the altar, and ringing the bells, which possession I certify that no one has opposed.

Given in the church of Fort Louis the day of month and year above, in the presence of Jean Baptiste de Bienville, lieutenant of the king and commandant at the said fort, Pierre du Q. de Boisbriant, major, Nicolas de la Salle, clerk and performing function of commissary of the marine.

(Signed) DAVION, BIENVILLE, BOISBRIANT, DE LA SALLE.

Everything now again looked bright, and the census of this year was promising. There were one hundred and eighty men capable of bearing arms, two French families with three little girls and seven boys, and six young Indian slaves, — for slavery had also taken root, copied from the Indians themselves. Pickett says the first Creole, that is native French, was born this year, the son of Claude Jousset, a trader. This may be, but the first in the baptismal register is Jean François, baptized by Huvé on the day of his birth, October 4, 1704. His father was Jean de Can, if we rightly read the entry, who was a locksmith of the settlement, and his mother was Magdelaine Robert, — for a wife is always, as here, called by her maiden name. Later in the same month was born a son of François Le May, but he died and was buried on the day of his birth. The next recorded Creole is Jacque, in August of next year, son of Jean Roy, master cannoneer (*maître canonier*), and Renée Guilbert his wife. The sponsors (*parain* and *maraine*) were Le Conte, master carpenter, and Gabrielle Savary, wife of Saucié. Thence on such births, although not numerous, are not uncommon.

The allotments of land had borne fruit. There were eighty one-story thatched houses, and in this 1704 census are fourteen cows, four bulls, six calves, and, while no horses appear, nine oxen performed some of their duties. There were also one hundred hogs, three kids, and four hundred chickens.[1] One

[1] Pickett's *Alabama*, pp. 195–199.

INDUCTION OF LA VENTE

can somewhat understand that the merchandise sent out was to be sold for royal account, but it seems odd to read that five of the oxen and one bull belonged to the king. The baptismal register credits him with a slave, too. Was he in the stock business, or was some of the land that was cultivated near the fort his private domain? Or perhaps this is the first instance on our soil of advances, — Louis XIV. being the merchant!

But the Pelican had touched at St. Domingo and brought also yellow fever. What a visitation that for the little colony! Half the crew of the Pelican, thirty of the newly arrived soldiers, Father Dougé, Le Vasseur, and, worst loss of all, Henri de Tonty, died in that September of 1704. The site of the cemetery has been lost, but we may imagine it in the woods behind the little town. There in an unknown grave near the Mobile River they laid the remains of Tonty, one of America's great men, with sobbing pines to keep his vigil. The first epidemic, — perhaps in proportion the most fatal.

An Indian war between Choctaws and Chickasaws now began, but, fortunately, the enfeebled French were only anxious spectators. Boisbriant and twenty Canadians were sent to take through the Choctaw nation seventy odd Chickasaws who happened to be at the fort. He shielded them as best he could, but in one town, by a stratagem, the male Chickasaws were murdered and the females enslaved. Boisbriant was himself wounded accidentally, but was brought back to the fort by an escort of three hundred Choctaws, "in mournful procession." He recovered, however, and lived to do much service, for he was a dashing cavalier. Not much later, a Lady Superior fell in love with him, and became angry with Bienville because he broke up their intended marriage.

There came now a concentration of the colonists. The fort near the Mississippi mouth, which St. Denis had commanded since Bienville was promoted on Sauvole's death, was finally abandoned. Lack of supplies and the non-healthfulness of the spot may have caused this, and, at all events, the troops were withdrawn to Fort Louis. St. Denis, however, soon tired of post life and withdrew to Biloxi, where he settled, — to stay until other adventures, which we shall recount, called him to new fields and pastures green.

Colonial life now fully centred at Fort Louis.

CHAPTER VIII.

FORT LOUIS had now been founded, influence obtained among the Indians, the Mississippi valley guarded and in part explored, and the future of Louisiana seemed assured, despite temporary disasters like famine and fever. Wise perseverance was all that was necessary.

And yet much depended upon the one man who was as influential at Versailles as on the Mobile. Affairs were always in better condition when Iberville was by young Bienville's side.

It was at this time that he came upon the Loire with the ever needed supplies and oversaw for a while the affairs of his colony. But it was as when one sets his house in order. His health had been bad for some years, for the southern climate had enfeebled his Canadian constitution. After his departure, Bienville and all Louisiana received a rude shock in his death at Havana, in 1706, of yellow fever.

With him died not so much his plans as the power to carry them out. Bienville succeeded, but he stayed in America, and did not, like Iberville, visit Pontchartrain at Versailles and give and take the enthusiasm that carried all before it. Bienville had his brother's name and his own energy behind him. The last was to be neutralized by dissension in the colony, the other by time; but the greatest hindrance was the long war of the Spanish Succession, when the generals of Louis unsuccessfully contended with Eugene, and Marlborough in command of allied Europe. France suffered many defeats, and her treasury was too exhausted to take care of her colony.

On the removal of the man in whom all had confidence, the colonists, too, became restless and factious, while the court itself was indifferent if not suspicious. The great policy of Iberville for wholesale rearrangement of Indians dropped out of view, and what was actually accomplished was to maintain

Mobile as a point of observation and influence, the port for a large but ill-organized trade among the Gulf and Mississippi River savages. A few interior trading-posts there were, but for the present no other colonies, and the agricultural resources of the country were almost entirely neglected.

The plan of royal colonial government provided that a commissary of marine, or *commissaire ordonnateur*, as he was sometimes called, had control of public property, and with the governor attested public acts, such as grants. In 1704, Nicolas de la Salle, whom we met at Massacre Island, is called secretary (*écrivain*), performing the function of commissary of marine. He was certainly active, but got on ill with Bienville. From 1706, he constantly complains to the ministry at home of the governor and those he deemed a clique of Canadians. He said the governor was undignified, withheld salaries, speculated in royal property, appropriated public funds, and, in fact, was a grand rascal generally.

The curé La Vente joined this opposition, and it is possible to understand his feeling without altogether sharing it. He justly disapproved the profligacy of the men and the sale of liquor to the savages.[1] But violent opposition was not the way to win them back or advance his cause. Bienville in his turn accused the curé of keeping shop like a Jew, and of stirring up the commissary against him.

It is impossible to doubt that part of the trouble arose from Bienville's partiality for Jesuits. His father had been in their employ, and the boy had been brought up with love for them. He thought they made more sacrifices than the other clergy, and, in 1706, had a mind to put in La Vente's place Gravier, the Jesuit who had been driven away wounded from the Illinois flock.[2] Gravier went to Paris to have the Illinois arrowhead extracted from his arm, and on the way took occasion, in a letter to France, by accident, as it were, to praise the location of the colony, its management, and its governor.[3]

Bienville was, perhaps, on more friendly terms with his Spanish neighbors at Pensacola than with his commissary and curé. But he frequently had to lend them provisions, some-

---

[1] Shea's *Catholic Church in the Colonies*, p. 551.

[2] *Ibid.*, p. 552.

[3] King's *Bienville*, p. 156.

times when his own colony had little enough to spare. Penicaut tells us that on January 7, 1706, Señor Guzman, governor
of Pensacola, came to spend four days at Mobile,[1] and we
know that he was there also in 1709, for he attests the register
of a baptism then in a bold hand as "Dom Joseph de Guzman." On one of these occasions, if in fact they are not the
same (for Penicaut's dates are not always accurate), our chronicler tells us that the Spaniard was received with salutes and
entertained in great state. He was godfather at a christening,
and at another time distributed Spanish money as largess with
no sparing hand. In his honor prisoners were released, and
at his departure powder was again lavishly used.

Bienville complains that his salary of twelve hundred livres
had to pay for such entertainments. There was always at
least a diplomatic quarrel, however, as to the boundaries of
the two colonies, even when Spain finally acknowledged the
de facto existence of the French at Mobile. The Spaniards
claimed to the east bank of the Mobile River, the French to
the Perdido, and this last prevailed. But probably to the
dispute we owe the naming of one branch of the Mobile (our
Tensaw), even on French maps, as Spanish River.

In 1706 there was again great dearth of provisions at Mobile, and Penicaut tells us they lived by hunting, until in February, 1707, the Eagle arrived under command of Bienville's
uncle, M. de Noyant, with supplies and dispatches. The vice
of the whole system was in not making the colony agricultural,
at least in part. On or near rich lands, the colonists yet had
periodic famines. The government retained Iberville's plan
of making the settlement commercial, but gave up the Indian
diplomacy which would have made it pay, and did not encourage agricultural pursuits which would at least make the colony
self-sustaining. There were no regular grants of land, except
possibly the little town-lots, and of the eight oxen the king
owned half. No wonder the Canadians preferred the woods.
The annalist notes that there were too few horses for successful
farming.

Indeed, the census of next year shows none of these essential animals. As given by D'Artaguette, there were one hundred and twenty men in garrison, including the priests, and

---

[1] 6 French's *Historical Collection*, p. 98.

one hundred and fifty-seven colonists, besides sixty unattached Canadians. The colonists consisted of twenty-four men, twenty-eight women, twenty-five children, and eighty Indian slaves. Of domestic animals there were fifty cows, four bulls, fourteen hundred hogs, and two thousand chickens. Pickett allows fewer soldiers and specifies eight oxen. There were two priests besides the curé.[1]

In this year, 1708, came an Indian war, which all but had disastrous consequences. The Alibamons during these early years, as we have seen, were frequently in arms against the French, despite Milfort's legend that the French protected them, and reconciled them with the Creeks after centuries of war and wandering. The Cheraquis, Abecas, and Cadapouces (Catawbas) from the northeast formed an alliance with the Alibamons and descended the river four thousand warriors strong. But two Mobilians who had married among them gave warning, and the French were on their guard. Their courage failed the invaders for some reason, too, and the army, which could easily have driven the French into the sea, contented themselves with burning *cabanes* of the Mobilian Indians six leagues above Fort Louis, and then retired without attacking the fort.[2]

This was a formidable alliance, and included nations away east on the borders of the English colonies, Virginia and Carolina. The Alibamons were the tribe of the Muscogee confederacy furthest down the river, and thus most in contact with Fort Louis, while the Abecas were the Creeks furthest up the Coosa River, showing that the whole confederacy was aroused, possibly by English influence.[3] The Catawbas, also, are well known. They inhabited the Alleghanies on what is now the line between North and South Carolina, and were at this time a powerful people. They were in constant hostilities with the Iroquois, the Shenandoah Valley being the seat of the counter raids; but they and the Cherokees west of them were uniformly allies of the English. There was early a trading-path from Petersburg to the Catawbas and Cherokees, and we know that the Tennessee River was a regular route of English traders to the nations beyond.

---

[1] King's *Bienville*, p. 176 ; Pickett's *Alabama*, p. 202.

[2] Penicaut, 5 Margry, *Découvertes*, pp. 477, 478.

[3] Gatschet's *Creek Migration Legend*, p. 124.

This great army had melted away as those of the savages always did after a short while, but the French did not let the matter drop. Penicaut tells us that Chateaugué, in an expedition to the neighborhood of Pensacola, killed a number of Alibamons, and captured nine warriors and brought them to the fort. There their heads were broken (*l'on fit casser la teste*), a mode of execution employed by the French no less than by the savages.[1]

Diplomat and master as he was in Indian affairs, Bienville was to suffer in France after Iberville's death. The accusations of La Salle bore fruit at court, and on February 10, 1708, the Renommée arrived at Massacre Island with royal orders for a change in the administration. The new governor, De Muy, had died at Havana on the way out, however, and so Bienville was not, in fact, superseded. Diron D'Artaguette came as the new commissary in La Salle's place, with instructions to make full investigation and report, as well as change the name of the place to something more stable than "Mobile." For on the map of Delisle, in 1707, the old native name for the waters had even been adopted officially.[2] D'Artaguette, in jest or earnest, actually suggested a change to *Immobile*, but Pontchartrain to the contrary notwithstanding, Mobile it has ever remained. D'Artaguette's (or Bienville's) change of name of Massacre to Dauphine Island, however, was more permanent,[3] and, in order to secure better communication with that port, D'Artaguette built, in 1709, a boat of sixty tons to carry merchandise,[4] perhaps due in part to the arrival there of a vessel from Havana, which, the first Spanish boat ever on that mission, came to bring provisions, brandy, and tobacco for trade.

This year was also marked by a change of base of some Choctaws. We are told that Choctaw refugees came to the fort and Bienville settled them on Mobile Bay. They may have fled from the Spaniards, as Penicaut says, for the Choctaws claimed territory as far east as the Escambia River, and

---

[1] 5 Margry, *Découvertes*, pp. 478, 479 ; Gatschet, *Creek Migration Legend*, pp. 87, 225.

[2] Scaife's *America*, p. 163.

[3] King's *Bienville*, p. 184 ; 6 French's *Historical Collection*, p. 77.

[4] 5 Margry, *Découvertes*, p. 481 ; 1 Martin's *Louisiana*, p. 169.

Bienville never lost an opportunity of ingratiating himself with the savages. This immigration may have had sóme connection with an expedition led by Bienville to aid Pensacola against an attack by Alibamons and English.[1] An interesting feature of this migration is that he put them below his fort, and on the site of the present Mobile. It may be conjectured, however, that it was near our Frascati, for it was on the bay, and the marshy cape near there between river and bay has from French times borne the name of Choctaw Point.

The irregularity of supplies after Iberville's death had hampered attempts at a colonial forward movement, and yet something had been done. The Alibamons were at least kept at bay, the many Choctaws were friendly, and the nations immediately near the fort devoted to the French. The abortive expedition from the east showed that the French name was already known and feared as far as the mountains of Carolina. The Mississippi, too, was secure for French traders, and knowledge of the valley was growing. Slaves at the fort were from tribes on and even beyond the great river, and thus indicate distant expeditions; and in 1708 there was even talk among the officers of exploring that great tributary which we call the Missouri. The trade in skins and furs was already a growing one. Probably every ship that came to Dauphine Island took away peltries, and that port itself was of value. It was soon to be important enough to need both church and fort of its own. Louisiana was not a failure.

[1] Gatschet, *Creek Migration Legend*, p. 76 ; 1 Martin's *Louisiana*, p. 169.

CHAPTER IX.

UNKNOWN to almost all but their immediate custodians, there lie, in the residence of the Catholic bishop of Mobile, some old books covered with cloth and marked, "Baptisma." Opening the first, 1704 to 1778, one sees that it is made of a number of thin volumes, like ledger indices, bound together. The entries are in French and brief, giving little more than baptisms, and are in different handwritings. Some of the hands are very indifferent, too, the spelling archaic and often incorrect, the paper poor and blotted. It is just such a book as one would think fit for the fire.

Looked at with the eye of an historian, however, what a treasure do we find! Here are the church records of the first permanent settlement of the Gulf coast, the French Louisiana, with signatures of many of its leaders, and side lights on their lives.

Here, for instance, is the signature of Père Davion, the gentle but heroic missionary to the Tunicas, who had joined Bienville at Biloxi. As *missionaire apostolique* he officiated at the settlement on Mobile River, as we have seen, until 1704.

Davion baptized after that, too, but as before he only signs, never writing the entry in full. His signature is in back hand, not unlike that of Treasurer Spinner of our own times. La Vente has an illegible monogram or series of flourishes about the initial "R" of his name. He alternates with Alexandre Huvé as curé in the entries until 1710, when La Vente's name occurs no more. Nothing indicative of dissension between curé and governor is found in this register. Huvé (or "Huué" as he has it) all but prints his letters, and his entries, which are found as late as 1721, are easy to read. His first name is always distinct, but he runs together the letters of the second.

Let us investigate the credentials of these clergymen.

Until 1722 Mobile's ecclesiastical history is connected with that of Canada, for Louisiana was part of the diocese of J. B. de la Croix, commonly called St. Vallier, the second bishop of Quebec. He ruled from 1688 to 1727, and to his strict discipline, requiring registers, etc., we no doubt owe our Mobile chronicle.

Gravier succeeded his fellow Jesuit, Allouez, when that missionary to the Illinois died in 1689, and St. Vallier at first constituted the superiors of that order his vicars-general in those parts. But afterwards, despite Jesuit protests, he made the superior of the Seminary of Quebec his vicar-general for the banks of the Mississippi.

The first priest, a missionary of this seminary, was, as we have seen, Henri Roulleaux de la Vente, of Bayeux, with a salary of one thousand livres, and his curate was Alexandre Huvé, whose salary was six hundred. Gravier was in Mobile in 1706 and 1708, but has no entries. F. Le Maire signs an entry there on January 30, 1708, as priest and apostolic missionary, and his small, close hand occurs at intervals for several years. He had resigned a parish charge in France and come out at the instigation of Gervaise, a wealthy young priest, who piously wished to found a chapel. Gervaise, indeed, sent out three years' provisions and workmen to build a house and chapel; but when on the point of sailing himself with Le Maire, was restrained of his liberty through the influence of an uncle. Doubtless to Gervaise, then, was due the most commodious residence for the priests, built in 1707 on an eminence to the left of old Fort Louis. Le Maire was friendly to Bienville. Huvé, who had come over in the Pelican in 1704, was not really the Mobile pastor. He was missionary to the Apalaches, and chaplain at the Dauphine Island church, where he almost lost his life in the English attack. He, too, was to go to the Mississippi when that began to be settled, but, shocked with the levity of his countrymen, went to preach to the Indians. He finally returned to France, almost blind, in•1727.

There is a delightful absence of the restraints of orthography, rules of capitalizing, and everything else in these pages, and the side lights on people and place when Mobile was capital of half a continent are full of interest. It is a relief, a positive pleasure, to turn from the quarrels of leaders, which will much engage our attention, to study the private life of the settlement. On this we have a good deal of information from this church baptismal register. The marriage and death records begin later, but the register preserved often gives rank and occupation of parents and sponsors.

An interesting feature about this old Mobile register is that frequently the baptism is lay (*ondoyer*), perhaps by the midwife, in case of danger, although the priest afterwards supplies the usual church ceremonies, if time permits. Indians, too, are often baptized conditionally (*sous condition*).

The first thing that attracts notice, after baptism by Davion of the little Apalache before La Vente's arrival, is the prevalence of Indian slavery. On the 18th of September, and thus before his induction, La Vente baptized a little savage slave of ten to twelve years, living at the house of Poudrié. The child was extremely ill, and, in fact, died and was buried on the same day. Huvé the next day baptized one of thirteen or fourteen who had been living in the colony for a year and belonged to La Vigne. On the first of October were baptized two other slave children, belonging the one to M. de Chateauguay, the other to Minet, and towards the end of the month another of Chateauguay that died three days later. And thus it runs through the whole period. Many colonists, from Bienville and Manteville and the missionaries down, had Indian slaves, of whom not a few were only from one to three years old. Of course, to these, removed from their homes, death came often. Boutin had one of two months from the Tensas in 1708. Why they should have been taken so young it is difficult to understand, unless with the view of training them in the French interest. The king owned such slaves also, but his were adults. Sometimes they were given names, — witness Hypolite in 1707, slave of M. Poudrié. The nationality is not often mentioned, except Schittimacha from 1708 and 1709, and from the latter year an occasional Alibamon and Tensa. In 1710 was baptized Alexandre, a Padoka (Comanche) slave of the priests of Fort Louis. A Natchitoche and a Chicacha are also mentioned.

The Indians themselves held slaves. The chief of the Apalaches in 1710 had his Paniouacha slave of three years baptized as Marie Susanne. The Apalaches we know were Christians, and their names occur often in the records.

Negroes were not numerous at old Fort Louis, but there were some. The first mentioned was a little seven-year-old slave of Bienville in 1707, named Jean Baptiste, but where he came from is not stated. Bienville had another of three years, baptized the same year as Joseph. Chateauguay had a negro named François Jacemin, who the same year was declared to be the father of Anthoine, born October 26, of Bienville's negro woman Marie. This is the first recorded birth of a negro on the Gulf coast, although these other children may have been born here. Marie stood godmother later for Marie, a Sitimacha slave of Bienville. The names are sometimes odd. Once a man is Bon Tems, and another is Vin d'Espagne.

Generally it is not stated whether a slave is Indian or negro, but, as the records are often precise as to degree of negro blood, it is to be supposed the slave is Indian unless otherwise given. The importation of negroes in quantity began some years later.

We find named only one mulatto child, Marie Anne, belonging to Sieur La Tour. As she was eleven in 1710, she was not born at Fort Louis, however. Of mixed Indian and white blood (*mestifs* in the later registers), there were hardly more. Sieur Charli, merchant, admits he had a child in 1709 by an Indian slave. Huvé mentions one, Jean Baptiste, with bated breath, July 26, 1710. It was a child of an Indian female of Sieur D'Arbanne, and the curé adds, "Cujus filius non tantum rumore publico habetur, sed et ratione spontanea matris." The church did not sanction marriages with Indians, but we shall see such unions in later years, and find them even in the church records called *mariages naturels*.

Of the occupations recorded, the military would naturally rank first in importance. Chateauguay is early spoken of as captain, Blondel as ensign in his company, Valentin Bareau as surgeon major, and besides Roy we have, in 1707, Jean Louis Minuit, and in 1711, Jean Louis, as master cannoneers. Simon de la Salle was a cadet of the company Vaulesar in 1708, and Bernard Diron of Chateauguay's company the next year. Jean Colon was the sergeant of Chateauguay's company, and La

Violette is later mentioned as also a sergeant. Michel Danti is named as a private soldier.

René Doyer and Jean Bon are *maîtres arquebusiers*, gunsmiths, — an important trade and semi-military. Doyer could not write. Hardly less important was the occupation of master pilot, which was Simon Coussot's business, and that of tool sharpener (*maître taillandier*), which was Pierre Alein's and also Philippe La Briere's somewhat later. Besides Jean De Can, we find in 1709 Jean Le Camp as a locksmith, and in the same year Sieur Boie as armorer.

In a semi-official capacity we see from 1707 M. Poirier named as keeper of the royal stores (*garde magasin*), an important position in a colony which depended on the home country for almost everything. Jean Claude Poirier was a merchant in 1716. We find early mentions of Les Sœurs and their house, and March 29, 1710, they are named as Sœurs Grissot and Linand. Elsewhere we find mention of Marie Linant, certainly the same, but it seems improbable that Sœur Grissot should be the Marie Grisot, midwife, named in 1708. It may be conjectured that they are the two "Sœurs Grises" (gray nuns) who chaperoned across the ocean the marriageable girls who came on the Pelican. Was it one of these two that wanted to marry Boisbriant?

Among the purely civil avocations, tradesmen (*marchands*) easily lead in number. The first named as such is Jacques L'Allemand in 1707, although Gabriel Savary, wife of J. B. Saucié, is mentioned in 1705, and we learn in 1708 that he was also merchant. In the same year Gme. Boutin is described by Le Maire as *marchand à la Mobile*. The wives of merchants are also named. Boutin's wife, for instance, was Louise Marguerite Housseau. It was at the baptism of their child that the Pensacola governor Guzman signed his name with so many flourishes. J. B. La Loire is a *marchand*, and his wife's name is also given, — Marie Nadant. François Trudaut is often named, and his wife also, Jeanne Burelle.

La Tour is a Sieur, but is *marchand*, too, in 1710, as also Claude Trepanier, whose wife was Genevieve Burelle. Mr. Joseph de Lery was another in that same year; his wife, Hippolite Mercier.

There were, however, other trades. The constant complaint

was of lack of mechanics, but we find at least several carpenters. Le Conte was a *maître charpentier* in 1705, and in 1707
we find Jean Prot another, a man of family, although he could
not write. It was not by any means every person who could
in those days. Next year we find as carpenters François
Trudault, a married man, and André Penegault also. This
last name sounds like Penicaut, our literary friend, but the
master carpenter was a married man, while the author probably
was not at that time, from the adventures he described. This
lady was Marie Prevot. It might be added, too, that if André
had written a book as badly as he did his name, it never could
have been deciphered.

Cabinet maker (*maître menuisier*) is the only other trade
named, and there is but one in that business, Jean Alexandre.
Of course the fact that it is not given in these defective registers is no certain evidence a business did not exist; but this
fact probably shows at least that the man was not of family
and not popular.

Many residents (*habitants*) are mentioned, but they would
be mere names to us. The Le Sueurs, however, may be spoken
of. Mlle. Marie Le Sueur and her mother Le Messier, the
widow Le Sueur, are often sponsors. Marie could not write.
The widow had also a son, Jean Paul, whom we shall know.
All of course owned slaves, — who did not, indeed, that had
the means?

Signatures of well-known men are there as witnesses to baptisms, for father signs, and godfather and godmother, as well
as the priest. The induction of La Vente in 1704 is attested
by the clear hand and flourish of Bienville, lieutenant of the
king, the cramped signature of Major Boisbriant, and "De la
Sall." Poor Nicolas de la Salle! He was removed from
office in 1708, and in March of that year an infant of his was
baptized, and another on August 24, 1709; but the record
notes the burial of the latter in the parish cemetery six days
later. On May 18 is the striking signature of Philippe Blondel, later commandant at Natchitoches. He stood godfather
for the child of a cannoneer. The free hand and bold flourish of Chateaugné, — spelled by the priests Chateauguay, like
the domain in Canada, — occurs several times.

Naval stores are not named, but existing tar kilns, overgrown with large trees, testify to this industry near there during French times. Whether the sawmill and tannery planned by Iberville were established, we do not know, but Sawmill Creek not many miles away had that name at least long before the American period. Hunters are not named, for probably all hunted, and of the French names of places given, at least one indicating a hunt has survived. Just behind Twenty-one Mile Bluff is a corner or low ground still bearing the name of "Fondlou," — Creole for Fond de l'Ours, Bear Ground. Somewhat lower, Bayou Conner is a corruption of Bayou Canon, named, it is said, from cannon thrown overboard in some expedition, on account of low water or otherwise, while across the river Bayou Registe commemorates some forgotten Frenchman.

Such were some of the people and their occupations at the "vieux fort" on Mobile River. Where pass steamboats loaded the one way with provisions and for the return trip with hundreds of cotton bales from the upper rivers, then sailed Iberville and his compeers, pioneers and gentlemen of France. From those now neglected shores looked out men and women like ourselves, founding indeed an empire for Louis XIV., but often amid hunger and danger, sometimes yearning for beautiful France and straining the eye to catch the first glimpse of the boats from Dauphine Island, coming from the Loire, or other vessel expected from the old home. There, on the land where now grow pines, and where the silence is unbroken except by the distant locomotive or passing steamer, was the town clustering about Fort Louis, in streets and lots, where civil life began with its joys and sorrows, lights and shadows, private loves and public enmities, almost two hundred years ago, never to cease forever, despite change of site, of flag, and of race.

CHAPTER X.

THE GREAT CHANGE OF BASE.

PENICAUT tells us that early in the year 1709 a rise of the river occurred, which overflowed both town and fort, and left uninjured only high elevations. This was a serious and unexpected event, and of course might happen again. In our own day high water has flowed all around Twenty-seven Mile Bluff. It had the calamitous result in Bienville's time of destroying the crops of the Indians, on which, to some extent, the French were dependent.

It was necessary to make a change of base, and to move the site of the colony to some place not subject to overflow.

Bienville therefore selected, doubtless with the assent of D'Artaguette, who was friendly to him, the land which he had given the fugitive Choctaws, and he determined to build there his new Fort Louis. This is the site of the present Mobile. The Choctaws he removed to Dog River, and directed Aide-Major Pailloux and other officers to mark out a place for the new fort and barracks, and land for each family. The city lots should be twelve and a half by twenty-five toises, say seventy-five by one hundred and fifty feet each, and the priests were given a square to the left, facing the "sea," for the church, — of course Catholic. Such is the account of Penicaut, who was on the spot.[1]

The same authority tells us that they worked at the new fort for a year, and that in 1710 movables and merchandise were brought down in canoes, cannon and munitions by floats. The inhabitants were all moved, and the old fort abandoned entirely.[2] This was followed by migration of their old Indian neighbors, too, and the new city was to have surroundings of the old site. A new feature, however, was having two batter-

[1] 5 Margry, *Découvertes*, pp. 481, 482.
[2] *Ibid.*, pp. 484, 485.

ies outside the fort, of twelve cannon each. As these commanded the sea, we may imagine that, unless they were just outside the fort, as is probable from Dumont's later mention of half-moons, one perhaps was at Choctaw Point and the other on the higher land to the north of the city afterwards called Round Top.

The new city was founded in a time of scarcity of food, due to the flood. In this year, 1710, Bienville disposed his unmarried colonists among the savages. Lieutenant Blondel, on this occasion, went with thirty soldiers to live among the Choctaws, and Sieur de Valligny (or Walligny) with his twenty-five French, recently arrived on the Renommée, and eight Apalaches departed to Fish River across the bay, — the first mention of this stream. This was not a quartering of soldiers on the natives, for Penicaut's account shows that the Indians, especially the young women, enjoyed it as much as the French. It was really a stroke of policy.[1]

We now reach modern ground, and it would be interesting and important to ascertain the exact site of Bienville's town relative to the existing city. No plan has ever been published, and none is known in city or American archives. But the author has been able, through courtesy of the French Minister of the Marine, in 1895, to secure a photograph of a manuscript map by Sieur Cheuillot, discovered for him in the Archives of the Marine at Paris, and this is now for the first time printed.

A description in old French script is at the sides of the plan. A translation of this document of 1711 is given below. The toise is a measure of six feet, but it must be remembered this French foot is 12.78933 English inches, and thus longer than our own.[2]

"DESCRIPTION OF THE CITY AND OF THE FORT LOUIS.

"A. Fort Louis, fortified with an exterior length from one point of bastion to another of 90 toises, and with this length they have given to the faces of the bastion $23\frac{1}{2}$ toises, to flanks $12\frac{1}{4}$, to gorges 5 toises, and to the curtains 40 toises.

"The fort is constructed of cedar stakes 13 ft. high, of which $2\frac{1}{2}$

[1] King's *Bienville*, pp. 179, 205 ; 5 Margry, *Découvertes*, p. 485. Cf. p. 443, etc.

[2] 2 *Public Lands* (1838), p. 715. For original French text, see Appendix.

PLAN DE LA ·VILLE·ET·FORT·LOVIS·DE

·LOVISIANE·ETABLIES·PAR·LES·FRANCOIS·EN·1711·

Nouuelle Etablissement cottées par lettres Alphabetique

SVITE·DE·LA·DESCRIPTION·
De La Ville et du Fort Loüis.

E·   DE·   LA·   MOBILE·

are in the ground, and 14 inches square *de paisseur*, planted joined
the one to the other. These stakes end on top in points like palisades.
On the inside along the stakes runs a kind of banquette in good slope,
two feet high and one and a half wide.

"There is in the fort only the governor's house, the *magasin* where
are the king's effects, and a guard-house. The officers, soldiers, and
residents have their abode outside the fort, as is indicated, being placed
in such manner that the streets are six toises wide and all parallel.
The blocks are 50 toises square except those opposite the fort, which
are 60 toises wide and 50 deep, and those nearest the river, which are
50 toises wide and 60 deep.

"The houses are constructed of cedar and pine upon a foundation
of wooden stakes which project out of the ground one foot and might
be called piling, because this soil is inundated, as you see marked on
the plan, in certain localities, in times of rain. Some people use to
support their houses stone which is a kind of turf (*tufle*), very soft,
and would be admirable for fine buildings. This stone is found 18
leagues above the new establishment along the bank of the Mobile
river. The houses are 18, 20 to 25 feet high or more, some lower,
constructed of a kind of plaster (*mortié*) made of earth and lime.

"Note : — This lime is made of oyster shell found at the mouth of
the river on little islands which bear that name.

"They give to all who wish to settle in this place land $12\frac{1}{2}$ toises
wide, facing a street, by 25 deep.

"The stone used to support the houses is scarce and not common
for lack of the means of water transportation, such as flat-boats, which
do not exist, nor are there persons who wish to go to the expense [of
building them]. This would be a great aid, for those whose houses
rest only on wooden stakes are obliged to renew them every three or
four years, because they decay in the ground."

The lettering connected with the fort is thus given in the
margin of the map : —

"B. House of the governor, C. Warehouse (*magasin*) of the king,
D. *Poudrière* or powder magazine, E. Guard-house (*Corp de Garde*),
F. Prison, G. Bastion where they place the flag, H. Bastion in which
is a bell (*cloche*), there being no *chapelle* in the fort."

At the top of the plan is the heading, "Names of Officers
and Principal Inhabitants who Occupy the Sites (*emplacements*)
of this New Establishment Indicated by Letters of the Alpha-
bet," and with that guide the plan is very interesting.

We read: "I. Church and parish (*L'église et paroisse*)," but there is no "I" on the plan. There are a number of unlettered lots, and a building, unmarked, to the north of the fort, not to mention twenty-eight squares projected, quite in modern American style, through the piney woods (*Pinierre*). We know that in 1713 Remonville was to find it expedient to build a church for the colony,[1] it may be on the lot of the Seminary priests. So that any building in 1711 must have been only temporary. It would seem probable that, even if temporary, the unmarked building by the fort is the parish church, for it is in a central place, convenient to garrison and inhabitants, as near the bell as the swampy ground admitted, and separated from the residence of the Seminary priests (V) only by that of M. de Grandville (z), and from the cemetery (R) only by that of M. de Bois Brillant (&). It seems to have been Bienville's policy in this arrangement to have the prominent officers live around the fort. He himself had a whole square (X) next south, — probably that afterwards occupied by the Eslavas on Royal, extending from our Theatre to Monroe streets, and as far west as St. Emanuel. Near the northeast corner of this square is (Q) "a little moat made to carry off water," emptying into the river, and itself with a bridge.

On the two blocks west of the fort we find, beginning at the south, (h) M. de Clos, *ordonnateur*, (q) one of the several places marked as occupied by inhabitants and *voyageurs*, (m) Jean Louis, *maître cainonier*, and on a corner (e) the celebrated M. de St. Denis. As we shall see, streets have been much changed since then, but this paladin must have lived near the west side of St. Emanuel, about the middle of the block running south from our Church Street. Next north of St. Denis, separated by a street, was (c) M. de Valligny, then (z) M. de Grandville's second and smaller lot, — for he had a larger one, where he more probably lived.

Next north of Grandville's smaller lot, and, like all others about the fort, facing on what seems to be a double row of oaks around the esplanade, comes (&) our friend M. de Boisbrillant (or Boisbriant), occupying the whole southwest corner of the streets as then platted, — now more likely the site of Christ Church. Back of him on our Conception was (R) the cemetery, and the rest of that block was occupied by (S) sol-

---

[1] King's *Bienville*, p. 195.

diers, — as were the whole of the two cleared westernmost
squares of the city, where they were perhaps thought of as a
protection on that side.

On the corner across the street from Boisbriant was (g) M.
des Laurier, *chirurgien major*, and at the north end of his
block, near our southwest St. Emanuel and Conti, are (p)
people in the pay of the king, and then going north a block of
(S) soldiers again, and back of them about our Conception and
Dauphin (L) the hospital, near where it will be found in
Spanish times.

The Seminary priests, then, were about Royal and Conti,
and across what corresponded to Conti we find (y) M. de Chateaugué, Bienville's brother, and one of the most active and
famous Mobilians. Next north of him came (l) Sieur Poirrier,
"Garde magasin du Roy." Near the north end of town, —
which was about our St. Louis Street, — was (f) M. de St.
Helesne, Bienville's younger brother, but rather a scapegrace.
However, he may have been put near the north end of town
to protect it. Not far off, about the northeast corner of Bienville Square, was (b) M. Blondel. This completes the list of
notabilities north of the fort. The others are called employees
or inhabitants, without names.

South were fewer people, although eight squares are laid off
there, as in the other direction. About our Madison, between
Royal and St. Emanuel was (a) M. de Mandeville, and next
east of him, facing on Royal, was (T) the "logement des
prestres." These must have been the Jesuits Bienville favored,
placed here with Bienville, Grandville, and the whole fort between them and the Seminary priests. Across the street north
was (d) M. de Paillou, the accomplished engineer who laid off
Mobile, and was to design other cities, too. This plan, however, is marked as "Levez & Dessignez par le Sr. Cheuillot,"
— otherwise unknown, but for this valuable document worthy
of being held in lasting honor.

No explanation is given for lot (r). The other lots so far as
marked belong mostly to (p), who as we have seen are royal
employees of different kinds, or (q) inhabitants and *voyageurs*.
There is one curious exception. South of the fort, across west
from Bienville, next to Dr. des Laurier, in the midst of the
soldiers at the intersection of our Dauphin and St. Emanuel,

and, in particular, over the rear third of the square occupied in front by Grandville and the Seminary priests, occur lots with the letter (n). On the explanation we have only, "Emplacement occupées par plusieurs femmes."

Other signs are on the chart. The river bank south of the fort is noted as (M) "marshy land, which occurs sometimes," and (P) is a wooden bridge serving as a wharf (*embarquadère*), extending obliquely across the marshy land at the northeast corner of the fort, say between Government and Church streets, to deep water. East of the river are noted (o) banks of sand, while on what is now Pinto's Island two pine-trees are represented.

Among the curious features of this map is the location of the fort. It extends much further east than the residences, and on all sides is surrounded by marshy land. Even if the interior was filled and raised, the surroundings would make the place unhealthful. This seems strange, when we reflect that the move from the older site was on account of overflows of the river. But it is to be remembered that there was a town as well as a fort, and that the garrison lived outside in houses, only the guard on duty having actual quarters inside.

Another odd thing is that no names are annexed even to the twelve dedicated streets, and such is the case with later maps, also. There can be no doubt, however, that this was the time when the streets were named. At this period were distinguished the family of Conti, who were of royal blood, being descendants of a brother of the great general Condé, who died universally lamented in 1686. Says Voltaire, "The first Prince de Conti, Armand, was brother of the great Condé. He played a part in the war of the Fronde, and died in 1666. He left by Anne Martinozzi, niece of Cardinal Mazarin, Louis, died in 1685, without issue by his wife Marie Anne, daughter of Louis XIV. and the Duchess de la Vallière, and left also François Louis, Prince de la Roche-sur-Yon, then Prince de Conti, who was elected king of Poland in 1697; a prince whose memory has long been dear to France, resembling as he did the great Condé in brightness (*esprit*) and courage, and always animated with the desire to please, a quality lacking sometimes in the great Condé. He died in 1709."[1]

[1] Voltaire, *Louis XIV.*, p. 476, Firmin-Didot ed., 1891.

For this prince, doubtless, patron of La Salle and of Tonty, was Conti Street named, important avenue as it then was. In 1711, this Conti, it is true, was dead, but he had a son, born in 1695, then alive, who outlived Louis XIV.

Parallel to Conti was Dauphin Street. The son of the king, the heir apparent, was called "dauphin," his wife "dauphine." The street and the island were probably named in 1711. Who were the pair at that time?

Louis XIV. lived with a number of women at one time or other, notably the Duchess de la Vallière, Mme. de Montespan, and Mme. de Maintenon whom he married late in life; but his only queen was Marie Thérèse of Austria, born 1638, married 1660, died 1683. Louis and she had but one child, the dauphin Louis, born 1661, died April 14, 1711. Of him, called Monseigneur, it was said, — "Son of a king, father of a king, king himself never." Not knowing exactly when the names were given, for they might well have been brought with the settlement from up the river, we cannot say the name of our shopping street was not for this prince, distinguished only for scandal. But remembering that it would take some time to settle down, it seems more probable the name is for the eldest son of Monseigneur and his wife, Marie Anne Christine Victoire of Bavaria.

This Louis, called Duke of Burgundy, was born in 1682, and his wife, the dauphine after April 14, 1711, was Marie Adelaide of Savoy, daughter of the first king of Sardinia. This dauphine, according to Voltaire, was well educated, just, peaceable, enemy of vainglory, a worthy pupil of Beauvilliers and the celebrated Fénelon.[1] For them, then, were our street and island named.

The closing years of Louis XIV. were marked by private grief as well as public disaster, and 1712 brought home losses which humbled even the great king in the dust. Nemesis it may be, but one cannot help pitying the man. In that year died Louis, the seven-year old child of this dauphin, then February 12 the loved dauphine, and six days later, of smallpox, the amiable dauphin himself, to the sorrow of France and of all Europe. And the loss was even greater than it seemed. A man who would have been a good king was gone, and the

---

[1] Voltaire, *Louis XIV.*, p. 473.

new dauphin was the two-year-old child who was to be the dissolute Louis XV., in whose minority came the regency of Philip of Orleans, the friend of John Law.

Remembering the pitch reached by royalty under Louis XIV., it is natural that the principal street, the one fronting the river, should be Royal Street. St. Louis was run many years later through swampy land, but its name shows its French origin, and, whether then built up or merely important as the north boundary street, it too must date back to Bienville's time. But unless St. Francis be another, only the four streets above given seem to retain now their French names. The present streets south of Government are certainly American, and St. Emanuel, Conception, (St.) Joachim, and St. Michael were almost as certainly renamed by the Spaniards, and their French names are not now known.

Our plan does not show the two-story house Chateaugué built on his lot, and we do not see the name of Commissary La Salle nor of Curé La Vente. Indeed, these last two never exercised authority on the soil of present Mobile. La Salle died in 1710, probably up the river, and La Vente in October of that year returned to France in a dying condition.[1]

Le Maire, the new curé, was friendly to Bienville and often enjoyed his hospitality, and in D'Artaguette the governor had also a friend. D'Artaguette showed Bienville the charges against him, and this induced him to write a spirited remonstrance to Pontchartrain, which D'Artaguette took with him to France in this year, 1711, when he returned home on the Renommée to exculpate the governor.

[1] Shea's *Catholic Church in the Colonies,* p. 552.

CHAPTER XI.

When Bienville moved his colony to its final seat, the brilliant reign of Louis XIV. was drawing to its dark close. The vaulting ambition of the French monarch had overleaped itself. Although he outlived his great opponent, William of Orange, and still annexed provinces on the Meuse and Rhine, Marlborough and Eugene had filled the place of the Dutch-English commander, while the French Condé and Turenne were dead. An honorable peace was finally patched up at Utrecht, but the rest which followed was the sleep of exhaustion. Money was gone, men were gone, — all gone, save honor. The king could not carry out his old American dreams.

On March 17, 1713, the frigate Baron de la Fosse, commanded by De la Jonquin, arrived at Dauphine Island, firing salutes. She brought the news of this Peace of Utrecht, but news, too, much less acceptable to the colonists. There was to be a complete change of system.

The aid which had come in the Renommée two years before had been the private enterprise of Remonville, always a friend of the colonists, and the government had now improved on that experiment, and farmed out the whole colony. Antoine Crozat, a rich merchant, — Marquis de Chatel he was then, — had leased the country for fifteen years from the king, and intended through mining and commerce with Mexico to make his venture pay. The total population was four hundred, including twenty negroes,[1] and he was obligated to bring over colonists, and also introduce slaves from Africa. He was to be represented by a governor and directors, while the king on his side was to maintain a sufficient military force.

Bienville was not satisfactory to the new proprietor. He believed in agriculture, not commerce, and had taken D'Artaguette to the Mississippi to urge an establishment there. So

[1] Penicaut, 6 French's *Historical Collection*, p. 113.

Crozat sent over a new governor on this frigate in the person
of De la Mothe Cadillac, who had already served with distinction in Canada. With him came his wife, sons, and daughters,
as well as twenty-five young girls from Brittany. Cadillac
was interested in Crozat's venture as in some sort a partner.

The transfer of the government could not have been either
lengthy or formal, and no doubt occurred in the fort at Mobile.
The new governor lived outside, however. For, as Chateaugué's house was the best in the town, Cadillac proceeded to take
possession of it for his large family. Chateaugué complained
to the government at Paris, but apparently without effect.

History has not dealt kindly with La Mothe Cadillac, and
yet he had his merits. In August, 1701, he had founded
Detroit from Three Rivers, and for some years was an important character in Canada. For his Detroit stockade, named
Fort Pontchartrain, held for France the passage between the
upper lakes, whose fur trade was controlled from Michilli-
mackinac by the Jesuits, and the lower lakes, whose trade at
La Salle's Fort Frontenac and British Fort Oswego was disputed between the French and English. He had been hampered there by Pacaud's Compagnie du Canada, which held
a monopoly of the trade at Detroit and Frontenac, and Detroit
was destined not to be able to compete with Mackinac in trade.
This company was practically abolished after a few years, but
not before its monopoly had helped Louisiana by driving down
to the Gulf the *coureurs de bois* and their peltries.[1]

So that when Cadillac was put in charge of the interests
of Crozat, he knew something of his business. The northern
end of the Mississippi, even the Illinois country where the Ohio
empties, was not in Crozat's charter. It was in a measure independent, and in fact always oscillated between Canada and
Louisiana. Exploration had by this time opened up much of
the interior, and the designs of Cadillac covered trade with the
Spaniards, as well as with the Indians of the Mississippi and
Alabama valleys, and the working of mines wherever found.

Among his first endeavors from Mobile was to open an over-
land trade with Mexico. For it he selected Jucheran de St.
Denis and sent him with ten thousand livres of Crozat's goods.
The adventures of St. Denis as detailed by Penicaut were

---

[1] Winsor's *Basin of the Mississippi*, pp. 72, 116.

less important for commerce than geography. He penetrated almost alone up the Red River region, where he had
once explored with Bienville, and made his way to the Spanish
post of Presidio del Porto. He was sent forward to Mexico
and well treated, but obtained little satisfaction in the way of
trade. The same result followed St. Denis's second and larger
trading expedition through the Natchitoches country, this time
on his own account. But he at least won a Spanish wife, if he
did have to stay in jail for some time.[1] The same repulse followed the mission of Durigouin by sea to Vera Cruz. Cadillac
had to give up the idea of Spanish trade, but the French at
least gained a foothold among the Indian neighbors of Mexico.

Indian relations were generally happy. On the Mississippi,
in one of those Indian wars of extermination that devastated so
much of our country from time to time, the Tensas were, in
1714, driven away from their homes near Bayou Manchac.
They were then persuaded to move to Mobile, and were settled
two leagues north from the fort, where the Chaouanons and
Taouatchas had been.[2]

On the Mississippi the French were all but supreme. In
1714, they found an English officer exploring that river, and
they captured him and brought him to Mobile. Some give his
name as Hutchey, some Young, and Penicaut calls him M.
You.[3] He was released at Mobile, but was not wise enough
to leave for the Atlantic coast. The Tohome Indians recap-
tured him and "broke his head."

The enterprising English were taking advantage of the Peace
of Utrecht and penetrating everywhere. Long before this the
Tennessee River had been the route for Carolina traders to
the interior tribes, and the English were now even among the
Natchez. The Catawbas and Cherokees were always friendly
with the Atlantic colonies, and it was a great security to these
to have peace, particularly with the latter. For the Cherokees
dominated all the eastern tribes south of the Iroquois. But
the relations with the Yamassees and Tuscaroras were not so
satisfactory, and from 1711 there was war with the English.

---

[1] Penicaut, 6 French's *Historical Collection*, p. 133 ; 5 Margry, *Découvertes*,
pp. 495, 527 ; 1 Martin's *Louisiana*, p. 204.

[2] Penicaut, 6 French's *Historical Collection*, p. 126.

[3] 5 Margry, *Découvertes*, p. 509 ; 1 Martin's *Louisiana*, p. 185.

Colonel Moore finally drove the Tuscaroras northwardly to become the sixth nation of the great Iroquois confederacy, and by 1713 all was quiet.[1] But all was not friendly, and this hostility seems to have driven the neighboring Creeks and Alibamons into the arms of the French. The French were ever the better diplomats.

We are told that in the year 1714 the "emperor" of the Indians near Carolina and the principal chief of the Alibamons came to Mobile and proposed to Cadillac that he erect a fort among them. This commercial and political chance was not to be lost, and he sent Captain de la Tour with a hundred men and built Fort Toulouse, near where the Coosa and the Tallapoosa join. Other accounts make Bienville the builder of this first extension of Mobile's influence. The fort, by whomever erected, was of logs, and had four bastions, with two iron cannon in each. It is said the name was at first Alabama (in some more French spelling, no doubt), but that it was by Bienville changed to Toulouse in honor of the Comte de Toulouse, an admiral of France, and at this time director of the colonies. The usual name of post and district in the church records, however, we shall find to be "Aux Alibamons." The first garrison was of thirty soldiers, commanded by Marigny de Mandeville; but the fort, not less judiciously than beautifully located, had an importance far beyond the actual number of soldiers within its ramparts.

From both a commercial and military point of view it controlled the warlike Creeks, and covered the approach around the southern flank of the mountains from the Atlantic not only to Mobile, but also to the Mississippi. From this time it is that Coxe in his contemporary work on "Carolana" dates the decline of English influence among the "Allibamons, Chicazas and Chattas," although he mentions Fort Louis itself rather than its outpost. In fact, a general Indian war with the English followed, extending even to the Chickasaws, where Bienville's kinsman St. Helene was killed. Characteristically enough, it was as he stooped to light a cigar.[2]

On the Mississippi the French already had a post among the Natchez. It was a warehouse or factory, and may have been

---

[1] Winsor's *Basin of the Mississippi*, 20, 133, 168.
[2] 1 Martin's *Louisiana*, p. 186.

due to fear of M. You and the English traders Penicaut found, in 1714, among those Indians. The station at first met with misfortune, for the Indians murdered Frenchmen on the river and plundered the warehouse. But Bienville went there in 1716 for redress. He seized the chiefs by stratagem, and compelled the execution of the offending warriors. A site for a fort was also conceded, and Paillou, who had built Fort Louis, now superintended the erection of Fort Rosalie there on the Mississippi. Such was the origin of Natchez.

The French long cherished De Soto's dream of mines in the interior, and to this was due much of the misfortune of the colony. Lands lay rich about them, but they did not attempt agriculture. Commerce with the Spaniards had not succeeded, and that with the Indians, on which Iberville had so counted, was not sufficient. It was one of Crozat's original plans to develop the mineral wealth of the country.

Le Sueur, years before, had built his short-lived Fort D'Huillier on Green River, high among the sources of the Mississippi (where Penicaut had wintered with him), and thence taken to France his green earth. In 1702, M. D'Eraque had been driven from the fort by Mascoutins and Foxes. Now Cadillac was to investigate the silver ore which was brought him from mines in the Illinois.[1] He was deceived, of course, for it had been brought from Mexico. But he staid in the upper country almost a year, and had, on his return in 1715, very little to say about his discoveries.

He said enough about everything else. His reports from the beginning were blue. The colonists were irreligious, the country unproductive, mines a myth, and commerce with the Spaniards not permitted by them. On the other hand, the commissary Duclos praised everything, Bienville in particular.

Relations were always strained between Cadillac and Bienville, and one half suspects that Bienville put some of his friends among the wood rangers up to palming off that ore on the governor in order to take him away for a while.

And yet Bienville, in a letter to his brother, the Baron de Longueuil, as early as 1713, had mentioned Cadillac's "grown daughter, who had a great deal of merit," and whom he

[1] Winsor's *Basin of the Mississippi*, p. 99 ; 5 Margry, *Découvertes*, p. 416 ; 1 Martin's *Louisiana*, p. 184.

thought of marrying, although he disliked her snarling father.[1] This marriage was never consummated; but no authority has been discovered for the old story that she fell in love with Bienville, and, when Cadillac offered him the hand of the daughter, he declined it.[2] It would be more likely that the jealousy between the two men drove the romantic attachment out of Bienville's heart.

Cadillac's complaints to France finally bore fruit, — but only in his own recall. Crozat wrote him that the disorders he complained of were due to his own maladministration, and selected L'Epinay to succeed him. Meantime Bienville was to act as governor *ad interim*. Cadillac then complained that he was treated discourteously at Mobile. We may hope it consisted, for one thing, in being forced to give Chateaugué back his house. At all events, on March 9, 1717, the Duclos, Paon, and Paix, Crozat's vessels, arrived at Dauphine Island, bringing the new governor and Hubert, the new commissary. Bienville received the cross of the order of St. Louis and grant of Horn Island as his property, but was disappointed at not becoming governor himself.[3]

The whole colony had but seven hundred inhabitants, according to Du Pratz, and the change of governor was to make little difference. One important change, however, was made in the fort which caused it to survive until this century. It was reconstructed of brick, traditionally said to have been made in the forest not far from Dr. Ketchum's residence on Government Street, and carried to the fort by Indian squaws. A stone bearing the date 1717 is said to have lasted until American times, but this valuable relic has disappeared. The dimensions show that the new fort was smaller, for the ditches hardly reached to where the first stockade had run.

This show of activity was almost the last. Crozat soon found that the new fort and the new governor made little improvement in the returns. The disappointed old man at last, in this same year, prayed the regent to accept a surrender of the colony, and he consented.

[1] King's *Bienville*, pp. 190, 200.
[2] Pickett's *Alabama*, p. 225.
[3] Penicaut, 6 French's *Historical Collection*, p. 134 ; King's *Bienville*, p. 228.

CHAPTER XII.

On February 9, 1718, the Dauphine, Vigilant, and Neptune arrived at Dauphine Island, bringing Boisbriant as royal lieutenant, commanding Mobile and Dauphine Island, and a commission for Bienville as governor, all dated September 20, 1717. This, says Penicaut, "gave general satisfaction, as no one better knew the wants and resources of the colony."[1]

But there was one who thought he knew them better, — John Law, the first great "promoter" of modern times. Scotch gambler, outlaw from England, introducer of the game of faro, French banker, intimate of the notorious regent, the Duke of Orleans, head of the Mississippi bubble, outlaw again, then a wanderer on the face of the earth until his death, — the life of this brilliant man reads like a romance. Whoever has read Gayarré's picture of Law in his glory, with princes kicking their shins in his anteroom when the Mississippi project was at its height, can never forget it.

Law was undoubtedly a master of finance, but he raised a spirit of speculation which he could not lay. From banking he went to "booming" Louisiana. His Western Company of August 17, 1717, obtained a charter for twenty-five years, and was designed to develop the agriculture of the country. Prospectuses, however, painted too brightly the fertile soil, balmy air, and golden sands. The company tried to develop in a few years what needed a century.

Bienville believed in the scheme, and did all he could to further it. He had always favored a settlement on the Mississippi, and now determined to make it. Hubert opposed him, and was to succeed in forcing a compromise on New Biloxi for a time. But Bienville believed he was right, and he

[1] Penicaut, 6 French's *Historical Collection*, pp. 138, 139 ; 2 White's *New Recopilacion*, p. 436, etc., which gives the commissions in full.

was yet to succeed. It was in this expansive spirit that in the
year of his appointment he examined the Mississippi and picked
out the site of New Orleans, shown on the Company's map
of this time as only a portage. He sent the brave Blondel as
commandant to a post now established at Natchitoches, and
Boisbriant, who had been knighted, as governor to the Illinois
region, where in 1718–20 he built Fort Chartres, on the Mississippi above the Ohio, to become the chief seat of French
influence in that region. At Mobile itself, however, we read of
desertions, in 1719, of soldiers who made their way overland to
Carolina.[1]

The Company was anxious to induce immigrants of every
class, and to this we owe some maps. One, beautifully drawn
and dating from the beginning of Law's enterprise, gives a
clear idea of Mobile Bay, which still, as with Delisle, is not
named as such. It shows the Old Fort (Vieux Fort) about
opposite where R. Espagnole leaves the Mobile River, and
near Isle Dauphine it notes, " jadis Massacre." It is based on
Delisle, and has the same names that he has and the same general arrangement, but lacks his bay soundings.[2]

An early map gives "Chaeteau Bienville" on the bay above
Dog River. It was no doubt the place mentioned by Penicaut as built in 1719 by the governor on the bank of the sea a
league from the fort. This would locate the château in Garrow's Bend, but its exact site is now unknown. Tradition is
silent, too, but somewhere on the present Shell Road, Bienville
had this " fort belle maison avec un jardin." According to
French's version, he lived there all the year round for his
health, and had orange-trees in his orchard. Margry's text,
however, says nothing of oranges, which are thought to date
from a later régime.[3]

Bienville was to ask for a fief on Pearl River to bear his
name, and get Horn Island instead in socage tenure.[4] The
desire to perpetuate his name was not unnatural, but he was
as unsuccessful as his older brother. For Iberville had asked

[1] Penicaut, 6 French's *Historical Collection*, pp. 138–141 ; 1 Martin's
Louisiana, p. 207.

[2] Winsor's *Basin of the Mississippi*, p. 423.

[3] 5 Margry, *Découvertes*, p. 487 ; 6 French's *Historical Collection*, p. 106.

[4] King's *Bienville*, p. 228.

that the country on upper Mobile Bay, from Dog River around
to below the great bluffs of the eastern shore, be granted to
him as the Comté de d'Iberville, two leagues deep at all points.
He said he would undertake to settle it.[1] Had this been done,
how different might have been local history!

These particular grants were not made, but land was liberally divided out among *concessionaires*, who should as a condition of the grants settle colonists on them. In March, 1719,
the warship Comte de Toulouse arrived at Dauphine Island
with one hundred passengers, and a month later other vessels
under Serigny with more, as well as soldiers and workmen,
and also "two hundred and fifty negroes, who were sent to
Dauphine Island and distributed among the concessions."[2]
This was the first large importation.

Serigny brought also news of war with Spain. Bienville
and Chateaugué accordingly got together an army of eight
hundred French and Indians at Mobile and marched overland,
while Serigny sailed for Pensacola with four vessels. Invested
May 14, it soon succumbed, and Chateaugué was left there
with a garrison of three hundred. The Spaniards in Cuba
received the news from vessels that carried the garrison as
agreed, and, seizing these ships, speedily recovered Pensacola.
They even captured Chateaugué and took him to Havana.

This was not all. A powerful Spanish armament sailed for
Mobile. It was twelve days before Dauphine Island, where
St. Denis commanded, but his forts, two hundred troops and
Indians, drove them off. A Spanish gunboat did enter the bay
and land men, who plundered a place called Miragouin; but on
their repeating this attack, Mobile Indians were on the watch
and killed thirty and captured seventeen. These captives
fared badly. The Indians took them up to Mobile, clubbed
them to death, and threw their bodies into the bay. As many
captured deserters were shot at Mobile.[3]

Miragouin we can identify. Maringouin, probably the same,
we are told by Penicaut in another place, is the name of a
small biting insect, — which we recognize at once as the mos-

---

[1] 4 Margry, *Découvertes*, p. 616.

[2] Penicaut, 6 French's *Historical Collection*, pp. 145, 146.

[3] Penicaut, 6 French's *Historical Collection*, p. 148 ; 1 Martin's *Louisiana*,
pp. 212–215.

quito.   It was the name that we see on old French maps for
a place on the bay front of our Monlouis Island.

Bienville and St. Denis by land and Champmeslin by sea
now reinvested and captured Pensacola.   There they found
forty deserters, of whom they hung twelve on board, but
peace came in 1720 not long after, and the old flag of Spain
at last regained its place, to remain there for generations.
Chateaugué and his companions were released, the Spaniards
borrowed provisions as usual, and old ties were renewed as if
that port had never been a French capture.

Ships continued to bring colonists in great numbers to Mobile
Bay for the different concessions, and the population required
creation of courts beneath the Superior Council in the persons
of directors or agents with local assistants.   No vessels except
the Company's could come or go.   The Company fixed the
price at which the colonists should buy and sell, and either
transaction could be only with the Company.   On the price at
Mobile and Dauphine Island, five per cent. was added for goods
delivered at New Orleans, ten at Natchez, thirteen at the
Yazoos, twenty at Natchitoches, and fifty at the Illinois and on
the Missouri.   The Company in turn bought colonial produce
at its warehouses in Mobile, Ship Island, New Orleans, and
Biloxi.[1]

For Biloxi (on the new site) was again important.   At the
close of 1720, the headquarters of the company were removed
there,[2] as nearer the Mississippi, whose fertile shores were
being peopled.   Mobile was for a time to continue to be the
largest city, but ceased to be the capital.

For a while it kept on as usual under the old inertia.   The
fort was renamed Fort Condé by an order of the Company of
October, 1720,[3] that arrived on the Mutine.   Early the next
year, M. De Pauger set out from Biloxi to make a plan of
Mobile and a survey of Mobile River to the white bluffs thirty
leagues from Mobile and six from the Chicachas River.[4]   La

---

[1] 1 Martin's *Louisiana*, p. 218.

[2] Pickett's *Alabama*, p. 257.

[3] La Harpe, *Historical Journal*, pp. 82–84 (3 French's *Historical Collection*).

[4] La Harpe, *Historical Journal*, pp. 84, 85 (3 French's *Historical Collection*) ; 1 Martin's *Louisiana*, p. 256.

MOBILE BAY AND COAST, ABOUT 1732

Harpe goes on to say that they are similar to those of St. Luke at Paris, and are two hundred feet high, being a continuation of interior mountains. From this it would seem the Tombigbee was called for the Chickasaws and the Alabama the Mobile, as indeed is shown by some maps, for the reference must be to the bluffs at Claiborne. As late as 1723, when the Spaniards were assisted with provisions, it was from Mobile.

In January, 1721, came three hundred colonists for the grant of Mme. Chaumont at Pascagoula, and then another with twenty-five prostitutes from the Salpetrière, a house of correction at Paris, sent as wives for the colonists. In March arrived one hundred and twenty negroes from Guinea in the Africaine, a warship, and also three hundred and thirty-eight in the Maire, and one hundred and thirty-eight more in the Neride. The mortality on these slave-ships was great, but none other had the story of the Neride to tell. Three hundred and fifty negroes had sailed in the frigate Charles from Angola. This vessel was burned at sea, many of the crew and human cargo perishing. The escaping seamen finally, almost crazed with hunger, killed negroes one after another for food.[1]

On June 4, the Portefaix arrived with three hundred and thirty German colonists, and also the commandant for the now provincial Fort Condé at Mobile. It was no other than Mandeville, become a chevalier of the military order of St. Louis.

But other familiar names now leave us. About this time Bienville was informed of the death, at Natchitoches, of Blondel, and on October 6 of this year, 1721, our chronicler, Jean Penicaut, was himself to leave the colony and sail back to France for treatment of his eyes.[2] It is with sincere regret that one closes the lifelike pages of this first literary Mobilian, and we cannot but hope Mr. French is wrong in his supposition that Penicaut soon died under operation in France. Two years later, although desiring a pension, Penicaut wished to go back to Louisiana, despite his eye trouble. He had left wife and slaves there, and, as owner of a concession near Natchez, describes himself as *Sieur*.[3] Serigny, too, in 1720, returned to France, where he became captain of a vessel and afterwards

---

[1] Pickett's *Alabama*, pp. 257–259.

[2] Penicaut, 6 French's *Historical Collection*, p. 161.

[3] 5 Margry, *Découvertes*, pp. 553, 584, 585, 689, 690.

governor of Rochefort. He died in 1734, and was the only one of the Lemoynes to found a family. His descendants have long been distinguished in French history.[1]

La Harpe, too, becomes less garrulous now, and soon goes to Europe. But it is from him we learn that the Portefaix on this June 4, 1721, had brought news of the flight of John Law from Paris, and of the collapse of his bank and of the Mississippi bubble. The universal panic and distress which ensued in France were to find their echo in Louisiana.

The currency was, with the colonists, a serious question after Law's failure. The Company went on, lasted ten years longer, but the paper money lost credit with the public. To restore confidence, the old notes were nominally redeemed and a new issue made. So Michel was set to work, in 1722, at Mobile to engrave the new obligations. These were called cards, and in due time the Mobilian turned them over to the Company, which hit upon the ingenious device (since copied by Chancery courts) of not redeeming the old claims after a published date. As the circulation was extensive, all of course were not presented in time, and the plan succeeded for a while. The next year Spanish pistoles and dollars were legalized, and thus the silver set in circulation that was for over a century to be the general medium of exchange. There was about this time struck a copper coinage also for the colonies. The portion for Louisiana was brought by Fouquet to Biloxi. It was current in Mobile.[2]

In this year, 1722, it is said, was the excitement of a military execution at the fort. The province was as deficient in food as in good money, and at Fort Toulouse up the river, as we shall see, most of the garrison mutinied. Commandant Marchand was murdered and the mutineers escaped. Villemont, however, second in command, pursued them, and, with the aid of friendly Indians, captured those whom he did not kill. Down

---

[1] White's *New Recopilacion*, pp. 655, 656.

[2] 1 Martin's *Louisiana*, pp. 247, 256 ; 1 Gayarré, *Louisiana*, pp. 282, 357 ; Pickett's *Alabama*, p. 267. A thin sol or sou dated 1721 has been dug up on Franklin Street, south of Church, by Mr. G. Pulliam, who still possesses it. I myself have one identical in all but the mint mark, Pulliam's having H, for Rochelle. On the obverse is a crown, and under it two capital L's, facing in opposite directions and crossing each other. Around is the legend "Sit [Nomen Domini] benedictum." On the reverse is the inscription, "Colonie Françoise, 1721."

to Mobile in canoes he sent them under charge of an Indian guard commanded by Ensign Paque, and there they were duly executed.[1] Meek says[2] one of the eight was even placed in a coffin and sawn asunder according to the rules of the Swiss company to which he belonged. The death penalty was probably enforced in the parade north of the fort, say on Royal between our Church and Government streets.

In years to come, one D'Aubant was to command at that Fort Toulouse and take thither the lady, once of Wolfenbüttel, who had only the year before this time arrived in Mobile and married him. She claimed to have been the wife of Alexis Petrovitch, the son of Peter the Great, but to have pretended death on account of his brutality and escaped to America. At all events, she met a lover and new husband in D'Aubant, an officer in the Mobile garrison.[3] Whether princess or impostor, her story reads like a romance.

In whatever vine-clad cottage they lived, under the pines or oaks of Mobile, with the little daughter born to them, they must have suffered like every one else in the years just succeeding Law's failure. And yet, speculative and careless of means as it was, Law's Company gave Mobile and all Louisiana a forward impulse. Slaves had been introduced by the hundred, the orange and fig successfully planted, never to die out, and, even if our princess is not quite above historic question, and many a Manon and much of the refuse of France were landed on Dauphine Island, there were not a few valuable citizens, too; and from John Law's time the colony developed as it never had before.

---

[1] Pickett's *Alabama*, p. 266.

[2] *Romance of Southwestern History*, p. 30 ; compare Bossu as to the Beaudrot execution. *Travels*, p. 325.

[3] Gayarré claims her for New Orleans (*History of Louisiana*, p. 270), but New Orleans was hardly habitable for a princess in 1721. Pickett relies on material found at Paris, and fixes the place as Mobile (*History of Alabama*, p. 259, etc.). Unfortunately, neither cites authorities, although it is said Gayarré relied on Voltaire. The probabilities favor Mobile. D'Aubant was in that garrison, and it was from here they would naturally leave to go to Fort Toulouse, which was an outpost of Mobile. Martin does not say, but places D'Aubant at Mobile. He says D'Aubant is called such by Bossu, but Maldeck by the king of Prussia. 1 Martin's *Louisiana*, p. 231. See, also, Meek's highly-colored account in his *Southwest*, p. 30.

CHAPTER XIII.

RELATIONS of peace or war with the Choctaws, Alibamons, and other large Indian nations will occupy much of our attention, indeed make up the principal part of our story, but as interesting, if less important, is the history of those nearer, smaller tribes who came to Fort Louis for protection, and from place to place followed the fortunes of the French. Among these the Mobilians, Apalaches, and Tensaws attained considerable civilization.

The most distant of these Mobile races were the Tohomes or Thomez, — "Little Chiefs." Their location has not been perpetuated by any surviving name of bluff or stream, and the French maps are so general as not to give much assistance. These early maps have a waving line for coasts and river bends, and creeks are liberally distributed where they will look best, but accurate topographical details are not given. The Thomez were eight leagues above the fort,[1] and we may fairly place this tribe about McIntosh's Bluff on the Tombigbee. We know their country was fertile and had good roads. Almost the first mention of them is in 1701, when Bienville sent from Biloxi to them to buy corn meal.[2]

The Tohomes were closely associated with the Mobilians, who lived two leagues below them. In his enumeration of Indians in 1702, Iberville classes them together. After the removal of Fort Louis to the present site of Mobile we hear no more of them, and it may be conjectured that they became absorbed into the Mobilians. They were not numerous. Pickett allows them forty huts; Iberville for his time but eight or ten.[3]

Next south came the Naniabes, or Naniabas, "Fish-eaters,"

---

[1] 4 Margry, *Découvertes*, p. 514.
[2] *Ibid.*, p. 504.
[3] Pickett's *Alabama*, p. 128 ; 4 Margry, *Découvertes*, p. 514.

who lived and gave the name to the high bluff and district on
the Tombigbee still preserved as Nanna Hubba, just above the
junction with the Alabama River. Not a great deal is known
of these. Like all the other native Indians west of the lower
Alabama, they were branches of the Choctaw stock, but the
Naniabas kept up an independent tribal organization, until
finally they, too, were absorbed in the Mobilians. Their
mounds are still seen in the woods, and bones are found about
the Seaboard wharf. Arrowheads abounded back of Beau-
fort's Landing on the line between Mobile and Washington
counties, and a little bronze pot has been picked up not far
away.

The Mobilians are better known. They, too, were Choctaws
by race, but are supposed to be the remains of the people who,
under Tuskaloosa, a century and a half before, had been driven
from their homes in Maubila up on our Alabama, by the stern
De Soto. Their misfortunes had not ended then. The French
found all over the Mobile delta evidences of a former large and
peaceful population, with roads and fields, and heard of recent
devastation by the Conchaques (Apalachicolas) from the northeast. Iberville estimated them in his day as even with the
Tohomes amounting only to three hundred and fifty families,
and we do not hear of their having then more than one large
settlement, although many of them lived scattered among the
islands as well as on the mainland.

This settlement was six leagues above Fort Louis,[1] and therefore not far from the junction of the Alabama and Tombigbee
rivers. Some maps show them above, about Mt. Vernon
Landing, but some later ones, also, below near Seymour's
Bluff. Five leagues above the fort the observing Penicaut saw
one of their religious festivals. The Naniabas, Tohomes, and
Mobilians united in this ceremony, in which they invoked their
deity in a cabin by *jongler.*[2] At their September feast they
had a custom which reminded our Frenchman of his classic
studies. Like the Spartans, he says, they whipped their children until the blood came, to make them callous to what their
enemies might do to them. If the child was sick, this treatment was visited on the mother.

They had clay gods, too, as we know from the figures of

[1] 4 Margry, *Découvertes,* p. 422. [2] 5 *Ibid.,* p. 427.

man, woman, child, owl, and bear found by Bienville on some
island, possibly on the great mound about Bottle Creek.
Thither they resorted at certain seasons to offer sacrifices, on
a hill in the cane-brake. Strange to say, we do not read that
Iberville's taking the figures away to France alienated the
Mobilians at all, and this perhaps lends color to his theory
that they were really foreign, of Spanish workmanship.[1] This
mound of fifty feet is a marvel of industry, as the dirt must
have been brought in canoes for miles.

The Mobilians occur several times in the church registers.
Victorin we shall meet as curé of them and the Apalaches, and
there are baptisms when no curé is mentioned for them. In
1715, Huvé baptized Jean Louis, by nation "Mauvila, commonly called Mobilian," with Jean Vallade, called Drapeau,
a soldier, and his wife as sponsors, and in the same year Le
Maire baptized Jean, son of Jean, a Mobilian, and Marie Magdeleine, his Sitimacha (Chetimacha) wife. The sponsors were
also French. Next after the long interval of twenty years Victorin baptizes two Mobilians. Then, in 1758, comes a little
slave belonging to the chief of the Mobilians, and in 1759
Therese, the little daughter of Antoine Abbe and Marie
Jeanne, Mobilian Indians, with Durand and Mme. De Rous-
seve as sponsors. As late as March 21, 1761, was baptized
Jean Baptiste, a Mobilian.

Of the Apalaches, also, we know considerable. The common account is that they fled from attacks of the Alabamas
(Alibamons) in central Florida and were given shelter by the
French at the first Fort Louis.[2] Shea says that they had been
living peaceably with the Spaniards, and had become Catholic
converts there, when Governor Moore, of South Carolina, made
a raid, cruelly harried the country, and broke up their settlement, massacring Indians, priests and all.[3]

---

[1] 4 Margry, *Découvertes*, p. 513. The shell banks about Mobile, particularly those on Bon Secours Bay, Dauphine Island, and at Portersville, contain ducks and animals and human heads, moulded in clay and burned, often
of artistic value. These banks are in layers, showing periodic, not continuous, use, and contain human bones and simple crockery. They may possibly
point to an earlier race than the red Indians.

[2] Gatschet, *Creek Migration Legend*, p. 76.

[3] Shea's *Catholic Church in the Colonies*, p. 461 ; 5 Margry, *Découvertes*,
p. 461 ; Williams's *East Florida*, p. 212.

At all events, they were settled near the French by 1704, and the very first entry in the parish register is the baptism of a little Apalache boy on September 6 of that year, by Père Davion. Nor did this stand by itself, for the entries during many years contain Apalache baptisms. Indeed, this tribe had a missionary and chapel of their own.[1] Huvé came over in the Pelican in 1704, and was to be their pastor. He is said to have been no linguist, and how he got along with them until 1721 is hard to imagine.

For their village, which Bienville had placed near the Mobilians, was broken up again by their old enemies, the Alibamons, and they sought shelter with new Fort Louis. Bienville this time assigned them lands on the River St. Martin, a league above the fort. This would be at our Three Mile Creek, probably extending to Chickasabogue, the St. Louis. Delisle's map seems to bear out this location. There they had a church, font, and cemetery with a cross.[2] Where now stands some busy sawmill, and ships take on cargoes, Huvé said mass before this, the only Catholic tribe.

Their great feast day was that sacred to St. Louis, for whom their parish was named, when all dressed in mask and danced the rest of the day after service, with French or Indians, furnishing their guests refreshment also. The women wore their black hair in one or two plaits down the back, like the Spanish women, and dressed in cloaks and skirts, and the men in coats, quite in civilized style. They chanted the psalms in Latin at service, and had mass every Sunday and feast day. Penicaut says that they were devout, and except their mixed language (of Spanish and Alibamon) there was nothing savage about them.[3] They were excellent Catholics.

The Apalaches are often mentioned in the church registers, and sometimes Christian Mobilians, Chattos, and Tensaws, too. Such entries are irregular, however.

The first mention after Davion's baptism is in the next year, when Huvé baptized, in the ordinary forms of the church, a little Apalache girl born in lawful wedlock, named Françoise by the second chief of that nation. Then comes a three years'

---

[1] Shea, *Catholic Church in the Colonies*, pp. 546, 552.

[2] *Ibid.*, p. 554.

[3] Penicaut, 5 Margry, *Découvertes*, pp. 461, 486, 487.

blank, until Salome, wife of the chief of the Apalaches, stands godmother for Alexander, a Schitimacha slave of fifteen belonging to the missionaries of Fort Louis, and in the same year Joseph, an Apalache, was godfather for a little Chatto girl, both before Huvé. The Spanish antecedents of the tribe appear more clearly in 1710, when Salome, daughter of Charisto and Thereise his wife, was baptized. The sponsors were Lasso and Salome again, and Huvé records that they were all "Appalaches." Towards the end of the year, their chief and his wife have baptized a little slave of theirs, a Paniouacha by nation, — for, as we have seen, the Indians held slaves, too. They named this one Marie Susanne.

The next year, and thus probably after their second change of site, we have several other Apalache names. In January, there is Jean, son of Trigours and Minita his wife, with Mia and Oussima as sponsors, and later in the same month Pierre Michel, son of Piro and Oussima herself, with Michel and Soussia as godfather and mother. In November, Le Maire baptizes also Laurent, son of Charles and his wife Therese, with Lazo and Salome as *parain* and *maraine*, and later in that month Jeanne, daughter of Jean and Luce. Le Maire, in naming her sponsors, translates Ouan (no doubt the Spanish Juan) into Jean, and Ouanne into Jeanne. In December comes Joseph, son of Sanchez and Ouanne his wife. The godmother was Mariane. In a preceding entry we see Laurence and Laurentia, too.

In 1713, Varlet mentions Joseph de la Rivière as interpreter of the Apalaches, and next year Huvé baptizes Marie Joseph, daughter of Ouan and Francisqua, his wife. The sponsors were Piro and Maria Iousipa. Later in that year he also baptizes Caterine. In 1716, we meet perhaps the last-named sponsors bringing their own child Michelle to the font, — "Piero autrement Pierre," and "Ousipa ou Josephe." The sponsors are René Salot, a soldier, and Anhile, an Apalache. In the middle of the same year is a son of Josef and Francisque, with French sponsors in Francis Carrière and the wife of Claude Parent, prominent people.

In 1717, we find four large Apalache children baptized by Le Maire with the names Emmanuel, Marie Therese, Alexandre Joseph, and Henriette Marie Salome. The second is worthy of note as the son of an Englishman and an Apalache, and as having Huvé for godfather. The sponsors of the last were Jean Baptiste Ouachita, a domestic of the missionaries, and Marie Therese, an Apalache. This was before the reign of the celebrated Austrian queen Maria Theresa, so that the name is not in honor of her. Later in the year, Huvé was to baptize four small Apalache boys, all of whose names are not decipherable.

From that time on, the register contains fewer Apalache baptisms, although some occur. In April, 1721, however, we have several entries by Father Charles, Barefoot Carmelite and "Curé des Apalaches," a title never used by Huvé. He probably kept a separate book for his Indian flock, for no Apalaches seem to be mentioned in the Mobile register when he acts in the absence of the regular curé, Mathieu.

This suggests the idea that probably at this time, when Law's Company was forcing the growth of the colony at an extravagant pace, came the third change of location of this friendly tribe. Their St. Louis tract we shall find granted others in 1733. We know that at some time they moved over across the bay from the city, where the eastern mouth of the Tensaw River still preserves their name. They seem to have lived in part on an island there, for in Spanish times it is mentioned as only recently abandoned. The first indication of this change on the valuable maps so profusely given by Justin Winsor is on Kitchen's of 1747, but it is also on a French coast map dated three years earlier. Their main seat was at and above what we now know as Blakely. Bayou Solimé probably commemorates Salome, so often named in the baptisms.

On November 12, 1721, Mathieu baptizes Michel, whose godparents were Pierre and Michel, all Apalaches, but there are no more then for several years. In 1726, the daughter of Christian "Appanaches" is mentioned, and next year is the baptism of Therese, a Catholic Apalache, with Indian sponsors. The following year we read of the baptism of Françoise, a Hiamase (Yamassee?) refugee among the Apalaches of St. Louis, a dependent of that parish. In 1734, we hear of Victorin, missionary apostolic of the Apalaches and Mobilians, who acts at Mobile in the absence of Father Mathias, and in 1737, Pierre Lorandini, sergeant, was to stand godfather for an Apalache boy. In 1741–42, we know Jean François was "curé des Apalaches," and two years later, "f. Prosper prêtre missionaire " to them. So they seem quite continuously to have had a missionary of their own. In 1751 was baptized an Apalache *sauvagesse*, born in lawful wedlock to Marc and Michelle, but this is the last mention of the race in the Mobile register. If there was an Apalache register, it has disappeared.

Their place we find named, in 1741, as "aux Apalaches," doubtless that across the bay from the city. The entry recites that one De Sorges was buried there, and two months later in the same locality his wife was found drowned. A sad family scene these entries indicate, — it may be a tragedy. Twenty-one years before was the baptism of Jeanne Marguerite, child of Pierre Desorges and Marguerite Celesar his wife. Now she loses both parents as she herself reaches maturity.

The death of Nicola Chatelin in the river of the Apalaches is mentioned by Ferdinand in 1762, and earlier in the same year is the loss also of Joseph Cook in the trip (*traversie*) from the Apalaches to Mobile.

While we thus know more of the Apalaches on account of their church records, traces survive also of other tribes near Mobile.

The Touachas were also refugees from Spanish Florida to avoid Alibamon inroads, although Gatschet derives them from Tawasa, a village on the Alabama River. Bienville, in 1705, established them a league and a half below the first fort, and on the change of base they were placed a league above the Apalaches. They seem to have been useful at least as hunters.[1] The only mention of them noticed in the church registers is where, in 1716, Huvé baptized Marguerite, daughter of a savage, slave of Commissary Duclos, and a free Taouacha woman. The godmother was Marguerite Le Sueur. What became of them we do not certainly know, but it would seem probable that as early as 1713 they had made some change of residence. The Creek Toucha, emptying into Bayou Sara some distance east of Cleveland's Station on the M. & B. R. R., or, according to some, into Mobile River at Twelve Mile Island, would seem even yet to perpetuate this location, which corresponds nearly

---

[1] 5 Margry, *Découvertes*, pp. 457, 486 ; Gatschet, *Creek Migration Legend*, p. 89 ; 1 Martin's *Louisiana*, p. 167.

with Delisle's map, and one of 1744. As Touacha, it occurs a number of times in Spanish documents.

In some manner, as we have seen, a tribe of Choctaws had once separated from the nation west of the Tombigbee, and settled among the Spaniards of Florida. But they, too, became refugees, — expelled, according to Penicaut, by the Spaniards themselves.[1] This seems to have been about 1709. Bienville welcomed this, as every other opportunity, of ingratiating himself with the Indians, and gave them lands on the bay coast in a large cove a league in circuit, — "l'Anse des Chactas," — extending from our Choctaw Point west around Garrow's Bend. They occupied the site of the present city of Mobile, and were its first inhabitants. Pickett gives them forty wigwams.[2] When Bienville selected this very ground for new Mobile, he had to recompense these Choctaws with land on Dog River. Maps of 1717 and later show them on the south side of that stream, sometimes near the bay, sometimes several miles up. Few mounds or other remains have survived, but their memory has survived, however, near the city; for from them doubtless came the name Choctaw Point, in use under the French, and the adjacent Choctaw Swamp. The church register mentions the drowning, in 1743, of the Indian Joseph, slave of Joseph Laprade, "vers la pointe des Chacteaux." Their bend below Frascati, however, was to become L'Anse Mandeville. A map of 1744 shows below them, at the mouth of Deer River, a settlement of Yamané, probably Yamassees from Carolina, of whom nothing is known except that, in 1715, that tribe had revolted against the English and been driven west.

Several "Chatto" baptisms are recorded. It is not certain the Indians of Dog River are meant, but this is probable, as these were the nearest and most closely allied to the French of all the Choctaws. That race at large is in the French papers spelled "Chactas," not "Chatto."

In 1708–9, and consequently while they were still living on the present site of Mobile, five Chatto children were baptized by Huvé. The first was named Ouan for his father, the godfather being Serate. The second was Pharesco, son of

[1] 5 Margry, *Découvertes*, p. 479.
[2] Pickett's *Alabama*, p. 128 ; Gatschet, *Creek Migration Legend*, p. 64.

Dominguo and Lucia (the godfather being Gaspar), and also an older daughter of the same parents, named Maria. The fourth was Theresia, daughter of Gaspar and Magdeleine. And then came Andrich, or André, son of Pierre and Marie, having as godparents Ouan, chief of the Chattos, and Hiacinta, widow of the deceased chief (Felician) of the same nation. In 1713, three more were baptized by Varlet, — Pierre, whose father had the same name, Paul, whose parents had no Christian names, and Anne, daughter of Francisco. The godfather was the Apalache interpreter Joseph. Next year were two, spelled "Chakteaux," — Hiacinte, daughter of Thomas and Marie, with Pierre Graviche, called Lionnois, as godfather, and also Marie, daughter of the little chief Augustin and of Marie. All this was in the Choctaw chapel, — "Le Tout," adds Varlet, "dans Loratoire du dit village des Chakteaux." No doubt at the same place shortly after was baptized Marie Claude, daughter of a negro of M. de Bienville living with the Chakteaux.

In 1715, Huvé baptized Jacques, a free "Chactat" Indian, who had well-known colonists for sponsors, thus showing, as often before, the kindly relations between the French and their Indian friends. Next year he performed the same service for five little ones at "the village of the Chattaux," indicating that it was at the well-known place on the south side of Dog River. The names, however, have ceased to be Spanish. Thomas, Françoise, Catherine, Louise, and Jeanne are thoroughly French. At the same time was baptized Marie, a four-year-old Schitimacha, belonging to the chief of the nation, the fruit, we may believe, of that war which brought so many Chetimacha slaves from the Mississippi to Mobile. The godfather of all was Lionnois again, stated to be resident of the village. Some years later there is a casual mention, too, of a M. Dubriel as among the "Chaquetaux."

These Indians are mentioned seldom after that. In 1720 is mentioned Marie, of a *mariage naturel* of a slave with a Chatta named Capinan. The church did not recognize these irregular unions, and it may be that it was with some satisfaction that Huvé added the note that Capinan had quit her to take some one else. In 1729, the record closes with the baptism of a "Chactau," whose mother was Christian.

There is, strange to say, no record of the burial of a Choctaw, nor indeed of more than half a dozen Indians altogether. But this is the less remarkable when we remember that the death register, even of the French, is very defective. Greater attention was paid to the more frequent births than to the deaths.

In many respects, more interesting than the Choctaws were the Tensaws, who also lived near the Mobile colony. They came originally from the Mississippi River. The Tensaws have been called a connection of the Natchez, and like them were sun-worshippers and kept burning a perpetual fire, but the two languages fail to show kinship.[1] At the destruction by lightning of their temple on the Mississippi, they threw their children into the fire to appease the offended deity. Seventeen were killed before Iberville, who happened to be present, could stop them.[2] Montigny was missionary, but an unsuccessful one, among their villages just about the Bayou Manchac. The aborigines nearer the future site of New Orleans, the Oumas, waged relentless war against these "Tinsas,"—so much so that Bienville in sympathy brought them, in 1713, to Mobile, and placed them where the Chaouachas (Taouachas?) had been.[3] Delisle gives both tribes at once on his map.

Before the nation was removed to Mobile, we find "Taensa" slaves there. In 1708, Le Maire baptized an infant of two months, belonging to the tradesman (*marchand*) Boutin. The age of this child, who was named Vincent, seems to show that he was captured in a raid against the tribe while hostile. Two years later, Huvé baptized a female Tança of nineteen, belonging to Jean de Can, whom we have met before. Next year the church registers show us also Jeanne, child of a Tensa female of Mr. Charli, baptized by Davion and Le Maire, too. In 1712 comes Marie, daughter of Sieur Rochon's Tensa slave, and on February 12 of next year is one of the few entries recognizing marriage between Frenchman and Indian. It relates the baptism of Claude, legitimate son of René Le Bœuf and Marguerite, a Tença, his wife. The sponsors were Claude Parent and the wife of Jean Louis.

---

[1] Pickett's *Alabama*, p. 128 ; Gatschet, *Creek Migration Legend*, p. 32.
[2] 5 Margry, *Découvertes*, p. 397.   [3] *Ibid.*, pp. 508, 509.

In 1714, we find Marie, daughter of a Chitimacha slave of Sieur de Chateaugué and a Tança slave of Sieur de Boisbriant, baptized by Huvé. By this time the tribe had been removed to Mobile, but, except Pistolet, in 1761, son of a "Thinsa," the priests of Mobile seem never to have baptized any of the nation unless as slaves, — when the Indians could not help themselves. They were joined to their idols. Indeed, in that long interval there is no mention of the tribe, except that, in 1760, there was baptized a negro belonging to St. Michel, "habitant des Thinsa."

They had also by that time settled across the Mobile delta and given the name to the great river corresponding on the east to the Mobile River on the west. Exactly when this was we do not know, but they are shown over there, on the west bank of the Tensaw, on a French coast chart of 1744. They numbered a hundred wigwams, and dwelt then more especially on a bluff, for a long time afterwards called for them, above the Apalaches, and not far from our Stockton.[1] The Tensaw River had before that been called Branche Espagnole, but Spanish River has since been limited to a branch extending from near the Tensaw mouth to the Mobile. The eastern arm of the Tensaw at its mouth is still called the Apalache, as we have seen.

In 1766, and consequently in British times, the register was to mention the death of Ph. Klimpetre on his habitation at the Tensaws (*des Thinsa*), where he was also buried, and the same mention was to be made later of François Colin.

Such were the near neighbors of the French at Mobile. It is a tribute not less to the justice of the colonists than to the amiability of the Indians that no trouble occurred between the white and red men. Peaceably they lived side by side for many years, and in fact, when the fortunes of war brought a change of flag, these Indians went west with their protectors. Even as late as the early part of the nineteenth century, Tensaws, for example, were still to be found in Louisiana.

The others, however, have lost their identity and cannot be traced. The exact site of their Mobile domiciles, indeed, is now difficult to fix. All changed their locations from time to time as they exhausted the hunting-grounds, soil, or pasture, to

[1] Pickett's *Alabama*, p. 128.

which the "old fields" and "old towns" common in their names and country still bear witness, and the evidences of the Choctaws, who lived less in towns than the Creeks, are often scanty. Experience taught them to keep near bluffs in order to avoid the freshets of the rivers, but they did not always live on these exposed places, and certainly preferred to cultivate lower lands.

Beyond mounds, which mark the Choctaw rather than the Creek races, Indians leave few permanent memorials. As with their tracks through the forest, which the last warrior conceals, the next coming civilization obliterates the traces of the red man. Where they fished and hunted are still the same waters, trees, and landscape, but the natives have gone, and only an occasional name survives to recall the first occupants.

PART III.

THE DEPARTMENT OF MOBILE.

1722–1763.

CHAPTER XIV.

WITH the removal of the capital from Mobile, that city lost many inhabitants as well as much prestige. She was no longer the point from which the Mississippi valley was explored and settled. She sank to a place second to New Orleans, although Dauphine Island for a while still remained perhaps the favorite port for immigration.

But Mobile continued to be the centre of Indian influence and diplomacy. There the annual congress was held, and on account of the dependent posts up its rivers, it was the point from which the English Atlantic colonies dreaded French inroads.[1] The geography of the country favored it. It must be remembered that south of the east and west Ohio valley there was a north and south one, whose largest rivers, draining from the Alleghanies on the east to near the Mississippi River itself on the west, emptied into the Bay of Mobile. Smaller than the disputed basin of the Mississippi, or even that of the Ohio, what we have called the Alabama basin was as fertile as either, and in the Chickasaws, Choctaws, and Creeks had Indian tribes larger and braver than any south of the Great Lakes and west of the mountains. By 1721, between Carolina and the Mississippi were about nine thousand warriors, of whom over a third had been weaned from English influence by the French. Mobile could not fail to be an important place. Bossu mentions its trade in tar and furs, the last monopolized by the officers in his days, and says that quite a trade in provisions was carried on with the Spanish in Pensacola. The inhabitants, he says, were industrious. He mentions in connection with the Indians, maize, millet, beans, potatoes, melons, and gourds, also. The watermelons he pronounces delicious.[2]

---

[1] Winsor's *Basin of the Mississippi*, p. 170.

[2] Penicaut, in 5 Margry, *Découvertes*, p. 579 ; Bossu's *Travels*, pp. 221, 224, 230.

But Mobile, when Charlevoix wrote in 1722, was already suffering from the emigration to the Mississippi. He describes the River Maubile as narrow and winding but rapid, although but a small boat (*pettiaugre*) could ascend when its waters were low.

"We have on this river," he says, "a fort which has been a long time the principal post of the colony; yet the lands are not good, but its situation near the Spaniards makes it convenient for trading with them, and this was all they sought for at that time." He goes on to speak of the reported discovery of a quarry, which might prevent its entire desertion. The inhabitants were unwilling to cultivate a soil which did not answer their pains. "Nevertheless," he says, "I do not believe that they will easily resolve to evacuate the fort of Maubile, though it should serve only to keep in our alliance the Tchactas, a numerous people, who make us a necessary barrier against the Chicachas, and against the savages bordering on Carolina. Garcelasso de la Vega in his history of Florida speaks of a village called Mauvilla, which no doubt gave its name to the river, and to the nation that was settled on its borders. These Mauvillians were then very powerful; at present there are hardly any traces left of them." [1]

Mobile was one of the nine districts into which Louisiana was, in 1721, divided by the Company, the others being New Orleans, Biloxi, Alibamons, Natchez, Yazoo, Natchitoches, Arkansas, and Illinois. In each of these was one or more forts or trading stations. At Mobile and the first three places named, goods were sold at fifty per cent advance on prices in France, but at the others higher. Toulouse was in this favored class because of Carolina competition. Leaf tobacco and rice were bought for the company at the warehouses in Mobile, New Orleans, and Biloxi. [2]

At the annual Indian congress, Bienville met and feasted the friendly tribes and distributed presents. As a matter of policy he did not permit them to come to the new settlements at Biloxi and New Orleans, and Mobile was thus always the great rendezvous for the savages. [3] Choctaws they generally

---

[1] Charlevoix's *Journal*, p. 190 (3 French's *Historical Collection*).

[2] Gayarré's *History of Louisiana*, p. 273.

[3] Bossu's *Travels*, p. 221.

were, but the Alibamons also often came and exchanged talks and smoked the decorated calumet of peace with the French. Penicaut says Mobile was retained from its connection with Fort Toulouse and the Indians.[1]

The failure of Law had embarrassed the Company, and the forcing process with all its monopoly was not remunerative. The directors were dissatisfied, and Bienville knew it. But he certainly did the best with the materials sent him, and, despite the character of many of the colonists, Louisiana as a whole was improving.

By the twenties, the culture of indigo had been added to that of rice and tobacco, while the fig-tree had been introduced from Provence, and the orange from Hispaniola. Slavery was of much aid in developing the country. The Company had at least succeeded in giving Louisiana a good start.[2] One evidence was the need for legislation. Bienville issued in March, 1724, a short code to cover almost all their relations, and it has gone into history as the Black Code.

It had intolerant features, of course. It banished Jews, and established Catholicism alone, while an ordinance of the same year severely punished maiming stock. But the name of the Code really relates to its main subject, the negroes. It forbade marriage between the whites and blacks, and regulated slavery. It was in effect a copy of Louis XIV.'s code for St. Domingo,[3] a French conquest of the preceding century.

But this was the last act of the governor. Bienville was recalled. He and Chateaugué came over to Mobile, and thence to Dauphine Island, to sail for France on the Bellona. Their baggage was ready, and on that Easter Monday, as the little boats that were to take them aboard reached the shore, the ship fired signals of distress. She suddenly began to sink before their eyes. Down she went in fair weather, with many of the crew, without a warning, and there she doubtless now lies in the shifting sands southeast of the island.[4]

The two brothers returned to New Orleans. They soon found other shipping, and finally arrived safe in France. There Bienville was to remain for several years, and of Cha-

[1] 5 Margry, *Découvertes,* p. 579.   [2] 1 Martin's *Louisiana,* p. 265.
[3] King's *Bienville,* p. 273.   [4] *Ibid.,* p. 274.

teaugué we only know that he was afterwards governor of Cayenne.

Boisbriant was called from the Illinois, where he had been since 1722,[1] to command Louisiana *ad interim ;* but soon Perier was appointed governor, and, in 1726, he came out. All of Bienville's friends, Chateaugué and Boisbriant included, were removed from office. There was a new deal, a new political slate. If the charges against Bienville were true, improvement should immediately follow.

With Perier's administration, which consisted largely in severity towards the Natchez, we have little to do, except so far as that misguided policy aroused the Chickasaws, and even after a while a faction of the Choctaws, too, and was to make life in the Mobile district unsafe. It brought on, in 1729, the massacre of the garrison at **Fort Rosalie** on the Mississippi. Of this he notified Mobile by courier. A war of extermination by the French was to follow.

In February, 1728, the Company sent over, for marriage, some girls who were of virtuous raising. They were each provided with a little trunk (*cassette*) of clothing, from which they received the nickname of *cassette* girls. Descent from these was in after days to be held a mark of good family.[2] Not many of them could have come to Mobile, for the population there was diminishing. It held at this time but sixty families, besides the thirty of the Apalaches near by, while New Orleans had increased to six hundred families.[3]

In 1722, Mandeville was commandant at Mobile, and on his death, about 1727, Diron D'Artaguette, son of the old *ordonnateur*, succeeded. We find Beauchamps in command in 1731. We know that the return of Bienville as governor the next year was hailed with delight, for he was ever a favorite with the colonists. He came as a royal governor, too, for, in 1731, the Company, as Crozat before them, had surrendered Louisiana to the crown. The venture looked more like war than money-making, and they were glad to let the regent take charge again. The administration was to be through governor and a reorganized Superior Council of thirteen members. Be-

---

[1] 2 White's *New Recopilacion,* pp. 439, 655.

[2] Pickett's *Alabama,* p. 273 ; 1 Martin's *Louisiana,* p. 264.

[3] Shea's *Catholic Church in the Colonies,* p. 567.

sides officials, the Council was made up of six councillors, an attorney-general, and a clerk. To aid the colony, the king in 1731 exempted imports and exports from duty for ten years, to be prolonged to thirty.[1]

While Bienville was taking up the cares of office, he found his old home, Mobile, in great distress. In 1733, D'Artaguette writes from there that the smallpox is virulent, and that, too, right after a disastrous hurricane had swept over the place and destroyed crops and provisions.[2] D'Artaguette was commissary then, but commandant next year. It was in 1733 that he received a grant of the extensive St. Louis Tract between our Three Mile Creek and Chickasabogue, but we do not learn what use he made of it.

D'Artaguette had returned from France with Bienville, but was not to prove of much assistance. Not but that he was brave enough: Bienville could hardly keep him from marching with one hundred French and numerous Choctaw allies against the threatening Chickasaws. This would have been the kind of adventure his daring Swiss lieutenant Grondel, famous for duels, would have delighted in. Could he have suggested it?

The governor came over himself and held a heated Choctaw congress at Mobile. He found British influence had in his absence invaded even his old allies, and in Adair we learn how this was accomplished. Adair was an Indian trader from Charleston in 1735 and for many years afterwards, and takes all the credit for securing the Choctaw chief Red Shoe. Adair was then among the Chickasaws, whom he supplied with English arms and goods from Carolina by a route north of Forts Toulouse and Tombecbé. He was also commissioned to open a trade with the Choctaws, and was enabled to do so on account of the resentment of the chieftain of Quansheto, Shulashummashtabe or Red Shoe, at discovering a Frenchman from Tombecbé in adultery with his favorite wife. Red Shoe visited Adair by invitation, and became convinced of the advantages of an English alliance. A long Choctaw civil war was to be the result.

[1] Gayarré's *History of Louisiana,* pp. 279 ; Pickett's *Alabama,* pp. 263, 330 ; 1 Martin's *Louisiana,* pp. 269, 292, 320.

[2] Gayarré's *History of Louisiana,* pp. 457, 461.

The Choctaws were thus partly alienated, and D'Artaguette represented matters worse than they were. People became uneasy, then alarmed. They went to mass with guns in hand, and finally even prepared, in 1735, to abandon the place and retire to New Orleans. But Bienville knew the value of Mobile. He forbade this, and reprimanded D'Artaguette for thus terrorizing the people.

On July 16 of this year, a smuggling vessel from Jamaica entered the bay. De Velles was sent against her with thirty men, but, in the battle on the water twelve miles from the fort, was worsted. Seventeen French were killed, and the British vessel escaped. This only increased the breach between D'Artaguette and the governor.[1]

Bienville took up his residence in Mobile this summer, and there again met the Choctaw chiefs in grand council. He became satisfied finally of their coöperation, and busied himself in preparations to attack the Chickasaws from Mobile. Provisions were to be supplied from New Orleans, artillery from France, and troops from several forts. Everything was well planned.

But much miscarried during that fall. The means of transportation were not promptly furnished, half a cargo of rice was lost overboard, and the cannon were never shipped. At Mobile there was a delay, too, until bread could be made by the bakers.

At last all was ready (except the cannon), and the expedition embarked. Five hundred soldiers were there from the garrisons of Natchitoches, Natchez, and Mobile, including, too, a company of volunteers from New Orleans and another of unmarried colonists, besides forty-five negroes under Simon, the brave free black.[2] They embarked in front of Fort Condé in thirty large pirogues and as many flatboats. Mobile River had never seen so stirring a sight as the expedition that gayly rowed off on the morning of that first day of April, 1736. The glint of the lilied flags on the boats bearing Bienville and his staff was answered by the waving banner of Fort Condé, and the salute of the cannon awoke the echoes of the islands in front. But gradually the flotilla got out of sight, the seabirds

---

[1] Pickett's *Alabama*, p. 333 ; Adair's *American Indians*, p. 314.
[2] King's *Bienville*, pp. 294–296.

settled back to their haunts, and the people dispersed to their occupations. For two months they dreamed of victories.

We have somewhat lost the thread of the development of the Mississippi valley since Mobile ceased to be the capital, but in this Chickasaw war we see something of what had been accomplished in the mean while. For Bienville was not relying upon his own force alone. He had arranged that D'Artaguette, brother of the commissary, should coöperate with three hundred men from his post in the Illinois. They were to meet him in the enemy's country.

Bienville selected as his base of supplies what is now Jones's Bluff, where the A. G. S. Railroad crosses the Tombigbee, in Sumter County, Alabama, above the confluence of the Black Warrior. Thither he had dispatched De Lusser to build a fort, the one so long useful as Fort Tombecbé. It was in the Choctaw country, near the Itomba-igabee Creek, which gave its name to the river, and but a few days' march from the Chickasaws. There bread was to be baked for the expedition, but little was done until Bienville arrived and built three ovens in addition to the one there.

On the arrival of Bienville's army at the unfinished fort, after a trip of twenty-three days from Mobile, there was a final conference, May 1, with the Choctaw chiefs, — the faithful Alabama Mingo and the English-favoring Red Shoe among them. D'Artaguette was not heard of, although Bienville had sent him word of the change of date, and therefore the governor thought D'Artaguette must have had a battle with the savages and returned to Fort Chartres.

By arrangement at the conference, the chiefs were to meet the French in force higher up the stream. This part of the river journey was accomplished by May 22, and, after building there a small fort called Oltibia, the united army of French and Choctaws struck through the woods in rainy weather to attack the Chickasaws.

No good feeling prevailed between the French and Choctaws, for the English had sown dissension even among these Indians. They were more intent on injuring the Chickasaws than aiding the French, and precipitated an action against Bienville's judgment at Schiouafalay, the first of the fortified villages which they reached.

This, the battle of Ackia, was a disaster from the first. The Chickasaws were always brave, and now the English flag floated over one of their villages, and Englishmen actively aided the savages in the conflict. The men led by Chevalier De Noyan were routed, and left that gallant leader alone. De Lusser was killed, and Grondel, of the Karer grenadiers, all but dead, was rescued only after several of his followers had been slain trying to recover his senseless body. The Choctaws, for their part, did more howling than fighting. The repulse of the French was complete.

Now it was that the absence of artillery was most felt. It was sacrificing men to send them to attack the palisaded villages protected by loopholes, and Bienville had no cannon to batter the defenses.

He finally determined to retreat, and did so with difficulty, but fortunately was not followed. The water was so low at Oltibia that they could hardly descend the stream to Fort Tombecbé.

Thence Bienville went on to Mobile, learning on the way of D'Artaguette's fate. This soldier set out with one hundred and forty whites and about three hundred Iroquois, Arkansas, Miami, and Illinois Indians. They duly arrived at the Chickasaw Bluffs (near Memphis), and then learned of the change of date. In order to retain his allies, D'Artaguette marched into the enemy's country. He was outnumbered, and when most of his Indians took to flight, the wounded D'Artaguette, the Jesuit Senat, and a few others were captured. Their fate was horrible. All were burned alive, but died without flinching.[1]

The loss of these men was bad enough, but even worse was the capture of D'Artaguette's papers, revealing Bienville's plans, and thus enabling the Chickasaws and English traders among them the more easily to defeat at Ackia the expedition from Mobile.

D'Artaguette, the brother left behind, was almost crazed with grief, and Bienville had to face there many whose homes were darkened by the losses of this first Chickasaw war. For others, too, in Mobile had to mourn the loss of friend or kin. The Swiss De Lucer, or De Lusser, who had been sent

---

[1] Bossu's *Travels*, p. 311.

forward to build this Fort Tombecbé at Jones's Bluff,[1] did not come back, nor did De Juzan and many others. The daring Grondel (later to command the Swiss of the Halwill regiment in Fort Condé) had been thought dead, too, but although it was long before his desperate wounds were healed, he lived, destined for the cross of St. Louis, and was to be at Mobile for over twenty years. Indeed, he was to be in the Bastile in 1765, and to outlive the terrors of the French Revolution.[2]

The Translated Records, in 1736, speak of Jean Belzaguy, deceased, the widow Verneuil, and apparently of a dead sergeant, Beauvais. These may be other reminders of the fatal day of Ackia. Terrepuy sold Girard, for two hundred livres, the lot he had acquired at auction of the Beauvais property. If this included a house, as seems intended, pilot Girard's purchase would show that the defeat had much depressed real estate at Mobile. Beyond its rear, fronting the woods, we have no means of identifying this or the few other city places which we know of. The grant, in 1737 and 1738, to Mme. De Lusser of the island in Tensaw River, which had been abandoned by the Tensaws, and that on the mainland are more easily located, but could hardly have been then of much use or value. Were they intended as a pension to the soldier's widow?

Bienville realized better than any one else the disastrous result of the Chickasaw campaign. It was undertaken because the Chickasaws had sheltered the fugitive Natchez; it must be retrieved because they had defeated the French. For this meant not only the emboldening of the Chickasaws, but that the English would through them secure a foothold on the banks of the Mississippi. The defeat would also encourage the growth of the English faction of the Choctaws, Creeks, and other friendly tribes, and thus possibly cause great danger to the whole French colony.

Bienville therefore determined on another expedition, and spent several years in preparation. As it was by way of the Mississippi, however, it is somewhat outside the scope of our story, and we can only note that it was made in 1740. Although, from a soldier's point of view, it was not brilliant and

---

[1] Pickett's *Alabama*, p. 334.

[2] Gayarré's *History of Louisiana*, pp. 475, 489, etc. ; Bossu's *Travels*, p. 312.

even hardly creditable, it impressed the Chickasaws.   It at
least resulted in their pacification and the safety of the colony.

It was, however, disappointing to Bienville, and he did not
conceal the fact.   He wrote to the minister that in some way
his plans of late years all miscarried, and that he would like
to retire.   His request was granted, and Louisiana was soon
to lose in him her governor and father, too.   Although they
did not know it, the Chickasaws really drove Bienville into
private life, for, unlike his two involuntary retirements in the
years before, his resignation this time was finale.

CHAPTER XV.

ALTHOUGH Mobile, after it ceased to be the capital, was at first cut off from the active competition with the English colonies which we find in the Mississippi valley, yet this also at last reached the Alabama basin. As the English were pushing over the mountains into the Ohio valley and giving the French uneasiness in the lake region, so in the south their influence increased. The Georgia colony, under the sea-to-sea charter of 1732, was a distinct advance in this direction. Under that we find Oglethorpe, on January 20 of next year, on the site of Savannah and making treaties with the Creeks, Cherokees, Chickasaws, and even Choctaws. On the 1st of August, 1739, he even held an Indian conference at Coweta among the Creeks of Alabama. The English were thus pushing around the south end of the Apalachian ridge towards the French on the Gulf of Mexico. This was an easier route than the old one over the Carolina mountains, and it was thus more efficacious. To this was due the division even among the Choctaws.

This success of the English was the easier that the experienced hand of Bienville was about to be removed. Although not a great general, there is little doubt that, as a negotiator among the Indians, he was unequaled in his day.

While he was quietly preparing to leave, and making matters as smooth as possible for his successor, Vaudreuil, tornadoes devastated the Gulf coast. It was as if nature was angry at Bienville's recall.

September, 1740, is one of the blackest months in the history of Mobile, for then the place was visited by two destructive cyclones. Crops, warehouses, and shipping alike felt their force, and the distress from the lack of food and shelter was heart-rending.[1] The storm on September 11, from east southeast, lasted for twelve hours. It blew down houses, among them Bizoton's store and sailors' refuge (which we may conjecture was near the wharf), and floated off flour and other provisions. The port at Dauphine Island was also much damaged. Half the island was washed away by the storm, and three hundred head of cattle were destroyed. A cannon was blown eighteen feet.

It was about this time that a traveler describes Mobile. In a survey of the posts in Louisiana, Dumont says that Fort Mobile, as he calls it, is "built of brick and fortified by four bastions, on Vauban's system, with half-moons, a good ditch, a covered way, and glacis. It contains a storehouse, barracks for the numerous garrison always kept up here, and a pavilion for the commandant, who was, in 1735, the Sieur D'Artaguette, royal lieutenant of the province."

Dumont goes on to say that he does not understand the utility of the post. All supplies are brought from the capital, New Orleans, as this place produces only firs and pines and a few vegetables, not of the best. The climate, however, is mild and healthy, and there is facility for trading with the Spaniards. Game is abundant in winter, but in summer the heat is excessive, and the inhabitants have to live on fish.[2]

There is no doubt that the removal of the capital and the Indian troubles had injuriously affected the place. In 1745, the population, outside the garrison, had decreased so that the white males were but one hundred and fifty, and negroes of both sexes two hundred.[3] But this seems to be an increase on the sixty families of some years before, and the garrison was large, and the place, as ever, the seat of the great Indian congresses.

The new governor, Vaudreuil, on March 22 of this year, met twelve hundred Choctaw chiefs in council here, and by presents cemented the alliance with the French. Red Shoe was still an English partisan, and was to divide even the Choctaws into hostile camps. His following was not large, but they did much damage, and great was to be the relief felt in Mobile

[1] 1 Gayarré's *History of Louisiana*, p. 515.
[2] Dumont's *Memoirs*, p. 40 (French's *Historical Collection*).
[3] 2 Gayarré's *History of Louisiana*, p. 28.

when, in 1748, the death of this active Indian was announced. He was shot by a Choctaw for a reward said to have been offered by the French.[1] Vaudreuil's negotiations ended the revolt, which Bossu says he managed by cutting off supplies of ammunition from the friendly Choctaws until they forced the hostiles to peace.

It was in Red Shoe's time that Vaudreuil found it necessary to palisade Mobile. It had never been done before, so far as we know. But 1747 had witnessed a hostile expedition down the Mississippi of Chickasaws and Muscogees, and even the Choctaws were not all loyal now. For a while the French even thought of abandoning Fort Tombecbé. The Indians were bolder, the colonists more timid. For Bienville was gone.

Despite Indian troubles and palisading, it was from this time, the year of Red Shoe's death, that we have the first expansion of the town beyond its original limits in the grant of a tract two arpens and four toises wide by twenty-five arpens deep on the west to Mme. De Lusser. This land probably fronted the river at first south of the inhabited town, say about the foot of our Eslava Street, and we know extended west even across Broad Street south of Dauphin. Its course is perplexing to us, cutting diagonally across our existing streets, but it is easily explained. It was merely continued straight in the line even Eslava Street would take, if projected according to its course at the river. The fact is, that the modern city developed best north of the fort, and the streets there were run out first; so that when the southern part built up west of Conception Street, its streets had to change their course to conform to the river bend above. This De Lusser tract, the one surviving French city grant, shows how the streets would have run if the town south of the fort had developed first.

In fact, the De Lusser marked a decadence, for it was an abandonment of the old plan of 1711, which ran out streets and squares far to the west. This grant was a recognition that, while land a few hundred feet south of the fort might do for farming, it would not now be needed for city purposes. In fact, Mme. De Lusser cleared only such as she needed for her slaves, and built cabins in which she lodged them.

[1] 2 Gayarré's *History of Louisiana*, pp. 30, 41 ; Bossu's *Travels*, p. 316. See Adair's *American Indians*, pp. 320, 328.

For some years little of interest is recorded. So much so that early history even was not always remembered. Dumont may have never been in Mobile, and, indeed, from his description, this seems to have been the case. But passing strange it is that, in his introductory sketch purporting to give the history of Louisiana, he seldom if ever mentions Mobile, and speaks of Dauphine Island as the first seat of the colony. While this leads one to distrust his book, it seems also to show that the place had much declined for an inquisitive stranger not to learn of its famous history. And yet its fort was still the finest in Louisiana. In 1751, we read that the troops there numbered four hundred French and seventy-five Swiss.[1] Vaudreuil was not content merely with fortifying Mobile against the Choctaws, but he also undertook, in 1752, an expedition from there up the Tombigbee against the Chickasaws.

His fleet of boats followed Bienville's route up the river to Fort Tombecbé, where he remained some days, and then up to where Bienville had disembarked at Cotton Gin Port. From that point he, too, marched across the country, and with French and Choctaws attacked the Chickasaws. He destroyed cabins and crops, but met defeat like his predecessor, and made a similar retreat. Bienville had had no artillery, while Vaudreuil probably had, but he seems now to have abandoned his cannon in the river on account of low water.

The French halted at Fort Tombecbé, which they enlarged and strengthened, and then returned to Mobile.[2] The early expedition of Bienville and this of Vaudreuil sixteen years later were almost perfect counterparts in design, route, and method, except that Vaudreuil had greater resources and knowledge of the country; but the result was the same in each case.

Let us turn to more peaceful occupations, and see what can be learned of lands and people during this troubled time.

We shall in another place study in detail such deeds as have survived, but from the fact that one of this time refers to a street by name, it is of interest here.

In 1749, Alexis Cartier and wife sold to Louis Flandrin a lot of the usual twelve and a half by twenty-five toises, and the latter, seven years later, deeded it to J. B. Boisdoré. In this

---

[1] 2 Gayarré's *History of Louisiana*, p. 56.
[2] Monette's *Valley of the Mississippi*, p. 300 ; Pickett's *Alabama*, p. 358.

second conveyance the land, with its house of wood covered with bark, apparently adjoins on the one side royal property, and on the other that of the widow Barthelemy, "making the corner of Rue Conty," or Coucy. It is interesting but difficult to study out its location. In the later papers we learn that it was "at the corner of the square opposite the commissary's office," and also that it faced the river. It must therefore be one of the corners made by Conti with the west side of Royal. As the block was opposite the commissariat, it would seem to be the southwest corner, but the fact that this would be in the barracks square makes it difficult to understand how it could on one side be bounded by private property. The price, in 1759, was fifteen hundred livres.

The land records go on all through this period; indeed, are more voluminous now than earlier. Not a great many have survived the ravages of war and time, and no government grants of city lots are found. But there are private sales and exchanges between the inhabitants before Dubourdieu or other royal notary, often signed by cross. The notary in 1749 was Dupuisier, 1756 Marcellin, 1759 Duparquirien. The land is described with reference to other lands and owners, and to street by name only the one time just named, although "streets" are often spoken of. How tantalizing this to the antiquary seeking to trace the origin of street names! Former owners are given, sometimes back to the first settler, and it would seem that the original deeds were deposited in the register's office, and a copy given to the owner.

CHAPTER XVI.

By the middle of the century, the Mobile country had been well explored and settled, both about the sound and bay, and far up the rivers, too. Indian disturbances would play their part, but names would remain even when some of the plantations were abandoned.

Almost all the names about Mobile, particularly of the watercourses, were given by the French, and are found on their maps and in their private and public documents. Strange to say, the Tombecbé is not on many French maps. It is almost always called Mobile River, — so on Homann about 1720, Dumont, Du Pratz 1757, and others. Sometimes it is named for the Chickasaws among whom it rose, and by the English Coxe for the Choctaws, but only occasionally it received the name Tombecbé, which became usual under the British. The Alabama, however, almost uniformly was called R. des Alibamons, except by Coxe 1722, who names it Coza, or Coussa.

Delisle is the real founder of modern geographical science, and his maps of Louisiana, for instance 1703, are valuable. Danville's map of Louisiana, 1732–52, is for Mobile points the best of all.[1] It calls for Baye de la Mobile, has Pte. de la Mobile, and the now familiar Baye Minet, Ecor Rouge, R. aux Poissons (low down on which some maps give a waterfall), Isle Dauphine, with Islets aux Grands Goziers out towards the channel entrance, and our Little Dauphine Island is Isle à Guillori, with I. aux Herons nearer Pte. aux Huistres. There is also Pte. aux Pins, and R. à Derbanc is not yet changed to La Batterie. Les Jones (grass islands) show the breakwaters of Portersville Bay, but Isle aux Herbes (Coffee Island) is not given, nor the Passe à Barreau to the east. The bay at

[1] See it in Winsor's *Basin of the Mississippi*, p. 59 ; as to Delisle, pp. 63, 74.

Choctaw Point is marked two fathoms, and all below is three, —an improvement on Delisle's two and a half. Miragouane seems nearer Grosse Pte., but Bellefontaine between Rivières aux Poules and Chevreuil and R. aux Chiens are the same. Chacteau Bienville in our Garrow's Bend we have seen, but Chacteau Sauvagé with two village marks, one on each side of Dog River, at different places, would seem to point to the Choctaws, whom Bienville had transplanted there.

Of the people, we of course know more of the residents of Mobile town, but, besides Boissy near our Toulminville, the Baudins on Miragouane or Mon Louis Island, and the Carrières over near Bay Minette, we find traces of some of the many settlers up Mobile River still mentioned even after the change of flag.

Most of their names are lost to us, but, as a southern Acadian race, they tilled the river banks, and the smoke from homes of thrifty settlers rose amid the figs and vines from Mobile up beyond the fork of the rivers. Gayety was not lacking, and pirogues carrying pleasure parties would pass the farmer or the hunter taking his products to town, or hail the solemn Indian in the bayous.

We should naturally expect to meet them mostly about the bluffs, not on the swamp lands predominant below Twenty-one Mile Bluff, and so it was. This, the first highland, was occupied by Beauchamps, who sold to Grondel, for whom the plantation was called St. Philippe, and a little promontory almost making up a part of it is even yet sometimes called for La Prade. Lizard Creeks across in the delta were long named for Beauchamps, and Bayou Registe a little above we have noticed as at least certainly French. Creole Dubrocas, including the Brus, have long lived near Twenty-one Mile Bluff, although the French grant places B. Dubroca south of Bayou Sara.

About the site of the old fort we do not find settlers, but the well-known La Tours seem to have been near the river bend a mile above. Bayou Mathieu across in the delta may commemorate the curé of this name, and Krebs Lake perpetuates some one of that family.

The De Lussers, at the close of the French period, certainly lived at the north end of the delta. Where the Tensaw leaves

the Mobilians and Apalaches, one plan shows the Parents, and
not far away was Favre.

Eleven leagues from Mobile, and therefore near what is now
called Chastang's, the Le Sueurs at one time had a plantation
at a bluff on the west side of the river. It was afterwards
the property of Narbonne. The description, owing to court
proceedings, has survived in some detail. In 1756 the house
was new, thirty feet long by twenty wide, a filled-in frame of
posts, and roofed with bark. It had six windows and two
doors and a clay chimney, with a gallery at one gable; there
was also a lean-to (*appentif*) kitchen with chimney. To one
side was a chicken house, and to the right of the yard (*cour*)
a large structure sixty by thirteen feet, surrounded by posts
and piling, covered with bark, used as a lodging for slaves.
On the other side was a barn, twenty-five by eighteen feet,
with lean-to and chimney. The whole was inclosed by piling
(*pieux*), making a yard twenty-five toises square. The place
faced on the river fifteen arpens by two deep, and across the
river there was another field (*desert*) ten arpens front by two
deep.

To this time we must assign the adjacent Chastang settlement near Chastang's Bluff, still represented by the large and
interesting colored Creole colony who live in the vicinity.
They claim descent from Dr. John Chastang of Spanish times,
but really go back to the French period, of which their *patois*
is an interesting reminder.

The church registers give the history of some families quite
in detail, and of these it will be interesting to select for fuller
notice the Le Sueurs and De Lussers, whose out-of-town homes
we have just noted.

In the fascinating pages of Penicaut we learn of one Le
Sueur who, in 1700, went from Biloxi in charge of an expedition
up the Mississippi to the Falls of St. Anthony and to the Sioux
west of our Lake Michigan, in order to find a copper mine on
Green River, of which he had known in previous years. He
had had a post on the upper Mississippi in 1695, and discovered the Minnesota, which he named St. Peter River. These
former expeditions must of course have been by way of Canada. He had come to Louisiana on the voyage of 1699, but
had spent several years among the Sioux, and it was on account

of his knowledge thus acquired of the Indians that Iberville so highly recommended him as suited to induce the vast resettlement of nations which this leader planned. The Canadians slyly intimate that the partiality was due mainly to their connection by marriage, Le Sueur having married the other's cousin-german.[1]

We do not know much more of Le Sueur, except that he spent the winter at the north in his Fort D'Huillier, where his name is perpetuated by a county in Minnesota, and in 1701 came back with thirteen hundred pounds of green earth, which he took to France. The result of the assay Penicaut does not know.[2]

The church registers throw light upon the subsequent family history, for it must be his widow, Bienville's cousin-german, whom we find in 1708 as the mother of Jean and Marguerite, who act as sponsors for a Barraud child. Next year the son's name is given as Jean Paul, and a sister Marie is mentioned, who, by the way, cannot write her name. Marguerite we find still mademoiselle in 1722, but Marie was two years before wife of Sieur La Tour, captain of a company, probably the commandant of Fort Toulouse. La Tours were later to have their residence on a plantation up in the Mobile delta, although this one is mentioned, in 1727, as then major at New Orleans.

Six years before this, we find a Mr. Pierre Le Sueur named as officer of the garrison at Mobile, and then, years later, mention of a Captain Le Sueur whose full name is not given, and J. P. Le Sueur seems to have been, perhaps casually, at Fort Toulouse in 1736, when Pechon died. Whether the commandant at Tombecbé was Jean Paul or Pierre must therefore remain uncertain, but the dates well admit of Jean Paul's commanding in the twenties at Dauphine Island, and in the thirties and later up the Tombigbee. We know that before his death at Mobile, in 1751, he was major as well as chevalier of the order of St. Louis. He must, therefore, have been a man of experience in the service.

Another family worthy of study is that of the De Lussers.

[1] 5 Margry, *Découvertes*, pp. 400, 401 ; 4 *Ibid.*, p. 607 ; Winsor's *Basin of the Mississippi*, pp. 32, 51, 52 ; 1 Martin's *Louisiana*, p. 155.

[2] 5 Margry, *Découvertes*, pp. 419, 423, 426.

It has been the romantic dream of antiquaries that the land-owning Mme. De Lusser was the widow of the gallant victim of Ackia, and that town-lots and, later, more extensive lands were grants in the nature of a pension by a grateful sovereign. But the recitals of his heirs seem to point to the husband as surviving the wife, and enjoying what he (like others of a more commercial epoch) put in his wife's name.

And yet there is good reason to believe that the romantic story is true, and the family tradition wrong.

We have seen that Captain Joseph Christophe De Lusser was killed at Ackia in 1736, and there is nothing to point to any other De Lusser in Mobile except his wife and children, unless a Captain Joseph in the baptismal records be other than his son. His wife, and widow, was Marguerite Bouras. They had three children. Of these, Marguerite Constance was born and baptized September 10, 1720; Marie Joseph was another child, but her baptism has not been noticed in the church records. She, like her sister, was old enough in 1734 to attest the baptism of a son of engineer De Vin. On June 4, 1724, was born the third child, Jean Baptiste. He was *ondoyé* by Father Claude at the time of his birth, but for some reason the baptismal ceremonies were not supplied until February 4, 1735. Then they had a great time of it. Governor Bienville was godfather to the boy, who bore his name of Jean Baptiste. Dame Barbe Bonnille was godmother, and among the dozen witnesses were Le Sueur and Beauchamps.

Captain De Lusser was a large slave-owner, and every now and then the register shows he had one baptized. After his untimely death, his widow continues to acquire slaves, and as Mme. De Lusser has them baptized. Sometimes her daughters act as godmothers or witness the ceremony, — as October 1, 1736, where Constance signs as godmother, and March 7 of next year, Marie, who always writes her pet name, Manon. By 1737 we find J. B. Lusser, officer, witnessing a baptism; in 1742 again as *enseigne d'infanterie*.

Constance became the wife of Captain Pierre Nicolas Annibal Chevalier, Sieur De Velle, and April 17, 1740, we find young Lusser, his mother, and several others witnessing the baptism of the first De Velle child. Marie soon afterwards married Lieutenant Francis Marie Joseph Hazeur, and their first child was baptized in 1742. Both lived to raise large families, and ultimately moved to New Orleans.

We find no mention of children of Jean Baptiste, and the children of his sisters Constance and Manon were to claim his property on the ground that he left no direct heirs. But it would seem that the property he was to leave was acquired of his mother, Marguerite Bouras, for the land was given to the owner of the slaves, and the owner of the slaves was the Ackia widow, mother of Constance, Manon, and Jean Baptiste. How he inherited from their mother we do not know, but may well have bought out his sisters' interests when they moved away.

Suffice it, however, that the Mme. De Lusser, from whom came the De Lusser Tract and other lands, was probably the mother, not the wife, of J. B. De Lusser.

Another prominent family was that of François Cesar Bernoudy, long *garde magasin* and royal attorney (*procureur*) at Mobile. His wife was Louise Marguerite Belzagui. He was dead by 1757, when she signs as Veuve Bernoudy, but they seem to have had a large family. A daughter called for her was wife of Captain J. B. Aubert, François is named as *cadet Suisse*, and at the same time Mlle. Marguerite and Mlle. Françoise Bernoudy also appear in the church records.

"Endless genealogies" could be made of many city families, some noble, some bourgeois, but these will suffice. Of families that will later meet us, however, may be named Charles Rochon and his son Pierre, Landry, Delalande, Jean and Simon Favre, Durand, Duret, Jusan and H. E. Krebs. Colored offshoots of the Bernoudy and Favre families were to perpetuate those names in land grants. The Pechons, Beauchamps, Mandevilles, and others of rank were to disappear with the French flag.

CHAPTER XVII.

WE have already examined somewhat in detail the history of the church at the first Fort Louis, and it will be not without interest to see who officiated at the new settlement and learn what they did. They have left full records, and we can realize their surroundings.

Le Maire was the curé first after the change of base to the present site of Mobile, although from 1712 we find Huvé generally acting, and good Davion's name also occurs in 1712, in 1713, and, in fact, as late as 1720, when he signs as the vicar of "Kebec." But evidently he was at Mobile only on visits, for the regular priest is Huvé.

In 1713 we find Varlet, and after that his name as apostolic missionary and then vicar-general occurs. Dominique Mary Varlet of the Seminary of Quebec was vicar-general of St. Vallier, and became afterwards the Bishop of Babylon. His views, however, were unorthodox, and later, when setting out for the east, he was discovered to hold Jansenist doctrines and was recalled. He did not recant, and was a prominent schismatic in Holland.[1] His full, good-natured face is preserved in Shea. He looks like a man who saw the bright side of things, — even of heresy.

It would be interesting to have a portrait of Alexandre Huvé (called Huet by Penicaut), who so long went in and out at this Gulf city. He baptized and buried French, Indians, slave and free, and negroes, too, and often married the French, and it is much to his credit that with so long an incumbency and under so many rulers we hear no complaint of him. In 1715, he speaks of himself as priest performing for the present the function of curé at Fort Louis, and sometimes as missionary apostolic in the church of Fort Louis. To officials and the

[1] Shea's *Catholic Church in the Colonies*, p. 556.

public, officers and soldiers, freemen and slaves, he ministered for several years, and we can imagine his task, particularly after Law began to send his colonists, no easy one. He knew every one and every one's business and relations, and was often in their homes.

His last entry at Mobile was his baptism, January 13, 1721, of a negro child. We are told that he went to the Mississippi and afterwards had a mission among Indians, but his lack of power to acquire language, and his increasing blindness, impelled him, in 1727, finally to return to France.[1]

As Louisiana could not well be governed in civil affairs from Canada on account of the distance, so the same difficulty had to be met in religious matters. Bishop St. Vallier could not from Quebec directly supervise the great Southwest, and in course of time various expedients were devised to meet the case.

First, the Capuchin Louis Francis Duplessis De Mornay, of Meudon, was made coadjutor of Quebec. He never came to America, and so personally did not solve the question, although he succeeded Bishop St. Vallier in 1727. He naturally turned to his own order for missionaries, and from 1721 we find at Mobile, instead of Huvé, the Capuchin Brother Jean Mathieu. Huvé was the last of the missionaries of the seminary, and from now on we have the regular orders only, generally Capuchins.

Mathieu signs as "prestre religieux missionaire apostolique." At the beginning it is as performing the function of curé, but afterwards as curé of Mobile. In 1722, the Western Company, whose charter of 1717 pledged it to build churches and care for the religious instruction of the people, free and slave, by agreement with De Mornay divided the province into three districts. The Illinois (including afterwards to the Natchez) went to the Jesuits, New Orleans and west of the Mississippi to the Capuchins, and the Mobile district, extending from the Mississippi to the Perdido, from the Ohio to the Gulf, to the Barefoot Carmelites. Except Charles, who in the preceding year was among the Apalaches, no Carmelites came to this district, and it is said that therefore Mobile, also, was then by St. Vallier given to the Capuchins.[2]

[1] Shea's *Catholic Church in the Colonies,* p. 553. [2] *Ibid.,* p. 564.

Dividing into districts was but a partial relief, and the great question still remained, should the country be a vicariate apostolic, dependent only on Rome, or a vicariate of Quebec? Mathieu, in 1722–23, signs himself as vicar apostolic, and he seems to have applied to Rome for the province, containing, as he said, fifteen missions. This, if granted, was but temporary. Indeed, when St. Vallier created a regular line of vicars-general, he seldom selected Capuchins, and so, too, under Bishop Pontbriand the position of vicar-general was usually held by Jesuits, despite the outcry and opposition of the Capuchins. For on February 20, 1726, the Company made a treaty with the Jesuits for their services in the Mississippi valley, including also the Chickasaws, Alibamons, and Choctaws.[1]

Beaubois was the earliest vicar-general, perhaps, — a man to be famous as the founder not only of the Jesuit mission in Louisiana, but also in 1727 of the useful and long-lived Ursuline convent at New Orleans. Mathias, it is true, was vicar-general afterwards, but from 1739 it was Pierre Vitry, and from 1757 Michael Baudouin, both Jesuits again. Baudouin had previously labored eighteen years on the Choctaw mission.

After the removal of the capital to New Orleans, the more rapid growth was transferred from Mobile, but its curé had to make visitations over considerable territory. There was generally a missionary to the Christian Apalaches, but outside of that the parish of Mobile was a large one. We find the Mobile curé often at Dauphine Island, and sometimes at Pascagoula and among the Choctaws. In 1728, even the Apalaches of St. Louis are mentioned with Pascagoula and Dauphine Island as dependent on the Mobile parish.

On January 20, 1720, the directors-general of the Company of the Indies supplied a book of forty-eight pages for a register. Up to page twelve was to be for baptisms, then to twenty-six for marriages, and the remainder for deaths. This division, however, was not observed. Baptisms and deaths are in separate books, while there is no regular record of marriages, although many are found in the baptismal register.

The earlier church registers had been kept without special rules by the parish priests. There was a long ordinance of

[1] Shea's *Catholic Church in the Colonies*, p. 582 ; 1 Martin's *Louisiana*, p. 261.

1667 bearing on the subject, but it does not seem to have been at first regarded in Louisiana. On January 21, 1726, Fleuriau at New Orleans delivered to Mathias a blank register for baptisms, marriages, and burials, containing ninety pages, numbered and initialed, and prefixed is an extract from that ordinance. Fleuriau signs as Royal Councillor and Attorney-General to the Superior Council of the province.[1]

The ordinance directs that two registers be issued each year, paged and initialed (*cotté et paraphé*) by the royal judge of the place, the one to serve as a minute-book to be preserved by the curé or vicar, the other to be delivered when filled to the *greffier juge royal* as an engrossed record. The church shall pay for both.

In baptismal entries shall be mentioned the day of birth and names of child, father and mother, and sponsors (*parain et maraine*). In those of marriages there shall be given the name, age, quality, and residence of each of the bridal couple, if of family, and four witnesses, who shall declare whether they are relatives, and if so on what side and of what degree. In burials shall be mentioned the day of death, and there shall sign two of the nearest relatives or friends who assist in the procession (*convoy*). If any one cannot write, he shall so declare. The priest shall ask this question and make mention of the fact. All entries shall be in one register according to date, without blanks.

Six weeks after the end of the year, the priest must take or send both books, signed and certified as correct (*veritable*), to the royal clerk and judge who issued them, who must receive them, noting the date. He shall give a receipt after comparing the minute or blotter and the engrossed copy. The clerk shall cross out all blanks in both, without charge. The minute-book is to remain with the curé or vicar, and the copy shall be preserved by the clerk for reference.

This entry is signed by Fleuriau, and also what seems to be Delarivière Flamont.

How far the regulation as to original and copy was carried out we do not know, but it is certain the minute-book was left with the parish priest. The books ever since in the custody

---

[1] 1 Martin's *Louisiana*, p. 293, gives the name as Fleuriau, but he writes it more like Fleuviau.

of the church at Mobile are evidently originals. But it is also certain the books were not annually issued, for each one of the volumes covers several years.

It is in the time of Mathieu that we find the first records of abjuration of heresy. We learn only that on November 14, 1722, he received the abjuration of heresy of Magdelaine Moyennant, native of the vicinity of Geneva. The lady could not write, but five witnesses attest her mark. On the 23d of the next month, Monsieur Jean Baptiste de Roy likewise acknowledged the error of his way, and seven witnesses seal his abjuration. Among them are Carrière, De Beauchamps, and Durand, so that it was evidently a matter of uncommon importance.

During a short period succeeding 1723, we find several priests named at Mobile. In that year it is Brother Claude, also Capuchin, and in March, 1725, Reverend Father Beaubois, Jesuit, superior of the Illinois, officiates, possibly during some temporary absence of Claude. In February, 1726, we find an entry by Brother Raphael de Luxembourg, as vicar-general of Monseigneur of Quebec. This was probably a visitation from New Orleans, for a few days later we see the Capuchin Mathias de Fidau (Sedan?) signing as curé. He was to retain the position for some time.

Mathias was, in virtue of powers from the Bishop of Quebec, to receive an abjuration on September 8, 1727. Edward Hurcksall of the English province of Quainte (Kent?) made profession of faith in the religion of the Catholic Apostolic Roman Church and publicly abandoned his former Protestant heresy, with the prescribed ceremonies, in the presence, amongst others, of the Jesuit Petit and of Monsieur Diron, chevalier of the order of St. Louis, colonel of infantry, and commandant of Fort Condé, — himself apparently of the Reformed (*reformé*) faith. This last may seem somewhat strange in view of the fact that Bienville's Black Code of 1724 had prohibited all worship but the Catholic; but even this code had not gone the length of banishing Protestants as it did the Jews. No doubt a Protestant could remain, if he did not worship in public.

The next year we find the first mention of a churchwarden (*marguelier*). It was then Robert Talon, master cabinet-maker, the first Creole of the colony, as we learn at his death in 1745.

The office is to be mentioned at intervals from that time down to the present time. In 1737, for instance, it was M. Prevot, and three years later Charles Marie Delalande, the well-known *garde magasin.* By 1755 there were several, as Antoine Colon is then noted as first *marguillier.*

Mathias, like all the curés, was to be absent occasionally on different missions, and others then took his place. Thus we find Brother Victorin Dupui, a Recollect, in 1730, and at other times, Pierre Vitry, the Jesuit, in 1732, and on another occasion the Jesuit Petit. Victorin was at that time missionary to the Apalaches near Mobile, and easily accessible for such calls.

In 1732 we begin another book, prepared by paging and initialing for the use of the curé. This one was of fifty-eight pages, and to be limited to baptisms, contrary to the ordinance above quoted. The official who had thus *cotté et paraphé*, was De Cremont, ordinary commissary of the marine, second councillor of the Superior Council of Louisiana, and first judge of Fort Condé of Mobile.

Two years later, we have record of Mathieu's supplying the ceremonies of baptism to a daughter of Sieur Noel de Prououd of Mobile River. She had only been *ondoyée* by Victorin, on account of lack of sacred oil.

It is in 1734 that Mathias signs himself as vicar-general of Monseigneur of Quebec, a position which this Capuchin held for five years. It occurs first during a visitation of the coasts of the Bay of Mobile. He continued to perform the functions of curé at Mobile, however, through April 5, 1734, when, after a break of about a month and a half, the Capuchin Jean François begins his ministry.

In November, during some absence of Curé Jean François, we find an entry by Brother Guillaume Morand, Jesuit, as apostolic missionary. We shall see him again at Fort Toulouse as his regular post. A year later, Mathias as vicar-general acts again, and then Prosper and Felix sign each as curé at Fort Condé within ten days of each other. From December, 1737, to the middle of the next March, Felix acted as curé, and in April comes Brother Agnan, with a curious hand. From August begins Brother Amand, a Capuchin, regularly. Is this fluctuation of pastors a reflection on the religious side of the uncertainty on the civil due to the fatal Chickasaw expedition?

Amand was curé until 1742, and it was during his administration the entries are made in 1741 that the church, never having been dedicated and being completely rebuilt (*toute à neuve*), received the benediction the day of the nativity of the Holy Virgin. On that account he dedicated it to the Holy Virgin by special commission sent him by Reverend Father Pierre, Capuchin, then vicar-general of Monseigneur of Quebec, who ordained that the anniversary should be celebrated every year. From that time the church is known as Notre Dame de la Mobile.

Jean François was curé of the Apalaches, and occasionally acted for Amand, and on December 23, 1743, he succeeds Amand as curé. Occasionally we have entries by Prosper, missionary of the Apalaches, and Seraphim, who even signs as curé quite frequently in 1744, but Jean François acts oftenest.

In 1744 begins another register, this time of forty-four pages and for baptisms alone, of the parish of Notre Dame de la Mobile. It is numbered, and each page initialed, with many flourishes, by Bobé Descloseaux, commissary[1] and controller of the marine, exercising the function of judge at Mobile. This book was to outlast the French régime. The companion death register was issued by Descloseaux in 1754, and its forty-eight pages were to suffice even through 1803.

During the time 1748–52 we have Brother Pierre as curé, but Jean François as missionary acts almost as often. It is difficult to say which was the real curé. From then on for two years we find Hilaire, Barnabé, and Sebastien alternating. In 1754–55, we have Maximin and sometimes Barnabé, but usually Jean François acts as curé, until, in 1756, the Capuchin Ferdinand begins. The indifferent but characteristic handwriting of this curé outlasts the French period, becoming gradually more uncertain and feeble. Occasionally Jean François comes, as at the baptism of negroes of the mission in 1760, and the Capuchin Valentin, missionary apostolic, two years later; but Ferdinand is the parish priest. He holds the position perhaps longer than any of his predecessors, acting even

---

[1] 1 Martin's *Louisiana*, p. 333, seems only to know of him as *commissaire ordonateur* from Auberville's death in 1758.

under the English, and to his entries we owe much of our knowledge of his times.

The church was southwest of the fort, near our St. Emanuel and Theatre streets. There these priests said mass, baptized children and slaves, married the living, and buried the dead with the imposing ritual of their church, forgetting their French home and earthly ambition in ministry to the people of this far-away American parish.

IN 1760, one Phelypeaux made a plan of Mobile which has
outlasted the several flags that have floated over its resting-
place. It gives a clear idea of what the town had been for
years before, — for we know it did not grow much after Vaudreuil succeeded Bienville in 1748, nor after Vaudreuil was, in
1753, promoted to be governor of Canada, and Kerlerec, captain
in the royal navy,[1] succeeded him in Louisiana. Of Phelypeaux we know nothing except that this was the family name
of the Pontchartrains.

The plan is headed, "Veritable plan de la Mobille; Tous
les Batimens; Marqué de rouge appartienne au Roy; ou les
occupe; fait a la Mobille le 20 8bre 1760 — Phelypeaux."

The general identity with the plan of 1711 is evident, but
the fort, marked as "Fort Condé de la Mobille," is drawn back
more from the river and has a wharf in front to deep water.
Around it is an open "Esplanade." There are, in two rows,
six blocks south of it instead of eight, the two west of the fort
are split through in an irregular way to provide for a red cross,
evidently the church, and "Terrein conservé Pour leglise;"
while the blocks north have grown from two rows of four each
to three rows of six blocks each, there being now a third row
pretty much in continuation of the one furthest west behind
the fort. In front of all runs a "Quay," bordering a marshy
shore. The land to the south is marked as high, that to the
north as low. Before, the streets bore no names, and there is
but one exception now. Our Conti west of St. Emanuel is
"Rue de Tournée."

The hospital square we find at the extreme north end of the
town, the buildings at about the northwest corner of our St.
Louis and Royal, perhaps the site of the old English house

---

[1] 1 Martin's *Louisiana*, p. 324.

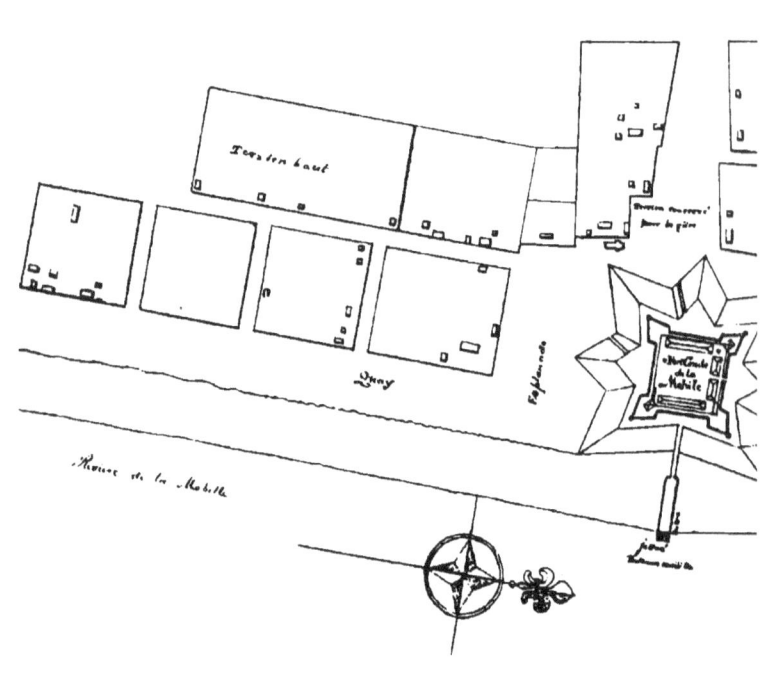

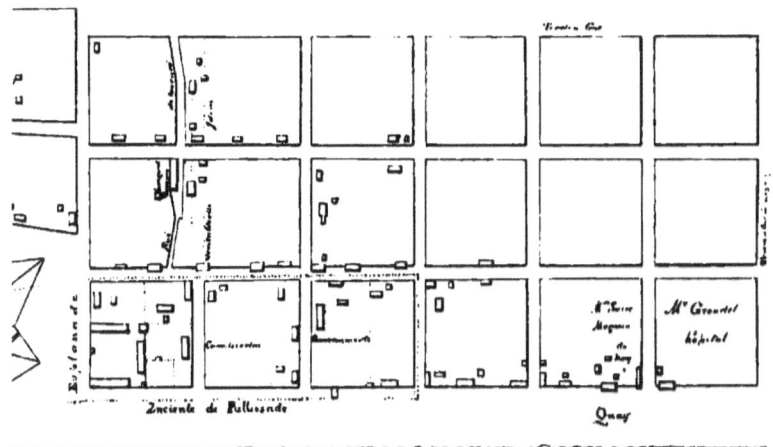

Riviere   de   la   Mabille

Plano que se ha hallado en la Sonda Sola.
merlifica ci maya 1760   Carlos Trudenes

formerly on a high lot next to the Electric Lighting Company. This ridge ran along the west side of Royal Street, and no doubt determined the location of the city. On this, overlooking the mud flats of the river, the houses were built. In the same square with the "hopital" we find "Mr. Grondel," but no line of demarcation for individual ownership from the red buildings, which indicate the king's. Under the British régime we shall find that Mme. Grondel was the acknowledged owner of the hospital house and grounds. This tends to show that it was not the daring cavalier's wife, as they lived abroad from 1758. The half block next south is indicated by a red dotted line as the king's, and in red there is a long building on St. Louis and a thicker one on Royal (besides three small outbuildings), marked as "Magasin du Roy." West of them is "Mde. Socier" (Madame Socier, rather than M. de Socier, as Monsieur is abbreviated "Mr."), and under the next government we shall see she claimed to own the site. This was a magazine for provisions, and was built in part of brick, covered without by planks, and shingled. At one end was a mill for "the shelling of rice," with necessary appurtenances.

The three blocks from St. Francis Street south to the fort moat corners are inclosed by a yellow dotted line, marked "Enceinte de pallisade," running through the centre of St. Francis, St. Joseph, and Royal streets. There, then, was Vaudreuil's palisade of 1748, inclosing principally royal property, — the "Gouvernement" (civil officials) on the north side of Dauphin, extending from Royal to St. Joseph; the "commissariat," seemingly without buildings, on the north side of Conti, extending west from Royal Street; and what are clearly barracks, occupying almost all the square from Conti to Government streets, and from Royal to St. Emanuel. This commissariat was, like the hospital grounds, laid off in walks and probably trees. The map gives no indication of the ownership by the De Lussers of the street corner of the commissariat under the recent grant. The palisade seems to have several gates, one on Royal Street at St. Francis, two at the intersection of Dauphin with St. Joseph and Royal, respectively, and one on the Quay, at what is now Royal and Government. The hospital and warehouse were too far off to be inclosed.

In each of the three palisaded squares were some private

houses, — the southwest quarter of the barracks block, for instance, being marked "Mr. Pechon." Of him we know little, and indeed in the record history of this interesting lot at·the northeast corner of Government and St. Emanuel we do not find his name. It had been granted by the French government to Grondel April 19, 1757, the year before he left, and after the English occupation it was the residence of Major Farmer.[1] Behind Pechon's two houses, with its end on St. Emanuel, is a royal building facing the south side of Conti. A fair conjecture is that it was the bakery of the king, which existed somewhere in this square. Indeed, there were two, of brick with shingled roof, one having two ovens, and another, new, with four. This corner we knew was the site of the "Bakehouse" of Spanish times. The barracks of this square were in a quadrangle open to the south. They were glazed and for officers.

Possibly the most curious thing about the map is the Rue de Tournée (our Conti), which is very irregular, and, just west of what we call St. Emanuel, widens and then as suddenly is contracted by a house in red, which with a smaller one is marked "hangard," "sovager." The words "gard" and "tournée " may have some connection with circuit of the watch, or a guard-house, but it cannot be doubted that "sovager" has some reference to the place in which were held the Indian congresses. Here in British times was the "Indian House," and we shall see that there was nothing new then built. So that it may be supposed in this house and open place was held that congress, for example, in December, six years before Phelypeaux's map, when the pleased savages voted Kerlerec "Father of the Choctaws."[2]

There is no indication of the recent grant to Mme. De Lusser of the lots on Royal and Conti, nor of the De Lusser Tract, which ran west from south of the fort. Taking the town as a whole, we count one hundred and thirty-one houses outside the fort, of which twenty-three pertain in one way or another to the government. Some, no doubt, are shops, and others so small that one conjectures them to be some kind of

[1] 3 *American State Papers*, p. 398 ; *Hallett* v. *Eslava*, 3 St. & P. (Ala.) pp. 105, 108.

[2] 2 Gayarré's *History of Louisiana*, p. 78.

outbuildings. But even then there would be perhaps seventy-five dwellings. If the family should average four persons, that would mean a population, in 1760, of three hundred, outside the fort. Most were to the north, there being but thirty-five houses south of the fort, and these all in the eastern tier of blocks.

The town had thus already built up north of the fort to the neglect of the lower land below it, a tendency still seen in the fact that the business part of the city, the handsome buildings of old times, all lie north of Church Street. The slight curve to the southwest now shown in all north and south streets at some point from Church to Canal is seen on this map, and must have been true in 1711, although not on that plan. For it is due to a bend in the river in front of the fort.

The square fort — Fort Condé de la Mobile — is shown on this plan in full Vauban splendor, as detailed by Dumont.[1] From tip to tip of the bastions is fifty toises, three hundred feet, while it will be remembered the original palisade fort of 1711 was ninety toises, five hundred and forty feet square. The brick fort of 1717 thus contained less than one third the superficial area of the wooden one; indeed, from point to point of the glacis was ninety toises, and so the whole new works, glacis and all, were within the lines of the palisade Fort Louis.

No explanation is attached, but a soldier has no difficulty in determining the use of the structures given. There was access slantwise the glacis on each side to the brick-faced covered way, on the east it being from the wharf and on the north from the palisaded inclosure; but entrance into the fort proper was only from the north. This would be to the west of the rear of the present court-house, for the still existing foundations mark the location of the fort. Its interior was pretty much within the lines of the block bounded by Church, Royal, Theatre, and St. Emanuel, although the east bastions extended across Royal, and the west ones across Church and Theatre just east of St. Emanuel.

Crossing the moat (about where Mrs. Voorhees so long had in our day a boarding-house), one entered through the brick scarp wall. This wall was about sixteen feet from the bottom to the cordon, above which rose a thin brick parapet four and

[1] Dumont's *Memoires*, p. 40 (5 French's *Historical Collection*).

a half feet high. In the curtains of three fronts at least were brick casemates for cannon. Passing between two buildings, one of which was the officers' quarters and one the station of the guard, the visitor came to an open square, probably with staff in the centre floating the lilies of France, — the yard now of the city street department. On the east and west of this parade were two long one-story barracks for about two hundred and sixteen men, but the warehouse of Dumont's time was now up town. On the south side of the parade were two wells. Walking by the bristling cannon standing upon wooden platforms, one would notice at the northwestern and southeastern corners entrances to two subterranean rooms in these bastions. The first was a brick bakehouse and the other the powder magazine, while at the northeast corner was some outhouse on Royal Street, near the present Armory. From the eastern parapet one would look out on the single wharf of the city, narrow in part across the miry bank of the river, but wider towards the eastern end. Where it reached the river (near the present Water Street) were boats at anchor, a hundred yards from the fort but under its guns. From the ramparts on the other sides lay in full view the bark or tiled houses of Mobile.[1]

Such was Fort Condé in 1760, such the city it guarded.

[1] The description of the public buildings has been drawn in part from a report on their condition made up shortly after the British occupation in 1763. Everything was then in want of repair, but the arrangement under the French had not been changed. This report is in the *Haldimand Papers*.

The plan was made in 1760, and in one corner Carlos Trudeau, the Spanish surveyor, has written, " Plano que je ha hallado en la tomada de la Mobila, 4 Mayo, 1780," — plan found at the capture of Mobile, May 4, 1780. What next became of it no one knows, except that it is now in the Department of the Interior, bearing the signature of United States Surveyor-General Freeman, and that in 1842 it was referred to in the case of *Watkins* v. *Holman*, 16 Peters Rep. pp. 30, 52 ; but no copy was actually made a part of that record. On the first organization of Mobile under the Americans, attempts were made by the local authorities to find the plan of the city. Money was sent to New Orleans on the report that a notary had it there, and then to Pensacola, but in vain. This map was afterwards found in New Orleans, and apparently purchased by the United States authorities for $500, in order to lay off the fort property for sale.

CHAPTER XIX.

FEW grants and deeds have come down to us, and of these the earliest preserved in full was a grant by Cadillac, in 1715, on Dauphine Island; but, although the actual grant has perished, we have a pretty full history of an earlier concession, possibly made at the first Fort Louis. This was of what we know as Mon Louis Island, practically the mainland opposite Dauphine Island. There is then a gap until 1733, when come for some years a number of grants and town-lot deeds. At the end of the French régime we have papers which are rather certificates of long occupancy and ratification of claims than original grants themselves.

Major Farmer of the British army was to claim that he had difficulty in preventing the removal of the records by the French, and from the few French ones now in the Mobile Probate Court it would seem that other custodians have been even less successful. In point of fact, some few have been found in the Haldimand Papers, and so were removed by the British themselves.

The books of Translated Records at Mobile are the more accessible, but the original papers in the cypress boxes in the same Probate Court are the more interesting. Neatly packed away by dates, with wide margins made by creases, bearing the signatures of applicants and the French officials, and seals of state, these bundles of original documents have survived war and fire and revolutions of empire even until now.

Mon Louis Island comes first in date. Nicholas Baudin, the Sieur de Miragouine, we know lived at Grosse Pointe, near the centre of the east coast, and from this the whole island was at first called. The grant is the earliest we have, and bears date November 12, 1710, at Fort Louis.

Bienville as the king's lieutenant and D'Artaguette as commissary of the marine made the cession, but, for some reason, it was thought proper to obtain Cadillac's ratification September 15, 1713. The papers were duly deposited later in the archives of the Superior Council, and were to survive at least until 1783.

This property was of more importance when Dauphine Island was the port of Mobile than after that harbor was practically abandoned. It may be that to this fact it is due that the Baudins never alienated the property. It was to remain theirs under the English and Spanish régimes, and be finally confirmed by the United States to the descendants of the Sieur de Miragouine in 1829.[1]

The concession of land on Dauphine Island to Joseph Simon de la Pointe, whose name occurs often in the church registers as father of Mme. Krebs, was made November 12, 1715, by Antoine de la Motte Cadillac, governor of the province of Louisiana, and Jean Baptiste Duclos, royal councillor and marine commissary. They certify that they are vested by his Majesty the king, their lord, with the power to grant lands. It recites La Pointe's application, and was executed on Dauphine Island, and registered, as ordered, the same day by *greffier en chef* Raguet in the office of the Supreme Council of Louisiana, — which would indicate that this office was at the time also on Dauphine Island. The description hardly admits of modern identification. The line seems to run north and south a league, the land bounded south on Fish River, and has a west front of a league on the sea, facing the Grand Bay (*faisant face à la grande Baye*). The island now is not a league wide, nor could it ever have given a west front, at any point, of three miles. The widest part is at the east end, and at this time much of that was taken up by the fort and settlement, and there is no Fish or other river on the island. The proper description should probably call for a north boundary of a league, with similar south line, but the original grant, which has survived, reads as the translation.

The grant was for the purpose of enabling La Pointe to raise cattle, and was careful to except a cedar grove said to be near Fish River. The title was to be absolute, provided he cultivated the land for two successive years, but was subject

---

[1] 5 *American State Papers*, p. 130 ; 4 *U. S. Statutes at Large*, p. 358.

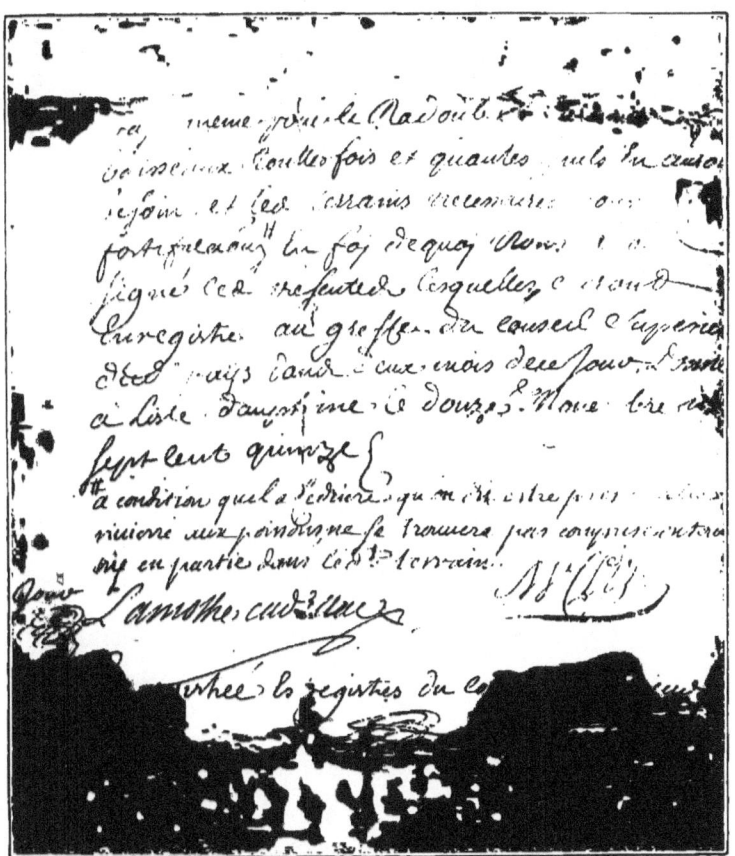

CADILLAC'S DAUPHINE ISLAND GRANT

not only to possible royal dues, but also to furnish timber for forts, repair of ships, and other public works, and the land could be taken for erecting fortifications. These conditions were common in all the grants, and but a proper instance of the right of eminent domain.

Quite different the private deeds. These were not papers signed by one party and delivered to the other, as with the Spaniards later and now too with us. The procedure was for both parties to go before a notary, and he certifies their appearance, and that the one declares the sale to the other for so many livres, paid before him, of a certain described piece of land, and that the other party declares his acceptance of the property. All sign, perhaps with witnesses, in the notary's office, and he annexes his signature, but all without seal. If necessary, the notary, according to ordinance, explains the transaction and the party makes a cross for his mark. The original deed is then deposited with the register, the parties receiving copies.

It was two years before Bienville's fatal Chickasaw expedition that James Philip Emard, May 23, 1734, exchanged his house and lot in the city for that of Thomas Asseline Fleury, and agreed to pay ten livres additional to Pierre Regnault on account of his vendor's claim. Fleury paid Regnault, two weeks later, one hundred and forty livres, the remainder of the purchase-money Emard had owed Regnault. Both transactions were before E. Dubourdieu, the royal notary at Fort Condé, — a frequent unofficial witness in the church records, as we remember.

These two houses cannot be identified, for, provokingly enough, the deeds never name the streets, but give other private places as boundaries. For instance, Emard's house thus sold to Fleury was opposite that sold by Verneuil to Robert, the master tailor, and adjoining De Terrepuy's house and Margaret Belzagny's vacant lot; but where were these? And the house Fleury sells is no better described, for it is merely said to be the one which he purchased of Jean Sarry.

Sixteen months later, after the Chickasaw expedition, we find Fleury selling this place for two hundred and fifty livres to Jean Girard de St. Jean and his wife Margaret Benoit before the notary De Flandre. The description gives the lot as twelve and a half toises wide by twenty-five deep, bounded on one side by a lot of grantor, and on the other by one of Jean Belzaguy, deceased, and fronting the house of the widow Verneuil, while to the rear are the woods.

De Terrepuy's lot next to this of De Fleury's had been acquired by him at the auction of the property of Sergeant Beauvais, and we find him selling it at two hundred livres on July 6, before the same notary, to Girard, pilot of the Alibamons, — no doubt the same man who bought from De Fleury. The description is equally vague, and we learn only that the lot was between the houses of Hamond and De Fleury. In what part of the town was this activity in real estate we do not know.

There were many grants in French times, of course, which cannot now be traced. Some were abandoned, but many, especially in the city, continued in uninterrupted possession of descendants or sub-grantees whose preserved deeds were not to antedate the Spanish domination. In the American State Papers we find Kerlerec's grant to Pechon of five thousand arpens on Mobile River, that of Bienville and Salmon, in 1737, of the five thousand and forty arpen island in Tensaw River to Margaret De Lusser, which had been abandoned by the Tensaw Indians. Corresponding is a tract on the mainland, to be certified by De Velle as property of Mme. De Lusser, granted her May 27, 1738, by Governor Bienville and Commissaire Ordonnateur Salmon. This had one league front on Tensaw River by sixty arpens depth, bounded north and south by creeks, about a league and a half above the Apalache Indians.

Many others were to be disapproved for one reason or other by the United States authorities, but among those which were to stand the test of time was the St. Louis Tract near Mobile. This is probably where the Apalaches had been located, and is that extensive and important region between Three Mile Creek and Chickasabogue. The last stream was called, under the French, the St. Louis River, possibly in connection with the Apalache parish of that name. It embraced about 22,500 arpens, and was granted to M. Diron November 7, 1733, by Bienville and Salmon.[1] After Diron left, we find it, before 1746, in possession of Charles Maria de Lalande, for Lalande

[1] 5 *American State Papers*, p. 130.

and wife in that year conveyed it to Joseph Barbeau de Boisdoré, whose heirs, in 1759, sold it to De Bonville (Bonnille?).
One of D'Abbadie's certificates of 1763 recognizes the ownership of this, under the name of St. Louis plantation, by
Bonville. From Bonville it was to pass to the De Lussers, in
1807 to J. B. Laurendine, and then in the same year to Joseph
Chastang, in whose representatives it was confirmed finally by
the United States. It was, in Laurendine's deed, described as
being one hundred and fifty arpens square.

To Bienville's grant to D'Artaguette, then, in his third
administration, do we owe the origin of that great tract extending from Bayou Chateaugué to Boguehoma and Chickasabogue,
from west of Whistler and Toulminville to Mobile River, now
the seat of so many railroads, mills, and industries.

De Velle was later to certify to another important grant to
Mme. De Lusser, — who turns out to be his mother-in-law.
This was what is now called the De Lusser Tract, the earliest
of the extensive concessions outside old Latin Mobile which
were to figure so much in the present larger city.

This tract now extends from about the northeast corner of
our St. Emanuel and Eslava out to a little across Broad Street
just south of Dauphin Street. At the time of the concession,
only the front, two arpens and four toises wide, was of any
consequence. The town did not stretch further west than Conception Street, and it is doubtful if any one knew or cared
where the twenty-five arpens depth would come out. It faced,
on the east, other lands of Mme. De Lusser and De Bonnille,
touching on the one side (north) property of De Morzier, and
bounded on the other (south) by the pine forest. This land
(*terrain*) Mme. De Lusser cleared in 1748, and when De Velle
wrote, in 1763, it was serving to lodge her slaves, for whom
she had built cabins. She could not have cleared much except
the front of this eighty acre tract.

Of Morzier's land we know nothing, and his title cuts no
figure afterwards. The lot opposite, however, had in later
years quite an eventful history. We next find both De Lusser
pieces in possession of Captain Jean Baptiste De Lusser, and
how it gets from her to him is one of the puzzles of the record
office.

Town-lots are recited to have been granted her by Governor

Kerlerec in 1757, also. They were two in number, making up a tract twenty-five toises square at the northwest corner of Royal and Conti, and consequently part of the commissariat property we find on Phelypeaux's plan of 1760.

Among the Haldimand Papers in the British Museum are preserved several deeds which passed to that British governor at Mobile in 1768. These give us the story of another piece of property from 1749 down.

We thus learn that Alexis Cartier was once the owner of a lot twelve and a half by twenty-five toises, and sold it, March 29, 1749, to Louis Flandrin. He in his turn, on May 15, 1756, sold it to Joseph Barbaud de Boisdoré. Flandrin's wife was Marie Louise Dinant, and all the parties were residents. The lot had on it a house built of posts (*potteaux*) and earth, roofed with bark. The place was contiguous on the one side to royal land occupied by M. Aubert, aide major, making the corner of "la Rue Coucy" (Conty?), and at the back (*sur le dernier*) adjoining the property of Widow Barthelemy. The consideration was not money, but fifteen cows and calves, one pair of oxen of three years, and a bull (*toreau*) of two years and a half, the whole to be delivered in two installments at the purchaser's St. Louis residence, — for, as we saw above, Boisdoré then owned the St. Louis Tract. All the purchaser's property is, as usual, mortgaged as security. Flandrin signs, with Joseph Chastang and Jean Boccard as witnesses, but Boisdoré could not write.

March 31, 1759, Boisdoré sold to Alen La Vergne, who likewise could not write, what is apparently the same property, situated at the corner of the square opposite to the commissary's office, for fifteen hundred livres, in the presence of J. B. Royot (Roujeot?) and Pierre Rochon. November 25, 1763, De Velle, former royal lieutenant, certifies to La Vergne's ownership of the house at the corner of the block (*isle*) vis-à-vis the old commissariat. Subsequent British deeds, as we shall see, make the property face the river, but do not otherwise help locate it.

The most reasonable interpretation of all this is that the lot was the southwest corner of Royal and Conti, and that, as the government had sold part of the commissariat to the De Lussers, it had also made the northeast part of the barracks square private property. Whether Cartier and Barthelemy were the original grantees or not, we do not know.

Three papers of this time connected with the estate of Barthelemy Monclin, deceased, have survived at Mobile in copies authenticated by their later Spanish custodians, and throw a good deal of interesting light on French procedure.

We learn that Monclin had been partner of Louis Flandrin, and that they owned the place once inhabited by Le Sueur up the river. The proceedings consist in an application, July 22, 1756, by Guillaume Marcellin as substitute of the general administrator (*procureur aux biens vacants*), for the sale of the interest of the deceased. This was addressed to Bobé Descloseaux, "Councillor of the King, Commissary of the Marine, Judge of the royal jurisdiction of Mobile." The petition was granted. The notice (*affiche*) is headed "De Par le Roy, Vente Judiciaire d'habitation," and says that the sale will be on three successive Sundays at the church door on the close of the mass service (*à l'issue de la messe*). This notice is signed by Descloseaux and by Marcellin as clerk (*greffier*), and says that the purchaser must pay cash, even if a creditor, and cannot receive possession until January, on account of the crop ·(*recolte*).

We are not told where the notices were posted, but the sale duly took place at the church door on the three successive Sundays. Descloseaux, accompanied by François César Bernondy, substitute of the royal attorney-general, and the clerk Marcellin, had Ceringe the crier (*huissier*) proclaim the sale in a loud voice, guaranteeing the title. A number of people assembled, and Olivier made the only bid, eight hundred livres, when the sale was adjourned. On the second Sunday, the sale starting with the eight hundred livres, Aubert bid nine hundred, and, there being no further bids, it went over. On the third Sunday the bidding was quite spirited and went up to 2520 livres, at which price the property was adjudged to Flandrin. Flandrin afterwards sold a half interest to François and Bernard Bernoudy, and, after Flandrin's death, one of them, in 1764, sells the half interest to Narbonne, who had married Flandrin's widow. This last sale was for four hundred piastres in hard Spanish money. "Robert Farmar" was one of the witnesses to this deed.

The next regular deed we find is a conveyance October 16, 1759, to soldier J. C. Mortall by J. B. Le Fleau as guardian of Francis and Réné, minor children of the late Marie Anne D'Agneau, and executor of his father-in-law, our friend Jean Girard de St. Jean, formerly royal boatman. The property is probably not that heretofore described, although Marie Anne D'Agneau had herself bought it originally from Terrepuy and Fleury. The land in our deed of 1759 seems to be bounded north by a street, — the second mention of a street, but, alas, unnamed, — and on the south by a lot of Lacage, while on the other side is the lot of Mme. Poupart. The price is eight hundred livres, payable within three years, drawing ten per cent interest, due every six months, all in current money of this colony. Right of reëntry is reserved in the deed on default of payment. A receipt and release by Le Fleau follows, executed May 23, 1763, before the same notary Roujeot, acknowledging payment in all of 2340 livres in full satisfaction. There is some mistake in the figures, however, for how the purchase-money even at ten per cent for about three and a half years could nearly treble itself is not easy to see. December 16, 1763, De Velle, ex-lieutenant at Mobile, and Director-General D'Abbadie, at New Orleans, were to certify to Mortalle's title to the property.

Among grants dating from French times may also be mentioned that of fifteen thousand arpens on Mobile River above Chickasabogue, granted in July, 1760, which under the Americans was to be confirmed to the extent of 5760 acres to Samuel Acre, who claimed it under Benjamin Dubroca. The original grantee of the tract is not known. The papers were much mutilated.[1] This grant extends from Chickasabogue north to Bayou Sara, and from a little east of the M. & B. Railroad to Mobile River.

The next document recorded is a copy of a translation of a petition by the Chevalier Montant de Monberault, January 3, 1763, for confirmation of his possession of a tract of land one league and a half up Fowl River in the *cul-de-sac* or turn called Lisloy (Goose Island), where he lived. The dimensions are not given, and indeed the description is confusing, as it is next said to take "its boundaries towards the sea from the

[1] *5 American State Papers*, p. 504.

River Barreau sometimes called by the name of River Labaterie, and on the other side ascending the river until the said
boundary reaches its spring or source." This is all quite uncertain, but would seem to point to a place between the headwaters of Bayou Labaterie and Fowl River. The northwest
confluent of Fowl River is still sometimes called "Isle aux Oies
River," and Lisloy is Bull Island. The land, he says, is
swampy and uninhabitable on account of the great number of
marshy rivulets called Bois Bleux. This must be a mistake,
as *bois bleu* is the titi-tree, which prefers low lands. Monberault wanted it for his business of cattle-breeding. He had purchased it from Mr. Petit, who got it from Mr. Dauriscourt, and
he in turn from a man named Lalime, the first settler, but
none of them had a title from the government. Wherefore,
says Monberault, "your petitioner finds himself in the same
situation with the greater part of the inhabitants of this part
of the country, who, in fact, have no other titles to the lands
which they occupy than the very incomplete and insufficient
right which arises from possession."

The governor, Louis de Kerlerec, chevalier of the royal
and military order of St. Louis, captain of the king's ships,
and Denis Nicholas Foucault, acting as *commissaire ordonnateur* of the province, considered this memorial, and on March
11, 1763, at New Orleans, granted the tract to Monberault in
fee simple, subject to the usual conditions, the same as set out
in Cadillac's grant to La Pointe forty-eight years before.

It cost nothing to enter public land in those days. There
was, in fact, in the troubled days of the Seven Years' war,
more land than colonists, and, as noted in several documents,
it was the king's will that all his subjects should settle in the
department of Mobile wherever they thought most convenient
and proper. But the will of the weak and dissolute Louis
XV. was on the wane in Louisiana, and in the latter part of
1763 his representatives were busy giving certificates to take
the place of grants which they could, after the Treaty of Paris,
no longer make.

Thus, on the fourth day of December, Pierre Annibal De
Velle, chevalier of the royal and military order of St. Louis,
ex-lieutenant of the king at Mobile, certifies that one Sanregret
Baptiste has held for many years an improved lot in Mobile

of twelve and a half toises front by twenty-five deep, adjoining that of Du Pont, who had lost his house by fire. Baptiste got the place from his wife, and she by inheritance from Joseph Sabatier, who acquired it originally by grant from Commissaire Ordonnateur De Cremont. D'Abbadie as royal director-general at New Orleans, thereupon, on the same day, certifies that the lot is the property of Baptiste, causes his seal at arms to be affixed, and the paper to be countersigned by his secretary at Mobile, Duvergé. This was the usual course, and, as De Velle's certificate at Mobile and that of D'Abbadie at New Orleans always bear the same date, it would seem that it was all done at Mobile at one time. Secretary Duvergé may have had this seal by him there which he attests as "By Monseigneur's command."

CHAPTER XX.

MASSACRE ISLAND we have seen explored by Iberville on his first voyage. Later Sauvole made some examination, and it was on his report that Iberville, in 1701, sounded to the east and found a good harbor, made by the intersection of Pelican Island. It was large enough for thirty vessels. Commissary La Salle describes it as having twenty to twenty-one feet of water at its entrance. He said it was better than Pensacola, and one of the best ports on the coast. La Salle thought it should have a fort, and Iberville, during the removal from Biloxi, did build magazines for merchandise and barracks for soldiers there,[1] which were probably more than temporary structures.

The port was always in use. There, and not in Mobile Bay proper, did the French vessels come, and, instead of directly sailing up to the river, ships all unloaded at the island, and cargoes were transferred to boats of smaller draught, like a *traversier* or a lighter, and taken up to town. It was indeed a dark time for Mobile, when, as sometimes happened, there was no regular communication with the island. On one such occasion, when the government finances were low, the officers of the garrison managed to buy a stray brigantine, which was put up for sale at Mobile, and thus reëstablished intercourse with their port. Du Pratz rather poetically calls Mobile the birthplace of the colony and Dauphine Island its cradle, but he was strictly correct in declaring that the two really made up but one place.[2]

By 1707, several families had moved there from Mobile, and we learn from the devout Penicaut that in this year Chateaugué

---

[1] 5 Margry, *Découvertes*, pp. 421, 425 ; 4 Margry, *Découvertes*, pp. 530, 533.

[2] Le Page du Pratz, *History of Louisiana*, pp. 17, 49.

rescued the survivors of St. Maurice's ship St. Antoine, whose impious sailors had thrown a figure of that patron saint overboard into the sea.

It was in 1709 that La Vigne Voisin, a captain from St. Malo, who some years later was to try to trade with the Spaniards, obtained permission to improve the place, and to him, says Penicaut, was due its fort to defend the harbor and the very beautiful church (*fort belle église*) facing the water, which attracted people even from near Mobile. This fort seems to have fallen into decay, or been ill located. At all events, L'Epinay was in 1717 to build another at half a gunshot from the sea.[1]

By 1710, all free persons from the ships settled on the island, and by two years later Cadillac found it necessary to build houses for the increasing population.[2] About this time it was that, during the long war between England and France, a pirate ship from British Jamaica, in 1711, raided Dauphine Island and the crew ruthlessly destroyed everything possible. The loss was estimated at fifty thousand livres.[3] Huvé was acting as priest at the time, and was himself all but killed.[4]

This, however, was the only English attack, and the island soon recovered. The port of Mobile was there, in the harbor formed by Pelican Island and the east end of Dauphine, and the many ships made the place prosperous. Colonists dissatisfied with the interior also drifted there, and the port now saw its palmiest days. When Cadillac was recalled, the chiefs of twenty-four Indian tribes went to Dauphine Island to welcome his successor, L'Epinay. Among them, according to Penicaut, were the Chaetas, Tonachas, Apalaches, Tinssas, Mobiliens, Tomes, *gens des Fourches* (Naniabas?), Capinans, Colapissas, Bayogoulas, Oumas, Tonicas, Chaouachas, Natchez, Chicachas, Nassitoches, Yataces, Alibamons, and Canapouces. The calumet-smoking lasted two months, as they could not arrange to come all at one time. The governor received them well, and sent them away with presents.[5]

[1] 5 Margry, *Découvertes*, pp. 482, 517 ; 1 Martin's *Louisiana*, p. 172.

[2] 5 Margry, *Découvertes*, pp. 485, 505.

[3] 3 French's *Historical Collection*, p. 37 ; Pickett's *Alabama*, p. 208.

[4] 1 Shea's *Catholic Church in the Colonies*, p. 553 ; 6 French's *Historical Collection*, p. 104.

[5] 5 Margry, *Découvertes*, p. 547.

The first church mention, for the Mobile priest visited it, seems to be the baptism on condition, in 1709, of a son of Jean Croix and Angelique Brouin his wife, inhabitants of Massacre. The second is when Le Maire next year at the island baptizes a number of people, when we learn that Bodin was a trader (*marchand*) there and that Roy was master cannoneer. Other names are mentioned also, besides slaves. Arnauld, Poudrier, L'Allemand, also a trader, and Grimauld seem to be among the inhabitants of Massacre, and D'Artaguette, commissary of the marine, at least had a slave who lived there. In 1715, as we saw, was the grant to La Pointe of a large cattle ranch on the island.

There comes in the church notices an interval of several years following the pirate attack from Jamaica, broken only by the baptism, in 1717, of Marie Marguerite, daughter of Jean Colon and Marguerite Prau his wife, inhabitants of "Lisle Daufine." This was the fatal year in which the Peacock entered in twenty-seven feet of water and was barred in, having to unload and go out by the Grand Goziers in ten feet.[1] Then again is a skip until 1721, when a daughter is baptized of the well-known soldier Pierre Danty and Marie Chatelier his wife, of Massacre, with the Alexandres as godparents. For Mathieu returns to the old name despite the change, in 1711, to Dauphine, and like the others seldom uses the word "island."

In 1719 came the Pensacola war, and it was in that year that occurred the Spanish counter-attack on Dauphine Island so vigorously resisted by Bienville and St. Denis with soldiers, savages, and *concessionaires*. The investment lasted twelve days, but the French were successful.[2]

Possibly no more interesting paper has come down to us from French times than a "Veue de l'Isle Dauphine" shortly subsequent to 1717.

In a clearing on the south side of the island rises from the beach the settlement, in two divisions. To the west, facing the open sea, high on the shores we see the bastioned, palisaded fort, in whose barracks lodge the troops. About it are sundry one-story houses, of which one within a fence is the powder-house, and behind a little embankment by the water's edge are cannon to defend the outer harbor.

---

[1] 1 Martin's *Louisiana*, p. 195.   [2] 5 Margry, *Découvertes*, p. 569.

Further east, beyond the fatal bar which in 1717 closed up
the entrance and joined Spanish (Pelican) island to Isle Dauphine, is the town (*bourg*). This is on a little cove and over-
looks the inner harbor, where ride, with full sail, the two-
masted Paon and the Paix, under the mouths of cannon
mounted on the strand. This settlement is a straight line of
some eighteen houses, almost all one-story, and generally in
square, picketed lots. The commandant's house is there,
facing the cove, and has a sentry-box in front. Two long
houses are *magasins* of the company, and adjoining is the guard-
house (*corps de garde*), while near the inner end of the line is
the *magasin* of the king. There is also a second but shorter
row of buildings behind, among which is the house which serves
for a church, — one of the few with two doors shown on this
plan. It may be the gift of La Vigne Voisin.

Across the island at the Shell Banks on the bay are still
found shell cement walls, not unlike those of the Spaniards
about St. Augustine, which some think the work of the French
after storms had injured the other settlement. It may be there
was a fort there once, but these particular walls are said by
old residents to be part of the kilns of De Vauxbercy in early
American times. This high spot commands a fine view over
the bay and Sound, and the Banks, crowned by cedars, must
always have been prominent in the landscape and a favorite
place of resort. The Shell Banks antedate the French, and
from them are still dug Indian skeletons, ornaments, and utensils.[1]

The closing of the port on the southern side of Dauphine by
the shifting bar changed the history of the island, and of
Mobile, too, but it had been anticipated by Iberville long
before.[2] In 1721 we read that several families left for New
Biloxi, and the Neptune was loaded with stores and families
for the Mississippi settlement.[3] Officers, soldiers, and magazines went, too, and the impression has prevailed that the
French completely abandoned the island. This is not true.
Danville's map, dating not earlier than 1732, shows the town,
and it was there that Bienville and Chateaugué came, in 1724,
to take passage on the Bellona for France, when the ship sud-

---

[1] So John Ladinier, now the oldest man on the island.

[2] 4 Margry, *Découvertes*, p. 509.   [3] 5 Margry, *Découvertes*, pp. 571, 572.

denly sank before their eyes. The church records also show
the port in use.

An entry, in 1722, by Mathieu shows Paul Le Sueur still
commandant for the king in Dauphine Island, "ditto Massacre." This was made during a visitation of that place. In
fact, a number of inhabitants and their slaves, too, are mentioned from time to time. In 1727, for instance, we find Jean
Arnauld, next year Mr. Renauld. Renauld is mentioned,
curiously enough, as of Massacre in the Isle Dauphine, as if
Massacre was the name of the town on the island. Arnauld
occurs again in 1736 and 1742. We have the marriage of J.
B. Baudrau, a creole of the island, besides mention of Nicolas
Rousseau and wife, and the baptism by Mathias, vicar-general
of Monseigneur de Quebec, of the daughter of Jacque Dupré,
a Canadian inhabiting the "Baye de la Mobile." This probably means the island, as the sponsor is J. B. Alexandre, creole
of the place, and there were Alexandres on Massacre. Later
we find Pierre Paques, inhabitant "deLabbaye." In 1740, we
again have Massacre named in the baptism of a son of Robert
Ollivier, another resident. Both in 1728 and 1742 the island
is mentioned as dependent on the Mobile parish.

No soldiers are given for a long time, but it would seem
there was often or always a garrison. In 1742, there was, for
we learn that according to report of officers and soldiers of
Massacre one J. B. Lozier, a private, was drowned in the
lagoon. He did not, however, give his name to this cove,
possibly that on which lay the settlement, as Derbanc had long
before to the river (now Bayou La Batré) where he perished.
Even as late as 1762 we find mention of the garrison of Massacre in the baptism of a child of Nicolas Bouvié, a soldier of
that post.

What we now call Little Dauphine Island we find on French
maps of 1732 as Isle à Guillori, and it was probably so called
for a resident, for in 1740 we have the baptism of the daughter
of Gregoire Guillory, described as both a native and inhabitant
of Massacre. His wife was Jeanne La Casse, inhabitant of
the same parish. Guillory was nine years later to lose a
daughter Louise, a younger child, and at this last date he is
mentioned as living at Fish River. But with the mention of
Bouvié, in 1762, the record closes as to Massacre or Dauphine

Island, although Point Chugae (Chateaugué?), Graveline Bay, Pont Vendigarde, and other existing names, indicate that there was more French history than we now know. Bon Secours Bay, beyond Mobile Point, was no doubt named on account of its security in time of storm.

Across Mississippi Sound on what we now call Mon Louis Island, granted to him in 1710 as Grosse Pointe, long lived Nicolas Bodin. It was practically a part of the mainland. Miragouin, we learn from Penicaut, was established the year before.[1] He bore this surname of Miragouin, — spelled differently at different times. It was regarded as his barony, so to speak, for Sieur de Miragouin is his common title and signature, too. The word seems to mean *mosquito,* and is not a strange origin for knighthood, — if sound plays any part.

It was this settlement which was attacked by the Spaniards, in 1719, to pillage the goods of *concessionaires* stored there, but on their second landing the invaders were beaten off by the Mobilians, Indians always friendly to the French. They killed thirty Spaniards and captured seventeen more, whom they took to Mobile. There they broke their heads and threw the bodies over into the river.[2] It was the usual method of savage warfare, and Penicaut does not say that the French interfered to prevent this massacre of the prisoners.

Our mosquito knight lived for more peaceful times, and we find him more than once in the Mobile church register. Possibly the first time was in 1729, when the Chevalier Jean Baptiste de Bulbulli, Marquis de Pisa, in a very shaky hand, signs as sponsor of two slaves of Miraguin. The name occurs on the map of the Western Company, and the word is shown on Danville's map of about 1732 near Grosse Pointe. Two years after that Bodin and his wife Françoise Pailliet are mentioned as "habitants" of the colony, and the same year is baptized a son, and later a daughter, of J. B. Alexandre, whose wife is Françoise Hyppolite Bodin. Both are creoles, and the godmother is Mme. Miragoine. We have the exact date of his death in the register as February 6, 1746, when he is described as a native of Mont Louis in the archbishopric of Tours, and a captain of militia of this coast. Hence no doubt his name Monlouis. Two slaves of his "succession" are mentioned the next year.

---

[1] 5 Margry, *Découvertes,* p. 484.   [2] *Ibid.,* p. 569.

The name continued in his descendants, for as late as 1762 there was baptized a son of "Louis Alexandre Bodin, dit Miragoine," and a slave of Monlouis is mentioned the next year. It may be that its belonging to one family prevented thick settlement of the country. Their home place was the well-known Miragoine on the bay, rather towards the northern part of the island, according to maps. This was at the Delchamps residence, if we may rely on tradition, and old pecans still mark the spot, while near have been found remains of houses made of frame and mortar. A little below is Point Juliet, named for a creole who married an Indian woman, and maps seem to mark this out as the Grosse Pointe for which the island was first named, although the cape in the sound at Pass à Barreau would better fit the name.

Above Mon Louis on the Bay Bellefontaine marks the spring known to the French no less than to the Spaniards, and on the island, above the Narrows, is the site of the traditional French Vineyard. Lower is Bayou Diable, called, it is said, for the exclamation of a man caught in that *cul-de-sac*, as he was trying to steal a boat and take it through the Narrows, and coming in from the west is Bayou Coulangué, named, it may be, for some forgotten resident. A Coulange we read of as active in Perrier's Indian wars.[1]

About the sound end of Mon Louis Island are a number of places indicating French ownership at one time, such as Pass aux Herons, Pass aux Huitres by Cedar Point, Heron Bayou, Pass à Barreau, and perhaps Maupers Island, but not necessarily showing settlements.

To the west on the mainland of the sound, Bayou Coden is but a barbarous form of "Coq d'Inde" (turkey), and Pointe aux Pins (pines) is yet preserved. Near that point Isle aux Dames is found on official maps, and Coffee Island has the alternate name of Isle aux Herbes. The occasion of giving most of these names has been forgotten, but Bayou La Batré we have seen called River Labaterie, and was probably named from a French battery on the west bank.[2] A mournful sound

---

[1] 1 Martin's *Louisiana*, p. 282.

[2] John Ladinier used to point out to J. J. Delchamps the site where he had seen such a colonial battery, and by the Tait place is still a mound which may be a part of a fortification.

heard from the waters of this coast is attributed by tradition to
the suicide of its native races by plunging into Portersville
Bay, — a story something like that of Pascagoula.

Pascagoula, too, was early settled by the French. On the
1732 map of Danville, Sr. La Pointe's place is shown about
the fine oaks above the present railroad bridge, although of
course the plan is not in sufficient detail to identify the exact
spot. Across the river and bay, somewhat higher up, is
marked the village of the Pascagoulas (Bread-eaters), and near
the great bend, where now is busy Moss Point, we find the
famous Chaumont concession. But the French settlement is
also shown prominently on the earlier map of the Western
Company, and may even have existed before then.

Tradition goes even back of the French, and Gayarré tells
the weird legend of a Spanish priest who came there after De
Soto's battle at Mauvilla and established a mission among the
mild Indians of that day. The cross, the bell, the mysterious
box gradually weaned them from their worship of a mermaid,
until once at midnight the sea and river rose in tidal waves
under the light of the full moon, and on their crest appeared
the maid pleading with irresistible music for her deluded
children to come back to her. And come back they did,
plunging one after the other into the water, leaving the distracted priest alone upon the shore. Laughing then, she disappeared, and the waters with her.

The father declared a crucifix, dropped in the river at full
moon, would break the spell, but that the priest who did it
would also die, and no one has ever dared to verify the prediction. But her music may still be heard, even in these prosaic
days, coming up from under boats of fishermen. For the
charm has never been broken.

The first entry in the Mobile records, curiously enough in
view of the legend, is the certificate of burial, in 1726, of several people found drowned in Fish River at Pascagoula, for
this settlement, too, was long dependent on the Mobile parish.
Then comes the baptism of the child of François Rilieu, of
Pascagoula, and, in 1734, we notice the marriage there of Ban-
drau, of Dauphine Island, at the house of La Pointe. This is
written on a loose slip of paper and announces that one ban
only was published after Sunday mass, the other two being

dispensed with. The reason of this doubtless was that Mathieu visited the place so infrequently.

Not until 1758 do we hear of Pascagoula again, except a casual mention of Rilieu and wife and child as resident there. There was once the baptism of the daughter of a Pascagoula Indian woman, but this was possibly at Mobile. In the year 1758 was baptized Joseph, son of Maturin Christian Cadner, an inhabitant of Pascagoula; but this seems to be the last church record of the place.

There is, in the registers, a mention or so of the death of sailors for the great company or the king, but the navigation between Dauphine Island and Mobile, and between the city and the river forts, was not managed by these *matelots*. In 1728 is mentioned the widow of Branquinier, late captain of *traversier*, and the next year we find Boudignon with the usual title for captain of small boats, — *patron*. He acted as late as 1746, when his wife is named as Anne Poirié. In 1731, Sr. François Harmon was master pilot, and next year "Theodore Robin dit Lanois" *patron* for the king.

A few years later the death of J. L. Vinant is mentioned, captain of a boat in the service of the king. In 1737, we first notice Francis Girard as *patron*, and three years later Jean Girard, his father, who was to act as such for so long a time. His print signature is very frequent in the registers. His wife was Marie Anne Daniau, creole of Mobile, whose death was to be subsequently noted. In the year 1737 we have the first name of a local boat, — La Marguerite, — whose "second captain" was Louis Pierre Sevet, and later is named Mr. Ællon as captain of the boat (*bateau*), but her name is not given. In 1758 was buried in the hospital cemetery André Miot, *patron* for the king, and in the same year died Jean Girard also, while a few years afterwards is mentioned a new *patron*, — J. B. Nicaise, called Vade Bon Cœur; the last of the French boat captains.

CHAPTER XXI.

FORT TOULOUSE AND FORT TOMBECBÉ.

As Massacre Island was the initial point of settlement and Pascagoula the furthest westward of the Mobile district, so up the rivers Fort Toulouse, four miles below where Wetumpka now stands, near the junction of the Coosa and Tallapoosa rivers, was the furthest inland the French reached in permanent occupation towards the English colonies on the Atlantic coast. It was built by Bienville in 1714, and was the cause of great anxiety to the English all through the French régime. Its first commandant was Mandeville, who had eight cannon and thirty men.[1] There were two cannon in each of the four bastions.

This was in the Creek country, in the immediate territory of the Alibamons. It was a depot for exchange of French articles for skins and other products, brought by the Indians from their hunting-grounds, and thence floated down the Alabama River by the *patrons* to the sea at Mobile. Its importance, strategically speaking, has been already noticed, and Adair habitually speaks of it as the "dangerous Alebahma." It was at the head of navigation of the Coosa and Tallapoosa rivers, and a bar to the invasion of the French possessions by turning the southern flank of the Alleghany Mountains. After Georgia was settled, those English colonists realized that it was conversely a menace to their own safety, and about 1735 they built a corresponding fort on the Tallapoosa at Okfuskee, forty miles away. This they maintained for several years.[2] At one time the Creeks much resented French interference in their matters, according to Adair, while Bossu says they brooked no English influences.[3] Bossu gives an account of

---

[1] 1 Pickett's *Alabama*, p. 223. [2] *Ibid.*, p. 316.

[3] Adair's *American Indians*, pp. 321, 338 ; Bossu's *Travels*, pp. 255, 270, 274.

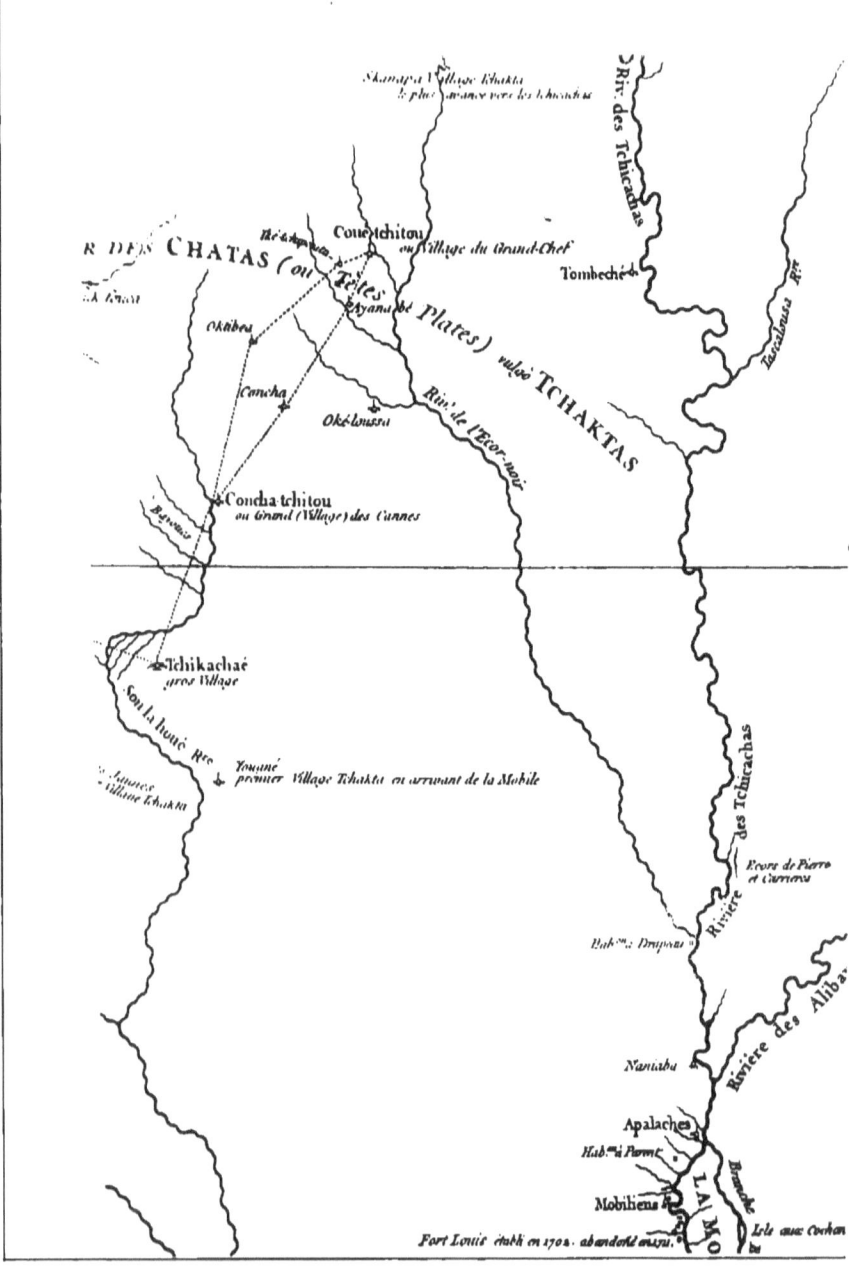

Shanapa Village Tchakta
le plus avancé vers les Tchicachas

Coue tchitou
ou Village du Grand-Chef

R DES CHATAS (ou Têtes Plates) vulgo TCHAKTAS

Tombeché

Riv. des Tchicachas

Tascalousa Riv.

La Craie

Oktibea

Concha

Ayanabé

Oké loussa

Riv. de l'Ecor-noir

Concha tchitou
ou Grand (Village) des Cannes

Tchikachaé
gros Village

Son la houe Ree

Amoné
premier Village Tchakta en arrivant de la Mobile

Amoeé
Village Tchakta

des Tchicachas

Rivière des Tchicachas

Ecore de Pierre
et Carrieres

Baketa Drapeau

Nantaba

Rivière des Alibas

Apalaches

Hab. a Pierret

Mobiliens

Branche

LA MO

Isle aux Cochon

Fort Louis établi en 1702. abandonné aussi.

its ou Fort à l'Ours

Isle ou françois

4 Isles

Sacré illé, l'Pecor mort

———

THE RIVER BASIN,

ABOUT 1732.

the visit of the Coweta "emperor" in his day, when the tutor or regent of the young eastern monarch disposed of the knife and fork difficulty by taking up his part of the turkey and declaring that the Master of Life made fingers first.

The name of the fort so established upon the Coosa River was Toulouse, but the church registers, as Bossu, too, almost invariably call it by that of the Indian district, — "Aux Alibamons." However, the first mention was in 1721, and the priests had then begun to use the Indian name Mobile, too, instead of Fort Condé. Besides, there is reason to suppose that the French called all of the Upper Creeks by the name Alibamons because that tribe of the confederacy was lowest on the river, and thus earliest and closest in contact with the post at Mobile, although strictly speaking not Creeks at all.

The Indian legend was that the Alibamons and Creeks were not akin, but on the contrary enemies, the latter pursuing the former all during the long flight from Mexico, until they were finally reconciled by the French at Mobile. But this last we know is untrue. Almost the first war of the French was that of Boisbriant, in 1702, against the Alibamons, and we remember also the great expedition of Alibamons, Cheraquis, Cʻaw-bas, and Creeks against the French in 1708. The French at first were their foes, not friends.

The Creeks or Muscogees were, in some respects, the most interesting of the southern tribes. Like the Chickasaws, they were expert deer hunters, and were brave fighters. Their Tustenuggee, or "emperor," sent around .. red club as a signal for war, although using red and white for war and peace and taking the black drink before battle was common to the Choctaws also. Each warrior carried in war a bag of parched corn meal, of which an ounce would make a pint of broth. Captured warriors are said to have been burned by the squaws in the public square, although modern Creeks deny this fact. These squares distinguished the towns from the villages, and there, too, was celebrated in July or August the busk, or feast of first-fruits. The square had about it the great house, council house, and the appurtenant playground for the games. Their ball play from descriptions might be termed a combination of tennis and football.

The Creeks had picture-writing and beads, and apparently

a female language different from that spoken by the men.
There was no sex to their nouns. Case was denoted by suffixes
more distinctly than with the Choctaws, although the Choctaws
had a more delicate phonetic ear. As with those kinsmen, descent was counted through the mother.

It would be interesting to map out the Creek country about
Fort Toulouse and show its towns. But these were not permanent, and their sites not all known. Beyond saying that the
country was along the upper Alabama and its sources and on
the Chattahoochee, and that of the towns Coosa (Cosa) in north
Georgia was the capital in and after De Soto's day, and Tookabatcha, near Fort Toulouse, the chief town in later times, it
would not be safe to go. Adair, in tracing resemblances to the
Jews, mentions old Coosa as in his time a "city of refuge,"
and at Tookabatcha were kept the mysterious brass plates
named by Adair. Tuskegee, Tallassee, Coweta, and many
other towns are known on these rivers; but their sites are not
always certain nor when they flourished.

French influence was long preponderant in this "Alibamon"
district. The Creek word for soldier, "sulitawa," is a monument of this fact, for it is taken from the French. The French
must have been just, for we learn that, in 1740, the commandant
had one of his soldiers shot for killing an Indian, as D'Erne-
ville similarly insisted on the death of an Indian for killing a
Frenchman. It was to Fort Toulouse that the sagacious
Priber, after five years' supremacy among the Cherokees, was
going, in 1741, on his way to Mobile, when he was captured by
the English and carried to Frederica, Georgia. There he died
in confinement. The Cherokees do not often concern us, but
the English suffered from them for eight years in South Carolina, and lay the blame on French and Jesuit influence in that
quarter. It was at Fort Alabama that Adair was imprisoned
a fortnight for activity among the Indians. He managed to
escape an hour before the king's boat left, which was to carry
him down to Mobile to be hanged. And it was from there
that Montberaut captured among the Indians those mutineers
who had killed Duroux of Cat Island in 1758, and sent them
down to Mobile under De Beaudin to be executed with Beaudrot.[1]

[1] Detailed references would be too numerous ; but much of the above is

The earliest church entry (1721) naming the French post is in the baptism by Mathieu of a daughter of Michel Mandré at Mobile, and mentions the grandmother as Mme. Catherine (elsewhere Genevieve) Raymond, wife of "Ecuyer Seigneur de Pechon, Major des Alibamons." The major signs the minute himself, and so was in Mobile at the time. Two years later Ecuier Crepin de Pechon and wife, mentioned as noble persons, themselves have a child baptized, Chateaugué, then lieutenant for the whole of Louisiana, and the wife of commandant Marigny de Mandeville acting as sponsors.

It is difficult to make the history of the Marchand mutiny, as generally given, fit into these entries, which clearly imply that Pechon was, during these years, a major and ranking officer of the post.

As told by Pickett, Marchand was captain there in command, in 1722.[1] Indeed, it is implied that he had been there several years, for he was by a natural marriage with the Indian princess Sehoy already father of a little girl, herself to be famous as Sehoy, mother of the celebrated chief McGillivray. La Tour, we know from Penicaut, commanded from 1717,[2] so that in any event Marchand must begin after him. In 1722, however, according to the story, supplies were scarce, and the garrison, part of whom were Swiss, rose in mutiny, and killed Marchand. They sacked the storeroom, burned the buildings, and made off with all they could carry towards Carolina.

The unnamed priest was absent, and only returned in time to mourn the ruin and bury Marchand. When Villemont, the second in command, came in, he called on friendly Creeks and pursued and fought the deserters. Many were killed, and eight prisoners captured. These were sent to Mobile by boat, and there promptly executed.

But the church registers make a change of date necessary, unless we are to suppose that two Marchands commanded the post. For Marchand de Courtel is mentioned after this as a captain at Mobile, and not as commanding at the Alibamons until 1727. A lieutenant and two sergeants of his company

abbreviated from Pickett's *Alabama* and Gatschet's *Creek Migration Legend.* See, also, Adair's *American Indians* (London, 1775), pp. 159, 242, 295, 343, 348, and Bossu's *Travels*, pp. 226, 250, 324.

[1] 1 Pickett's *Alabama*, p. 266.   [2] 5 Margry, *Découvertes*, p. 550.

are named at this same time, 1726–27, necessarily before the company were all shot or sawed to pieces.

Returning to Pechon, he, in 1725, was still major at the Alibamon fort, whose name Toulouse is mentioned. This occurs in the baptism by Father Claude of Marie Louise, daughter of this same Pechon Le Conte, — for the worthy major has his name different in the different entries. At the baptism of a daughter, in 1730, he is named as infantry captain and as *formerly* major at Fort Toulouse. His son Joseph Crepin de Pechon was baptized two years afterwards.

From a later act we learn something of Pechon's death. This instrument by Jean François was made. on the request of his son Antoine de Conte, Seigneur de Pechon, and certifies, on the testimony of M. Gondreau, J. J. Beauchamps, and J. P. Le Sueur, that Pechon died at Fort Toulouse on February 19, 1736. The family were prominent, and seem, in 1760, to have owned the place northeast of our Government and St. Emanuel streets.

The office of *garde magasin* was an important one at such a trading-post, and we have the names of several who occupied the position. In 1737, it was Michael "Gondeau," who the year before was surgeon-major as well, and at some time mystified the Indians by pouring out a little quicksilver, which they had never before seen. In 1751, Jean Charles Trouillet, who had married Marguerite Rochon, and, in 1755, if not earlier, Sieur Alexandre du Parquet held the place. Trouillet had died before that while descending the river, and was buried by the royal *patron*, St. Jean. The river *patron*, as La Rose earlier, is sometimes called *patron* of the Alibamons. It is to be hoped that the trip up did not usually consume fifty days, as with Bossu.[1] The land route was also in use, and we learn, in 1749, of the death and burial of one Fr. Melisan on the road (*chemin*) of the Alibamons. In 1759, Aubert, who was sick, came on horseback.

Of other officials we know Fr. Saucier as sub-engineer in 1751, and Laubéne (Lavnoué?) as interpreter later. Missionaries they seldom had. Such lack of minister is recorded in 1732, and the number of baptisms at Mobile of children born at Fort Toulouse proves it for other years.

[1] Bossu's *Travels*, pp. 226, 269.

We learn that about 1726 the Jesuit De Guyenne went, necessarily, by way of Fort Toulouse, on a mission to the Creeks, and built a cabin at Cusseta, as well as another at Coweta on the Chattahoochee. But the English, about the time they built their Okfuskee fort, induced the Indians to burn these and drive the priest back to Toulouse. After the Natchez massacre he labored among the Arkansas.[1] In 1740, the Jesuit Morand performed function of curé at the fort, and thence certified to the death there of Sieur Joseph Poupart of Mobile. Morand also went on a mission occasionally to Coosada, lower down, but, when the English under Oglethorpe were, in the thirties, founding Georgia and pushing actively into the interior even of the Alabama basin, this father was recalled to take charge of the hospital and nuns at New Orleans.[2] His full name was William Francis Morand. He was born 1701, and entered the society at nineteen in Lyons. He arrived in Canada in 1735, and died in Louisiana, 1761.

It was another father (Le Roi) whom commandant Montberaut drove away for complaining of him to the governor and then denying that he wrote the letter. Montberaut, in consequence, had to baptize when the rite was required. The church version of this difficulty, however, is that the priest opposed the sale of liquor to the Indians. Whatever the cause, Bossu describes Montberaut as an avowed enemy of these missionaries.[3] Max. Le Roi was born 1716, entered the society at seventeen, in what is now Belgium, and came to Canada in 1750. In 1763, he went to Mexico.

From 1754, until the expulsion of Jesuits from Louisiana by decree of the Superior Council, June 9, 1763, Father Jean Jacques Le Predour was on this mission, but he was the last.

The presence of Jesuits at Fort Toulouse, and, as we shall see, at Fort Tombecbé seems at first glance remarkable when we remember that they were excluded from Mobile, which belonged to the Capuchins. But in the division of 1722, they were allowed to keep a resident at New Orleans, and the flexible district of the Illinois was assigned them, and by the treaty

---

[1] Pickett's *Alabama,* p. 317 ; Shea's *Catholic Church in the Colonies,* pp. 572, 575.

[2] Pickett's *Alabama,* p. 317.

[3] Shea's *Catholic Church in the Colonies,* p. 584 ; Bossu's *Travels,* p. 228.

with the Company, of 1726, the Alibamons and Choctaws were
definitely assigned the Jesuits. The Jesuits on the Mississippi also occupied down to the Natchez, and apparently by the
bishop's consent.[1]

According to Pickett, also, D'Aubant succeeded Montberaut
in 1759, and his Russian princess wife and their daughter
joined him there. But the church records seem to contradict
this. Monbereau, as they spell it, was succeeded, in 1758, by
J. B. Aubert, and his wife was Louise Marguerite of the
prominent Bernoudy family. She died in 1759, and was buried in the church at Mobile. It seems a pity the story may
not be true, for it is romantic and interesting, but the church
records can hardly be gainsaid. Aubert might do for Aubant
(and Bossu says Aubert succeeded in 1759, although adjutant
at Mobile), but Louise Marguerite Bernoudy can hardly pose
for a Russian princess. Grand Maison is named after Aubert,[2]
and Lavnoué was the last commandant.

The site of Fort Toulouse was to be perpetuated by the fact
that Andrew Jackson in our century adopted it, and, repairing
the fort, used it in his war with the Indians. The relentless
plough has left little of it. It stood on a bold bluff of the
Coosa, but only one half-ploughed-up bastion, facing towards
the not distant Tallapoosa, now remains.

No trace is there of the landing-place or of the road leading
to it, but here it was that the French shipped peltries and
received supplies, in this fort traded with the Alibamons and
Creeks, and broke the English influence from the Carolinas.
Near by are many fragments of Indian pottery, some glazed,
some not, and other evidences that savages lived there under
the guns of the fort. The French cannon have long since disappeared, and all that is left is a little brass mortar, with
handles, on which some modern has cut the name "De Soto"
and "No. 12." Probably a Frenchman did it, for the piece
was only lately dug up, and acquired by W. P. Gaddis, of Wetumpka, but the piece itself may date back to Spanish times.

Further down the river is a large Indian mound about
twenty feet high and possibly two hundred in its irregular
circumference. It is abrupt on the side facing the Coosa, but

[1] Shea's *Catholic Church in the Colonies*, p. 567 ; 1 Martin's *Louisiana*, p. 261.
[2] Bossu's *Travels*, pp. 241 n., 250, 269.

slopes off on the opposite face. Some one once sunk a shaft in the top, and it is said bones, beads, and pottery have been found there. Certain it is, small pieces of pottery can still be seen all over the mound, generally rude and unglazed, but sometimes ornamented with lines. Stone hatchets are also there, and bits of flint chips abound. Trees and vines have covered the mound; but it remains a prominent object in the landscape, and remarkable as the only place in the neighborhood not submerged in recent floods.

Far to the west on the Tombigbee was another French outpost, — Fort Tombecbé. We saw it built originally by Bienville's order, as a base in his Chickasaw expedition, but it was not finished until later. From it went back to Mobile the defeated French, but it was essential to maintain the post permanently in order to watch the Indians and keep them in check. This wooden fort was a lonesome and dangerous place, and only brave men were fit to be its garrison, and supervise the trade and politics of the Choctaws.[1]

The site was above the confluence of the Bigbee and Warrior, near the present Epes Station on A. G. S. Railroad, and can still be traced. On White Rock Bluff, a part of Jones' Bluff, in present Sumter County, Alabama, eighty feet above low water, are visible remains of the embankment, about four feet high, with ditches almost as deep. The fort was in the angle between the river and a "branch" or brook emptying into it about one hundred yards above where the railroad crosses the Bigbee River. It inclosed, perhaps, one acre, now covered with a thick growth of cedars, two to three feet in diameter.[2]

The fort at its greatest extent faced the river 173 feet, the branch gully on the south 304, and on the north 231 and west 278 feet, with curtains about ten feet high. There were three gates, and a stockade on all sides. Inside the fort were oven, storehouses, interpreter's apartment, men's barracks, guardhouse, granary, and officers' building. Two of the houses there are given as 30×13 feet and 19×12 feet. There was also a house out of the fort intended for the savages. These were

---

[1] Pickett's *Alabama*, p. 335 ; Adair's *American Indians*, pp. 267, 285.

[2] Information derived from J. J. Hilman, of Epes, Alabama ; report of Ford in *British Colonial Records*, London.

Choctaws, and had a large town within a musket-shot of the fort.

The place was selected because of the river and the neighborhood of the Choctaws, being just below their boundary with the Chickasaws. They were the best friends the French had among the larger southern tribes, but we have seen that English traders finally succeeded in stirring up a long Choctaw civil war, in which the eastern division (Oypat-oocooloo, or small nation) contended with the western ones, called Oocooloofalaya, Oocooloo-hanalé, and Chickasawhays. They were less cleanly than the Creeks, their inveterate foes, and less aggressive in war; but in defensive hostilities their courage could not be questioned. They, too, had chunkey and the ball play, but they were unlike the Creeks in living less in towns. They were often called Flatheads from their compressing the heads of male infants. In hunting, they followed particularly the bear, wildcat, and panther. From pity they strangled their own incurable sick, and they did not torture their captives, but killed them outright and burned their remains. They slept around a war fire in a circle, while the Creeks slept in a row.[1]

In the time of the trader Adair, their principal town was Yowanne, apparently high up on Pearl River, although he also mentions seven towns as close together and towards New Orleans. He speaks of three trading-paths to Mobile. The westernmost was a horse-path from the Chickasaws and passed through these towns, the middle one by the "Chakchooma old fields," which with the one nearest the Bigbee was exposed then to Muscogee inroads.[2] The Yowanne path branched off from the Buckatunna a short distance west of Mobile. Romans places "Yoani" in his day (1771) on the Pascagoula River. He visited the place, and seems to be the author of the rather incredible statement that no other Choctaws can swim except those of Yowanne and Chickasawhay, — a peculiarity shown by the horses, too!

---

[1] This summary, like that as to the Creeks, is largely abbreviated from Pickett and Gatschet. See, also, Gatschet, *Creek Migration Legend*, p. 212; Adair's *American Indians*, p. 318, etc.; Romans' *Florida*, pp. 66, 73. Information as to Morand, Le Roy, and Le Fevre, was furnished from Jesuit archives by D. P. Lawton, of Spring Hill College, Alabama.

[2] Adair's *American Indians*, p. 298, etc.; Romans' *Florida*, p. 86.

One curious survival of French influence is that the Choctaws adopted from their "soulier" the word "shulush" for shoe. Red Shoe's Indian name of "Shoolashummashtabe" seems to incorporate the word. He, by the way, was a swift runner, and could overtake the active Spanish barbs which the Chickasaws and Choctaws rode.

Fort Tombecbé was important in the control of this race, whom the French managed by presents of arms and goods brought from Mobile.

Of one of these long river trips we have an account, for in 1759 Bossu went up the river with three boats to convey provisions and ammunition to the fort from Mobile. In a week he reached the Forks, near McIntosh's Bluff, where an alligator dragged him almost into the river. It was due to his sleeping on the bluff with a barbel wrapped up at his feet in his tent.

After going up about fifty leagues he struck very low water, and had to unload his goods, and even pull the boats along with lines. At some point on the trip they suffered for want of provisions, and he considered the relief providential. It was due to Indians cutting down a tree holding the nest of a royal eagle, and in this they found swans, rabbits, turkeys, grouse, partridges, and pigeons, which the parent birds had provided for the little eaglets. The Indians not only robbed the nest of the provisions, but killed the fighting eagles, and took the young ones. At Taskaloussas or White Mountain, probably near the mouth of the Black Warrior River, Mingo Howmas and some revolted Choctaws threatened them, but finally they pacified the savages and smoked the calumet of peace. Bossu much surprised French and Indians alike by lighting the pipe with phosphorus.

The rest of the trip was more pleasant on account of a rise in the river and assistance sent under De Cabaret from Fort Tombecbé. During the whole journey the travelers had to spend the nights on the banks, tormented by *maringoins* (mosquitoes), except so far as they could keep them off by sleeping under a linen cloth spread on bent reeds. They were certainly rejoiced to arrive at the fort, where Chabbert commanded. It had taken from August 20 to September 25 to accomplish the hundred leagues.[1]

---

[1] Bossu's *Travels*, pp. 279, 285, 317.

The first entry in the church registers at Mobile relating to Fort Tombecbé was in 1739, and was what might be expected after Bienville's unfortunate expedition. Le Sueur was in command, and, in default of a priest or chaplain (*aumonier*) there, the record is made at Mobile by Amand of the killing of a soldier by the Indians. It seems that this man, a Swiss named Aubergeron, was fishing in the river above the fort when he was assassinated in his pirogue. The first intimation of it to the garrison was when the current brought the corpse down to Tombecbé, where Le Sueur gave it proper burial and notified the commandant at Mobile.

We learn nothing more for several years. Then, in 1743, it is recorded that according to the report of officers of that post St. Hermand Fouke, soldier of the *convoye*, was drowned in the river of Tombecbé, and later in that year we are told that Mme. Pierre Mozel was buried at her home on the same river. Of them, however, we know only the names.

Adair says that to French influence at this post were due the Choctaw invasions of Carolina in the middle of the century, although the more immediate aim of Vaudreuil was to use the fort to keep the Choctaws in the French interest and hostile to the English-loving Chickasaws.[1] Except Le Sueur, we know little of any of the commandants, but the first and De Berthel, whom Bienville left there with a garrison of thirty French and twenty Swiss, and De Grand-pré in or before 1751. He it was that successfully carried out Vaudreuil's negotiations, which resulted in the pacification of the Choctaws after Red Shoe's revolt. De la Gauterais was in command at some time, and performed a remarkable feat. He built a raft of cedar which drew twelve feet and contained five hundred tons of timber, and took advantage of a freshet to float it to Mobile. In fact, it was not stopped until it reached modern Montrose. De la Gauterais came down on it himself, bringing four other men.[2]

Then we find Pierre Chabert, whom Bossu met, the last commandant under the French. *Gardes magasin* are oftener named. In the year 1743, in records of baptisms of Indian slaves, we learn that Cartier is *garde magasin* and Sieur

[1] Winsor's *Basin of the Mississippi*, pp. 264, 268. See Bossu, *supra*.
[2] Romans' *Florida*, p. 211.

Trouillet, called Argent, surgeon there. Three years later, François Lierle (?) is storekeeper, but in 1748 Trouillet occupies that position.

This office of *garde magasin* at Tombecbé seems to have changed hands often. In 1758 we learn from the entry of baptism of his daughter, Marguerite Felicité, that the incumbent was Alexandre Claude Du Parquier. The next year Valentin Dubroca was *garde magasin*, and we find him such through 1761, and he was there until the French abandoned the fort. His wife was Martha Fièvre, and during this time the Mobile register records the baptism of two of their children, — Marie Marthe, and Valentin.

But no record remains of the other officials, except that during Bossu's visit the chaplain was the Jesuit Le Fèvre. This was Nicolas Le Fèvre of present Belgium, who was born 1705, entered the order at eighteen, and came to Canada 1743. The year of his death is uncertain, but probably it was before 1764.

In 1726, when Guyenne went on the Alibamon mission, the Jesuit Maturin Le Petit went among the Choctaws. After Beaubois, the Jesuit superior, had been recalled, Le Petit succeeded him at New Orleans. The Canadian Michael Baudouin also came to Louisiana in 1726, the year of Jesuit activity, and we find him by 1739 on the Choctaw mission, where he was to be for eighteen years, assisted part of the time by the above Father Le Fèvre. He has been accused of immorality among his charge, but this seems unlikely, for he was, in 1747, promoted to be vicar-general of the bishop of Quebec, over the protest of the Capuchins.

But where was the seat of this Choctaw mission? Hardly at Fort Tombecbé, despite Shea's guess,[1] for we often find it without religious services, and, moreover, the Jesuits always lived among their flocks. It is more likely that it was on the site where Bernard Romans, in 1771, was to find a lightwood cross and the site of a destroyed chapel. This was at Chickasawhay, which was probably the Choctaw station shown even on early American maps as in east Mississippi upon the Chickasawhay River, some miles west of Fort Tombecbé. Romans says the priest could not convert the Indians, and this seems

---

[1] Shea's *Catholic Church in the Colonies*, pp. 572, 583, 585.

probable from their conduct.   He relates that when the English came, the Indians would mimic the motions of the Jesuits
and the sacred ceremonies of the church.[1]

[1] Romans' *Florida*, p. 78.

CHAPTER XXII.

WHEN Dauphine Island harbor was closed by a bar, and New Orleans later became the capital of the province, Mobile not only ceased to direct the development of the Mississippi Valley, but she largely lost touch with it. If Ichabod could not be written on the portal of Fort Condé, at least its glory was limited to the Alabama basin. As Matthew Arnold wrote of denominations differing from that to which he nominally belonged, Mobile was out of the current of national life. But, remembering the extent of its actual territory, it can hardly be said that her annals were merely hole-in-corner history, as the satirical advocate of sweetness and light said of the dissenters. Our story has now reached the point where we are directly concerned with the result of the struggle between the English and French colonies.

The two systems of colonization had gone on side by side. The English progressed more slowly, but with sure reduction and settlement of the land, while the daring French penetrated everywhere, but brought over few colonists, and cultivated little. Yet by Bossu's time, indigo, cotton, and tobacco were extensively produced. The standing argument of the French with the Indians was that the English wished to exterminate them and occupy their lands. True as this has proved, and powerfully as it generally acted on the savage mind, the English, nevertheless, attracted them by being cheaper traders, and even on Lake Ontario two beaver skins bought as good a bracelet from the English at Oswego as ten did from the French at Niagara.[1] The Indians sided with the French, but where possible bought their goods of the English.

The two nations had always been jealous, and their colonists shared the spirit. At first, when the English colonies hugged the seaboard and French emissaries penetrated everywhere, an

---

[1] Winsor's *Basin of the Mississippi*, p. 287 ; Bossu's *Travels*, p. 375, etc.

Iberville might indeed, with Indian help, have driven the Anglo-Americans into the sea. But by the middle of the eighteenth century the English had increased in numbers and occupied well back to the mountain passes. Germans had settled the interior of Pennsylvania, and Lord Fairfax was not the only landowner in the valley of the Shenandoah who gave work to young surveyors like George Washington. The thirteen colonies were divided, and indisposed to help in a war which Franklin felt was really for the benefit of English merchants.[1] But bolder counsels were finally to prevail, a union to be felt, if not actually organized, which was the precursor of the Confederation, twenty years later, against the English crown itself. When it is recollected that the English in America probably equaled a million and a half, while the French were less than ninety thousand, and that of these the inhabitants of Louisiana were too far away from the seat of war to be effective, there could be no doubt as to the result.[2]

The Peace of Utrecht determined, for a long time, the relations of France and England, for the French possessions in America were so vast that the loss of Acadia and Newfoundland was after a while almost forgotten. It is true that in the war of the Austrian Succession, beginning in 1740, the two nations were again opposed, and that English colonists helped in the capture of Louisburg and Cape Breton, but the Peace of Aix-la-Chapelle, in 1748, provided for a mutual restitution of conquests. And yet there was an hereditary antipathy, surviving, perhaps, from Roman and Teuton. It was felt that there could not co-exist two such colonizing nations. The world was not big enough, and a struggle for India and America must come at last.

France was weaker than in the time of Louis XIV.; England was stronger, particularly at sea. Pitt was the embodiment of the will of his nation, bent on the humiliation as much as the defeat of France; and while Louis XV., who had taken the reins of power in 1723, was exemplary at first, from 1737 he became bent only on his pleasures and mistresses. The final struggle in America came in the Seven Years' War, from 1757–63. Instead of a vast New France hemming in the English colonies between the mountains and the ocean, as had been

[1] Winsor's *Basin of the Mississippi*, p. 350.   [2] *Ibid.*, p. 347.

dreamed by Iberville, who was dead, and Bienville, who was still living, a private Parisian, the French were now to contend for their very existence in America. In Europe the war was fought for England by her Prussian ally, Frederick the Great, but in Asia and America she struggled hand to hand with her hereditary foe.

Clear-headed colonists realized well enough that Canada could not be permitted to grow up alongside them as a French dependency and thus involve the American colonies in every war between the mother countries. It was equally clear to such men as Franklin that the same was true of the Ohio Valley, in 1749 formally occupied by Céloron, and would ultimately become not less true of the whole Mississippi basin. The two portals to this basin were at Fort Duquesne, now Pittsburg, and down on the Tennessee River. The southern flank of the great mountain barrier could, we have seen, be turned through Georgia, as the northern was to be by Lake George and the St. Lawrence Valley.

In the first years of the war the French had the advantage, particularly shown in Braddock's defeat at Fort Duquesne. But mass gradually prevailed even over organization, and the St. Lawrence expedition under Wolfe finally settled the fate of the French in America. There was but desultory warfare south of Pennsylvania, for the southern colonies of neither side were strong enough to undertake offensive movements over the intervening wilderness. At the north the foes were closer together, and it was, moreover, instinctively felt that Quebec was the true key to all French America.

Little aid could come from Louisiana, although Mobile officers advocated invading Georgia and Carolina with Choctaws,[1] but all in that province watched the conflict with absorbing interest. News came only infrequently to Mobile, but we can imagine Grondel poring over such dispatches as arrived and the garrison of Fort Condé, from commandant down, eagerly discussing the war. Quebec fell September 12, 1759, and anxious must have been the little city on the southern gulf, when came the news that the capital, from which some had come, and to which all looked as the American Paris, was in the hands of the hated English, that Vaudreuil, so lately pro-

[1] Bossu's *Travels*, p. 292.

moted from among them, was a fugitive. Added to fears for the future, the southern colonists suffered much from financial mismanagement. As the war prevented bringing money from France, the governor-general was authorized to issue bills, called *bons*, in amounts from ten sols to one hundred livres, drawn on the royal treasury. Kerlerec negotiated some through Jamaica and other English colonies, but in October, 1759, the king by an edict suspended payment of them, to the amount of seven million livres. This paper made up all the colonial currency, and widespread ruin was the result, the more bitter as contrasted with the prosperity then prevailing and due to openly favoring importation of negroes.

Quarrels, of course, were not lacking between governor and intendant, as of old, and there was almost civil war when, in 1759, Rochemore seized two English smuggling vessels under the Jew Diaz Anna at New Orleans, and Kerlerec released them and permitted sale of their cargoes because the colonists stood so much in need of the goods they brought. Kerlerec arrested Marigny de Mandeville, Bossu, and other partisans of the intendant and shipped them to France. His conduct was disapproved at court, and this was ultimately to lead to his own recall and imprisonment in the Bastille.[1] He died of grief shortly after his release.

The end of the war came September 8, 1760, when Vaudreuil at Montreal surrendered Canada. Father Ferdinand, when he thought of his bishop a prisoner, could but pray that the storm reach not Mobile. And, in fact, it did not. While Louisiana was to be affected by the result, there was no fighting near its Gulf coast.

If the great commoner was to be influenced in his views of American aggrandizement by a book dedicated to him at the time, he would have not spent much blood or money to acquire Mobile.

The geographer of this era of English expansion was Thomas Jeffreys. In 1760, no doubt to show what American conquests might mean, he published at London the "Natural and Civil History of the French Dominions in North and South America," with maps of many places. Mobile has no plan, and

---

[1] Pittman's *Mississippi Settlements*, pp. 14, 15, 59, 67; 1 Martin's *Louisiana*, pp. 334, 343.

indeed little is said of it, and that little unfavorable. Du Pratz is his principal guide.

Approaching from the sea, we learn from him of Isle Dauphine that it enjoys a burning heat, the soil is barren, and the island is little more than sand so white as to injure the eyesight. It has one advantage in that one can find plenty of the finest fresh water by digging in this sand a very small distance from the shore, and again the seas are alive with excellent fish. Pines and firs abound, and there is a plant bearing *pommes de raquette* (prickly pear), which is a sovereign remedy for dysentery.

In his section on the products of Louisiana he describes the "Spanish Beard" (hanging-moss), acacia, wax-tree, cedar, canes, and many other trees and plants, as well as animals, but his reports of Mobile are so black that one is not certain he can mean that these advantages exist about here. The soil near this river is said to be extremely barren, but the interior is tolerably fertile. Fort Condé is barely named, and Fort Tombecbé, about one hundred and forty leagues higher, is important only for fine cedars and potter's earth. About Fort Toulouse, the "canton is said to be one of the finest countries in the whole world."

The soil on the coast is of sand as white as snow, with pines, cedars, and some green oaks. The river Mobile has a bed of sand, and is far from equal to the Mississippi in plenty of fish. The Mobile's banks are of gravel and earth and from its source equally barren, but the lands are somewhat better about the river of Alibamons. Like river, like people. "The lands and water of the Mobile are extremely unfertile, not only in plants and fishes, but, as the quality of both these contributes much to the decrease of animals, the same effect happens with respect to the inhabitants, many of the women having become barren on their settling in these parts; as, on the contrary, they have recovered on removing to the banks of the Mississippi. The interior parts of this country must be exempted from this quality common to many parts near the sea." [1]

Verily a doubting Thomas, aiming at truth, perhaps, — but at very long range! It would look as if he wished the conquests to take in the Mississippi, and was afraid the government might stop with Florida and Mobile.

[1] Jeffrey's *French Dominion*, etc., pp. 152–154.

At all events, this was exactly what happened. George III. had in this very year, 1760, ascended the British throne, and he wished to rule in fact as well as name. Pitt was in his way, and when this minister wanted war with Spain and rejected overtures from France for peace, and thus alienated his colleague Newcastle, the king widened the breach, and Pitt resigned in 1761. The complaisant Bute was made premier, but war with Spain came anyway, resulting in the capture of Havana and Cuba by the British fleet. The king abandoned Frederick, and in September, 1762, concluded peace. Negotiations continued for some time as to how much England was willing to leave to her rival, but the Treaty of Paris was finally made February 10, 1763.

By it Canada was confirmed to Great Britain, Florida ceded to her in consideration of the retrocession of Cuba and the Philippines, and Louisiana east of the Mississippi and north of the Iberville rivers also fell to Great Britain, despite protests and propositions of France for a buffer Indian country between. By a secret treaty the king of France ceded New Orleans and all west of the Mississippi to his cousin of Spain. Thus old Louisiana was dismembered, and the Mobile district was to go to England. Both Rochemore and Kerlerec returned to France, and D'Abbadie as director-general had, until the Spaniards should come, the powers of both intendant and governor.

Cession to the foreigner was bitterly regretted. We can well imagine how the hearts of his old colonists were to go out to Bienville again when, at the age of eighty-six, he appeared with their deputy Jean Milhet before the French minister De Choiseul to implore that Louisiana be not cut off from France. But they did not even reach the throne.[1] And it would have done no good.

The exemplary prince and promising king had become corrupted by his own court, and was now the greatest debauchee of them all. The vices of Louis XIV., not his virtues, had repeated themselves in his great-grandson. And all France was in ferment. Now it was intellectual; it might become political. Could he but make the royal structure outlast his time, never mind the deluge afterwards. As to America, that

---

[1] King's *Bienville*, p. 323.

was far away, — and the Pompadour so near! What cared Louis XV. for Louisiana? He had obtained peace, at all events, — never mind the cost! A *parc aux cerfs* was worth a dozen Mobiles and New Orleans. The cession was final.

It was to take some time, however, to make the world-wide transfers. New Orleans long did not know of the secret cession to Spain, and remained under French rule until 1766, but Mobile was surrendered October 20, 1763. As the lilies of France descended, a regiment of Highlanders from Pensacola entered, it is said, under Colonel Robertson, to the music of bagpipes, and a royal salute greeted the British flag as it was flung to the breeze.[1] The *proces verbal* of the transfer was signed by De Velle and Fazende for France, and Robert Farmar (or Farmer) for England, and was followed by Farmer's proclamation. The historic name of Fort Condé was changed to Fort Charlotte, for the queen of the young king of England.

The French troops with the ordnance and many of the people sadly withdrew to New Orleans. But the bulk of the inhabitants remained, for they loved the old home even better than the old flag.

[1] 2 French's *Historical Collection*, p. 62.

PART IV.

THE BRITISH DOMINATION.

1763–1780.

CHAPTER XXIII.

WHEN by the Treaty of Paris, February 10, 1763, Mobile became a part of the British possessions in America, it was not as a dependency of any of the thirteen colonies which would soon become famous. Georgia had, like others, claimed a charter from sea to sea, but the Treaty of Paris recognized the middle of the Mississippi as the west line of the British possessions. And the king curtailed the colonies yet further. By proclamation of October 7, 1763, he made crown lands of all from the Mississippi to the Alleghanies, and established south of the line of 31° two new colonies. East Florida was the peninsula, with St. Augustine as capital; West Florida was the country west of this to the Mississippi and Iberville rivers, with Pensacola as capital, and including Mobile in what was to be known as Charlotte County. The northern boundary of West Florida was next year shifted northwardly to the line running east and west through the mouth of the Yazoo River. These proclamations were probably, like one named by Adair, published by posting on the gate of Fort Charlotte.[1]

The crown lands extending to Canada were not erected into a province, but were reserved nominally for the use of the Indians until the further order of the king. This practically adopted the French proposition of an Indian buffer country, but under English control.

The first governor of West Florida was George Johnstone, who, according to Adair, was much respected by the savages. Its military, however, were subject to the orders of the commander-in-chief at New York, General Thomas Gage, who in 1763 succeeded Amherst in command of all America, — an

---

[1] Winsor's *Basin of the Mississippi*, pp. 428, 430 ; Adair's *American Indians*, p. 369. Much information in this Part IV. has been derived from the *Haldimand Papers* at Ottawa, and from an examination made in the *British Colonial Records* at London.

arduous position even in time of peace. He had been governor
of Montreal in 1760.

The military of West Florida was commanded until the
spring of 1767 by Colonel Taylor, and the post at Mobile consisted at first of the 22d and 34th regiments, which occupied
the place October 20, 1763.

Fort Toulouse, up the Alabama River, had been maintained
by the French as much as a check on the British of the Atlantic as for trade, and was now, when everything had become
British, of less importance. Farmer could not spare the men
to garrison it, but sent James Germany there to keep possession.
As late as August, 1764, we know from the Haldimand Papers
that flags were made for the Creeks, and in the next February
Germany was interpreter to them still. The British could
have found little of value in the fort, as Lavnoué spiked his
cannon, broke their trunnions, dismantled the work, and threw
all the property into the river before withdrawing to Mobile in
1763. The cannon remained, however, for many years.[1]

Fort Tombecbé, called by Farmer Fort York, was of more
value from its nearness to the warlike Chickasaws, and was
maintained, as Gage later frankly expressed it, for the purpose
of encouraging the Choctaws and assisting in Indian quarrels.

Thirty British soldiers under Lieutenant Thomas Ford had
taken possession November 22, 1763, and Ford reports that he
found it a strong post, but in need of repairs. We learn from
the major's contingent account among the Haldimand Papers
that Farmer paid Captain Chabbert for the French stores left
there £40 10s. 8d. There was immediately a draft on all the
fort supplies, for there was a Choctaw town within musket-shot,
and the Indians must be placated with presents. This was following the French policy, and also the order of Lieutenant-Colonel James Robertson. The bill of £235 1s. 5d. was ultimately
paid by Farmer. In March of next year there was a fleet of
"battoes" (*bateaux*) sent up there from Mobile, and for pilot-
ing them Anthony Narbonne was paid £3 14s. 8d. H. M.
S. Stagg had just arrived with supplies for Fort Charlotte,
and probably some were sent up the river. There was a good
garden at Tombecbé.

[1] See 1 Pickett's *Alabama*, p. 221, for their migration to Montgomery,
Wetumpka, etc.

THE COUNTRY OF THE SOUTHERN INDIANS, 1764

The next item paid by Major Farmer on this account is one of £9 14s. to W. Escott in August, 1765, for horse-hire and horses lost in carrying Lieutenant Smith, of the 22d regiment, to and from Tombecbé,—certainly a moderate charge even if only one horse was lost. Fort Tombecbé is not mentioned again until the quarrels between Ritchy and Lagardère, two officers of the post, in 1766. Adair deplores its precipitate abandonment, and says the Indian agent who remained was totally unfit to deal with Red Captain and the other Choctaws.[1]

Some of the Indians, like the Tensaws and a part of the Alibamons, were so attached to the French as to follow them west of the Mississippi. Two hundred Tensaws from Mobile were established on Bayou Lafourche, and Alibamons will be found on the Mississippi. Of the Mobilians, Tohomes, and Apalaches near Mobile we hear no more, and they no doubt retired among the Choctaws. Chickasaws, Creeks, and Choctaws remained, and the "Koosahte" (Coosadas) moved nearer Mobile, settling on the east side of the river, twenty-five leagues above the city.[2] The British, after some blundering, undertook an even more systematic Indian policy than the French, for they now had a larger territory. In 1762, Captain John Stuart (or Stewart),[3] a survivor of the massacre at Fort Loudoun, had been appointed the first Indian Superintendent for the South, and he convened at Mobile a great congress of all the tribes south of the Ohio River.[4] This was held in the spring of 1764, and resulted in a general pacification and alliance with the English of all but a few Choctaws and Creeks. As the Indians knew little English, the Frenchman Louis Forneret acted as interpreter for 196 days, at 4 shillings 8 pence per day, as we learn from Farmer's accounts. There we find also, for this year, three entries of beef for use of the Indians, aggregating £107, besides some wine, increase in Farmer's own table ex-

---

[1] Adair's *American Indians*, pp. 292, 310.

[2] 2 French's *Historical Collection*, p. 47 ; Adair's *American Indians*, p. 298. There is reason to class the Coosadas and Occhays, whom Romans found with them, as Alibamons and not Creeks.

[3] Brownlee's *Indian Races*, p. 402 ; Meek's *Southwest*, p. 85.

[4] John Stuart, of Carolina, long acted, and his cousin Charles was deputy at Mobile after the death of Mr. Henderson in 1769.

penses, and £1554 of presents for them paid to Dugald Campbell, the commissary. Farmer complained that he had to entertain five hundred himself at one time. Stuart afterwards expended £1200 a year on them at Mobile.

That fall, probably to some extent in consequence of the Indian pacification, Governor Johnstone, to carry out the aims of the home government, issued a glowing description of West Florida, designed to attract settlers.[1] Agriculture, timber, trade with Central America, were dwelt on, and analogies found to Tyre, Sidon, Carthage, Colchos, Palmyra, Amsterdam, Venice, and Genoa. "On the whole," we learn, "whether we regard the situation or the climate, West Florida bids fair to be the emporium as well as the most pleasant part of the New World."

The British must have credit for the first great extinction of Indian title in these parts, the beginning of that gradual process which was to make West Florida available for white settlement, give all the southern country to the whites, and culminate in our own century in moving the Choctaws, Creeks, and Cherokees to the territory west of the Mississippi. On March 26, 1765, was a cession by the Choctaws of land west from the Cahaba and Alabama rivers to the Buckatunna, and from there southward, including the coast. This important sale was consummated at a Congress in Mobile, attended by Governor Johnstone, Superintendent Stewart, and twenty-nine chiefs.[2] It was probably held in the Indian House, which was this spring repaired. Article 5 of this treaty runs as follows: —

"ARTICLE 5. And to prevent all disputes on account of encroachments, or supposed encroachments, committed by the English inhabitants of this or any of his Majesty's provinces, on the lands or hunting-grounds reserved and claimed by the Chicaksaw and Choctaw Indians, and that no mistakes, doubts, or disputes, may for the future arise thereupon, in consideration of the great marks of friendship, benevolence, and clemency extended to us, the said Chickasaw and Choctaw Indians, by his Majesty King George the Third, we, the chiefs and head warriors, distinguished by great and small medals, and gorgets,

[1] *Haldimand Papers*, Ottawa.
[2] *American State Papers*, p. 314, corrected by copy from the official papers in the British Record Office, " America and West Indies."

and bearing his Majesty's commissions as chiefs and leaders of our respective nations, by virtue and in pursuance of the full right and power which we now have and are possessed of, have agreed, and we do hereby agree, that, for the future, the boundary be settled by a line extended from Grosse Point, in the Island of Mount Louis, by the course of the western coast of Mobile Bay, to the mouth of the eastern branch of Tombecbee River, and north by the course of the said river, to the confluence of Alibamont and Tombecbee rivers, and afterwards along the western bank of Alibamont River to the mouth of Chickianoce River, and from the confluence of Chickianoce and Alibamont rivers, a straight line to the confluence of Bance and Tombecbee rivers; from thence, by a line along the western bank of Bance River, till its confluence with the Tallatukpe River; from thence, by a straight line to Tombecbee river, opposite to Atchalickpe; and from Atchalikpe, by a straight line, to the most northerly part of Buckatanne River, and down the course of Buckatanne River to its confluence with the river Pascagoula, and down by the course of the river Pascagoula, within twelve leagues of the seacoast; and thence, by a due west line, as far as the Choctaw nation have a right to grant.

"And the said chiefs, for themselves and their nations, give and confirm the property of all the lands contained between the above-described lines and the sea, to his Majesty the King of Great Britain, and his successors, reserving to themselves full right and property in all the lands to the northward of said lines now possessed by them; and none of his Majesty's white subjects shall be permitted to settle on Tombecbee River to the northward of the rivulet called Centebonck."

These boundaries can be identified, although most of the names have been changed. The grant begins on Mon Louis Island, extends along the coast to what is now the Apalache River, and up this, the Tensaw, Mobile, and Alabama rivers to the Cahaba, here called the Chickianose River. Thence the line runs to the junction of the Black Warrior, called the Bance, and the Bigbee, and up the Warrior to a stream near Tuskaloosa, whence it runs across country and over the Bigbee again at the village of Atchalickpe (Hatchatigbee) to the source of the Buckatunna, down which it runs to thirty-six miles from the sea, and thence west through all the Choctaw country.

This embraces all of the river and coast which has figured in this story except Fort Toulouse, but the treaty contains a singular limitation. By forbidding white settlement north of the "Centebonck" (now Santabogue or Cintebogue Creek, in lower Choctaw County), the treaty practically made that stream the northern boundary of the British possessions, with Fort Tombecbé as an isolated outpost above.

According to Adair, the policy of fixing a low scale of prices to articles to be sold the savages, and of general licensing of traders under bond and security, sanctioned by this treaty, was to ruin legitimate traders and permit introduction of so much liquor as to injure the Indians. He claims to have lost much himself by the new plan of operations. But at least it looked plausible, and probably failed because of insufficient supervision. Locally it would seem to have benefited Mobile, as the superintendent aimed at supplying traders even for the Chickasaws through Mobile, whose navigation, however, Adair — who has never a good word for the town — deemed inferior to Charleston's. The general tariff was 70 per cent. below that of the French up the Mississippi.[1]

The Indians were satisfied, and gave up their French medals and commissions, accepting those of the British king. The congress lasted from March 26 to April 3, and although they often numbered 2000 men, no damage was committed. Rev. Mr. Hart read prayers, but next year there was no church or parson at Mobile.

It was in the year of the congress, possibly at that time, that Hooma, or Red Captain, with forty Choctaw warriors, charged three hundred Creeks and drove them headlong through Mobile into the river. Hooma alone killed thirteen Creeks, even when fighting on his knees, but was slain himself by one of the retreating foe. On the river-bank, according to tradition at the foot of St. Francis Street, the pursuit ceased; for these Choctaws could not swim, while in this the Creeks were expert.[2] This was in the beginning of a six years' war between these tribes.

---

[1] Adair's *American Indians*, pp. 367, 370, 414.

[2] See *Scenes and Settlers of Alabama*, p. 20, where the flying Indians are called Seminoles. Romans' *Florida* dates this "not above six years ago," but he may have written some time before the 1776 imprint of his book.

Under the French, Mobile, after it ceased to be the capital, was still important as controlling the Alabama basin. This remained true under the British, and it now acquired also a new importance. New Orleans remained French (or Spanish), and Mobile now became, especially at first, a base of supplies and operations for the British control of the east half of the Mississippi valley.

Several English publications were devoted to the new acquisitions, but none of them grasped the importance of Mobile better than Roberts, — if he does prefix a Cockney "H" to the name of the main river. He says: —

"The Bay of Mobile forms a most noble and spacious harbor, running thirty miles north, and six miles broad, to the several mouths of the Halabama and Chickasaw rivers. It affords very good anchorage and is capable of containing the whole British navy.

"The French, perceiving the importance of this place, and the advantages that must naturally arise therefrom, erected, on the west side of this bay, a strong fort called after the bay. This place is now become to us of the utmost consequence, since all the country to the eastward of the Mississippi is ceded to us by the late treaty of peace.

"The advantageous situation of this harbor, to the very heart of the richest part of the country, is as it were a back door to New Orleans, and will ever remain an unmovable check, by inevitably cutting off all communication between the river Mississippi and Europe, and the French western islands. Yet this depends upon the seasonable measures taken by the government to put this country and harbor into a better posture of defense, by erecting a fort at its entrance, and sending colonies over."[1]

Almost on a line to the west of Fort Tombecbé, the British, in order to watch the French across the Mississippi River, had built at the Natchez Fort Panmure. Lower down, the Iberville separated West Florida from Spanish Louisiana; and making the Iberville navigable, so as to give continuous communication with the Mississippi, was the constant aim of the British. In January, 1765, Farmer paid Lieutenant James Campbell, of the 34th regiment, £326 13s. 13d. "towards de-

---

[1] Roberts' *Florida*, p. 952.

fraying the expenses of clearing the river Iberville," and the very next month no less than £863 6s. 8d. was paid Delille Dupard for the same purpose. Lieutenant Pittman, later to be connected with the great survey of Mobile Bay, on April 8 of this year we find mentioned in connection with surveying the Iberville. On that day Rochon was paid twenty-two and a half pounds for repairing a boat for Pittman "to survey the lakes with." Pittman was stationed there, and his verdict was that the river had got in worse condition than ever, because the drift logs had been cut up only near the Mississippi, and high water had blocked up the lower part with this material.[1]

This lake route was of value not only for watching the French and Spanish. Through this, or through the lower Mississippi, must pass all communication with the upper valley, and particularly the fertile Illinois region, which had been, under the French, the granary of Louisiana, and in part of Canada. Johnstone, therefore, had the Scots Fusiliers build, on the site of the workmen's camp, a fort to protect the passage. This was the origin of Fort Bute.

The French had always been powerful in the upper Mississippi valley, the Illinois, opened by their missionaries, and later its trade was contended for by the rival governments of Canada and Louisiana. Fort Chartres, founded 1718 among the Kaskaskias on the Mississippi above the Ohio junction, had become the principal post of a district containing 1100 whites, besides three hundred negro slaves. Altogether there were over two thousand French in the upper valley.[2]

The Treaty of Paris surrendered all east of the river to the English, but the reluctance of the French inhabitants and the hostility of the Indians under Pontiac and others made the cession at first nominal. Major Loftus, with 400 troops of the 22d regiment from Mobile, attempted in 1764 to ascend the Mississippi to take possession; but on March 20 these were driven back by Tunica Indians at Davion's Bluff before they had well started, with the loss of five killed and four wounded.[3] Part of the command then returned by the lake route to Mobile. Even the Indian pacification at Mobile was limited to the

---

[1] Pittman's *Mississippi Settlements*, pp. 31, 32.

[2] Winsor's *Basin of the Mississippi*, p. 268, chap. xxi.

[3] *Ibid.*, chap. xxiii. ; Pittman's *Mississippi Settlements*, p. 35.

southern savages, and taking possession of the Illinois was still in the future. An expedition to feel the way was necessary, and we read of an unsuccessful one by Lieutenant Fraser from Fort Pitt.

At this time there seems to have been at New Orleans the firm of Logan, Terry & Co. They were of assistance when English vessels, instead of taking the lake route, ascended from the mouth of the Mississippi, as they had a right to do under the treaty. This firm figures largely in the Farmer accounts.

The first item is a payment on August 22, 1764, to Pousset of 16s. 4d. for bunting and making of flags for the Illinois and Creek Indians. In November we find Hugh Crawford and Ludow^k Huckle mentioned as having a contract to conduct an officer to the Illinois; and Captain John Lind, of the schooner Charlotte, as bringing the king's *bateaux* from the Balize to New Orleans. About the same time Logan, Terry & Co. collected a large quantity of Indian goods for a new expedition to be undertaken by Lieutenant Ross, their bill being no less than £3247 5s. 4¾d.

Unless we are to suppose that Lieutenant John Ross's party was a different one, it would seem that the expedition did not leave for the Illinois until early spring, — and it would be strange to undertake a northern journey before that season. Then in March comes the payment to Messrs. Monsarts & Co. of £1405 18s. 8d. more for boats; and to Logan, Terry & Co., next month, one fifth as much again on account of "battoes" for the Illinois expedition. This seems extraordinary, unless the first set had been destroyed in some way. The Monsarts had already been paid in part by skins, as we learn in the curious entry of a draft on General Gage for repayment of the duty of almost 200 pounds sterling placed by the governor and council on these skins when imported into the colony. It is possible even yet to imagine the explosion when Gage heard of this tax! And on April 1 was paid £397 more in drafts from Monsart, met by Farmer through the Mobile house of George Ancrum.

Logan, Terry & Co. had supplied Ross with a sixteen-pound outfit himself, besides two horses for £12, and every now and then on his progress he draws on Farmer for some expense. Up among the Chickasaws he draws for £103 16s. in favor of the trader John Brown, who seems to have supplied guides from there to the Illinois, and this was in addition to the compensation of Francis Underwood, who acted as guide and interpreter too.   Daniel Clark makes presents of forty wampums (costing over £57) on the way; and Logan, Terry & Co. supply £350 of goods to pay the rowers of the *bateaux* employed by Captain Laganterais for the public presents to the Illinois.   These goods would seem to have been well protected, for we learn also that a barrel of tar from Mobile was used in making tarpaulins.

The result of this expensive expedition we do not know.   But it must have been exceedingly satisfactory to the Indians at least, and have kept Major Farmer busy paying out British gold from his strong-box.

The final occupation of the Illinois was in the fall of 1765, and effected by the operations of Captain Stirling with Highlanders, who penetrated the Ohio valley from Fort Pitt; while Major Farmer shortly afterwards, in December, led the 34th regiment up the Mississippi to join him.   The French commandant, St. Ange, then retired across the river to the village of St. Louis, and the English entered Fort Chartres.[1]

With this the British occupation of the Mississippi basin was completed.

[1] Winsor's *Basin of the Mississippi*, p. 457.

CHAPTER XXIV.

COLONEL WILLIAM TAYLOR was the commanding officer of the province, stationed at Pensacola. He seems to have drawn some of his supplies from Mobile. William Irving was contractor at Mobile, and frequently forwarded him fowl and other things, and at one time we find him soliciting a continuance in his agency. One D. Clark (deputy collector of customs in 1765) writes the general from there concerning his wood contract; and later we find Elias Durnford furnishing bark for barracks, and sending over cattle from Mobile. Favre was interpreter to the Indians. In fact Mobile, on account largely of its rivers and bay, was, until its healthfulness became questioned, of much service to the army, especially during the uncertainty of the long war which now began between the Creeks and Choctaws.

Major Farmer was in command at Mobile for a number of years. At first he was much embarrassed for money, for the merchants were so unused to the change of flag that they would not take his bills on New York. He was compelled to accommodate himself, most unwillingly, to the French-Indian policy and keep open house for twenty or thirty every day, — a vile custom, he declares.

As to the inhabitants, he construed the treaty strictly, and recognized only formal grants of land, and not the possessory right so common. He gave but three months' shrift to those inhabitants who preferred emigration to taking the oath of allegiance to King George.[1] This led to a petition by them to the home government, with favorable result. Farmer found ninety-eight French families, and of these about forty remained, withdrawing largely to their river and bay homes, and there raising cattle. Lieutenant McLellan was sent to New Orleans to induce the French to move to Mobile and Pensacola, but in this he was unsuccessful. Pierre Rochon, who was to

---

[1] 2 Gayarré's *Louisiana*, pp. 100, 101.

be the contractor that did most of the fort repairs, was of the Mobile French who remained.

For a careful examination was made by the new owners of Fort Charlotte (Condé), and a report dated November 30, 1763, showed many repairs to be necessary. All woodwork was old, glasses gone, the brickwork overgrown with grass, bake-houses and hospital in need of attention. The embarkation of French cannon and disembarkation of the English effectually ruined the old wharf. Evidently the French had for several years taken little care of what they did not expect to keep. The British claimed the French cannon, but D'Abbadie at New Orleans curtly refused to surrender them, as they were not fixtures.[1]

The British set resolutely to work, and shortly there was great improvement. New platforms were laid for the cannon; another flagstaff erected; the brick casemates repaired; the barracks, both within and without the fort, put in order; the ovens of the bake-house made serviceable; and the palisades, which seem then to have surrounded the officers' square (Government to Conti) and connected it with the fort, were renewed, lathed, and spiked. In the next July thirty-seven loads of scaffold poles were brought for the bake-house repairs. Adair speaks of the garrison prison as a "black-hole," even after these improvements in the fort, and mentions the imprisonment there of a local trader whom a "Choktah" accused of selling him a cracked brass kettle.[2] This instance of British justice may be supplemented by the official record of a white found guilty of the murder of an Indian in 1765. Next year there was still no secure "gaol," but later we find an allowance for a negro to keep one. Chimneys and five wells were also repaired, the officers' guard-room in the fort floored, and, like their barracks, whitewashed, besides repairs to roofs and sashes. An addition of six rooms to these quarters was in course of construction, besides partition, "two cupboards and skirtin boards put around some of the officers' rooms." "The late Com^t house" had four new floors and one repaired, beside hearths, windows, and doors put in order. The smith shop, too, had a new roof and the bellows mended; and the hospital had repairs to gallery, roof, hearths, and well.

[1] 2 Gayarré's *Louisiana*, p. 97.
[2] Adair's *American Indians*, p. 287.

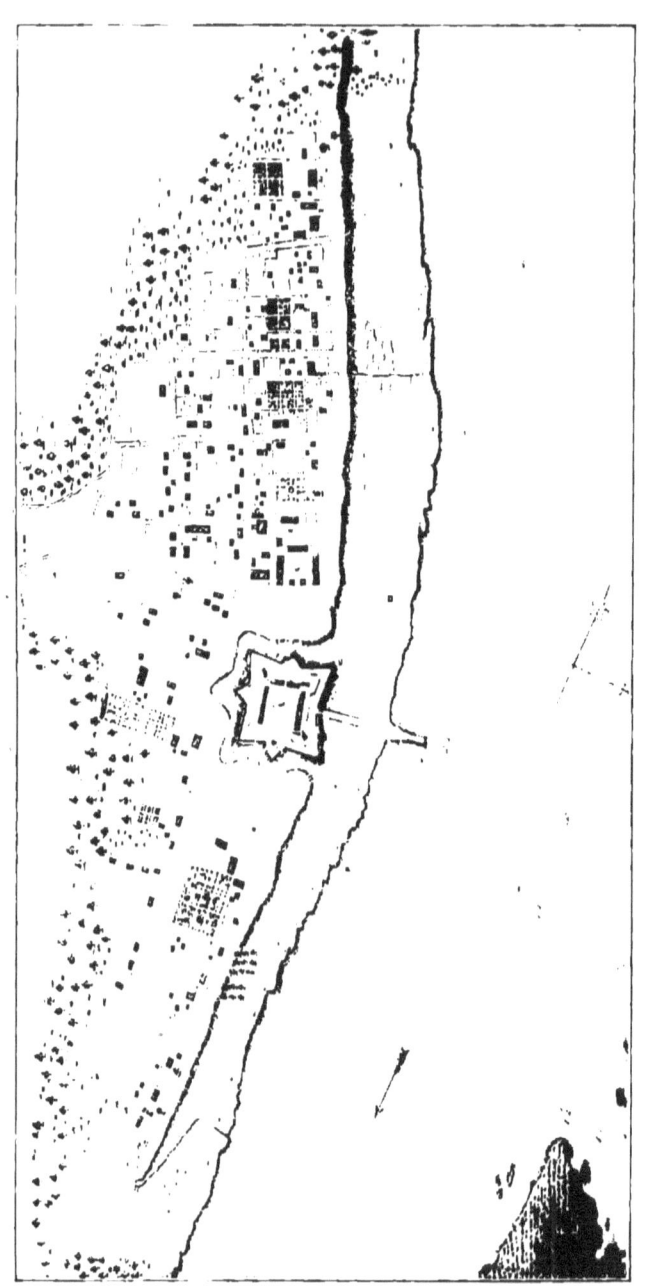

MOBILE IN 1765

A Fort Charlotte: B Government House: C Barracks: D Bake House: E Indian House: F Provision Magazine: G Hospital

The receipt of Pierre Rochon of April 9, for payment for all this labor, has also come down in the Haldimand Papers. It states that he did the work by order of Major Farmer, of the 34th regiment, and Farmer's account shows that Rochon received in all £2232. A certificate dated April 13, of officers of the 34th and 22d regiments, shows that the work was satisfactory.

The major complains that the French claimed everything outside the fort to be private property, the commandant's house included. The new-comers were bound to respect private property, and so we find Farmer renting from Mme. Grondel the hospital. On September 10, 1764, he bought it for £186 13s. 4d. The deed was at first taken to Farmer individually, but this was afterwards corrected. We learn later that firewood for the hospital cost fo'r dollars per cord.

In May he had already purchased of J. B. Roussève for use of the Indian interpreter another house and two lots, for which he paid £93 6s. 8d., or "four hundred dollars." The place Farmer bought in January of next year, as a lodging for artificers brought out from New York for government work, was a house of wood and clay covered with bark. J. C. Montal had sold it to Mr. Maloney, an English resident, for 430 "hard dollars," part on time. It may be on this account that Mr. James Hendrie, deputy vendue master, on July 25, 1764, certified that he had sold the place at public vendue, by order of the commandant, to Mr. Hugh Kennedy, for $266. In the next January, Hugh Kennedy Hoy, presumably the same man, sold it to Major Farmer for the use of his Majesty. The description of this lot of 12½ by 25 toises, fronting the river, bounds it on the one side by the house of Mr. George Ancrum, merchant, "on the other side making the corner of a street," probably Conti. The artificers did much work, for we know that Farmer paid them £537, if not more.

Major Farmer was, at the time of the surrender of Mobile, forty-five years of age. He was an interesting character. He had occasion to correspond officially with Aubry, the French governor, who had succeeded in 1765 on the death of D'Abbadie at New Orleans, and we have Aubry's impression of him in a dispatch to the home government : —

"This governor of Mobile is an extraordinary man. As he

knows that I speak English, he occasionally writes to me in verse. He speaks to me of Francis I. and Charles V. He compares Pontiak, an Indian chief, to Mithridates; he says that he goes to bed with Montesquieu. When there occur some petty difficulties between the inhabitants of New Orleans and Mobile, he quotes to me from the Magna Charta and the laws of Great Britain. It is said that the English ministry sent him to Mobile to get rid of him, because he was one of the hottest in the opposition. He pays me handsome compliments, which I duly return to him, and, upon the whole, he is a man of parts, but a dangerous neighbor, against whom it is well to be on one's guard." [1]

The major acquired from the Indians a piece of land facing the bay and extending over towards Pensacola, and from the government, at some time, Farmer's Island and his residence at what is the northeast corner of Government and St. Emanuel. This was his home until he moved over to the Tensaw River at modern Stockton.

In the fall of 1766 two traders, Goodwin and Davis, were murdered in the Choctaw country. The Nation disclaimed the acts, and tried to arrest the offenders. In fact, they sometimes put too much confidence in Indian traders; and it was in this year that the distinguished Choctaw "Minggo Humma Echeto" was with a number of warriors cut to pieces by the Creeks whom Englishmen had put on their guard.[2] But there was general uneasiness in exposed places, and, on the eastern shore of Mobile Bay, some apprehension also from the Creeks. We find F. Pousset in 1766 suggesting a fort over there, and the governor and council requested Colonel Taylor that it be large enough for thirty men and two officers. We do not know whether this was the flag-maker of two years before, but he probably was the Pousset who was later member of the colonial supreme court.

Pousset says he has consulted the inhabitants, and they agree "that a small post, somewhere above the Red Cliff near to Mr. Genty's, would be of great advantage to them, that whenever apprehensive of an Indian war they will leave their present habitation and settle themselves for the time being (with per-

---

[1] 2 Gayarré's *Louisiana*, p. 124.

[2] Adair's *American Indians*, p. 312.

mission of the governor and council) as near as possible together on the lands from Ge[nty's] to Fish River, which with
the Bay of Mobile forms a point of [land] of about ten leagues
in length and four in breadth. This would afford sufficient
pasture for all their cattle for a considerable [time], which they
would drive there together and protect them. They would propose to go out alternately in small parties and leave their wives,
children and slaves under the protection of the fort. Thus
they think they could cover themselves safely during a Creek
war, and be commodiously situated for providing Pensacola with
provisions. According to the information I have received,
there are from the highest to the lowest, on the east side of the
Bay of Mobile, seventeen plantations, thirty-nine white men
who can bear arms, thirty-two negroes of which twenty-nine
are men grown, twenty-one negro women and children. In
all, 124 souls and 2280 head of cattle. I hear they do not
want arms."[1] This project was not to be carried out, however, for several years.

It may be that Gage's disapproval of more posts, as expressed in his letter of August 11 to Taylor, had something to
do with this; perhaps also sickness among the Mobile garrison,
which led that summer to an encampment on Dauphine Island.

Gage's opposition to distant posts was such that he not only
wished to abandon the Mississippi forts, but even Mobile itself,
and draw the force in West Florida to Pensacola. He evidently had doubts about all the province. "The whole of the
trade in those parts," he says, "consists of skins only; the furs
come from above. You will know if the skin trade is of much
value. Many people at home think not, and that it does not
pay the expenses of Mobile and Pensacola."

This letter is also noticeable for the vigorous denunciation of
Governor Johnstone's idea that he was supreme over the military as well as the civil departments. The commander-in-chief
instructs Taylor to recognize no such claim. The opinion of
Attorney-General Arthur Gordon that control of his Majesty's
land was vested in the governor would hardly be contested,
except as a precedent later for a claim to own the very forts.
The dispute even affected the distribution of surgeons when,
in the fall of 1766, Mobile was unhealthful.

[1] *Haldimand Papers*, Ottawa.

The dissension dated back a year at least, when nineteen officers at Mobile signed a memorial against the governor, which Gage forwarded to Halifax at court. Farmer had thoroughly supported Gage, and thus incurred Johnstone's enmity and was now to feel it. Charges were made against the major of embezzlement, and a court martial was called for. Gage took up the matter, and on September 29, 1766, ordered a trial, sending the articles of accusation to Taylor, with direction to give a copy to Johnstone.

The articles read as follows and are serious enough: —

"Articles of accusation against Major Farmer of His Majesty's 34th regiment on which he is hereby ordered to be tryed at Pensacola or Mobile, as shall be found most convenient, as soon as a General Court Martial can be assembled for that purpose.

"For sending flour belonging to the King to New Orleans, and selling or attempting to sell it there, by means of one Pallachio, a Jew.

"For selling the Fort of Tombeckbee to Mr. Terry, a merchant.

"For misapplication of ten thousand pounds said to be expended on Indian presents, and on the Fortifications.

"For making a job of the Publick service, in the operation of the Iberville.

"For turning in a different channel the monies, which should have been expended on the Barracks, so that the officers and soldiers lived in a miserable condition.

"For insisting to charge five bitts p. barrel for lime, which could be made for three bitts and dividing the profits with the Engineer.

"For desiring the Engineer to bear a man extraordinary upon the works at *three shillings*. P. Diem; and to charge a laboring negro belonging to him the Major at three shillings more, both which was done.

"For employing the King's boat to his own emolument, and dividing the profits with the sailors."

In this may be some reference to the major's boat the Little Bob, in which during 1765 he sent beef and flour to New Orleans for the Illinois expedition. She brought back five barrels of claret at night and put them on the schooner Charlotte. For this she was seized by Collector Clark.

We find the names of Terry and of Pallachio in Farmer's accounts, and also items relative to large quantities of wood for lime-kilns (probably up the river), but nothing criminating. He handled in the two years in question something over £15,000. The trial lasted several years, and the dispute between civil and military departments meantime fills volumes of British records with complaints and counter-charges.

By a coincidence, the year of the Farmer articles was that marking the birth of the girl who was to become Mrs. Hollinger and live a long and honored life in Mobile. The inscription on her tomb in the " Old Graveyard " dates from 1836, and recites the changes of flag and the growth of her native city from her birth seventy years before.

CHAPTER XXV

THE brave and chivalrous Bouquet, famous for his energy in the subjection of the Indians of western Pennsylvania in Pontiac's war, succeeded Taylor in command of West Florida, but he died shortly after his arrival at Pensacola. The story goes that while he was absent on duty his fiancée, Miss Willing, of Philadelphia, married another man, and that the soldier grieved himself to death. His brick tomb was on the shore of Pensacola Bay, but has now disappeared, washed away by the waves.[1] Frederick Haldimand succeeded Bouquet.

Colonel William Taylor did not leave for his new post at St. Augustine until after Haldimand's arrival, but this general found everything in confusion. He set manfully about bringing order out of the chaos.[2]

His report to General Gage of April 31, 1767, says he was thinking of building a new road to Mobile. At Pensacola the water was bad, and he was issuing rum to the men at the doctor's suggestion, — a plan of which Gage disapproved. Instead of rum, spruce beer was to be manufactured.

Haldimand found the laws of the province an extraordinary compound; but this was the fault of his government in substituting English for the civil law where most of the people were French or Spanish. Gage was regretting that cattle were allowed to be taken from the country west of Mobile to Louisi-

---

[1] Campbell's *Colonial Florida*, p. 71.

[2] Frederick Haldimand was a Swiss, an officer of note in the British service. He was a methodical man and kept almost everything, leaving his collection at his death to a nephew. On the death of this gentleman in 1858 these papers were bequeathed to the British Museum, where they still remain. Haldimand after his service in the South was governor of Canada, and for this reason the Canadian government has, through the energy of Mr. Douglas Brymner, their archivist, had the whole collection copied, and thus made accessible in America.

ana, an act soon made unlawful, while Haldimand was scheming to get the French to come over the Mississippi and Iberville rivers into the Mobile country. The cession to Spain had at last been made public, and the Spanish governor, Don Ulloa, had arrived at New Orleans March 5, 1766. Discontent prevailed and was to culminate in revolution.[1]

Meanwhile Haldimand reports that the advantages of Florida had been exaggerated, and that he did not hope much from Spanish commerce; in fact, he did not see how all the past and future expenses could be made up to the nation. He rather favored the withdrawal of the troops, although this would be opposed from personal interests. Lieutenant - Governor Browne, in his reports, declares the trade to be large, including 150 hogsheads of peltry annually from Mobile alone, besides much else. Haldimand says the trade was small, and chiefly confined to the military and persons employed by the government.[2]

One important factor in commerce was the pilot. The first one was Samuel Carr, who lived on Dauphine Island. It seems the island had been in whole or part granted him, but he cut down the timber and killed the cattle to such an extent that the governor and council moved him over to Mobile Point. That was to be his headquarters, and a house was ordered built there. He was succeeded in 1768 by Captain Richard Harley, whose salary was £50.

The fort at Tombecbé was abandoned in January, 1768, in one of the severest winters on record, and the garrison brought to Mobile. Lieutenant Ritchie was left to settle the accounts of the post. Haldimand liked Johnstone as little as did the other military men, and writes Gage he thinks the governor and his friends wanted posts maintained for their own benefit. The grants of land, too, were extraordinary. The general retained three square miles around the forts, for otherwise the council would have made grants up to the very glacis. But

---

[1] 2 Gayarré's *Louisiana*, pp. 147, 205.

[2] It at least needed the annual visit of a vessel of 200 tons, filled with British manufactures and carrying back skins to London. The custom-house fees, however, were heavy, being sometimes half the freight of ordinary boats, and, while ships drawing thirteen feet could cross the bar, several feet less was the depth at the town

this can hardly refer to Mobile, where the fort always had been in the midst of a town. The grants by the governor to a field officer might be 5000 acres, and so on down, until a private man could get sixty acres.[1]

Johnstone left that spring, but was succeeded *ad interim* by the lieutenant-governor, Montford Browne, equally a *persona non grata*. It was infectious, — Taylor had the same trouble with Governor Grant in East Florida. And meantime Major Farmer's court martial was progressing as far as the evidence was procurable, but witnesses on both sides were scattered. Farmer made charges, too, against Lieutenant Pittman.

Pittman had already in February surveyed Mobile River by Haldimand's order; and shortly afterwards the general gives direction to Elias Durnford, the provincial engineer, to make a survey of the bay to join on to and continue Pittman's work. This survey is the most important act of the British occupation which has come down to us, and we owe it to Haldimand. It seems that Gould had done some of the work, but Durnford was to do the most.

On March 10 Durnford writes Haldimand from Mobile that he had since his arrival been making plans for officers' and soldiers' barracks in the square (which needed bedsteads for one thing), but that when the weather became settled he would begin the survey on the east side of this bay, so as to meet those of Pittman and Gould. Durnford had a plantation on the eastern shore near Montrose, and, while surveying about five miles below there, he was painfully wounded in the left thigh by the accidental discharge of a gun loaded with duck-shot, which temporarily laid him up.

Haldimand in a letter of the 18th said that he would not do anything more in the way of repairs to the barracks, and directed Durnford instead to lay out some healthy place at Red Cliff which would accommodate about two hundred men of the Mobile garrison, should the summer be unhealthy. This, it will be recollected, was the spot where Pousset some years before had wished to have a fort. Remembering the propensity of the governors for granting lands, Haldimand directs Durnford to reserve enough ground around the new post to supply springs and firewood. Haldimand adds that he has ordered

[1] See *Report of Senate Committee on Private Land Claims*, June 13, 1840.

Aikman, the Mobile commandant, to furnish such men as Durnford would need in this work, which was to include also cutting and hauling logs for the larger buildings. The trees were to be barked, as much, no doubt, to use the bark for the huts as anything else. In this work one Frenchman could direct twenty soldiers. Unless he has Rochon in mind in particular, it would seem therefore that Haldimand has a high opinion of the French in general. As soon as Durnford has finished at Red Cliff he is to go on with the survey of the bay, keeping at it as long as his presence was not needed in Pensacola "to represent the office of Chief Justice with Messrs. Hodge and Pousset." From which it would seem that Durnford was of varied accomplishments, and the first of the line of distinguished lawyers resident near Montrose.

Durnford, on the 21st of March at Mobile, acknowledged this letter, received by the hands of Mr. Waugh, probably the commissary. This correspondence, conducted in French by the general, in English by the surveyor, throws side lights on affairs. Haldimand orders fifteen barrels of Indian corn (*blé d'Inde*) and "chappons and canards" (capons and ducks). Durnford sends twenty-four barrels of Indian corn by Mr. Jones' sloop, besides twelve previously sent. Fowls or duck were not to be had right then, but would be sent if found in the course of the survey. Aikman had some to be sent "to you, Sir, by this opportunity." Haldimand we find returning his compliments to Rochon with thanks for the trees and oranges which he had had the goodness to send.

While the important survey was progressing here, however, General Gage at New York was preparing to withdraw all but three companies of the two regiments heretofore kept in West Florida. By letter of June 27 this determination was communicated to the acting governor, Browne, and it threw the province into consternation. The troops were to be taken to St. Augustine. Already, indeed, George Bryn had in March brought the garrison on the Iberville down to New Orleans and thence across to Mobile, getting also some of the deserters who every now and then escaped to New Orleans.

In July there was promise of moderation in the factional disputes of the province in consequence of the arrival in Pensacola of ex-Chief Justice Clifton, Attorney-General Wegg, and others. They seem to have brought the news of the appointment of Elliott as the new governor. The arrangements for moving the troops went on all summer, and shopkeepers and others at Pensacola held indignation meetings, and drew an address of the king praying for protection to this "Emporium of the West." Mobile had even more reason for alarm, since only the preceding spring a Choctaw conspiracy to massacre the inhabitants had been frustrated.

About this time the founder of Mobile died at Paris. He was buried in Montmartre. Mobile, as the baptismal record shows, was still essentially French, but so quiet had Bienville lately lived that it is doubtful if they even heard there of his death.

In November, Lieutenant Nugent with a detachment of the 31st relieved Farmer of the 21st, who marched to Pensacola, and next month the bulk of the stores and field artillery were taken away. Haldimand himself came to Mobile to make the final arrangements.

It may also be that he was here to keep a weather-eye on the French revolution over in Louisiana. The Spanish governor had not brought many troops, relying upon the French soldiers under Aubry, who were still retained but were paid by Spain. The amiable Ulloa had never been popular, nor had his beautiful but distant lady; and on October 29, 1768, the superior council at New Orleans had taken upon itself to expel him and hoist the French flag. The Spanish officials took refuge on their frigate and shortly afterwards sailed away, to the delight of the Louisianians, who now sought again the rule of Louis the Well Beloved.

While the many French at Mobile no doubt shared this love for old France, no effort was made at revolution. They realized that the English were very different masters.

In August, 1768, the court martial on Major Farmer had at last been concluded and the papers submitted to the king. The general-in-chief, in notifying Farmer, remarked that he could say nothing until the result was known; but in October the news came that his Majesty approved of the court martial acquitting the major. We can readily imagine the joy of the whole southern detachment at this victory over Governor Johnstone.

The major seems at the time of this trial to have withdrawn

from the active service, but we find him in 1769 recommended by the French to succeed Governor Browne. His family consisted of his wife Mary and five children, of whom Elisabeth Mary will meet us later. Through her marriage with Louis Alexandre de Vauxbercy, the Farmer blood has survived until the present day.

Even after his retirement, Major Farmer was in frequent demand for information as to Mobile matters. In January, 1769, for instance, Haldimand corresponded with him as to the house of Mr. Socié, taken possession of in 1763 as government property, probably up by the warehouse, and therefore supposed to belong to it. Farmer believed the private claim now set up to be fraudulent, but finally, in February, the house was surrendered by Nugent to Mme. de Socié on Haldimand's order. Haldimand did not give the order until the lieutenant-governor had made application, and the attorney-general had advised that it was private property.

When on the point of leaving Pensacola for St. Augustine in March, Haldimand wrote a letter to the expected governor, regretting not meeting him. But it is uncertain that Governor Elliott arrived alive. He had been reluctant to come at all, and seems to have committed suicide at sea, or shortly after his arrival, for reasons unknown, and Durnford, writing from Pensacola to Haldimand on May 16, tells of the funeral.

CHAPTER XXVI

A PECULIAR feature of the British tenure of Mobile was the recurring mortality every summer among the troops. The first of it was something like a plague among officers at a general court martial in the fall of 1764. All were taken and three died, and even shipmasters also suffered.

Next summer the 21st regiment relieved the 22d at Mobile and suffered much from fever. Their surgeon (Dr. Lorimer) attributed it to bringing unacclimated troops at so unseasonable a time, which was done despite his protest. It amounted to an epidemic.

The British foreign office thought the situation better in 1766, but if so it was because so many of the 21st were absent, and we know there was an encampment on Dauphine Island. A memorial from the inhabitants showed that three officers were dead and eleven absent, besides the deputy commissary of stores, the fort adjutant and barrack master, the chaplain, surgeon, minister, and schoolmaster, who were also absent from Mobile. The minister was Mr. Hart still, but early next year he resigned. He gave as reasons that he had no church building, parsonage, nor hope of promotion to chaplainship of the fort, and found it impossible to support his family on so inconsiderable a salary in a country where the expense of living was so extravagant.[1]

In 1767, Haldimand's report of April 31 dwells on the unhealthy condition of Mobile, where fevers were already pre-

---

[1] In 1768–69 there is an allowance in the British civil list of £100 for minister's salary, and £25 for that of a schoolmaster at Mobile. We learn from Von Eelking (*Deutsche Hülfstruppen in nordamerikanischen Befreiungskriege*, p. 139) that there was a minister also in 1779, the only one in the province. This was William Gordon, who acted from 1770 (at latest) all through the British period. He celebrated service also at Pensacola sometimes.

valent. The next year there were fifteen deaths in June, leaving but two officers fit for service.

This continued unhealthfulness was remarkable, for the French had had no such trouble. Haldimand gets at the root of the matter when he says the country is as healthy as any southern colony, and that temperate men have nothing to fear. Added to imprudence was the lack of medicine for the sick and the want of proper hospital accommodation. Surgeon Gray in August wrote, that, despite the increasing sickness and danger of "putrid fever," he had not the money to buy medicine. On the 21st of August, 1768, directions were sent Captain Stewart, commanding at Mobile, to order on board the Ledia upon her arrival all baggage, the sick, some officers and men; and Captain Brass of that sloop and Chambers of the Jenny were sent to Mobile to receive them. This consumed some time, but by the middle of September the soldiers — or rather this hospital, as Haldimand expresses it — were taken by sea to Pensacola. Four died even on the passage. Twenty-five men with officers, under Lieutenant Farmer, were all that were left as a garrison. Those who did not go by sea marched over by land. Fort Charlotte held fewer men than at any time since it was built.

Next year Haldimand detailed Lorimer to study the disorders at Mobile. He was to keep a journal and report precautions to be observed by troops and new settlers, "Mobile river being the most fertile and promising from its advantageous situation to be early settled." He desired Lorimer to impart to the new settlers any discoveries tending to preserve health, "by which means the credit of that place may in short time be restored from the bad report it hath lately lain under." [1]

Lorimer was duly assigned quarters in the garrison and spent the next six months studying the subject, being facilitated by Captain Crofton of the 31st regiment, whom Haldimand in February had put in command at Mobile.

In 1769, the garrison remained in the fort and connected square, and even by May the fevers had already set in. Dr. J. Lorimer, in a letter to Haldimand on the 30th, hinted that he would like Dr. Brown, of Pensacola, to exchange with him. He had given up his own room to the sick, but complains it

---

[1] Romans' *Florida*, p. 244, mentions "locked jaw" as also frequent at Mobile.

will all be in vain if money is not allowed for what is necessary
for their recovery. By July the detachment was very sickly,
and this continued all summer.

Lorimer's report in December is as follows: —

."There were scarce any sick until the month of June. The
bilious, remitting and intermitting fevers then set in, and continued by repeated relapses throughout the months of July,
August, and September. In the beginning of this last month
there were out of the small party stationed at Mobile twenty-
two men sick, that is about two thirds of the whole. At the
approach of the cold weather, the fevers abated, and they then
fell into fluxes, dropsias, and cachexies. . . .

"By the journal which I kept of the heat at Mobile it does
not appear materially to differ [from that] at Pensacola, the
thermometer rose [during] the month of April to the 28th of
June when it was at eighty-eight degrees of farenheit scale,
and I do not find that it has been above ninety this year, which
may be reckoned moderate; though till about the latter end
of September the heat continued the same as in July and
August. . . .

"At Mobile the acid in the air is not more abundant than at
Pensacola; iron and steel is therefore alike liable to rust at
either of these places, but the moisture and damp at Mobile are
very considerable, as I have found by several experiments.
Nay this is evident from viewing the sun in the evenings, which
about five o'clock begins to be a deeper hue and before he sets is
nearly of the color of claret. If one leaves off his shoes for one
day they are quite mouldy, and in the garrison or square the
hardest and best polished wood will gather mouldiness in a short
time. From the wells at Mobile they can only draw what we
call hard water, except it is after a considerable rain; and the
river contains innumerable impurities. . . .

"As to the situation of Mobile you very well know, that from
the east to the north of it, is entirely swamps and marshes, for
as far or even farther than the eye can reach. From the north
point round by the west and to the south it is inclosed with
pine trees and thickets, and from the south to the east is the
bay; though even in that direction some small islands and
marshy points are interposed before the town. The ground
upon which the town stands is as low or even lower than any

thereabout, and the fort is situated on the very lowest spot in the town. . . . There are too many obstacles now in the way, to think of removing it, though there might be several amendments made in the present situation, such as cutting down the woods, particularly towards the Choctaw point, so that from the ramparts of the fort the whole bay might be seen from side to side. The summer sun would then dry up the marshes about that point. The low houses in the fort should be converted into stores, and a second story raised upon them would overlook the walls and serve for barracks.

"The whole parade might be covered with green sod and the ramparts with the same. The outside of the glacis should be cleared, so as to prevent the water from stagnating there, and the earth taken from thence may be laid upon the broken parts of the glacis; thus the soldiers would live in a more cool, airy and healthy situation, at least than [that] of the people in town; but at present either in the fort or in the officers square it is as close and suffocating as if they were put into a great oven. If the wood is cut and cleared away a kind of bank will be found to run all along from the south side of the fort, almost to Mr. Stuarts house on the Choctaw plantation. The people then should be encouraged to take up lots of that ground about one acre each, under the condition of keeping the lower parts well drained, and the higher lands clear of trees or brushwood. They should build their houses in one row along the top of this bank, leaving a street of at least one hundred feet broad to be crossed by a small lane between every two lots. If the three mile creek was then made to run through the town according to a plan which was long ago proposed and for a moderate sum would have been executed, we might expect to see Mobile a very comfortable place to live in all the year round. . . .

"Much has been said concerning a post on the east side of the bay; and for that purpose the Cliffs are generally fixed upon. They are high and some runs of good water are near them; but such a situation would be extremely inconvenient on many accounts. As their situation is in the bite of the bay, they are entirely deprived of the southern breeze by the point below Mr. Wigg's plantation. There is however a bluff between Mr. Durnford's and the French village where the land is sufficiently high, and there are just by it on both sides some springs and small rivulets of the finest water I have seen in the country; and by a little cutting and clearing this point might be rendered more open to the breezes than any on the bay; and the building a blockhouse and establishing a village there would afford the best retreat for those that were attacked with the country diseases at Mobile. But to return; the close and marshy situation of Mobile at present is evidently the cause of these fevers, and the want of some little comfort and conveniences which are indispensably necessary to the recovery of the sick, is the occasion of their frequent relapses. I well know that this is the most disagreeable part of my subject, my duty obliges me to bear witness against the mode prescribed by you in that behalf. For though the commanding officers both at Pensacola and Mobile have always shown the utmost readiness to use any means in their power by which the sick could be benefited; yet while nothing besides the poor remaining pittance of the soldiers' subsistence is allowed, it will never do." The inhabitants, he says, suffer less because less confined and they have better food.

"Another very considerable cause of sickness, though little expected, arises from the small number of men in that garrison; for when there are only ten or twelve men fit to do duty, if any one misses the ague for three or four days, he is very naturally put on guard, and this is the occasion of a certain relapse.

"The small number of troops is likewise productive of another inconvenience, viz., that when fresh meat is allowed, they cannot consume a whole bullock in one day, and in the summer it will not keep till the next."[1]

There is nothing to indicate that any of these suggested improvements were carried out. The sickness in the garrison for several years had given the place a bad name. Adair in 1775 calls it "that graveyard for Britons," and a "black trifle." Romans states next year that the epidemic of 1765 entirely ruined the place; and the preface to Pittman's book says the swamps, dead fish in the marsh opposite the town, and the absence of wholesome water within a mile and a half, caused almost as much suffering in that year to the unacclimated 21st regiment at Mobile as the 31st experienced at Pensacola.

---

[1] *Haldimand Papers*, B., vol. xv. p. 78.

A number of people left from time to time, and few new settlers came, despite the rivers and soil praised by Pittman.[1]

New Orleans was troubled, but in a different way. Spain moved slowly perhaps, but deliberately. Her royal advisers debated what should be done with revolted Louisiana, and determined not to permit such a precedent to stand. Alexander O'Reilly, an Irishman in Spanish service, was sent out with an overwhelming force, and on August 18, 1769, landed at New Orleans. No resistance was offered; in fact O'Reilly was well received. He took firm possession, reorganized the government, and then had the chief revolutionists tried. On October 25 the talented Lafrénière, Pierre Marquis, Joseph Milhet, J. B. Noyan, and Pierre Caresse were shot by a platoon of grenadiers, Jeannot, the negro hangman, having struck off his own arm to avoid acting.[2]

The revolutionists had once planned a republic under the protection of Great Britain, but the British officials in West Florida did not encourage it. Now the British government became uneasy at the O'Reilly expedition, and determined to send the troops back to the old posts in West Florida to be ready for any emergency. Haldimand's opinion was, that the best defense of West Florida was by the fleet; and he thought the approach to the Mississippi through the Iberville River, which was dry in summer, not practicable. But plans now were all changed. Gage in February, 1770, directs him to return to Pensacola to meet the 16th regiment, and distribute them between that place and Mobile.

By the middle of March the troops had reached Pensacola, and Haldimand arrived about a month later. The whole province rejoiced over the return of the military.

They had been gone for a year, and much had taken place. The disorders following Governor Elliott's death had been temporary, and the only effect of the Spanish severity at New Orleans was to make it likely that many French would leave there for Mobile. Governor Browne usually resided at Mobile, and was constantly urging on the home government to intercept some of the Mississippi River Indian trade by building a road

---

[1] *American Indians,* pp. 310, 456 ; Romans' *Florida,* p. 10 ; Pittman's *Mississippi Settlements,* p. vii.

[2] 2 Gayarré's *Louisiana,* pp. 295, 342.

from Natchez to Mobile. He was probably more successful in his recommendation that Acadians from the Atlantic, who had been attracted by the Spaniards, be brought to Mobile. Père Ferdinand had been an Acadian, and was influential amongst them. He recommended that the government pay Ferdinand a salary of fifty guineas, but this was refused. Browne finally left the province after a duel with one man and calling out two others, who apologized. He had intended challenging others, but was bound over to keep the peace. This spring of 1770, Elias Durnford, thanks to Haldimand's influence, was acting governor.

Governor Durnford recommended to the home government that a substitute for Mobile be built at the Cliffs, between his land on the one side and Mr. Wegg's on the other. He urged the healthfulness of the site and the depth of water in front. But all that was done was the establishment of a summer resort for the troops. Captain Crofton built the long-talked-of resort at the Red Cliffs, and there such of the 31st as were not needed at Fort Charlotte were taken. Certainly a more healthful spot than those piny woods bluffs below Montrose could not be found, and, if it was near where the cliff near Rock Creek towers sheer a hundred feet above the bay, the wide view over the blue water would charm those in health as much as it would the invalids. Nothing remains of the camp and tradition has lost the site, but, on account of water for drinking, there near the creek it must have been.

By August the troops in Fort Charlotte were in miserable condition, and both Brown and Lorimer were employed either at Mobile or the new encampment, Croftown, where the sick were taken from Mobile as they could be moved. Haldimand approved the captain's acts, and sent him tools. Crofton in this month asks for molasses to make spruce beer, and reports the men recovering. We do not know whether he used local pottery, but Romans says the finest potter's clay he ever saw was at the village not far away on Mobile Bay, where the inhabitants, like the Indians before and the Americans after them, made domestic vessels.[1]

The civil and military authorities seem on this occasion to have agreed for once. It was as to establishing a ferry over

[1] Romans' *Florida*, p. 33.

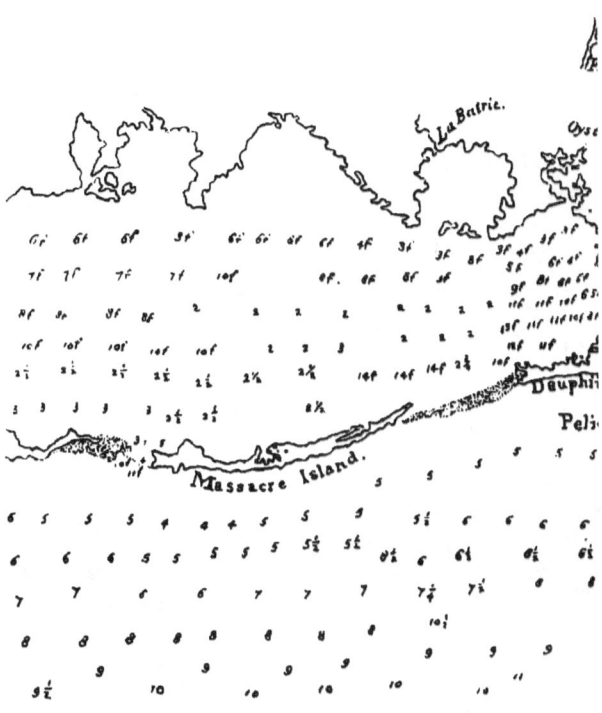

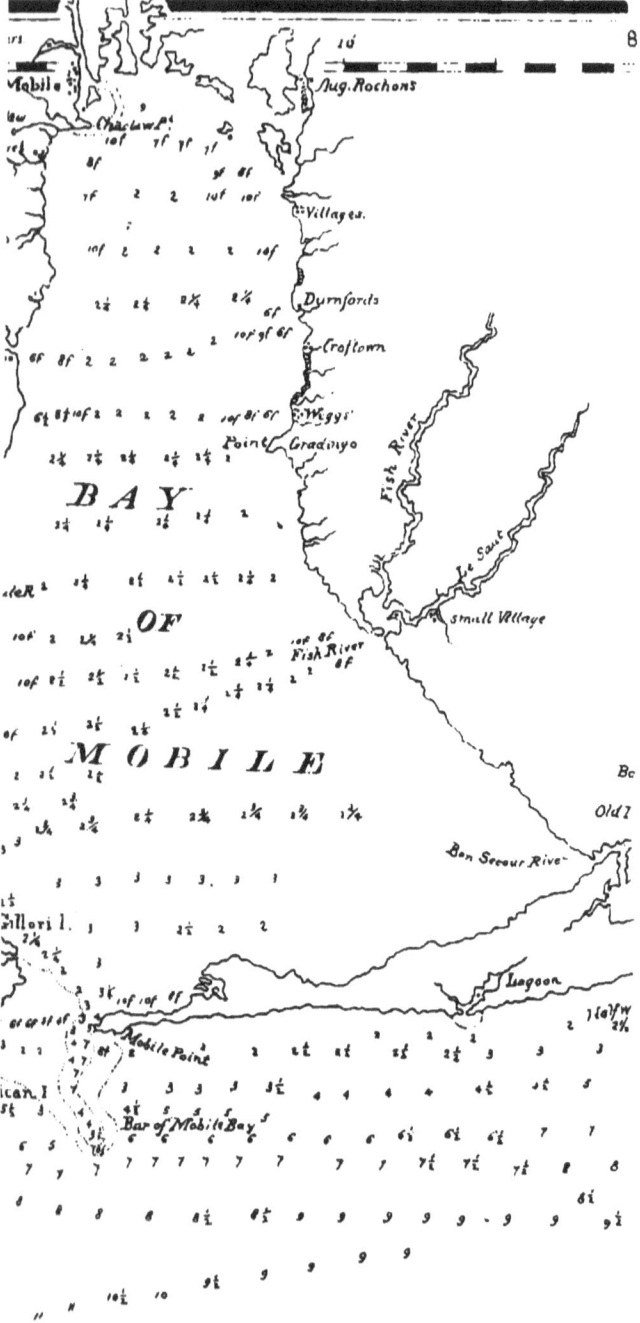

Mobile

Aug. Rochons

Chactaws

Villages

Durnfords

Croftown

Mggs

Point Gradingo

Fish River

BAY

OF

Le Saut

small Village

MOBILE

Fish River

Bc

Old I

Bon Secour River

Ellori I.

Lagoon

Mobile Point

ican I.

Bar of Mobile Bay

the Perdido and cutting the road from Mobile to Pensacola, long before designed by Durnford while engineer. It also embraced the canoe ferry once recommended by Farmer to be established between Mobile and Apalache Old Town. The authorities took care of the bridges, and also the Perdido ferry, but the Mobile merchants maintained the express to Pensacola to communicate with British packets.

We meet a little touch of modern times in November in the complaint of the widow Lemarque to Haldimand that certain officers had left without paying their board, — a shabby act, certainly. What the general did for her is not known. It is to be hoped he did not turn over to her the provision stores just reported to him by Strother as spoiled.

Before sending the troops to Mobile, Haldimand had a survey and report on the condition of Fort Charlotte from T. Sower, commanding engineer. He found that there was not a single building belonging to his Majesty but needed some repairs. All the picketing whatever was entirely decayed about the fort. So of the hospital in town, and "the Indian House, one hundred feet long and forty broad, wants its roof repaired." This was the "Savage House" of earlier times.

Of the fort he says: "The fort is a square with four bastions; has embrasures for thirty-eight guns. . . . The fort is built of brick; has four bastions; the curtains are casemated. Two bastions are likewise casemated. In the southeast bastion is a powder magazine, and in the west-northwest one is a bakehouse; both of these bastions are bomb-proof. The parapet, ramparts, and bankets are all of brick. The barracks are composed of upright posts put into the ground, with some framing to the windows and doors; the vacancies of which are filled up with clay and Spanish Beard, and whitewashed over; these two piles consist of nine rooms each."

The officers' square was then arranged as follows. On the left, as one entered, was the guard-room; on the right, the provision store. Near were the men's barracks, and on the north side of the square the officers' barracks, with adjacent kitchen. Opposite were two wells, shingled over, and behind the officers' barracks was a small building of four rooms, also meant for officers. All buildings in this square were of brick. The new bakehouse, of which we learned in 1763, had now gone entirely to decay for want of covering.

"As all the barracks in Fort Charlotte," he continues, "were found so much decayed as not to be worth repairing, and in order to save expense, it was judged necessary to repair the officers' square of barracks, formerly called so by the Spaniards, which is within one hundred yards of the fort, for the accommodation of his Majesty's troops, as all the buildings in the above mentioned square was good, being built with bricks." This had been Farmer's work, and he had begun a brick bastion over by the bakehouse.

"This square is fitted up for the reception of two companies with their complement of officers, which are now well lodged, and, by adding four small stockaded bastions to the corners of the square, could defend themselves against Indians. But as this square is not quite so convenient, nor large enough to protect the inhabitants which are now remaining at Mobile in case of an Indian war, I would recommend that the old communication between Fort Charlotte and the square be stockaded as it formerly was, which would save the inhabitants to retire to, with their effects, in case of any rupture with the Indians in that part of the country."

This shows that Lorimer's report had had the effect of the abandonment of the fort for residence of the troops. In March, 1771, the repairs were under full way, the contractor at Mobile, and at Croftown too, being the energetic Pierre Rochon. A great deal was done at Red Cliffs more particularly, and on April 1 Croftown was finished. It embraced a palisaded battery, with powder magazine and blockhouse in the rear. There Haldimand proposed to move some of the ordnance and stores from Fort Charlotte. Rochon was hard at work in Mobile, too, on the barracks and stockade, and on boats to be sent to Haldimand at Pensacola. It was all none too soon. There were Indian outrages reported. May 8 the inhabitants sent a petition, which was laid before Governor Chester, asking protection, and on the same day Captain Connor reported to General Haldimand that the Choctaws had become so hardy as even to strike the sentry of Fort Charlotte. Chester promptly called the attention of the general to the matter. Somewhat later, too, Choctaws destroyed cattle on Dugald Campbell's plantation. Another party robbed a trader within twenty miles of Mobile, and Creeks forced the abandonment of three plantations on the bay, near the pass of Dauphine Island. Other Indians, probably Creeks, attacked the house of Tryon on the Alabama fifty miles above Mobile, and also compelled Hamton, Fleming, and others to abandon neighboring places, claiming that the whites did not belong north of Apalache Old Fields.

It is pleasant to turn to the side lights in the correspondence between Rochon and the general. The contractor was compelled by his wife's illness in April to remain at Mobile, and from there he sends a few dozen fowls as a compliment. He was building boats, one a schooner for the government, but had to wait until the middle of May for a sailmaker from New Orleans. His own schooner was taken for carrying guns, but he has the policy to express himself as satisfied about it. He asks that his white workmen have rations at the royal tariff, which he will repay if not allowed. To Pensacola he sends over *diables*, — despite the name, the peaceful articles we call log carts, — and also two pairs of oxen. Once Rochon expresses the intention of coming to Pensacola after finishing his work at Mobile, which would be by the 20th of June. He was anxious to obtain further employment, in order to refit his house, spoiled by the bad conduct of his children; but he does not let us into the particulars of this domestic affair. This home may have been at Dog River, whence later letters are to be dated.

Pierre Rochon was also a slaveholder, and his clear, bold signature to the negro baptismal entries contrasts strangely with the cramped hand of Père Ferdinand, the Acadian. This good father continues his ministrations during the English times. The same forms, the same words, all in French as before, continue in this record, in the same thin book that had been paged and issued to him in 1757 by the French commandant. Forneret, R. Roi (the Indian interpreter), Montelimart, Lusser, Trouillet, Girard, A. Rochon as well as Pierre, Chastang, Demouy, Grelot, Carrière, Badou, Monlouis, and others, bring their children or slaves to him for baptism as in the old days, or attest his entries, as they chat with the father of French times and friends. The inhabitants were not able to support him, however, and about 1771 he retired to New Orleans. Twenty-six of them earnestly petitioned next year for his recall, and Governor Chester warmly recommended it, and that a salary be allowed him. We find him back at Mobile again, although Lord Hillsborough refused the salary, and we can imagine the good father's welcome home.

But they would soon come to notice, as we do even now, the trembling hand and almost illegible writing, at last the abbreviated entries, often unsigned, of the curé, seldom filled out now with the titles "capuchin priest, apostolic missionary," as he had once loved to write himself. Some time, it may be not long after that last signature under the marginal date 1773, the old citizens closed his eyes, and, in or near the church he had served so long, laid to rest with tears the beloved form which had connected for them this half-deserted British outpost with the Mobile of Grondel and Bienville. The church is gone, its very site uncertain, the grave and its contents now unknown; but somewhere near our St. Emanuel and Theatre, it may be in street, it may be by some home, lies the dust of Ferdinand, the last French curé of Mobile.

CHAPTER XXVII.

THE acquisition of Florida by the English caused the production of a number of books relating to the Indians, geography, plants and animals as well. Jeffreys, Pittman, and
Roberts we have already noticed, and have now to follow the
travels of Bernard Romans, who was an army captain; and later
we shall study those of William Bartram, a botanist. The
first went over the Tombigbee district in 1771–72 for Superintendent Stuart, and the other over the Alabama and Mobile
country some five years later. Both show the interest taken
in the new possessions, and the study to find out what could be
made of them for commercial purposes.

Romans says that after making arrangements with Superintendent Stuart, he left Mobile at four P. M. on Saturday, September 20, 1771, with a party of Choctaws. He spent his first
night "in pine land near a spring to the north of the path and
at the foot of a hill six miles from town, the west a little by
south." It is difficult to fix many of his locations, but there
can be no reasonable doubt that this first stop was at or near
Spring Hill. Thence on for some days they were crossing or
heading Dog River and other streams, and then arrived on the
banks of the Pascagoula River. Near there they found an
Indian "hieroglyphick," or picture-writing, of which he gives
an illustration, as he does also of one found a few days later.
The first was a Choctaw memorial of having killed and scalped
nine Creeks, and the second a Creek one showing that warriors
of the Stag family had at Hoopah Ullah scalped two men and
two women and rowed off in triumph.

Rain deterred them somewhat, but on the 27th they crossed
Bogue Hooma (Red Creek), the boundary between the English
and Choctaws, and three days later reached the Bogue-aithee-
Tanne (our Buckatunna), and at Hoopah Ullah, or Noisy Owl,

found the second "hieroglyphick." The country was alternately pine and oak, savannah, swamp, and hill; and they often
passed through hurricane lands, and frequently saw such marks
of Indians as paths, fields, and old camps, with occasionally a
head on a pole to remind them of the Creek-Choctaw war.
One day they saw three graves, — the first of a Tombecbé
soldier; one of a savage, after whom it was named Rum-drinker's Hill; and the other of a trader named Brown, who had done
considerable business in the "Chactaw" and Chickasaw nations.
Near the Choctaw town of Coosa they found peaches, "plumbs,"
and grapes.

November 4, they were aided by Indians in crossing the
Sookahanatcha (Sucarnochee), and at East Abeeka found
Choctaws exulting over a victory. There the travelers put up
at the house of Hewitt, a resident trader. This place had a
stockade fort, and like Abeetap-Oocoola was a frontier town
against the Creeks. George Dow now became their guide.
Amongst many Choctaw towns chronicled, Moka Lassa is a
familiar and important name; and Romans passed near the site
of East Congeata, destroyed in the Choctaw civil war. On
the 23d they reached Chickasawhay, and stayed at the house
of Ben James.

Romans made quite a circuit of the Choctaw territory, going
even to Yoani, and returning to trader Hewitt's house at
Abeeka. Thence he went to the Chickasaw nation, crossing
Nashooba (Noxubee) and Okatebbechaw (Oktibbeha) rivers on
the way. The Indian commissary treated him very cavalierly,
and awakened the captain's ire by taking away his horse.

He reached the Tombigbee at last, apparently near where
Bienville disembarked to attack the Chickasaws. On December
13 he, his servant, and Mr. Dow embarked on Town Creek, .
after catching beavers. Perhaps its name of White Man's
Trouble (Nahoola-Inalchubba) refers to Bienville's defeat. On
the first day they passed the site of an old French fortified trading-house on a bluff. His voyage took him by bluffs and lowlands, sand-bars, gravel islands, and pine banks; sometimes
running rapids, sometimes detained by logs, or cutting his
way through cypress-trees in the river. Romans was so unfortunate, after killing some ducks and teals, as to have his gun
torn from his hands by a snag, and see it sink beyond recovery
in deep and rapid water. This was near Aberdeen.

The weather was wretched, being cold, snowing, or rainy, often detaining them for days in camp. They passed the last branch of the Tombigbee (probably the Buttahatchie), then the stony Sonac Tocale,[1] and a number of creeks, none recognizable by his Indian names except "Old Town Creek," Okatibbehaw (Fighting Water, from being the Choctaw-Chickasaw boundary), and Eleven Mile Creek (Luxa-pali-lah, or Floating Turtle). He had an eye for the romantic, too, and described at some length a remarkable crescent bluff [Barton's], rising fifty feet above the water, and extending almost a mile and a half along the river. This was near the modern Columbus.

Before the 28th of December they had traveled fifty-eight miles and three quarters, having lately passed few creeks. On that day they began to see more rapids and high land than before, and had their first evidence of human life. Thence on, his journal will be given almost entire.

"An hour and a half after leaving camp," he says, "we saw a bark log, just landed on the west side, and evident marks of people having just landed; this was in a long reach, and we had seen a smoak, but when we came near the bark log the smoak vanished all at once. We soon found these people to be a war party of Creeks, who, perceiving our boat, had put out their fire, which on these occasions they make of hickory bark and other oily matters that yield little smoak. We therefore put on our hats, which we had not on before, it being a fine agreeable day and rather warm, and, laying on the paddles, did all we could to show that we were white people. It was fortunate for me that I had not brought a savage guide with me, which would have exposed us to a volley from these warriors: we did not see them, but we knew by the suppression of the smoak, that they had discovered us; they were undoubtedly on the top of a pretty high bank, in ambush, so we let the boat flow past them. N. B. We have discovered many of those bark logs, made of cones, both above and below this place, upon which the war party ferry over. Half a mile

---

[1] This means Hanging Kettle. For the more difficult identifications given I am much indebted to the learned Dr. W. S. Wyman, Captain Frank Stone, and to Messrs. Williams and Jackson, pilots of the river. In meanings of words these notes reflect the views of Dr. Wyman. The edition of Romans used is that of New York, 1776, pp. 303–334, etc.

lower down we saw the mouth of a middling large creek, on the east side. . . . The river is here above two hundred feet wide. Having come twenty-three miles, we encamped at four o'clock on a gravel bar. We saw many places that appeared like old fields, as having been formerly cultivated.

"29th. At nine o'clock proceeded. . . . We saw again some spots bearing marks of former cultivation, and more of drowned land; the river in general this day rapid, with many islands [perhaps Ten Mile Shoals]: at half an hour past three P. M., having . traveled thirty-five miles, we encamped on the east side in a lagoon, on a high bank, where for the first time we saw the rich ground clear of large canes; this being timbered chiefly with the shagbark hickory, ironwood, and Spanish oak.

"30th. This morning we had our boat loaded, but it began to rain, and thus were obliged to unload again. Here we found a canoe, which was well made, but had been by the savages, on account of the war, scuttled, and rendered unfit for use; however we found that, if we could make her anyways tight, she would be more safe than the one that we had, and this we effected by the help of wedges, clay, and leather. Our provisions beginning to grow scant, and having lost the only gun I had taken with me, I began to be uneasy, especially as we found the beavers become less plenty. The weather was uncommonly bad till the evening of the third of January, 1772, when it cleared up, and next morning,

"4th January, 1772, at a quarter before eleven o'clock A. M., we proceeded in our new craft. . . . The canoe proves very leaky, and on unloading we find a great deal of our bread spoiled. This day came twenty-two miles and an half; the canes and timber are very exceeding large.

"5th. At a quarter past ten embarked: high banks on both sides. At half an hour after eleven past the mouth of a river from the east: this is called by the savages Nashebaw [probably Sipsey [1] River, in Alabama]. The land here is exceeding rich, the canes very large; and we saw a species of phaseolus, in great abundance, along the bank. About a mile and a quarter below the creek, we met four savages from Abeka, in the Choctaw nation, to whom Mr. Dow was known. The river has risen considerably since yesterday; the current

---

[1] Meaning Poplar Tree. The Choctaw *Nashoba* means Wolf.

has been for these two days almost uniformly at the rate of three miles per hour. It is remarkable, that though the velocity of our way was not much above two miles per hour independent of the current, yet we had several instances of having evidently outrun the flood at night, in so much that it would scarce reach us again before morning. We came to camp near the savages above mentioned, having come seven miles and a half; they had a good canoe which I intended to purchase. The weather was very cold to-day. Lost a silver spoon at our last camp, which Mr. Dow proposed to go and fetch; but he found it impracticable to cross the Nasbehaw River. I agreed with the savages that they should hunt for us to procure provisions. At night it rained; our camp was on the east side, in a very rich spot. We have not yet seen any sand or gravel, except on the bars and islands in the river, the soil in general being clay, or loam, with a dry black mould.

"6th. After a great deal of persuasion, I bought the canoe from the savages; and they brought me in two deer and a turkey, for all which I gave them five yards of blue strouds, two powder horns, knife and some small shot. I described our last camp to them, and desired them to look for the above mentioned spoon, directing them to leave it in their own country with Mr. Dow's partner, who lived just by their homes, and gave them a note to him, desiring him to pay them for their trouble; but when they understood it to be the *white stone* (*i. e.*) silver, they declined going purposely for it; but promised, if chance led them to the place, to carry it as directed, for, they not being able to work it, in case the trader refused to pay them they would lose their labor; but had it been *the fat of the earth*[1] (*i. e.*) lead or pewter, in that case they might make bullets or ear-rings of it, and then they would not take pains in vain: towards evening they left us, and during night we barbecued our venison to preserve it.

"7th. At half an hour past seven o'clock A. M. embarked in our new craft; all day we passed between high banks, some steep, some sloping; several as high as eighty feet above the surface of the water; one of these has an extensive savannah on the top. At the end of nineteen miles and a half, on the west side, we saw the mouth of the river Noxshubby [Noxu-

[1] The Choctaw for these is *Talla-hatta* and *Yakne-em-belah*.

bee], or Hatchaoose;[1] its banks are high on both sides; here seems to be the true theatre of the war, for the bark logs are very numerous.   The river is widened now from two hundred to two hundred and fifty feet.   A mile and a half below the mouth of Noxshubby is the first bluff of arid ochre, like earth, very high and steep [Gainesville], and about eight-miles lower a white one, being a kind of stone almost as soft as chalk. . . . At four o'clock P. M. we came to camp on a low spot, on the east side, having gone down the river forty-two miles and a half; all day dull weather, and at night rain.

"8th.   Proceeded half an hour after 8 A. M. and having gone a little more than a mile, we reached the mouth of the creek called Ectomboguebé (*i. e.* Crooked Creek), on the west side; from this creek's name the French derive their Tombechbé, the name of the fort which stood here, and which has again given that name to the whole river [probably Tom's Creek].[2]   We went about half a mile further down, under a high and steep bank of chalky stone, and arrived at the ruins of the fort by means of which the French kept all the savages in awe.   I went ashore in the old fields, and drew a view of the ruins; this is about forty miles east from the town of Abeeka.   The river is not sixty feet wide here.   About a mile and a half below these ruins is a pretty high but sloping slaty bluff: having come about nine miles, we arrived at a hunting camp of Choctaws, on the west side, who invited us on shore, treated us very kindly, and spared us some venison, bear's meat and oil.   The afternoon being stormy, with hail and rain, we encamped at a small distance from them: the canes were not very plenty here, but the land rich: a great deal of the plant called Indian Hemp grows in this place, but the season deprived me of the satisfaction of knowing what genus it is of.

"9th.   At half an hour past eleven proceeded, and in an hour and a quarter we passed by Chickianoee,[3] a white bluff [Bluffport] with a savannah on its top, on the west side; it is upwards of seventy feet high above the water's level: we passed

---

[1] *Oka-nak-shobe* is Choctaw for " Water which has a foul smell," while *Hatcha-Use* means Pumpkin Creek.

[2] Wyman thinks the creek's name, *Ish-tam-bok* (Crooked Creek), was different from *Ectomba-ikbee*, Coffin-maker, the name of the river.

[3] *Chiki-anowah* would mean Chickasaw Walk.

several high bluffs, among which one is yellow like Ochre.
. . . Having travelled twenty-four miles, came to camp at
four o'clock P. M. on the east side, at the beginning of a steep
slaty bluff.

"10th. At a half an hour past nine, A. M. proceeded; we
went between high bluffs, and in two hours came to the mouth
of Tuscaloosa River [Black Warrior] from the east; and a
little below it is the steep, white, chalky bluff on whose top is a
vast plain [Demopolis], and some remains of huts in it; the
bluff is called the Chickasaw Gallery, because from here the
savages used to annoy the French boats going up to the fort, or
down from it. The river is hereabouts full of rapids and bad
passes: we came past a number of high bluffs, most of them
chalky. At half an hour past three we passed the mouth of
Sookhanatcha [Sucarnochee][1] from the west, and three miles
below it came to camp, at four o'clock P. M., at the foot of the
hill where formerly the Coosadas[2] were settled: this place
is called Suktaloosa (*i. e.* Black Bluff), from its being a kind
of coal: it is a great thorough-fare for warring savages; therefore we took the usual precaution of large fires, and hanging
our hats on stakes, which we had reason to think not in vain;
for in the night we heard the report of small arms. This day
we came thirty-six miles. It is worthy of remark, that although we have come near seventy miles from the ruins of
Tombechbé, yet by land the distance is not above twenty-four
or twenty-five miles. The land here is very fine, and Mr.
Dow told me that he had lived here with the Coosadas, and
that the common yield of corn was from sixty to eighty bushels
per acre; that they increased horses and hogs to any degree
they pleased; and that venison, turkies, and fish were uncommonly plenty.

"11th. Last night and this morning being rainy, we could
not proceed till eleven o'clock. All this day we passed through
the remains of the Coosada and Occhoy settlements,[3] being all

---

[1] *Shukha-nachaba*, Choctaw for Hog's Backbone.

[2] Some of the Coosadas, who were of Alibamon, not Creek stock, moved
west when the French abandoned Fort Toulouse. In 1766, they were at war
with the Choctaws and seem to have been worsted.

[3] The Okchays had been in the Coosa region. They were apparently of
Choctaw stock and accompanied the Coosadas in their migration. There is
a bluff in the northeast corner of Choctaw County still called West Okchai.

a fine tract of ground, of which much had been cleared; but it is now again overgrown with reeds; the grand, or public plantation in particular is an excellent tract. At four o'clock P. M. we encamped on a little plain, under a bluff, where was a large hunting camp, to appearance about two years old; here we saw some stones, having been deeply marked by the savages with some uncouth marks, but most of them being straight lines and crossed. I have since been led to conjecture, whether they were not occasioned by these people grinding their awls on these stones; yet they do not ill resemble inscriptions: this place is a pretty situation, and is nearly two miles below the deserted Occhoy town, which stood likewise near a black coaly bluff; the distance we made this day is twenty-one miles; we had fine weather during the day, but the night was showery.

"12th. At half an hour past 8 A. M. proceeded. All this day we saw marks of great fertility of soil, and much tolerably high land: at half an hour past ten we were at a creek called Abeshaï; at a quarter past eleven, at the last Occhoy field, by a creek called Bashailawaw;[1] at eleven A. M., at the hills of Nana Falaya,[2] on the east side, which rise steep out of the water about fifteen or twenty feet, then slope up into very high short pine hills. Some parts of the rock are red, others grey. Here we were overtaken by very bad weather, from which took shelter; at half an hour past one P. M. we encamped about three quarters of a mile below the hill, on the slope of a pretty high bank, where we found the remains of a camp that had been occupied lately by white people; we came about eleven miles and a half this day; the rain continued till two o'clock A. M. next day, when the wind shifting to W. N. W. it grew excessively cold.

"13th. At half an hour past ten A. M. proceeded; at one o'clock we came to a hill on the east side, with an old field on its summit; this hill is called Batcha-Chooka [Tuscahoma]; here we found a notorious gang of thieves, belonging to the town of Oka Loosa (Black Water), a town in the Chactaw nation.

---

[1] This seems to mean "boundary," but unlike Bashai Creek, in Clarke County, was on no boundary now known. .

[2] This means Long Bluff, *nunnih*, accented on the second syllable, denoting bluff. In a previous note Romans says that by pine he always means *Pinus Abies Virginiana, conis parvis subrotundis*, the Balm of Gilead Pine.

When we saw their raft, we took them to be a Creek war party; therefore, being hailed by them, and not choosing to be shot at, we went near the shore; but on discovering who they were, I refused to land; they still insisted we must, but my obstinate persisting to the contrary disappointed their sanguine hopes of plunder, and after some altercation I proceeded. This day the marks of fertility of soil are not so uninterrupted as on the former days. Our weather was clear, and a strong northerly wind prevailed; we came nineteen miles since morning, and encamped on the west side, in a low spot of ground.

"14th. Last night the frost was severe; at a quarter past nine A. M. proceeded; in half an hour's time we saw very high hills, at a mile, or better, from the river, seemingly covered with pine timber; these hills the savages call Nanna Chahaws.[1] Here is a steep place above forty feet perpendicular out of the water, and another steep above it; the last is a grey slaty rock; this place is called Tecakhaily Ekutapa, and the people from Chicasahay had a settlement here before the war. [Macarty's Ferry.] About a mile and a quarter from hence is a remarkable white sand hill on the east side; four miles lower, we came to Yagna-hoolah[2] (*i. e.* the Beloved Ground), which lies on the east side and is very high, continuing above two miles along the river bank; its lower part is steep and of a whitish grey, and at the end above two hundred feet high, reckoning perpendicularly [Witch Creek Hill]. A mile below this is a white sand hill on the west side; we saw the pine hills all this day, at various distances from the river, sometimes close to it, and the canes begin to diminish, and pine trees mix among the timber. The current for these two last days is very considerably slackened, and the river widened to above five hundred feet. We came about thirty miles and a half this day, and encamped at four o'clock P. M. on the side of a kind of bluff, about six miles below a branch called Isawaya;[3] all day cold, the latter part dull and hazy; at a quarter past nine proceeded. Eight miles

---

[1] Just below Wood's Bluff. This buhrstone formation makes up the most picturesque spot on the river. The meaning is High Hills, and the hills do not cease until at Oven Bluff, near McIntosh's.

[2] *Yakne-hulo,* Holy Ground.

[3] The Crouching Deer, far more romantic than the senseless Sea Warrior into which the Americans have converted the word.

below our camp we were at the mouth of Senti Bogue [1] (*i. e.* Snake Creek), having an island in its mouth, and coming from the westward.   Two miles and a quarter lower is Atchatickpé [Hatchetigbee],[2] a large bay or lagoon on the same side; at this place is the beginning of our boundary with the Chactaws, running from the west till it strikes Senti-Bogue, and then follows 'the course of said creek up to a certain sugar-loaf hill, and so over to Bogue Hooma and Bakkatanè.[3]   A mile below this, at the bending of the river, is a bluff, but not very high, of a dark grey stone: above this it rises gradually, sloping into a very high hill, variegated into small ridges.   We saw many spots of pines, and some white sand hills; but in general the soil has a better appearance than yesterday.   About an hour before we encamped, we came to the last rapids [McGrew's Shoals], or the first from below; here is a remarkable spot of yellow rock in the western bank, beginning with a high, perpendicular, white rock with some grass spots [near St. Stephens]; it is above fifty feet above the present surface of the water; its top is level and shrubby; in the middle projects a remarkable lump, which in coming down looks exactly like a buttress against a wall.   At four o'clock, P. M. we encamped on the east side in the low ground, above a mile below the rocks, having come thirty-one miles.   The weather has been clear and cold all this day.   Stout sloops and schooners may come up to this rapid; therefore I judge that here some considerable settlement will take place.

"16th.   Proceeded at half an hour past eight A. M.   Having come about fifteen miles, we saw the remains of the old Weetumpkee settlement: about seven miles below this, on the east side, is an odd rocky bluff, appearing to be sandy, and is covered with cedar trees [Carney's Bluff].   The river here is very crooked; and about six miles below, on the west side, we saw a spacious old field, and a smoak in one edge of it; but nobody near it; and two miles lower down, hearing a rustling

---

[1] *Sinte-bok.*

[2] This seems to mean Neck of Bottle Stream, possibly from expansion of the river into the lagoon, now long since filled and cultivated.   Old pilots remember the lagoon.

[3] Bogue Homa, or Red Creek, is a branch of the Buckatunna, which means " Creek on the other side."

in the canes, we looked that way, and saw a savage in a war
dress, lying flat; finding himself perceived, he got up and beck-
oned to us; but although we were within ten feet of him, we
seemed not to have remarked him, upon which he lay down
again: it is to be imagined that he was not alone, and that this
was a war party, who had been at the smoak in the old field,
and having perceived us had come to this place, knowing that
here we must come near the bank; but seeing that we were not
Chactaws, and thinking themselves undiscovered, kept close.
At a quarter past four o'clock P. M. we came to a camp on the
west side, which we supposed by the boats, etc., to be occupied
by white people, in which opinion we were soon confirmed.
When they invited us on shore, we found they were one Thomas
Baskett, with two white hunters and some Chactaws; we were
here well regaled with excellent meat and very good bread,
which, being prepared in an excellent manner, was a noble feast
to us. I purchased some bear, bacon, and venison hams of
them, and staid all night at their camp; the distance we came
this day was thirty-one miles.

"17th. Embarked at half an hour past nine A. M. and
proceeded, accompanied by two canoes with savages: we soon
passed by some high pine hills on the east side; and at their
end, having come about two miles, we were at the little creek
called Apé-Bogue-oosè [Choctaw for " little salt creek "],
which is a spring so intensely salt that, the savages told us,
three kettles of its water yield one of salt. Having then
proceeded four hours through low land on each side, we arrived
at the place called by the French The Forks, being a lagoon
divided into three branches [Three Rivers], whereof the first
is called Ape Tonsa, the second Beelosa, and the third Caänta-
calamoo: here the savages left us; we still proceeded for half
an hour more through low land, and then came to a large bay,
at the end whereof begins the Tomechettee bluff [McIntosh's],
where formerly a tribe of that nation resided; this is the first
time we have the real pine barren butting on the river; it is
very level.[1] About five miles below this place, we came to the
first islands that are of note [Bilbo's Island]; the land con-

---

[1] Romans does not mention this as the residence of James McIntosh,
Indian interpreter under the British ; but it was so at this or some other
time.

tinues low and pretty rich: here we see the first summer canes.[1]
At six o'clock P. M. we came to the Coosadas bluff, having
had the Naniabe (*i. e.* Fish Killer's Island) [Nana Hubba]
above an hour on our west side; this place was the last settlement of the Coosadas after they left Suktaloosa; and in little
more than half an hour we were at the mouth of the great Ali-
bamo River. We passed the Nita Abe, or Bear Killer's Bluff,
on the left, and at nine o'clock P. M. we came to the north end
of the island, which divides the branch called Dog River [the
Tensaw] from the west branch of the river. Here we stayed
all night at the plantation of the Chevalier de Lucere, but found
only three or four old slaves and children, the whole of the able
hands and the overseer being gone to make tar-kilns, so that
we had but indifferent fare. We came this day forty-two miles
and a half. N. B. These islands are very fertile, and have a
great many plantations on them, on the branches which lay out
of our way, particularly on the Taënsa and Dog rivers.

"18th. At a quarter past nine A. M. proceeded; passed
several plantations, as well on the islands as on the main,
particularly Campbell's, Stuart's, Ardry's, and M'Gillivray's:
at half an hour past eleven A. M. arrived at Mr. Favre's house,
where I stayed in order to get some refreshment; this being
the first Christian habitation I had been at since the 20th
September last year. Mr. Favre treated us in a most friendly,
genteel and hospitable manner. At one o'clock some boats
went up the river, which I heard were Mr. Stuart's people,
with a provincial deputy surveyor, going up to ascertain the
boundary between us and the Chactaws. At two o'clock some
gentlemen, among whom was Major Dixon, of the sixteenth
regiment, and Charles Stuart, deputy superintendent of Indian
affairs (to whom I described Atchatikpè and Senti-Bogue, where
they were to begin), followed them: they proceeded up to Mr.
Stuart's plantation, about three miles higher up the river. We
had come seven miles and a quarter this day. In the afternoon
it began to rain, and all night was a prodigious storm of wind
and rain, which I had the pleasure of weathering out under

---

[1] Romans presented Superintendent Stuart with part of a cane cut on
this trip which measured 47 feet from the third joint up. The joints were
20 inches long and above 5 in circumference. He says it was not an extraordinary instance.

a good roof; here we found several families of Chactaw savages.

"19th. At a quarter past nine A. M. we proceeded; went past Chastang's, Strother's, and Narbonne's plantations, having chiefly pine land on the main, and the rich islands on our left all this day. Having gone five miles and three quarters, we passed by the ruins of Fort Condé, or old Mobile [27 Mile Bluff], and near six miles lower down we passed by the ruins of a fine plantation, formerly belonging to the French Intendant at Mobile, now to Mr. Lizard at the same place [21 Mile Bluff [1]]: four miles and three quarters lower down, we met with the first marsh; the river being very full, we could not learn how far the salt water had its effect, the bay itself being fresh and good at this time; but Mr. Dow, who had been several times up and down this river, and had lived with the Coosadas for some years, assured me that the tide was very visible at the old Wetumpkee settlements, and in extraordinary tides even as far as Sukta Loosa, where, during his residence on the spot, he has frequently seen it ebb and flow about an inch. We came this day thirty-five miles and a half, and at nine o'clock P. M. we arrived at Mobile."

---

[1] This Mr. Lizard has given his name to the bayous east of this place at 21 Mile Bluff and obscured the earlier history. The French intendant, or more properly commandant, alluded to as the first owner, as Dubroca testifies in an existing Spanish inquest, was Beauchamps, for whom the bayou was named. Beauchamps sold to Grondel, in whose honor the plantation was called St. Philippe, which apparently has led to the idea of first Fort Louis' having that name. Grondel sold to Populus and he then to Pechon. On the coming of the English it was bought by Lizard & Co., who erected a mill there. After Romans' trip we learn that Lizard was murdered, and at an auction the place became the property of John McGillivray, the well-known British merchant at Mobile.

CHAPTER XXVIII.

SUCCEEDING years brought little change to Mobile. The fort and barracks were repaired and two companies were stationed there, but little advance was effected beyond trade with the Indians. Haldimand, in June, 1771, took twelve twelvepounders from Fort Charlotte to Pensacola, substituting, as he wrote Gage, "small pieces to satisfy the inhabitants, who, to obtain more troops, pretend to be afraid."

We do not read of so much sickness in the garrison this summer, although there was some; but in November we find Haldimand corresponding with Pierre Rochon the younger at Pensacola, who speaks of the death of his father. The mantle had descended on worthy shoulders, and the young man announces that he will carry out his father's agreements and intentions. Missing planks, for instance, will be supplied. The last letter preserved from the father was dated July 11, from Mobile. Haldimand no doubt missed his old friend when on November 28 he was in Mobile to attend a Congress of Chickasaws.

In January, 1772, Lord Hillsborough, for the British cabinet, wrote to General Gage from Whitehall to set at rest the old question as to control of the forts; for the popular Peter Chester, governor since 1770, had reopened it. It was decided in favor of the governor, and the general was to exercise authority only over the troops. This no doubt settled the question also as to the house which Chester maintained in the fort at Pensacola, always submitted to reluctantly by the military.

Haldimand writes Gage in February of another difference with the governor. Durnford had finished his surveys, — in fact the well-known admiralty chart dates from 1771, — and the general had sent the bill for expenses to Chester. These the governor insisted should be paid by the general, who retorted that the survey was for the good of the whole province, which received a sufficient subsidy. He had just visited the country. West of Mobile Bay he found it barren and liable to floods. There was only one settler on the river.

This was not to remain true long, for Chester's congress at the end of December, 1771, showed the Choctaws friendly. Almost two thousand were present, and, besides British officials, Robert Farmer, William Struthers, Alexander McIntosh, and Daniel Ward were there among the principal Mobilians. One matter of complaint by the savages would seem to have been the granting of lands to whites up the Alabama, this being beyond the Tensaw River, which they deemed the natural boundary.

Shortly after this the plan was seriously discussed of demolishing Fort Charlotte, and taking the brick to Pensacola for building some batteries contemplated there. Engineer Sowers estimated that there would be 16,000 brick thus available. Haldimand finally decided against such removal, although he favored putting bastions to the square; while about the same time, May, Governor Chester determined to destroy Fort Charlotte. The design was not carried out, but may be Chester would have had his way at last, — if, a few years later, Galvez had not had *his*.

A good deal of interest was taken in settling the banks of the Mississippi. Durnford was sent there to explore the Iberville River, but Gage declared it useless. The English, he said, must possess New Orleans in order to utilize the river, and he and Haldimand discussed from time to time plans for invasion of Louisiana in case of war with Spain. The Indians, too, were under constant surveillance. Charles Stuart or John Stuart made frequent expeditions to conciliate different southern tribes or to mediate their quarrels and wars, and often one or the other reports on the subject from Mobile. The Indian question was a very live one then, and the sale of rum to the savages was as now a great cause of trouble. Trade by canoe or pack-horse was important, and many savages, especially Choctaws, were on the streets of Mobile even at other times than during their congresses.

The exports at this time were principally derived from them, and if not large in volume were certainly varied in nature. Indigo and hides probably led the list, but we find also timber and lumber, staves, peltry, cattle, corn, tallow, bear's oil, tar and pitch, rice, tobacco, myrtle wax, salted wild beef, salted fish, pecans, sassafras, and oranges. Romans says vegetables, although not common at Pensacola, were raised in great abundance at Mobile, and that the only reason meat and fish were rare at both places was the indolence of the inhabitants, who let one or two butchers and three or four industrious Spanish hunters and fishermen fix their own prices. Bees came from the Atlantic colonies to West Florida only in 1772. This spring and fall of 1772 we see Rochon from Dog River (*Rivière aux Chiens*) sending loads of plank and of hay to Haldimand at Pensacola, and drawing for fifty dollars and other sums, — once for the total amount then due, in order to satisfy an execution; for, under the common law of imprisonment for debt, a civil execution was almost as bad as a military one.

Cotton has been noticed under the French, and now Romans speaks prophetically of its future.[1]

"Cotton," he says, "being so very useful a commodity that scarce any other exceeds it, and an article of which we can never raise too much (for, like all other things, the more it is multiplied the more its consumption increases), it therefore behooves me to mention it as second in rank. We, by following the example of the industrious Acadians, will do well to manufacture all our necessary clothing in Florida of this staple; and although it has not yet been raised in a sufficient extent to export a considerable quantity thereof, yet when we consider the number of manufactures in Lancashire, Derbyshire, and Cheshire that consume this beneficial commodity, either alone or in mixture with silk, wool, flax, etc., and that England imports all the rough materials from abroad (chiefly from the Levant) to so great an amount as near £400,000 sterling value, we may perhaps find it worthy of a more universal propagation. . . .

"Cotton will grow in any soil, even the most meagre and barren sand we can find.

"The sort we must cultivate here is the *Gossypium Anniversarium,* or *Xylon Herbaceum ;* also known by the name of green seed cotton, which grows about four or five feet in

---

[1] Romans's *Florida,* p. 139. See also pp. 115, 141, 171.

height. Give this plant a dry soil, and further it will cost you little trouble or attention; it must be planted in rows at regular distances about six feet apart: plant the seed in rainy weather, and in about five months' time the fibres will be completely formed and the parts fit together, which will be known by their being completely expanded; it must now be carried to the mill, of which take the following description.

"It is a strong frame of four stubs, each about four feet high, and joined above and below by strong transverse pieces; across this are placed two round well-polished iron spindles, having a small groove through their whole length, and by means of treadles are by the workman's foot put in directly opposite motions to each other: the workman sits before the frame, having a thin board, of seven or eight inches wide, and in length of the frame, before him; this board is so fixed to the frame that it may be moved over again and near the spindle; he has the cotton in a basket near him, and with his left hand spreads it on this board along the spindles, which by their turning draw the cotton through them, being wide enough to admit the cotton, but too near to permit the seed to go through, which, being thus forced to leave the cotton in which it was contained, and by its rough coat entangled, falls on the ground between the workman's legs, while the cotton drawn through falls on the other side into an open bag suspended for that purpose under the spindles.

"The French in Florida have much improved this machine by a large wheel which turns two of these mills at once, and with so much velocity as, by means of a boy who turns it, to employ two negroes at hard labor to shovel the seed from under the mill. One of these machines I saw at Mr. Krebs' at Pasca Oocooloo, but as it was partly taken down, he claiming the invention was very cautious in answering my questions, I cannot pretend to describe it accurately; I am informed that one of those improving mills will deliver seventy or eighty pounds of clean cotton per diem.

"The packing is done in large canvas bags, which must be wetted as the cotton is put in, that it may not hang to the cloth and may slide better down; the bag is suspended between two trees, posts, or beams, and a negro with his feet stamps it down; these bags are made to contain from three hundred and fifty to four hundred weight; with about twenty slaves moderately working, a very large piece of poor ground might be finely improved so as to yield to its owner a fine annual income by means of a staple which is much in demand in England, and here is raised by no means inferior in whiteness and fineness, as well as length of fibres, to that of the Levant."

The summer of 1772 was again a sickly one for the garrison. On August 15, Haldimand writes Gage that the whole of the garrison would soon be in hospital. He had already sent a third doctor, and would forward a schooner to relieve the troops.

But the schooner was not to arrive very soon, for it encountered the great September storm, which lasted from August 30 through September 3 on all the Gulf coast. This was probably the schooner which was driven westerly as far as Cat Island, where she anchored until the water rose so high that she parted her cable and floated over the island. This relief detachment of the 16th regiment was compelled to remain on a desolate island for six weeks until themselves relieved by a smack. The Mobile garrison improved before they arrived, but the storm injured the wharf, fort, and town severely. The hurricane drove vessels, boats, and logs out of the bay up into the river, and through the very streets of the town. There was such an accumulation of logs on the lower lands of the place that the inhabitants needed no other fuel during the ensuing winter. Spray was carried far inland,[1] and salt water was forced over the gardens, destroying the vegetables. All the houses were filled several feet deep with water, and one inhabited by a joiner was run through by a brig which had broken from the moorings.[2] The greatest severity of the storm, however, was felt by Krebs and the Germans near Pascagoula River.

We can readily imagine that Rochon was now in great demand, and by November we find the patriotic British at Pensacola up in arms about this Frenchman's taking their business away. John Cambel files with Haldimand a written protest against the preference given to Rochon and other Frenchmen when reasonable offers were received from others who could better supply the articles. This entailed, he said,

---

[1] 3 Gayarré's *Louisiana*, p. 48 ; Romans' *Florida*, p. 4.
[2] 2 Pickett's *Alabama*, p. 11.

discharge of local carpenters and injury of shingle men. Haldimand was a foreigner himself and had the good sense to refer the matter to General Gage, who promptly decided in favor of Rochon as the cheaper.[1] Lieutenant Cambel rather sided with the civil authorities in the disputes with the military, and receives sharp reprimands from both Gage and Haldimand. He appears finally to have claimed a court martial, and to have been sent to New York.

Charles Stuart, the deputy superintendent, writes from Mobile on May 1 about the doings of the Chickasaws on the Illinois, and in July communicates from Mobile the result of his investigation into the murder of whites by Indians in the interior, where three had been killed. The Upper Creeks and Choctaws had been at war as usual, but negotiations were then in progress looking to running a new line. Some murders of Georgians and the defeat by Creeks of Georgia militia, however, rendered affairs critical for a year or so, the more so as reports came of a general alliance of the southern tribes. The assembly of Georgia in March, 1774, petitioned for imperial aid; but Superintendent John Stuart at Charleston found a way by November to settle disputes with the Creeks, the real disturbers of the peace. Mobile was in little danger, as the Creeks were far away, although on the Alabama River, and the Choctaws remained friendly. Indeed, they were ready and willing to fight their inveterate foes the Creeks in order to aid their British allies. They complained through John McIntosh, an Indian agent at Mobile, of the traders' bringing in rum, a wrong spoken of also by Charles Stuart in July in connection with the Chickasaws, who had on the whole remained friendly. Stuart had been lately among both tribes. As return visits to him meant not only talks but presents, we can readily understand his remarking on the expense of so many Indians coming to the Mobile station.

But here the valuable Haldimand Papers fail us. General Gage had to go to England in 1773 for some purpose, and Haldimand was promoted to take his place at New York. Thence he superintended his old department, but only as he did the rest of North America, and local information is rare. Chester interested himself in the purchase of Haldimand's

---

[1] Campbell's *Colonial Florida*, p. 104.

house in Pensacola; but from those papers we learn nothing of
Mobile beyond the implication in the statement of 1773 that
settlers were coming into West Florida.

Gage returned to America in 1775, and when the Boston
Tea Party and other troubles came he was in command. It
was thought inexpedient that a foreigner like Haldimand should
be prominent in dealing with the colonists, and so he was sent
to the West Indies for a while. He was never again in Mobile
or Pensacola. He was governor of Canada for the ten years
following 1778, and to Canadian interest in that fact we owe
the existence of his papers in America.

Few documents survive in the Mobile archives of this period,
and the one deed in the Translated Records is so indefinite in
description as not to be of much aid. But its form of "grant,
bargain, sell," and the rest of it, with the "To Have and To
Hold," is at least an agreeable reminder of English procedure.

One paper is dated February 2, 1775, and by it, for $100,
Augustin Rochon buys three lots, with a house all falling to
pieces. The sellers are Margaret Belluque, Francis Fieurs
(Fievre?), Martonne (Martha?) Dubroca, and Louisa Rochon.
The property is a double lot, that is, extending east and west
from street to street, bounded south by Henry Driscol. North
it is bounded in part by the vacant lot also conveyed and the
lot of J. B. Lefleaux, the vacant lot in turn being bounded
north and west by unnamed streets.

This property was the subject of litigation in American times
between the omnivorous Kennedys and the heirs of Rochon,
and in this way we learn its location to have been at the southeast corner of Conception and Government. It would seem that
the original grantee was B. F. Fievre, probably the ancestor
of the parties selling to Rochon. Rochon married Louisa
Fievre, and she as his widow resided there, with her yard,
fruit trees, and park overlooking the common, at least until
1780. Whether she was there later or not was the point in
the suit, which depended on whether U. S. Commissioner
Crawford reported in 1814 that she had lived there "thirty-
six years" or "thirty-six years ago."[1] Marie Jeanne Simon
Lapointe, mother of the wife of Orbanne Demouy, must have
been the first wife of Rochon.[2]

[1] *Kennedy* v. *Rochon*, 26 Alabama Reports, 390, 391.
[2] Will of Maria Rochon, 1 *Mobile Will Book*, p. 14.

There has been also preserved at Mobile a contract of sale by one Walter Hood, but the land is bounded by unnamed "streets" and cannot well be identified. It shows in an indorsement the signature of the firm of McGillivray & Struthers. There is also an English deed of a lot·in 1770 by John Favre to Joseph Bouzage, bounded north and east by unnamed streets, west by widow Parisien, and south by Juzan and Livoy.

A much longer document, dated August 10, 1777, has also survived among the Mobile records of these times, which throws much light on other things besides titles. It is an original sealed deed-poll, on genuine parchment, by Arthur Strother, one of the masters in chancery of West Florida, conveying to Daniel Ward, Esq.. the plantation of Lis Loy, also translated "Goose Island." The present instrument takes up the history of it as held by Monberault, and carries it almost through the British domination.

The Chevalier de Montaut de Monberault obtained his grant from Governor Kerlerec March 11, 1763, and with one Fontenot, who was also interested in the property, sold it on July 9, 1765, to Samuel Israel, Alexander Solomons, and Joseph Depalacios, merchants and copartners at Mobile. These merchants seem from their names and Farmer's articles to have been Jews. They were indebted to a merchant of Pensacola, John Thompson by name, and so for £1,157 18s. 1d. they in October of this same year mortgaged to him Lis Loy, with its dwelling, outhouses, and barn. The debt was not paid, and Thompson next February filed his bill for foreclosure and sale in the West Florida Court of Chancery. Where this sat is not stated, but a final decree was rendered August 11, 1767, Hon. Montfort Browne being then chancellor. The sale took place at Mobile in the spring of the next year before Elias Legardere, a master in chancery, and Daniel Ward, of Fish River, was at $107 the highest and best bidder. He paid the money and turned the title papers over to Thomas Hardy, attorney at law, in order to have his deed drawn. But Hardy died, and the papers could not be found.

"By great good luck," the executor ran across these and other old papers in 1776 in an old rice-barrel, and Ward filed a petition in the same "High and Honorable Court of Chancery" to have a master directed to make him a deed. This was granted by Peter Chester, Esq., chancellor, and Arthur Strother ordered to make the deed, which he accordingly did, reciting the facts as above related.

Deeds nowadays often contain unnecessary words, but do not call for as many appurtenances as this one; for Strother sells the "Plantation or Tract of Land, generally called Lis Loy, aforesaid, Situated about a League and a half up the River called Pool [*Poule*] River aforesaid at the Cul de sac or turn called Lis Loy or Goose Island, Together with all Houses, Out Houses, Buildings, Orchards, Gardens, Lands, Meadows, Commons, Pastures, Feedings, Trees, Woods, Underwoods, Ways, Paths, Waters, Water-courses, Easements, Profits, Commodities, Advantages, Emoluments, Hereditaments, Liberties, Priviledges and Appendages." The contents run somewhat over one large page, but by an ingenious device the master so affixes with tape an additional piece of parchment that he can still sign and seal the instrument on the main page.

Such is a report of the first known chancery foreclosure within the limits of the present Mobile County, — the cause of John Thompson, complainant, *v.* Samuel Israel *et al.*, defendants, with ancillary proceedings on the petition of John Ward for a deed, all before the governor of West Florida sitting as chancellor. It is almost the only instance surviving of British procedure; for, although we have also the indictment of Richard Painter in 1765 for stealing clothing from the warehouse of the merchant John McGillivray, this is all that is known of the case; and of the Court of Requests we learn only that in 1768 its clerk received a salary of £20.

CHAPTER XXIX.

BEFORE the American Revolution, a Dr. Fothergill, of London, commissioned one William Bartram, son of the distinguished botanist John Bartram, to search the Floridas and the west parts of Carolina and Georgia "for the discovery of rare and useful productions of nature, chiefly in the vegetable kingdom." He certainly selected the right man, and the travels of the observing and enthusiastic botanist contain a mine of information. He embarked in April, 1773, for Charleston, and after arrival, spent until January, 1778, exploring the southern country. In 1777, he was much in and about Mobile.

He came from Georgia by way of Talase on the Tallapoosa, the northeast great branch of the Alabama or Mobile River,[1] and crossed the Schambe (Escambia), which carried waters to Pensacola,[2] draining a dark and bloody border-ground between the Indians. After a while he "arrived at Taensa, a pretty high bluff on the eastern channel of the great Mobile River, about thirty miles above Fort Condé, or City of Mobile, at the head of the bay." Below Taensa he found low, flat, and rich islands for twenty miles, "well cultivated, having on them extensive farms and some good habitations, chiefly the property of French gentlemen who reside in the city, as being more pleasant and healthy." For the last ten or twelve miles were grassy islands, too low and wet for cultivation.[3]

Then he arrived at the city, which impressed him very favorably. "The City of Mobile is situated on the easy ascent of a rising bank, extending near half a mile back on the level plain above; it has been near a mile in length, though now chiefly in ruins, many houses vacant and mouldering to earth; yet there are a few good buildings inhabited by French gentlemen, English, Scotch, and Irish, and emigrants from the Northern Brit-

[1] Bartram's *Travels*, p. 394. [2] *Ibid.*, p. 400.
[3] *Ibid.*, pp. 401, 402.

ish colonies. Messrs. Swanson & McGillivray, who have the management of the Indian trade carried on with the Chickasaws, Choctaws, Upper and Lower Creeks, etc., have made here very extraordinary improvements in buildings.

"The Fort Condé, which stands very near the bay, towards the lower end of the town, is a large regular fortress of brick.

"The principal French buildings are constructed of brick, and are of one story, but on an extensive scale, four square. encompassing on three sides a large area or court-yard; the principal apartment is on the side fronting the street; they seem in some degree to have copied after the Creek [Greek?] habitation in the general plan: those of the poorer class are constructed of a strong frame of cypress, filled in with brick, plastered, and white-washed inside and out." [1]

He was in Mobile on July 31, when he records the thermometer as at 87°, with excessive thunder and heavy showers of rain all day.

On August 5, he went in a trading-boat to Taensa Bluff to visit Major Farmer. That worthy gentleman had invited him to spend some days in his family, and may be he saw the diamond buckles and heavy gold ring treasured by his descendants, and doubtless met Mary Elizabeth, who as wife of Vobiscey (or Vauxbercy), of Orleanist connection, was to be the mother of Mrs. Curtis Lewis of American times. "The settlement of Taensa," he observes, "is on the site of an ancient town of Indians of that name, which is apparent from many artificial mounds of earth and other ruins." Farmer had many French tenants, and he enjoyed a spacious prospect over his extensive plantations on the opposite shore. Bartram observed there many curious vegetable productions, particularly a species of *Myrica inodora*, the odorless wax myrtle (for our botanist is always exact), which the French inhabitants call the wax-tree. It was grown nine to ten feet high in wet, sandy ground about the edges of swamps. Its berries are nearly the size of bird cherries, and are covered with a scale of white wax, which is harder than beeswax and more lasting in burning. Above in the fields he found a rich, yellow bloom, a new species of *Œnothera*, our evening primrose, "perhaps the most pompous and brilliant herbaceous plant yet known to exist." It is seven

---

[1] Bartram's *Travels*, p. 402.

or eight feet high, with a daily succession of petals over five inches in diameter, of which there are several hundred in all on a plant.

Making an excursion in a boat, he found farther up the river ruins of ancient habitations, with loaded peach and fig trees, the figs a dark-blue purple and the size of pears. The canes and cypress also were of astonishing magnitude.[1]

On this trip he would land from time to time as anything attracted his attention, and on one occasion goes into ecstasies over the prospect. Nowhere in literature is there a more naïve description.

"What a sylvan scene is here! The pompous Magnolia reigns sovereign of the forests; how sweet the aromatic Illicium [star anise] groves! how gaily flutter the radiated wings of the Magnolia auriculata [cucumber-tree], each branch supporting an expanded umbrella, superbly crested with a silver plume, fragrant blossom, or crimson-studded strobile and fruits! I recline on the verdant bank, and view the beauties of the groves, Æsculus pavia, [red-blooming buckeye], Prunus Nemoralis [wild plum], floribus racemosis, foliis sempervirentibus, nitidis, Æsculus alba [spiked buckeye], Hydrangia quercifolia [seven barks], Cassine [youpon], Magnolia pyramidata, foliis ovatis, oblongis, acuminatis, basi auriculatis, strobilo oblongo ovato, Myrica, Rhamnus frangula [yellow wood], Halesca [silver bells,] Bignonia, Azalea, Lonicera [woodbine], Sideroxylon [gum elastic], with many more."[2]

Near the confluence of the Tombigbee or Chickasaw River with the Alabama or Coosau he beheld alligators, and just within the capes of the former "fine river" he found a lagoon containing a green, wavy plain of water-lilies, some being seven or eight inches wide and of a lemon yellow. The seed of this *Nymphæa nelumbo* (sweet-scented-water lily, water chinquepin) are eaten as a laxative. Up the river, at a steep red clay bluff, he saw an old field, with a young forest growth on the plantations, still preserving the corn and potato ridges, — *zea* and *batata*, in Bartram's vocabulary. He supposed "this to be the site of an ancient fortified post of the French, as there appear vestiges of a rampart and other traces of a fortress, perhaps Fort Louis de la Mobile; but in all probability it will

---

[1] Bartram's *Travels*, pp. 403, 405.   [2] *Ibid.*, p. 406.

not remain long visible, the stream of the river making daily
encroachments on it by carrying away the land on which it
stood." [1]

This is the more worthy of quotation because some have cited
Bartram as locating Fort Louis on Dog River, below the present city. [2] The fact is that he does no such thing. He locates
the fort — and does not make the modern error of calling it
St. Louis — near St. Stephens. This is too far up, but at least
shows that tradition in his time correctly placed the fort north
and not south of the present Mobile.

Opposite this Tombigbee fort was a swamp, enthusiastically
described as the richest perhaps anywhere to be seen. Ascending the river, he saw on bluffs, as he went along, deserted
plantations, houses burnt, and ancient Indian villages.

He returned to Major Farmer's, and had a touch of fever,
broken by tartar emetic. The major then furnished the botanist with a negro and horses to go in search of a medical plant,
which he learned was thirty miles up. He found it, too, and
says that it was a species of *collinsonia* (citronella tea), diu-
retic, carminative, and a powerful febrifuge. An infusion of
its tops was ordinarily drunk at breakfast, and exceeding pleasant in taste and flavor.

After some time he left Taensa and descended to the city in
company with Dr. Grant, a physician of the garrison. From
him he learned that there were few or no bees west of the isthmus of Florida. There was but one hive in Mobile, and that
lately brought from Europe, the English not finding any there.
Which was indeed curious, as Bartram says they were then
numerous on the whole Atlantic coast, even in wild forests. [3]

Bartram then arranged to sail from Mobile to Manchac.
He had to wait for a boat, and seized the opportunity of a
vessel to Pensacola to explore the coast. He sailed early one
morning, and, having a brisk leading breeze, came to in the
evening just within Mobile Point. They smoked away the
mosquitoes with fire from driftwood, and rested well that summer night on the clean, sandy beach.

At Pensacola he met Dr. Lorimer of the council, Secretary

[1] Bartram's *Travels*, pp. 407, 408.

[2] Pickett's *Alabama*, p. 191, n.

[3] Bartram's *Travels*, p. 411.

Livingston, and "soon after the governor's chariot passed by, his Excellency returning from a morning visit to his farm a few miles" off. He was introduced to Chester, who commended his pursuits, "nobly offering to bear my expenses." [1]

Returning to Mobile, he caught his boat, that of a Frenchman, the general interpreter for the Choctaw nation. This gentleman was going to his plantations on Pearl River, and had three negroes along to row in case of necessity. Six miles below (and therefore near Dog River), they spent the night with a Frenchman, and, setting sail next morning, made extraordinary headway. "About noon they came up abreast of a high steep bluff, or perpendicular cliff of high land, touching on the bay of the west coast, where we went on shore to give liberty to the slaves to rest and refresh themselves. In the mean time I accompanied the captain on an excursion into the spacious level forests, which spread abroad from the shore to a great distance back; observed vestiges of an ancient fortress and settlement, and there yet remain a few pieces of iron cannon; but what principally attracted my notice was three vast iron pots or kettles, each of many hundred gallons contents: upon inquiry, my associate informed me they were for the purpose of boiling tar to pitch, there being vast forests of pine-trees in the vicinity of this place." [2] Bartram goes on to observe that in Carolina they make the tar in pits.

Continuing southwardly, they passed later between the west point or cape of the bay and entered the channel Oleron. Bartram had left Mobile sick. He was to learn that beautiful swamps and sylvan scenes and piroguing the lower rivers in August is not very prudent. When he sailed, he had a pain in his head, and his eyes were running. He finally could not see, and at his request was taken to Rumsey's, on Pearl Island, where cantharides (fly blister), applied between his shoulders, gave him a new experience. When he awoke, after a twenty-four hours' sleep, he was weak, but had no pain and was in a heavenly frame of mind.[3] At Rumsey's he met ex-Governor Montfort Browne, and was much more pleased with him than Haldimand had been.

Farther we cannot follow him so closely, as he is getting

[1] Bartram's *Travels*, p. 413.　　　[2] *Ibid.*, p. 417.
[3] *Ibid.*, pp. 418, 419.

beyond our jurisdiction, although his visit to Manchac is full
of interest. There he found a large establishment of Swanson
& Co., Indian traders and merchants. The Iberville had a
wooden bridge over to the Spanish possessions, but the stream
was then dry and its bed twelve to fifteen feet above the Mississippi. Two miles above, he saw Alabama, a village of the
remnant of that Indian nation "which inhabited the east arm
of the great Mobile River which bears their name to this day."
They came from about Fort Toulouse.[1]

Bartram's eyes still troubled him, and he determined to re-
turn home. Sailing back to Mobile, his boat ran aground on
sunken oyster-banks between Dauphine Island shoals and the
West Cape of Mobile Bay; but the next day a south wind
raised the sea and they got off, and finally reached Mobile.
As his route would be overland through the Creek nation into
Georgia, he shipped his botanical treasures by sea from Mobile.
He says: "I made up my collections of growing roots, seeds,
and curious specimens and left them to the care of Messrs.
Swanson & McGillivray, to be forwarded to Dr. Fothergill, of
London." He says nothing of the Revolutionary War in these
parts, — for there was none, — but is a little uneasy at hearing
of the murder at Apalache, by the Seminoles or Lower Creeks,
of emigrants for Mobile. He therefore joined a caravan destined for the nation. Before leaving, he observed in a garden
two large trees of *Juglans pecan*, and also the *Dioscorea bul-
bifera*, which bears fruit in the leaves two to three feet from
the ground and tastes like the yam.[2]

His servant or companion was a Mustee Indian, who had been
in the Choctaw nation and learned their songs and dances, but,
not conforming to their customs, he had been chased by them to
Mobile, whence he was going to the Creeks. Bartram's horse
gave out, and, to keep up with his companions, he had to buy a
new one from some traders whom they met. It cost him ten
pounds. The custom of traders is to let their horses graze at
night, he says, and they do not get ready to start in the morning until the sun is high. Then they decamp, the loaded beasts
falling into single file, urged on with whip and whoop.

At this lively pace he continued his journey for several

---

[1] Bartram's *Travels*, p. 427 ; Pittman's *Mississippi Settlements*, p. 24.
[2] Bartram's *Travels*, p. 437.

days, but, when he passed the line of 33° on Mobile River, where the Illicium groves cease to perspire oleaginous sweat, we leave him, although our interest follows until he arrives, *via* sea voyage, at his father's on the Schuylkill in January, 1778.[1]

[1] The expedition of Bartram to the South is one of the important events in botanical history, and his book among the classics of that science. The edition quoted is the Dublin one of 1793, but it was published in 1791 at Philadelphia, where his father had established the earliest botanical garden in the United States, one which has recently been purchased by the public authorities on account of its beauty and value. William Bartram died there in 1823.

All of his plants have not been certainly identified, but the vernacular equivalents given above are those of that accurate and learned botanist, Dr. Charles Mohr, of Mobile. He it was that rediscovered Bartram's *Myrica inodora;* and for him it was that the *Halesea* was renamed *Mohrodendron,* when the other name was found to have been already appropriated by a West Indian plant. He says that Bartram's *Magnolia auriculata* has disappeared from the Mobile forests.

CHAPTER XXX

POLITICS.

INTEREST during the next few years has so centred in the Boston rebels, the Continental Congress of 1775 at Philadelphia, Bunker's Hill the same year, the Declaration of Independence in the next one, Valley Forge in 1777, and the French alliance the year after, that we are apt to forget there was any America outside of the United States. Most of the other southern colonies expelled their royal governors in 1775, but Governor Chester was in no danger, and presided over the council the same as ever.

Mobilians were in the council. Terry is mentioned in 1766, and one of them in 1772 was Jacob Blackwell, also collector of customs of the port. He left for London in that year on account of his health, and never returned. He died in 1775, and Chester appointed his own private secretary, Philip Livingston, Jr., to the vacant position. In this year we find Charles Stuart a member of the council, although also deputy superintendent of Indian affairs at Mobile. Dr. Lorimer and Elias Durnford are also mentioned as members later. The functions of the council were in part executive. The minutes show grants of land, consideration of the Indian question in all its phases, regulations as to commerce, roads and pilots, elections and military posts. When there was an assembly, the two bodies sometimes united in a "representation" to the home Board of Trade and Plantations on public matters. The principal use of an assembly seems to have been to vote supplies.

There has been an impression that there were no assemblies before Chester's time, but this is an error, as we learn from Romans, and otherwise. We know that there was one in 1766, and that the next assembly, on January 2, 1767, passed an act to erect Mobile into a county, and to establish a court of common pleas therein; but five years later this was disallowed by the Privy Council at London. At a meeting of the council in 1767, an election was ordered for another assembly, to be held at Mobile on August 11, at Pensacola on the 19th, and at Campbell Town on the 25th, returnable on October 11. In 1766, Pensacola and Mobile returned six members each, and Campbell Town two, although no law existed before 1778 governing the matter. This apportionment continued until 1771, when the writ was withheld from Campbell Town, because it was almost deserted. An act of 1771 with Chester's approval made an appropriation for bridges and ferries on the road from Pensacola to Mobile, via Perdido River and the Village. But then began the political trouble.

The origin of it is not altogether clear. Governor Chester later explained it by reporting to Lord Germain that the gentlemen of influence at Mobile did not want an assembly, for fear that it would pass an act regulating the Indian trade, in which they were all interested. Such an act would restrain their traders from taking profuse quantities of rum into the Indian nations, as had been customary, or at least give these traders and their sureties in Mobile much trouble by prosecutions at Pensacola. He says the Mobile members seldom attended when there was an assembly.

On the other hand, the facts seem rather to show popular dissatisfaction over the apportionment of representatives and certainly with the term of the legislature.

A writ of election was given to the deputy provost marshal, Alexander McCullough, in 1772, and, after due publication by him at Mobile February 29, by majority vote of the freeholders of Mobile and Charlotte County, William Struthers, John McGillivray, Alexander McIntosh, Robert Farmar, Henry Lizard, Daniel Ward, Edmund Rush Wegg, and Benjamin Ward were elected representatives. But the freeholders would not execute the required indenture, except with a provision limiting the assembly to one year, and a special return of the writ had to be made to the council. Four of the six Pensacola representatives sympathized to such extent that they would not meet without those from Mobile. The governor prorogued the assembly twice in vain hopes the Mobile members would attend, and then, on the advice of the council, dissolved it April 23, on account of such usurpation of the royal prerogative by

Mobile. His action was approved by the Earl of Dartmouth in the name of the king, and Chester was instructed to omit Mobile from the next election writ.

Chester got along without an assembly for some years, meantime, in 1777, inserting Robert Farmar, John McGillivray, and Michael Grant in the commission of the peace for the town of Mobile. Next year an assembly was needed to pass militia and Indian bills. The apportionment by the government then was of four representatives to the districts of Natchez, Manchae, Mobile, and Pensacola, each, besides four more to the town of Pensacola, because it was the capital; but the town of Mobile and Campbell Town were omitted. It was to no avail, for the "cantankerous" assembly, as Chester called it, protracted their session to thirty-four days without passing the bills, and obstructed all business in order to force the governor to reënfranchise the two places. They even presented, on November 25, 1778, a memorial to the "King's Majesty in Council," begging that Mobile be reënfranchised, declaring that it is "by far the most important of any in the province, for its antiquity, commerce and revenue to the Crown, it paying upwards of £4,000 annually in the custom house of London alone." The representatives of the district at that time were Daniel Ward and Peter Swanson, "elected in the room of Robert Farmar, deceased," E. R. Wegg, and the speaker, Adam Chrystie. The conduct of the assembly was thoroughly approved at Mobile, as was shown by a letter a few days earlier from the principal inhabitants to "the Speaker and Members of the House of Assembly," thanking them for their action in the matter. The signers of this paper were Peter Swanson, Buckner Pittman, George Troup, Daniel Mortimer, Thomas Strother, Jean Louis Maroteau, James McGillivray, L. Maroteau, James Dallas, Lavall, Charles Roberts, Francis Roberts, William Gordon, L. Carriere, William Struthers, Pierre Guilliory, John A. Austin, François Fieury, Thre Benoist, Jean Favre, Jean Bapt⁰ Lusser, John McIntosh, Louis Lusser, Walter Hood, Barthelemy Grelot, James Colburt, David McCleish, Thomas Baskett, Bertrand Nicolas, William Cocke Ellis, George Dow, Gilbert Hay, John McIntosh, Jr., Cornelius McCurtin.

The dispute led ultimately to a memorial in May of next

year to the king against Governor Chester's administration, and among the signatures of inhabitants are a number of those Mobilians.

The colonial administration was controlled by the home government through the Privy Council, sitting at St. James'. This body was what was left of the feudal royal council after courts and parliament had developed into separate institutions, and its powers were limited to commerce and the colonies. But its committee, the Board of Trade, which made commercial regulations, about this time went to pieces in consequence of an attack by Edmund Burke in 1780, and its Mobile acts were among the last.

In 1766 was one requiring the inhabitants to keep their lots and half of the street opposite clear of weeds and nuisances, under a penalty of forty shillings fine and the hire of a laborer, and also authorizing the Quarter Session to compel them to clear off the surrounding woods not exceeding half a mile from the town. Three years later, another act of the Board of Trade provided for the election by the freeholders and householders of Pensacola and Mobile, at their respective churches, of two church wardens, two sidesmen, two overseers of the poor, two way wardens, and two appraisers. These made up the vestry, and chose parish clerk and sexton, and could make a poor-rate not exceeding £10 for Mobile and £30 for Pensacola; but people of a different religion providing for their own poor were exempt. Power was also given to use the negroes of citizens three days in the year to clear and drain the swamps around Mobile, under a fine of four "ryals" per day. In the same year was another act to prevent the burning of herbage at improper seasons, to keep hunters from leaving carcasses of deer near plantations, and extending to Mobile a colonial act to prevent danger from fire and accidents in the streets of Pensacola. This last seems to have forbidden the carrying of fire in the streets unless covered and secured, under penalty of a dollar fine or three hours in the stocks, or twelve lashes, if a negro. There was also a fine of two dollars for firing arms in the streets, or riding or driving cattle through the streets at more than a walk. The substance of some of these police regulations still survives.

This section was positively benefited by the eastern revolt. Tories driven from Georgia and South Carolina were the first white settlers of what are now Washington, Clarke, and Baldwin counties, the ancestors of the half-breed McIntosh, Manac, McQueen, McGirk, and other families to be of note. The minutes of council in 1777 show a number of grants on Mobile waters to people who were probably fugitive Tories. On the "Tombeckby," lands were granted to William Jackson, John Mathews, Robert Abrams, Jesse Wall, William Wall, and John Low, mainly near "Basket's Creek." Charles Roberts, of Pennsylvania, received a grant on the same river higher up, and Alexander Cameron, of South Carolina, one at or beneath Black Rock on the west side of Mobile River. Moses Kirkland petitioned the council for several tracts, which were granted, amongst other lands on the west side of Tombeckby River, about six or eight miles below the Indian line at the mouth of Tallow Creek. We learn from the minutes that he was late a colonel of militia and justice of the peace in Ninety-six District of South Carolina, and embodied four thousand volunteers to serve the king on the outbreak of the rebellion. He escaped to Charles Town, but was afterwards taken and imprisoned by the rebels. He finally made his escape to Earl Dunmore's fleet, and brought General Howe's dispatches to East and West Florida.

Before 1776, Alexander, the son of the rich Scotch trader Lachlan McGillivray and Schoy Marchand, was already a power among the Creeks. This Lachlan "McGilivray" and George Galphin had had greater influence there than any other men. Through Alexander the Creeks now opposed the revolted colonists of Georgia, who, after Lachlan sailed to Scotland with the British on the evacuation of Savannah, confiscated his property. John and Farquhar McGillivray (no doubt connections of Lachlan) had commercial interests in the loyal colony of West Florida. At Mobile, Swanson & McGillivray (afterwards Swanson & Strothers) were the great Indian traders, and had posts at sundry places even to the Mississippi. Adair tells us, however, that the grant of indiscriminate licenses for trade cheapened goods too much, and made the Indians independent and insolent, while it ruined profits; quite unlike it was in the good, monopolistic times before the cession.[1]

Charles Stuart held a satisfactory congress with the Indians in May, 1777, although they complained very much of the pro-

[1] Adair's *American Indians*, p. 366.

fuse introduction of rum.   The Indian trade was now confined to West Florida on account of the revolt of the eastern colonies.

The council, as early as 1776, had fears that those rebels had designs upon Mobile.   Nothing in the way of repairs to the fort had been done since Mr. Sowers' adverse report some time before, but Durnford, as engineer, was now directed to put it in at least provisional repair.   His estimate called for $930 of material, especially for gun platforms.   The council recommended the governor to undertake this and also reinforce the post on account of its importance.   The defence works were accordingly carried out and munitions sent over.   As the 60th regiment was made up of raw troops, then sickly, too, no men could be spared, but the proposition of John McGillivray was accepted to raise companies at Mobile.   This was done, but on a smaller scale than anticipated (being six captains, but only sixty-seven privates), despite Chester's offer of the same pay as Colonel Stuart's rangers and the same quantity of land at the termination of the rebellion as was promised the provincial troops serving under Sir William Howe.   This pay seems to have been, for privates, rations and £2 per month, out of which they provided their own clothing.   McGillivray was to "embody" all whites at Mobile and in the Indian country that he could find, and accept savages, too, and then march to assist the people at the Natchez.

In 1778, the leading inhabitants of Mobile energetically petitioned Dickson, then in command there, to secure reinforcements, and the council thereupon asked the governor to do everything possible.   Next year we find General Campbell notifying Lord George Germain, of the home government, that he had on account of the commanding and "centrical" situation of Mobile ordered such repairs to the fort and barracks as were absolutely necessary.   The expense was about £4000, while a thorough rehabilitation would have cost over £50,000.   The council resolved that the inhabitants of Mobile and Pensacola take the oath of allegiance before their respective magistrates. These as well as those of the Tensaw, however, are noted by the governor as showing great readiness in forming volunteer companies.   But all may not have been so loyal, and even earlier we read of deserters from Pensacola who assaulted and robbed John Murray, the ferryman at the Perdido.

CHAPTER XXXI.

ANOTHER visitor was preparing to come to West Florida and to take in Mobile, but his errand was less peaceful than Bartram's. It was Don Bernardo de Galvez.

The successor of O'Reilly in Louisiana had been in 1770 Don Luis Unzaga, who in 1776, much to the regret of his former subjects, was promoted to be Captain-General of Caraccas. On the 1st of February, next year, Galvez, the young colonel, entered on the duties of his office. He was but twenty-one years old, highly connected, and full of energy. Haldimand and Gage had been discussing the best method of invading Louisiana, and in the first year of his governorship Galvez in turn is contemplating the conquest of their West Florida. He sends home to Spain in July, 1777, minute statements of the fortifications of Mobile and Pensacola; but, although their relations were sometimes strained, no war was declared between England and Spain until 1779. There was no alliance with the revolted colonies, but the Spanish agent Miralles got word to Washington of the contemplated invasion of West Florida. The Spaniards wished the British conquerors of the southern colonies to be checked by the Americans, and Washington hoped the invasion would make Georgia and the Carolinas untenable for the English, whom Lincoln was instructed to keep busy.[1]

From the time Galvez became governor, Oliver Pollock had regularly supplied the Americans from New Orleans. The Natchez district of West Florida, like the rest of it, remained loyal, and the American captain James Willing in 1778 made little progress, and indeed had a battle with the inhabitants from the river, but was driven off. He then sailed to the Tensaw settlements, and we can imagine the reception he would get from Major Farmer and his tenants.

[1] 3 Gayarré's *Louisiana*, p. 111 ; 6 *Washington's Works*, pp. 475, 542.

It is said that Pollock came with Willing to Mobile, and brought the Declaration of Independence for distribution. This famous document was then contraband of war, and Willing soon found himself a prisoner in Fort Charlotte. He remained in irons there until exchanged in 1779 for Colonel Hamilton, of Detroit.[1]

The governor was Peter Chester still, and the general in command of the province Campbell, with headquarters at Pensacola. A brave man he certainly was, but not of the best judgment. The Campbell papers — if they exist — would show no such careful supervision of Florida from the Mississippi to the ocean, no exploration of routes or sounding of bays, as with Haldimand. Campbell in peace was careless, if in war a fighter.

He had no very high opinion of his troops. He wrote Sir Henry Clinton that his 16th regiment was composed of seven companies of veterans almost worn out in the service, and of German recruits, and that the eight companies of the 60th were "chiefly Germans, condemned criminals, and other species of gaol-birds." He said none were to be depended on except the veterans, and desertions were numerous. The provincial troops he thought even more unfit, being composed mostly of Irish vagabonds, deserters from the rebels. Some, if not all, of these Germans came from the principality of Waldeck, whose prince rented them to the King of England to subdue the rebellious Americans.

Max Von Eelking published at Hanover in 1863 a history of the experiences of the Waldeckers, taken largely from the journal of the chaplain, Steuernagel. They were sent south by Clinton to serve in the expected war with Spain, and we learn that they arrived in January, 1779, at Pensacola, of which town of two hundred houses he gives an unflattering account. The whole province he found little more than a wilderness, inhabited principally by Indians, whose scalping propensities excited the horror of the Germans. One of the chiefs was Brandenstein, a Waldecker himself.

On the Mississippi, Lieutenant Dickson had 500 men, and so pressed Campbell for reinforcements that the Waldecker grenadiers and a number of foot were forwarded thither. At the

[1] 2 Pickett's *Alabama*, p. 36; Meek's *Southwest*, p. 90.

same time, on August 19, the Spanish authorities in New Orleans recognized American independence and began hostilities with about two thousand men, of which fact the English in Pensacola had no suspicion.

In September, 1779, Galvez, immediately after having amid great enthusiasm taken the oath of office as Spanish governor before the council (*cabildo*), made a secret dash from New Orleans at the Mississippi forts, and captured them successively before reinforcements could arrive. After five days, Fort Bute at the Iberville was carried by storm. Dickson had withdrawn his main force nearer Baton Rouge. At this post he was attacked, but repulsed attempts at storming. After Galvez undertook a deliberate siege, Dickson surrendered, giving up Baton Rouge and Fort Panmure at the Natchez; but his bravery secured full honors of war.

The news of this traveled slowly, but we can imagine the consternation at Mobile in October when the tidings came. A courier was sent on to Campbell at Pensacola, but he would not believe the report, calling it a Spanish ruse to draw him out of Pensacola. On the 23d, another courier arrived there, but Campbell for a while still took the same view. He gave orders to sail, then countermanded them, and hesitated what to do. He finally strengthened Pensacola, but left Mobile to its fate. Fortunately, Galvez was content for that season with his Mississippi captures, and returned to New Orleans to spend the winter in further preparations.[1]

A report shows that the garrison of Mobile, all told, consisted of 279 men, besides Mr. Gordon, the minister, who was quite active, Commissary Thomas Strother, and the surgeon's mate, probably Dr. Grant. There were seventeen negroes as officers' servants, and thirty-five more used in one way or another, whose owners afterwards claimed compensation from the crown. There were represented the engineers, artillery, 4th battalion of the 60th foot, sixteen of the "United Provincial Corps of Pennsylvania and Maryland Loyalists," fifty-two volunteers from the inhabitants (of whom fifteen deserted), and twenty-one artificers. Among the volunteers are included Captain Walker's provincial dragoons and Captain

[1] 2 Von Eelking, *Die deutschen Hülfstruppen in N. A.*, pp. 140–143; 2 Pickett's *Alabama*, p. 40; 3 Gayarré's *Louisiana*, p. 126.

Rees' militia in three canoes, who arrived at a critical time.

On February 5, 1780, Galvez sailed from the Balize for Mobile with two thousand men, made up of regulars, militia, and a few companies of free negroes. He had to encounter a hurricane, and some of his eleven vessels were stranded and his provisions and ammunition were damaged. But, as with the Mississippi expedition, he did not let the elements deter him. Despite imminent shipwreck, he persevered, and on the 9th captured the victualer Brownhall, of sixteen guns, carrying to Mobile the presents brought by the ordnance ship Earl of Bathurst for Superintendent Cameron's proposed Indian congress. Galvez finally succeeded in landing in the Bay of Mobile just below Choctaw Point, probably near our Frascati. It was in such disorder, however, that even Galvez at first felt inclined to retreat by land and leave his baggage and artillery. But he soon learned that Campbell was not expecting him, and acted accordingly.[1]

Meantime there was even greater confusion in Mobile, and the citizens hurried into the fort. Galvez erected six batteries north and west of the fort and began a brisk cannonade. The intervening houses were burned, one of them being the late home of Major Farmer, with valuable papers, and possibly the church also. We know that the home of the widow of Augustin Rochon (southeast Government and Conception) was burned at this time by the English, no doubt to enable the fort the better to command the neighborhood.[2]

Galvez was aware of his having superior forces, and from Chakto Point, on March 1, sent a polite request, in French, to Durnford to surrender, saying that after a battle he might not be able to grant so favorable terms.

Durnford's manly reply was as follows: —

"I have the honor to acknowledge the receipt of your Excel-

---

[1] 3 Gayarré's *Louisiana*, pp. 135, 136 ; 2 Martin's *Louisiana*, p. 52.

[2] *Kennedy* v. *Rochon*, 26 Ala. 390. The house of Rev. William Gordon, too, was burned by Durnford to prevent shelter to the enemy while erecting batteries. It was in the heart of town, near the fort, and worth $2,000. As Mr. Gordon was loyal and active, besides being a widower with four children, it is to be hoped that the claim for reimbursement, which Durnford indorsed for him in London next year, was favorably considered by Lord George Germain, of his majesty's government.

lency's Summons to surrender immediately the Fort to your Excellency's Superior Forces.

"The difference of numbers I am convinced are greatly in your favor, Sir, but mine are much beyond your Excellency's conception, and was I to give up this Fort on your demand, I should be regarded as a traitor to my king and country. My love for both and my own honor direct my heart to refuse surrendering this Fort until I am under conviction that resistance is in vain.

"The generosity of your Excellency's mind is well known to my brother officers and soldiers, and should it be my misfortune to be added to their number, a heart full of generosity and valor will ever consider brave men fighting for their country as objects of esteem and not revenge."

In his account of it to Campbell next day he says: —

"Soon after I sent Land Express, a flag was perceived in the wood, and I sent an officer to receive it at some distance.

"This, as I expected, was a summons to surrender to Don Bernardo de Galvez's Superior Forces, a copy of which you have inclosed, with my answer thereto. The Flag was brought in Person by an old acquaintance, Colonel Bolyny, who sent me a polite card wishing for the pleasure of an interview if possible, and Profession of Friendship, although we were National enemies, on which I sent Mr. Barde to conduct him into the Fort with the customary ceremony, where he dined and continued until near five o'clock, drinking a cheerful glass to the healths of our King and Friends.

"During our conversation I found that the Report of the Shipwreck was true; he acknowledged that they had undergone great hardships, but would not allow to have lost any men, and informed me that they were about 2500 men, but by trusty Indians who were sent by me into the camp in the morning I learned that a great number were negroes and mulattoes, and that they had landed no cannon.

"Bolyny confirmed that we had cut the cable and just hit the Row Galley, but we are certain that three nine pounders shot hit her, and as she is gone off I suspect she is well mauled, for yesterday morning she was seen opposite the Chactaws on a heal, and I suppose is gone to Dog River to repair the damage received from our shot.

"As soon as Colonel Bolyny left me I drew up my Garrison in the square, read to them Don Galvez's summons, and then told them that if any man among them was afraid to stand by me that I should open the gate and he should freely pass. This had the desired effect, and not a man moved. I then read to them my answer to the summons, in which they all joined in three cheers and then went to our necessary work like good men.

"I really believe their (the enemy's) force is greatly magnified."

Later he wrote: —

"Your great good news hath just arrived. I thank you, dear Sir, for the consolation it affords me. I need not say I will defend Fort to the last extremity. The vessels I can see from this are in the mouth of the East Pass, about two miles distant from the Fort. And the Galvez Brig is one, and Pickler's Florida the other. Near to the Dog River are five ships or Pollaccas, and I am informed that three or four are in Dog River besides the Row Galley."

Campbell on March 5 sent the 60th regiment, and on the next day the remainder of the Waldeck regiment, from Pensacola, to relieve Mobile. This was probably Durnford's "great good news." He followed himself with Pennsylvanians and artillery. He had 522 men in all. It was a march of 72 English miles through a wilderness without a single human dwelling. He arrived at Tensa on the 10th, but spent too much time building rafts; for after several days a breach had been made in the walls of the fort, and in the morning, March 14, the garrison capitulated upon the same terms which Dickson had obtained at Baton Rouge. Captain Durnford marched out his small command with flags and drums, and they grounded arms outside the fort, the officers retaining their swords. Hunger and lack of reinforcement from Campbell had had as much to do with the surrender as the cannonade, for only one man was killed outright, and eleven were wounded, of whom two died of their wounds. Durnford wrote, "No man in the garrison stained the luster of the British arms." When Galvez saw how small a garrison had so long resisted him, he was greatly mortified. But he kept his agreement to take them

to a British port and land them, upon their promise not to
serve against Spain or her allies for eighteen months.[1]

Campbell's return march is described as a terrible journey.
It rained almost continuously, and the troops had to wade
through mud ankle-deep or through ponds. They could pass
swollen streams only in single file over fallen trees, and whoever slipped was lost. At night they were surrounded by wild
animals, the wolves howling frightfully.[2]

Mobile remained in Spanish hands, and was now, as in Bienville's time, to become a base of operations against Pensacola.
But Galvez was too cautious to attack the capital at once. He
spent a whole year in preparation, obtaining troops and vessels
from Cuba. Campbell could muster but 800 men, and the
Creeks, Choctaws, and Chickasaws, who remained loyal and
steadfastly refused Spanish overtures, were sometimes more of
a trouble and menace than a help. The two hundred Choctaws
and Chickasaws were useful just after the fall of Mobile, in driving back the Spaniards who had crossed the Perdido and overpowered the British advance posts in order to drive off horses.

In January, 1781, General Campbell showed some activity at
last. On the 3d, he sent Captain Von Hanxleden with 100 in-
fantrymen of the 60th, eleven militia cavalry, 300 Indians, and
sixty Waldeckers to drive the Spaniards out of their intrenchments at the French village. This was on the coast, below
where the Apalache or Tensaw empties into Mobile Bay.[3]

Von Hanxleden arrived on the morning of January 7, and
several times attempted to storm the intrenchments at the point
of the bayonet, but in vain. The Spaniards resisted manfully,
while the Indians were of little use. The English did not give
it up, however, until Captain Von Hanxleden and Lieutenant
Stirlin of the Germans and the English lieutenant Gordon
were dead on the field, and two other officers wounded. The
Spaniards also had suffered severely and lost a magazine by
fire. The expedition then retreated to Pensacola, but not be-

---

[1] Campbell's *Colonial Florida*, p. 119. The correspondence is preserved
in the British Record Office, and has been published in part by William
Beer, of the Howard Memorial Library, New Orleans. See also Campbell's
report to the home government.

[2] 2 Von Eelking, *Deutsche Hülfstruppen*, pp. 144, 145.

[3] 2 Von Eelking, p. 147, places it on the Mississippi, but the dates and con-
text show this is a slip of the pen for the Mobile waters.

fore doing honor to the dead. "The body of the captain," says Von Eelking, "was in silence laid to rest. The grave mound, which was made in the wilderness under a great tree, is said later to have been surrounded with a fence by the gallant Spaniards, who duly honored the bravery of the fallen."

In March of this year 1781 came the unequal struggle at Pensacola. At first the Spanish admiral from Havana refused to cross the bar and insisted on Galvez' proceeding by land; but the general shamed him into coöperation by leading the way in a little Louisianian schooner, exposing himself to the full British fire. The British fleet, too, was not inactive. A sloop captured near Mobile and brought in to Pensacola as its prize a Spanish vessel whose contents showed careful war preparations. It had Galvez' baggage and necessaries, among them twenty thousand dollars in silver, silver plate, excellent wine, and all the utensils for a good kitchen.[1] But after a long siege, Campbell surrendered in May. Galvez granted him the same terms that he had to Dickson and Durnford, and the general, Governor Chester, and the troops found themselves prisoners of war aboard Spanish vessels bound for New York.[2] The capitulation was displeasing to the Americans because it permitted the conquered British to serve against them in the critical times about the Yorktown campaign; but Washington afterwards expressed himself as satisfied with Galvez' acts, believing him a true friend of the cause.[3]

At all events, the war was over on the Gulf. West Florida had become a Spanish province.

[1] 2 Von Eelking, *Deutsche Hülfstruppen*, p. 149.
[2] Campbell's *Colonial Florida*, pp. 135, 140 ; 8 *Washington's Works*, p. 176.
[3] Campbell's *Colonial Florida*, p. 137 ; 8 *Washington's Works*, p. 176.

PART V.

UNDER THE SPANIARDS.

1780–1813.

CHAPTER XXXII.

(Commandants, — Grimarest, 1781 ; Favrot, 1785.)

THE first Spanish commandant of Fort Charlotte seems to have been José de Espeleta, who with the local forces assisted against Pensacola. But he was in command during the war only, and, when the Spaniards had secured undisputed occupancy of all West Florida, affairs settled down generally to a peace footing. From 1783, we know Espeleta was acting captain-general in the absence of Galvez.[1]

It would be interesting to know more details than have been preserved of the new government of the place. On the Pacific coast and in New Mexico the Spanish settlers were either grouped about a *presidio* or fort, and so under military rule, or in an organized *pueblo* or municipality, with council (*ayuntamiento*) and civil judges (*alcaldes*). In the latter part of 1781, after Pensacola had been captured and the British troops withdrawn from the province, the title of Grimarest changes from "governor *ad interim*" to "Political (or Civil) and Military Governor of the Town of Mobile and its District," so to remain with all his successors. This would seem to show Mobile as partly a *presidio* but mainly a *pueblo*, and indeed in later years (under Salazar) the commandant was to sign himself as "captain of the pueblo infantry regiment." To the east of our Blakeley River on a Spanish map are found two or more settlements marked "pueblo," and the word occurs in the archives at Mobile. But this was evidently in a popular rather than a political sense. The usual name, even in official documents, was "Plaza de la Movila," although notary Saussaye used often the word *ciudad*, city.

Spanish rule was the same everywhere, for the paternal government from the time of Ferdinand saved its colonists respon-

---

[1] 2 Martin's *Louisiana*, pp. 56, 71.

sibility by defining all offices and prescribing the duties of every one. The fatherly love of the king is often officially mentioned in the archives. In old Louisiana the change was only gradually made, although formally Spanish law prevailed from O'Reilly's time.[1] French law and customs were too deeply rooted to be easily eradicated, and it is a fact now too often forgotten that Spanish rule was mild and the inhabitants well satisfied.

The commandant in each district, such as Mobile, was supreme in military and political matters, governing the soldiers, appointing inferior judges called alcaldes, or syndics, and himself supreme judge, notary, and custodian of deeds and records. There were no taxes except customs duties, but repairs of roads could be compelled. The governor and record-keeper received fees, — fifty cents per signature and half as much again per flourish, — which tends to account for the number of notices, decrees, certificates, etc., in the records.

With Henrique Grimarest's incumbency begin the regular series of grants and deeds still preserved, with the judicial proceedings, in heavy cypress boxes in the Mobile Probate Court. The deeds, but not the proceedings, have been rendered accessible to the public by two manuscript volumes of Translated Records, completed in 1840 by Joseph E. Caro, under commission from Governor Bagby of Alabama. The act of the Legislature was passed January 9, 1833.[2]

The earliest documents relate to Pass Christian, Cat Island, Biloxi, and other places in old West Florida, and were therefore regulated from Mobile. The procedure was by petition to

[1] 2 Martin's *Louisiana*, p. 14. See Blackmar's *Spanish Institutions in the Southwest*.

[2] The records at New Orleans were sadly abused and many destroyed or taken away by Federal troops in the American civil war. A fire at Pensacola on October 24, 1811, destroyed much that was there, and pirates more. The sub-delegate, Colonel Don José Masot, was instructed on closing the intendancy there to remove the archives to Havana, but he failed to do so. When Jackson captured Pensacola in May, 1818, it was agreed that the archives should be taken to Havana, and Masot duly embarked with them on the United States schooner Peggy. Corsairs overpowered the Peggy and threw the papers overboard, except one box which they kept. So it seems nothing ever reached Cuba from Pensacola except some inventories brought the preceding year by Don Francisco Gutierrez de Arroyo, the only part of the removal order which Masot had permitted him to carry out. Pintado in 2 White's *New Recopilacion*, pp. 340, 341, 370.

the governor-general (Galvez until 1786), who either granted directly, and instructed Charles Laveau Trudeau, surveyor-general of the province, or Grimarest, the governor of Mobile, to put the applicant in possession, or perhaps he commissioned the governor to do so if on investigation it seemed the land was vacant. Trudeau had Vincente Sebastian Pintado as deputy from 1796, and was succeeded by him in 1805.[1]

The first grant near the city was December 18, 1781, to Pierre Juzan, his Majesty's commissary for the Indians in the Town of Mobile, upon his petition for a tract one league in extent on both sides of the river, formerly possessed in British times by Henry Lizard and Thomas McGillivray. It is said to be bounded on one side by Bayou Cannon and on the other by Laprade's Bluff, and thus easily recognized as our Twenty-one Mile Bluff. Juzan says that he has no land, and in consequence of severe losses he desires to go to stock-raising on his river tract.

This is the first instance in these records of re-granting what had been British property. The Versailles treaty of peace of September 3, 1783, was to allow eighteen months for British subjects to sell and leave, and the time was extended six months longer; but this treaty was not yet concluded. While West Florida was Spanish in fact, the war continued elsewhere until that treaty recognized the independence of the United States, and at the same time confirmed East and West Florida to Spain.

The most prominent re-grant was that by Governor Grimarest of Dauphine Island to Joseph Moro, the origin, in fact, of the existing title to that historic spot. Moro's petition of July 31, 1781, is dated at New Orleans, and says that he is an inhabitant of that city. Galvez the next day directs Grimarest to investigate the matter, and if the land is vacant to put Moro into possession and return the proceedings made out "in continuation" with the commission, — a substitute for the indorsements on original papers by officials in our practice. September 21 of the same year there was a report by Charles Parent, Orbano Demouy, Dubroca, and Louis Carriere, who had been called on for evidence.

For some reason the matter was held up over two years, until

[1] 2 White's *New Recopilacion,* p. 338.

after peace was declared; for Grimarest's concession to Moro bears date December 5, 1783, after J. B. Lamy had made a settlement in the centre of the island. In 1785 we find the king maintaining there a pilot and four sailors at an expense of $696.00.[1]

There seem to be no grants or deeds of town lots while Grimarest was in command at Mobile, but several times its old inhabitants were thus called on in determining what was royal domain and what not. In October, 1782, Messrs. Lusser, Duret, and Dubroca certify that the small island known as Chucfe and "Camp of the Grand Bay," distant a league from the town, had never been owned, and they are granted provisionally to Joseph Colomb. So in December, 1783, Chastang senior, Dubroca, and Duret similarly certify that Round Island has been possessed by no one except Mme. Maurau, who was in possession in 1752 without title. This leads to the absolute grant to Francis Krebs, whose memorial sets up that Bienville had permitted Mme. Maurau, mother-in-law of Krebs, to occupy the island in 1745, and that Galvez had once stopped there on returning from Mobile and Pensacola and promised Mme. Krebs a grant.

December 3, 1782, Louis Francis Baudin, called Monluis, was granted thirty arpens east of grand Bayou Mathew, bounded north by a small bayou called Haron, it "being owned by the English and consequently by legal right . . . the property of the Royal Domain." This grant, like others, was provisional, until some general regulation concerning land claims should be established. He had to withdraw slaves from his old place, he says, because of the danger from Talapoosy Indians, that being too far off from Mobile. It is not named as occupied after his death in 1787, however. The successful petition of Jacques de la Saussaye about a fortnight earlier for a tongue of land shows that this vicinity (opposite Twenty-seven Mile Bluff) had until recently been inhabited by the Indians. The neighborhood was much sought after, for we find Grimarest on April 29, 1783, granting to Daniel Ward thirty-five arpens on the west of Bayou Mathew, opposite the field of Monlouis, near Narbonne's. It would therefore seem as if others than Saussaye thought the Indians would keep their promise of solemn peace.

[1] 2 Martin's *Louisiana*, p. 81.

We find Saussaye acting as notary to the first private deed, March 30, 1786, when Favrot, as attorney in fact for Grimarest, sold Daniel Ward for $240 a plantation of four arpens front on Fowl River, six leagues from Mobile. Grimarest had bought the place a year and a half before, and we may imagine lived there in the summer, but he had been succeeded (*ad interim* at first) before August of 1785 by our second Spanish governor, Pedro Favrot. This was possibly the beautiful place now known as Parker's, whose oak seventeen feet in circumference has a spread of over one hundred feet. There still exists an irregular inclosure, possibly for cattle or a bull-fight, surrounded by an earthen wall, and pieces of a cement floor are dug up near the fine bluff.

Favrot was a captain in the army, and, if he was the French captain who had been wounded in 1736 at Bienville's disastrous battle of Ackia, he must have been now an old man. Just before the change of flag, Louis XV. had conferred on him the cross of St. Louis, but he would seem to have remained at New Orleans and entered the Spanish service.[1] With him the title "Civil and Military Commandant" takes the place of "Governor of the Town of Mobile."

When the eighteen months allowed the British by treaty to change their religion and allegiance, or sell out and leave, had expired, the regulation of lands was confided to the governor-general at New Orleans. Galvez had been promoted in 1784 to his father's position of viceroy of Mexico; and Stephen Miro, colonel of the royal armies, was civil and military governor of the provinces of Louisiana, Mobile, and Pensacola. The first act recorded of his was confirming to Antonio Bassot of Mobile, a volunteer in the infantry regiment De Soria, a lot of land in that town on or near Galvez Street, with a front of one hundred and forty steps by two hundred deep, each step being two and a half feet. The lot had been granted him by Galvez on the conquest of the place, and he had built a house on it. In the same year, 1786, Bassot sold it to one Fargg. This seems to be the southwest corner of our Dauphin and Conception streets, the former street being probably called during a short time for the conqueror, who in this year died in Mexico of chagrin. He had built a place at Chapultepec, which excited

---

[1] 2 Gayarré's *Louisiana*, p. 109.

suspicion that he contemplated a revolution, and his direct method of doing everything was inexplicable to the bureaucracy of Spain.

By deed of October 19, 1786, F. Fontanilla (who some years later describes himself as laborer or peon in the commissariat) conveys to J. Colomb a house and lot on Royal Street, doubtless on the east side, "cornering on Dauphin Street," and bounded by the river. This is the first Spanish mention of those streets. The lot has ten toises front by twenty-six toises (156 feet) deep, inclosed with pickets, and there are other buildings besides the house. The price is $200, of course in Spanish silver dollars. The transaction would seem to be connected in some way with the sale on the same day by Colomb to Fontanilla of another house and lot on Royal Street. This last deed may be found interesting as giving the usual form of private conveyance. It reads thus : —

"Know all men by these presents, that I, Joseph Colomb, an inhabitant of this city, do hereby covenant that I sell really and truly to Francis Fontanilla a house of my own, lying and being in the city on Royal Street, opposite the house of Augustin Rochon, erected on a lot of ground bounded on the river, containing fifteen toises in front by twenty-six toises in depth, and having in said house a billiard table with all the apparatus appertaining to the same; and it is the same house, lot of ground and billiard table, together with all the buildings thereon, that I sell the said Francis Fontanilla for and in consideration of the sum of one hundred and fifty dollars cash to me in hand paid, by a note payable in three months from the date of these presents, the receipt of which note is hereby acknowledged, renouncing the benefit of the law *non numerata pecunia*, and of all others thereto relative : In virtue of which, I relinquish and divest myself of the right of property, possession, useful dominion and ownership which I had and held in and over the premises above conveyed and described, and cede, renounce and transfer the whole unto the purchaser, or his lawful representatives, in order that he may as true owner thereof enjoy, possess, sell, alienate, or dispose of the same at his will and pleasure. In virtue whereof I make this deed in his favor in token of real delivery, whereby it is shown that he has acquired possession thereof, without the necessity of any further proof, of which I relieve him; and I bind myself to the eviction, security, and warranty of this sale in all the form of law, with my property present and to come, granting hereby as inserted the clause of guarantee, renouncing the laws in my favor with the general [provision] in form prohibiting the same. And I, the said Francis Fontanilla, being present at the execution of this deed, do accept it in my favor, receiving therefrom as purchased the said house, billiard and lot of land, for the sum and as sold to me, acknowledging the same to be placed at my disposal, and grant a formal receipt. In testimony whereof, the present is done at the Town of Mobile on the nineteenth day of October in the year of our Lord 1786.

"FRANCIS FONTANILLA. (Seal)   JOSEPH COLOMB. (Seal)
    Witness, CHASTANG, JR.   Witness, DUBROCA.
Before me, SANTIAGO DE LA SAUSSAYE,   (Seal)
                                    Notary Public.
"Approved, PEDRO FAVROT." (Seal)

A well-known name in the southern part of the present county of Mobile is Bosage. The original settler of that ilk was Joseph Baussage in 1786 (for the name is variously spelled); and the petition and grant in his case, while fairly illustrating the procedure as to country lands, certainly rank among the curiosities of official correspondence. In full they are as follows: —

"To his Excellency, Stephen Miro, Colonel of the Royal
    Armies of his Catholic Majesty, and Governor-General of
    the Province of Louisiana, etc.

"Joseph Bousage, an inhabitant of the jurisdiction of Mobile, has the honor to represent to your Excellency, that he has been compelled in consequence of the state of his misery to retire with his wife and children on a piece of land situated on Bayou Battree, bounded on the east by Lisloy and on the west by Pine Point, which makes a distance of one league in front, for the purpose of fishing and planting some corn for the support and maintenance of his family; he further represents, that the said land has never been claimed by any person, except some prisoners who were living on it without title, possession, or right, and who have abandoned it a short time afterwards, and by Barthelemy Grelot better than eighteen months ago, who then moved to Bay St. Louis: wherefore your petitioner dares to hope that his unfortunate situation will appeal to your Excellency's feelings, and you will be pleased to grant him the said tract of land, in order that he may live thereon undisturbed, and conceal from the eyes of the world his poverty and misery; taking also into consideration that he is a poor father of a family of seven children, who is in trouble and his wife sickly; and lastly, this desolated family stretch their arms towards your Excellency and humbly entreat your Excellency to grant them your Honor's protection. In acknowledgment of which they will not cease in offering the most passionate prayers to God our Lord for the preservation of your Excellency's health and prolongation of your days, and of all those who are dear to your Excellency.

"I remain with profound respect and entire submission, Excellent Sir, your most obedient and humble servant, Mobile this sixth day of October, 1786,

"Joseph Bouzage."

Favrot approved these facts, and Miro, on November 7, directs that "the commandant of Mobile, Pedro Favrot, shall permit the petitioner to establish himself on the tract of land which he solicits situated on River Batteree, bounded on the east by Ocas Island and on the west by Pine Point."

Bosage duly went into possession of his Bayou la Batré property and made improvements. He considered his forty arpens depth as beginning, not at the marshy seashore, but at the line of tillable land, and acted accordingly. This was saving up more "misery" for his family. Ten years later, after he had died, his widow, Louisa Budro, was threatened with the loss of the back part of the tract in the application of some one else for a grant of it. She petitioned the governor-general, and, being backed up by the commandant, the Bosage grant was corrected so as to begin with the dry land as occupied.

Most of the new settlers wanted country lands, not in order, like Bosage, to hide themselves and their misery from the world, but to raise stock, or corn, or tobacco. And it was a fine opportunity. The British had largely abandoned the country, leaving their well-cleared farms on the Tensaw or "Tombagbe" to become Spanish royal domain, and thus liable to be granted to the first comer, in substantially this form: —

"The Surveyor-General of this Province, Charles Laveau

Trudeau, will put the petitioner in possession of the tract of land for which he prays a grant, containing twenty arpens in front with the usual depth of forty, at the place designated in the preceding memorial: provided that the same is vacant and without causing injury to a third person; under the express conditions, that he will make the customary road and clear sufficient ground thereon within the term of one year, and further that this grant shall be void unless the said tract of land shall be actually occupied and cultivated within the exact period of three years, during which time the petitioner shall not sell or in any other way alienate the said land. In consequence thereof, let the proceedings of the survey of the said tract of land be made out in continuation herewith, and, when completed, let them be transmitted to me, in order to provide the petitioner with a competent title in due form."

In this way on August 16, 1787, Cornelius McCurtin, who married Euphrosyna, one of Bosage's children, acquired Major Farmer's place on the Tensaw River, having a front of eighty arpens on each side of the river, bounded north by Mme. Milon and south by Chastang. The only consideration named in the petition is that McCurtin had already gone into possession and at considerable expense built a house, which would seem to show that the hospitable roof which sheltered Bartram had been burned, or otherwise destroyed. Farmer, he says, had "abandoned" the place, and, as the major died before the Spaniards came, this was true enough. A petition of James Fraser for lands of Farmer on the "Tombagbe" shows that he knew of this fact, for he ascribes the abandonment of these lands to Farmer's widow. An even clearer case of abandonment, perhaps, was that of Walker, whose lands on the Mobile River were granted about the same time to John Joyce. Favrot solemnly certifies that Walker did "abandon" the place, and the petition to which he refers leaves no doubt of it. It recites that Walker was killed by his Majesty's troops at the time of the siege of Mobile.

In this way Simon Landry, a mulatto from Baton Rouge, gets river lands of "McGilleveray," probably at Seymour's Bluff. "Seymour's" is the nearest the unromantic Americans could get to pronouncing *Simon's* French name. Here it is that the river makes that remarkable goose-neck or double horseshoe curve, coming back after several miles to a few hundred yards from its starting point, and from the height one has a beautiful view up and down the stream. This has long been the home of the Andrys, and near there many live, intermixed with Chastangs, but in their French patois claiming descent from the Creole Simon Andry (or L'Andry).

Peter Juzan thus acquired lands of Dugald Campbell north of Bayou Cedrera, Peter Trouillet those of Strahan at the mouth of the "Tombacbe," and John Turnbull those of Formand on the same river. George Walton under the next commandant gets McIntosh's Bluff of twenty arpens front on the Tombagbe. Next south had lived a Mr. Sunflower, and his land also went to some one desiring, probably, to put in corn and tobacco.

Only one instance is on record where the petitioner did not get what he wanted, and that was when Dominique Dolive asked for forty or fifty arpens of Michael Grant's for cattle-raising on the east side of the bay, between the widow Rochon on the north and the widow Dupont on the south. The refusal was not from any consideration for Dr. Grant, but because Dolive wanted too much. The general rule was now laid down by Miro on July 2, 1787, that grants would not be made, except for some very satisfactory reason, of more than twenty arpens front by the usual depth of forty. Dolive, like a wise man, then filed a new petition for twenty arpens front, and obtained the nucleus of the Dolive possessions at the mouth of the Apalache River.

Somewhat higher up was the De Lusser Tract on Tensaw River. This Louis Duret bought later of the heirs for forty dollars on time. Outlying property was sometimes undesirable because of fear of Indian outbreak.

And yet as a rule the Spanish succeeded to the friendship which the savages had generally entertained for the French. In the winter of 1781–82 there was a visit of Creeks to Mobile. LeClerc Milfort was a Frenchman who at that time lived among them, and was later to return to France and publish a book on his experiences. Among the Indians he was chief and in France a general, so that his book has a unique value. He tells of the traditional origin of the Muscogees in caves on the Red River, and of this expedition which he now led to visit the aboriginal seat of the race. His followers consisted of two hundred braves from Little Talassee. After a time they went on west, hunting by the way, and returned home next spring by way of the Ohio River.[1] On June 22, 1784, a vast congress of Indians was held at Mobile, presided over by Miro. Here were represented almost all of the tribes which had been previously identified with our history. Among them were prominent even the Chickasaws, as well as the Choctaws and Alabamas, and treaties of alliance were made with all.[2] The Indian trade rapidly became important.

But foreign commerce was all but dead. Spain's policy always was to forbid her colonies to trade with any other country, and at the same time she prohibited every industry, like raising tobacco, olives, or grapes, which would compete with the mother country.[3] This system was a severe one for Mobile and old Louisiana generally, and in fact the regulations were more or less evaded, even by the provincial authorities. In 1782 changes were made in the matter in favor of New Orleans and Pensacola, where were custom-houses, while no mention seems to be made of Mobile. But a better time was coming. July 24, 1784, a trade concession was granted in favor of James Mather, of New Orleans, he contracting with the government to employ two vessels under the Spanish flag and supply all that was needed for the Indian trade at Mobile and Pensacola. We soon find Mather confining himself to Mobile and William Panton operating at Pensacola, where he lived, after being driven by the American Revolution from Carolina and Georgia. Their vessels loaded at London, for the Indians had learned to prefer English goods, and they took the place in business left open by McGillivray's flight. The local trade, too, must have been something, as in 1785 Mobile's population was 746.[4] The next year the home government, against the protest of Mather and Panton, much curtailed commercial privileges. And yet it was rather as to source of supplies than from any niggardliness; for we find the crown supplying annually for the Mobile Indian trade, doubtless for presents and other subsidies, $10,000. The local expenses of

---

[1] Gatschet, *Creek Migration Legend*, p. 230.

[2] 3 Gayarré's *Louisiana*, p. 160.

[3] Blackmar's *Spanish Institutions in the Southwest*, p. 297.

[4] 3 Gayarré's *Louisiana*, pp. 153–156 ; 2 Martin's *Louisiana*, p. 77.

the king in 1785 were about \$11,000, as follows: governor, \$2,000; chaplain, \$360; sacristan, \$180; chapel, \$50; English interpreter, \$180; storekeeper, \$600; adjutant, \$300; guard, \$180; adjutant of artillery, \$300; armorer, \$360; surgeon, mate, and nurses, \$1,140; *patron* and hands, \$1,296; besides \$1,080 also mentioned for commissary and armorer.[1]

[1] 2 Martin's *Louisiana*, pp. 81, 83.

CHAPTER XXXIII.

In three years since the last census the population of Mobile doubled, for in 1788 it is given as 1,468, against only 265 at Pensacola, which had fallen off one half. This should indicate prosperity, but at all events land was not dear even in town. Ruiz, a free negro, in 1788 sells John Joyce a house and lot on the corner of St. Charles (St. Joseph) and St. Francis (St. Michael), opposite Mr. Orbanne's, for $100. Joyce in the same month of April buys a lot ten toises front on Royal, and extending twenty-six toises to the river, for $25 cash, and has a house thrown in. This was situated second north of our St. Michael, opposite Narbonne's lot, and south (north?) of Dubuisson's.

Next year the heirs of Jean Baptiste de Lusser, deceased, — viz., Cabaret de Trepy and Hazeur de Lorme, of New Orleans, — seem to have sold all the De Lusser land south of the fort.[1]

The names of all the De Lusser heirs are not given. De Trepy and De Lorme seem to represent them under a "letter of attorney." Pierre Marie Cabaret de Trepy was a chevalier of the order of St. Louis, and is in the title as husband of Marguerite Chevalier De Velle, probably daughter of Constance De Velle. Louis Francis Xavier Hazeur de Lorme, on the other hand, is grandson of Captain (Joseph Christophe) De Lusser, and also his executor. De Lorme must be a son, therefore, of Manon Hazeur. On May 14 they made a private deed to Louis Duret, of course before Folch, wherein, for a note of forty dollars due at one year, they sell a lot of the usual dimensions, bounded north by land purchased by Miguel Eslava at public auction, and on the south by Duret. This lot would

---

[1] *Mobile Translated Records*, p. 96 ; 2 Martin's *Louisiana*, p. 99.

therefore seem to be in the square west of our Royal and south
of our Eslava Street.   Duret was a lieutenant of militia, and
died in 1790.   Folch, at the request of the same De Trepy and
De Lorme, five days after the private deed, decrees the sale of
the other lots of J. B. Lusser, and they were accordingly sold
at auction, all being east and across the "street" from Eslava's.   The purchasers, beginning from Duret's on the south
and coming north to the esplanade, were as follows, each
extending from the street eastwardly to the river: [1] —

(1) Fifty feet front, bought by Alby, the fort carpenter,
for $45; (2) Forty feet front, by the negress Mary Josephine,
for $30; (3) Fifty-four feet front, by John B. Ham, for $54;
(4) Sixty-two feet front, by the negro Joseph the blacksmith,
for $40; (5) Sixty-two feet front, by the mulatto Honoré
La Pointe, for $40;   (6) Seventy-six feet front, by the mulatto
Petit Jean, for $30.   Four years later Honoré, who had
moved away, sold his lot, with a house on it, to William
Mitchell, for $120.   The average price, therefore, for the
river front at this point, — the site now of the Wilson power-
house and of many buildings, — was considerably under a dollar
a foot.

Eslava lived to be not only an important official but a large
landowner in this part of the country.   Family tradition describes him as a tall, soldierly man, without beard, and says
that he came originally from San Sebastian in Spain to the
City of Mexico, where he was manager of the mint, and thence
went to Natchez.   In a later petition he says that he was public
storekeeper (commissary) for the king of Spain at Natchez,
1782–84; and we learn from this and other papers of his that
he occupied the same position (*Guarda Almacen General*) at
Mobile from 1784 through all the Spanish rule.   In addition
he was also at some period collector of customs, and in 1793
"*Ministro Principal de la Real Hacienda*," or treasurer, at
Mobile.[2]   He had to be present officially, according to the archives, at all public acts affecting royal property and contracts.
Such presence is spoken of as his "intervention."   He was
also superintendent of the hospital.

There is something perplexing about his early purchases,

[1] *Mobile Translated Records*, p. 97.
[2] See 3 *American State Papers*, p. 560.

which were mainly at auction. Although in 1789 he had a house, said to have been brought from Spain, two years later we find him petitioning for land between the De Lussers and public lands, in order to build and thus escape the "exorbitant rent" which he was paying. The lot granted on this occasion was but sixty feet front by one hundred and twenty feet deep; while the tract on which his house was built had over seven times as large a frontage, being no doubt the auction purchase. It extended from our Royal to St. Emanuel, and from our Monroe to Eslava. The description of his place, the site now of homes of all degrees, in a deed of 1794 is picturesque, and reads thus: —

"A high house erected on a certain lot of land containing four hundred and sixty-two feet in front, on the side of the river, by three hundred and twenty-six feet in depth, fronting on the woods, bounded on the north by the fort of this town, and on the southwest by house of the deceased Duret. The land is enclosed by new cypress pickets, with all the fruit trees, gardens, kitchen and all other buildings thereon."[1]

Rations originally were distributed by him, as general storekeeper, to the troops and government employees, from a house on St. Charles Street. But when it became old, Eslava with the permission of the commandant abandoned it, and erected one south of the fort, near his own residence. This was a good move, and nearer the warehouse of 1793. On July 16, next year, we find the original lot granted to Mary Aygue.

There was a mysterious transaction, probably connected with an official valuation of 1793 still preserved, by which Eslava sells his own place to Leonard Marbury. The consideration was $4,060, of which $2,560 was cash, and the balance was to be paid on the arrival of his schooner from the north, which was to be about the end of the year. And Marbury's ship came home, for next year he sold the place for ten dollars less to John Joyce. But in some way Eslava repurchased it.

Eslava was to have considerable trouble with his titles in American times. The De Lusser purchase, even where he lived, was unfavorably regarded, and required a special act of

---

[1] *Mobile Translated Records*, p. 150. For map see Deed Book 27, N. S., p. 527.

the Congress of the United States, May 21, 1824,[1] for its vali-
dation in the hands of his heirs.

We now first meet William Fisher also, who was in later
years to become, like Eslava, a great landowner. In May,
1790, he buys for $500 cash from John Arnot, who got it from
P. Jusan, a lot on the south (west?) side of St. Charles, at the
corner of St. Francis, having one hundred and thirty feet front
by seventy-one deep.

Captain Manuel de Lanzos seems to act as commandant at
Mobile from 1790, and in 1792 Baron Francis de Carondelet
was governor-general. Lanzos was, during his two or more
terms, to become thoroughly identified with the place. He is
said to have come from Valencia in Spain to Peru, and thence
to Mobile. After his incumbency he lived in New Orleans.

As a witness to a deed of June 12, 1792, we now first see
John Forbes, to be, not many years later, so important a factor
in Indian trade. His house, Panton, Leslie & Co., may even
before this date have operated in Mobile, but apparently they
had not yet become landowners. It is not until 1795 that
we find him mentioned as a landowner, having on St. Charles
some small cabins at the corner of a street which we take to be
St. Francis.

In August, 1793, was an auction sale in Mobile of the lands
of another non-resident named La Fargg, at the instance of
his attorney in fact, Francis Durel.

"In the town aforesaid, on the fifth of the month of August,
1792," according to the Translated Records,[2] "Francis Durel
having requested the sale and transfer of the lot of land and
cabin conveyed by Antonio Bassot in favor of the above named
La Fargg, and desiring to make sale thereof; Therefore I, the
Commandant, attended by two official witnesses, went on this
day at ten o'clock A. M. on the lot above recited, and on order-
ing the sound of the drum the said Durel prayed by saying:
Is there any one who wishes to purchase a lot of ground with a
small house thereon, the said lot measuring one hundred and
twelve feet in front, be it more or less, by the corresponding
depth, as the property of Mr. La Fargg? In consequence of
which, James Nadeau offered most for the said premises, and
the same was thereupon struck off to him for the sum of $150

---

[1] 6 *U. S. Statutes at Large*, p. 311.   [2] *Mobile Translated Records*, p. 132.

cash as specified above. In faith whereof, the said James Nadeau, the two official witnesses, and 1 the said Commandant,
have signed the present act of sale," etc.

Thereupon Durel made a deed to Nadeau, but Pierre Juzan
afterwards bought from Nadeau at a trifle less.

Miro had granted Pierre Trouillet, of Mobile, a lot of ground
on Royal Street, "fronting the Government House," which
later maps show to have been at the southeast corner of Royal
and Government streets. Lanzos interfered and refused to
put him in possession, because it was too near the fort, — which
Trouillet admits is the case. But the lieutenant bought a forty-
foot lot adjoining from Nadeau, and then obtained a grant of
twenty feet of the lot before refused him.[1] This Trouillet property thus seems to be an encroachment on the esplanade of the
fort, — the first of record. Although, as to country lands, from
this time the duty of putting in possession again devolves on
Trudeau or his deputy, the commandant still acts in regard to
city lots. But a few months later, Lanzos, under commission
from Carondelet, puts F. Baudin in possession of a lot sixty
feet front on Royal, between Trouillet and the fort. And yet
the fort might be important again.

What has been called the Spanish Conspiracy has excited
much interest, particularly in Kentucky, where it blasted several characters. For James Wilkinson, the United States
general, was its head, and John Brown, representative in Congress, Judge Sebastian of the Court of Appeals, Hary Innes,
and other prominent men, were deeply implicated.

In its beginnings it might be called a patriotic movement, if
patriotism consists of love of home and country, and not in the
worship of a flag which then represented seaboard and not
Kentucky interests. The colonies had just achieved their independence, and the pioneers who had won a home in the wilds
felt that the government across the toilsome mountains was,
in courting the aid of Spain, willing to leave the Mississippi
closed and Kentucky shut off from her only commerce. Even
Virginia, they thought, was reluctant to have them become
independent of her, and the movement begun in 1785 for
Kentucky's admission to the Union was finally realized only in
1792, after nine conventions.

[1] *Mobile Translated Records*, p. 138.

Spain encouraged the movement for independence, and endeavored by pensions, promises, and concessions to win the leaders, with the object of having the district become either a part of her Gulf provinces or an independent country under a Spanish protectorate. Spain had made no treaty recognizing the United States, but had an agent, Gardoqui, in the east.

The plan was originally suggested by Navarro when intendant, adopted at Madrid, and carefully engineered by Governor Miro, who after Navarro's departure in 1788 made himself intendant, too. Miro was very popular with the Americans and Spanish subjects alike.[1]

The pensioners went on receiving money, but, from the time when the new American government under the Constitution of 1787 felt itself firmly in power and a national sentiment developed, the conspirators gradually lost their hold. Some, like Wilkinson, were able to turn coat and sail with the new wind; others went on blindly to their own destruction. The danger in Carondelet's time was of an invasion of Louisiana by the Americans, not of the Spanish annexation of Kentucky planned by Miro.

From 1793 the Mobile deeds, and among them one of Pierre Trouillet, contain militia titles, — lieutenant, captain, etc. It was at this time that Governor Carondelet regularly organized the local military over Louisiana and West Florida, and Lanzos had masons at work on Fort Charlotte. An inspection of "Fuerte Carlota" was made in August, 1793, by Nicolas Mangoula, Josef Barriales, and Juan Beson, while Miguel Eslava was present with others. This seems to have been in addition to a general overhauling by John Joyce as contractor early in the year, which, after formal examination by Juan Alvi and Antonio Espejo as carpenters, Nicolas Mangoula and Charles Lalande as masons, and Bertrand Nicolas and the free negro Josef Lusser as smiths, had been duly accepted by Lanzos for the crown. We find Orbanne Demouy now contracting to supply troops and hospital with meat at $3\frac{1}{2}$ silver "sueldos" per pound; and oath of allegiance was exacted from foreigners, like Nadeau and Langevin of Mobile, and J. B. Martin of Fish

---

[1] 2 Martin's *Louisiana*, p. 100; 2 Gayarré's *Louisiana*, p. 192; Green's *Spanish Conspiracy, passim.*

River (*Riviera de Pescado*). A new wharf and warehouse were built. Everything was military.

The events of this year were momentous. France a republic; her king imprisoned and then guillotined; and all the other countries looking on aghast, or combining to crush the revolution. The Spanish king declares war against France at Aranjuez in March, and the *cedula* was published at Mobile in August. This and other proclamations call on the people to contribute themselves and their means to oppose the disorder and impiety of that country. A royal proclamation, published at Mobile as elsewhere, invited back deserters from the army and navy; and we find the woods near the town cleared, no doubt for military as well as for the sanitary reasons named by Lanzos. The people of the United States were in sympathy with the new republic, and the French ambassador Genet carried things with a high hand over in the States. He was even planning to raise an American army and reconquer Louisiana for France.

It was to meet this that Carondelet was active, fortifying forts and raising troops. At Mobile two companies were thus mobilized, — one of infantry and one of cavalry. All classes seemed loyal to the Spanish cause; but perhaps the old French remembered O'Reilly at New Orleans.

CHAPTER XXXIV.

THE many official proceedings by the commandants which have survived would, if given in detail, furnish material for several volumes; but even a selection will show much of the public customs of the time and the private life of the people.

For the first few years transactions are in French, or in French and Spanish too; but, as the hold of Spain grew stronger, hers became the sole official language. The Trouillet division of 1786, before Favrot, was in French, but the partition of Louis Duret's estate in 1795, for instance, was altogether in Spanish.

We find the commandant exercising jurisdiction, often a very summary one, over almost every kind of dispute, including contract, attachment, and damages, and are enabled to follow up the procedure on account of the convenient practice of writing out even the original papers "in continuation" on consecutive sheets. Where a petition requires notice, the commandant's order, therefore, comes next after the petition; then the notary, or later two official witnesses, gives notice and certifies that fact. At the trial the testimony is taken down in writing under oath, and the decrees and subsequent proceedings follow in order, — all these papers being stitched together and preserved as archives.

We are told that the court (*tribunal*) was informal, but quite the reverse was true in Mobile, at least under the early commandants. We do not find lawyers in the American sense, but clerks or notaries aided the parties in their petitions where the cases were not *viva voce*. Criminal causes were tried before the same courts as civil, perhaps with official defending counsel. On giving security for costs, appeal lay to the supreme tribunal at New Orleans, thence to St. Jago de Cuba, and thence to Spain. In criminal cases the appeal was only in capital offences, and, from the expense, practically did not exist. Punishment was mild, generally a fine or stocks, and serious crimes were rare. The alcalde, like our justice of the peace, heard civil and criminal causes summarily and without written proceedings. His jurisdiction was limited to complaints in which the matter in dispute did not exceed twenty dollars.[1]

On March 15, 1786, we find Pierre Trouillet petitioning for dissolution of the partnership with his brother Jean and for division of the property, Pierre wishing to leave for New Orleans.

The business in which they were engaged would seem to be naval stores, at least in part, for one of their assets was a claim of 10,779 piastres against the king for "brais et godrons." Their account has also survived for such supplies to a number of vessels during the years 1782-85, all as furnished under a contract with Commandant Favrot. The slaves were valued at an average of 500 piastres, horses at sixteen piastres, cattle at twelve each. There were a number of accounts due them, a note of Mr. Miguel Eslava for 381 piastres for one, and they owed considerable also. They owned a house, a frame filled in between the posts and covered with bark. It was five feet above ground, with cellar below, which had a brick wall. The building was ceiled and composed of two rooms, hall, two closets, a double chimney, and had a gallery all around. Outside were kitchen and garden. The whole was within a picket fence, and on the corner of the street. This place was valued at 450 piastres, and went to Jean in the division.

The proceedings began with a petition to Favrot, the appointment of Genier and Dubroca as commissioners on the nomination of Pierre and Jean respectively, all in the presence of Santiago de la Saussaye, the notary public. Then was made out a list of debts due to and those due by the firm, signed by parties, commissioners, commandant, and notary; and next one of some twenty-eight slaves, with values varying according to age, and also including house and animals. It was thus found that each should receive 8,985 piastres $6\frac{3}{4}$ escalins, and the equivalent was allotted them respectively. Both brothers on March 24, 1786, signed at the end in token of full satisfaction.

[1] 2 White's *New Recopilacion*, pp. 693, 697.

In the course of the proceedings it is noted that there was a difference of forty per cent. between hard money and the paper current in the colony; but where necessary the paper values are reduced to coin, and the settlement is made on that basis.

Commandants sometimes exercised very summary powers in the collection of debts. In this same year, for instance, we find Favrot enforcing a claim against William Loyson, then a trader in the "Tinsa" country, although in British times he had been a silversmith at Mobile.

Loyson had mortgaged some negroes to Dé Lande Dapremond, of New Orleans, and did not pay the debt. John Linder, Jr., of the Tensaw district, became his surety for speedy payment, taking a hypothecation of the negroes, according to which on forfeiture the negroes should be sold at the gate of the fort. It appears that he made default, and in consequence Favrot sent the notary Saussaye and three soldiers over by canoe to Tensaw to imprison Loyson and seize his property. This was done in the presence of John Linder, lieutenant of police, and all of his property inventoried and brought to Mobile, where it was appraised and sold. He had deerskins, money, bear oil, draft of Charles Hall on John Joyce, etc., valued in all at 266 piastres, 4 reals, hard money, which then varied fifty per cent. from paper. Of this there were in gold two "portugaises," a coin worth apparently something over $12\frac{1}{2}$ piastres. The expenses of this five-day trip were thirty and a half piastres, of which Genier, who owned the canoe, received three, and the three rowers three piastres each. The notary charged thirty reals a day.

After all, the slaves were not sold, for the two Linders were in Loyson's debt for merchandise, and he was permitted to return home until the younger Linder came back from New Orleans. When that happened, the affair was settled and the slaves returned. Loyson's attachment became a matter only of record, — signed by himself, the Linders, and Favrot.

The proceedings in the matter of François Robert in 1786 further illustrate the extensive powers of the commandant. Thomas Durnford, of New Orleans, on June 29 petitioned Pedro Favrot, alleging that he had delivered to Robert goods to be sold on Durnford's account to the value of 438 piastres and two escalins, besides advancing him 296 piastres and three escalins; but had been informed by John Linder that Robert had abandoned his boat, the St. Françoise, and had with one Simon left the country to go among the Indian nations. Annexed is an invoice of the goods delivered, including tafia, sugar, mahy (maize?) in grain, pieces of Marly (gauze), tobacco, colored linen, pepper, plates, and wine. The advances were in part through a draft on Messrs. Mather & Strothers for 190 piastres.

Favrot lost no time in the matter, and in fact seems to have acted upon earlier and independent information. He knew François Robert from having granted him a passport to trade in the country of the "Tinsas," and was notified June 27 of his decamping by the same John Linder, civil lieutenant of that district. Linder's note is in English. The commandant betook himself to the boat with Saussaye, the notary, and seized it and its remaining contents. The cargo was inventoried, and deposition of the mate, François Olivier, taken to the fact of flight and fraudulent bankruptcy. Favrot found that one Lafond, who had come from the Ohio (*Belle Riviere*) under Miro's pass (for passes were necessary for travelers), and Simon, of the Tensaw district, had disappeared at the same time, the three men carrying off a canoe of Mr. Linder and five of Simon's own slaves. They had apparently taken the Tombigbee route to reach "Fort Comberland."

Claims to the amount of 768 piastres were filed with the commandant, who sold the cargo for 546 piastres, and the boat, including sails, tackle, and anchors, to Durnford for 200 more. The fees paid were as follows: To the commandant as judge, for four sittings, including writings and signatures, twelve piastres; to the notary for four sessions and writings, nine and a half piastres, besides six and a half more for copies. A transcript and the receipts are annexed, and the whole file, with inch margins, makes up a respectable booklet of rough-edged paper, which is preserved entire.

Pretty much the same proceedings were taken against François Simon, the depositions being in English before "John Linder, J. P." Among the claims is that of Turnbull & Joyce, merchants, for 42 piastres for goods, such as soap, blankets, fishing-line, powder and tobacco. The goods were bought in 1785 and 1786 of Mather & Strothers, but Turnbull & Joyce receipt, apparently as their successors, for the forty-two dollars and a "picaillon" (picayune), or half rial, in paper.

The commandant paid the debts out of the proceeds of property of Sieur Simon found by Saussaye and witnesses at his place, "Bonne Eau," four leagues from Fish River. The goods seized were clothing, furniture, cows, etc., but the house (*cabanne*) was worthless, and the bread in the furnace was spoiled by the rain. At the appraisement and sale Jean Chastang was present, having been appointed to represent Simon, and acting under oath as "Deffenseur." Notices were publicly posted, and the sale opened with the drum at the usual place. Old pantaloons, coats, socks, cups, boiler, mill, vinegar, salt, cows, seine, and the other articles went to various bidders, realizing a total of 404 piastres seven escalins, which was twenty-nine dollars six escalins more than the debts. This balance was held subject to the order, not of Simon, but of Governor-General Miro.

Simon was captured by Ben James among the Choctaws, near the mouth of the "Black Warrior" River, and imprisoned at Mobile, where Saussaye induced him to acknowledge the claims paid as substantially correct; but the file closes without indication of his fate. The other two whites escaped safely to the Chickasaws. Mr. Bely Chaney (also called Baley Chené, Bailey China, etc.) figures considerably in the Tombigbee land titles, but he previously lived in the Tensaw district and was involved in several controversies now difficult to understand. On one occasion he accused Haisel McWilliams of stealing a negro, and McWilliams in reply had Josiah Fletcher in 1787 make before John Linder, J. P., an affidavit in English which shows up his accuser in a remarkable light. The paper reads as follows: —

"Mr. Josiah Fletcher Declares and Says that M. Bailey China took a Negro Girl and headed her up in a hogshead to keep her concealed at St. John's Bluff on board of a Vessel in East Florida about four years past, where her Master, Mr. Summerling, found her in his possession, and further the Deponent declares and says that after said Negro was found in the possession of Said China he the Said Deponent saw a place where [which] the said China had made underground in his house where he might hide himself in case of necessity and had undermined a passage to make his Escape, and had two guns placed at the inside with springs so as to do Execution in case any one entered at the door, while he escaped at said passage underground."

Some of the transactions in which Chaney was concerned at least illustrate the uncertainties of border life. He once had some controversy with George Phillips about the title to a negro boy named Ben, "swapped" for another in Savannah before his coming to Mobile, as testified to by Gerald Byrnes. At another time he got back a stolen slave. One James Danley met a trader named Balay in the Talapuche (Creek) nation and exchanged negroes with him, but on reaching Mobile found himself sued by Bely Chaney for the newly acquired slave. Cheney proved to Favrot's satisfaction that he had previously bought this Moses from William Tibbs at St. Augustine, East Florida, for 200 piastres. The Creek trader Balay had exchanged stolen property for good, and the commandant compelled Danley to give up the negro to Chaney. The trader, however, had some thirty or forty head of cattle in the Tensaw district under the charge of Charles Hall, and on Danley's petition the commandant directed John Linder to sequestrate the cattle until Balay returned Danley's negress or her value.

The names of a number of Americans are given in these papers as bad men who steal horses, guns, and the like, and make off among the Choctaws to hide. Many papers relate to the sale of negroes, and others show them stolen and taken to the Indian nations, where it was difficult to recover them. Some proceedings also indicate that the commandant received negro testimony even against white. It was in this manner that the widow of William Lanham recovered some of the property which Thomas Bates had received from her husband, and was trying to retain on the pretext of having lost the things by theft.

It would seem that Lanham had gone to "America," — the common Spanish name for the United States, — had been killed there by soldiers, and that Bates had brought his property from East Florida over to Mobile. The inventory embraces slaves, wearing-apparel, and apparently goods of a dry-goods stand. In the list we find, of course, pantaloons, coats, shirts, socks, etc., and also silk gauze and dresses, white linen, muslin handkerchiefs, table-cloths, napkins, skeins of silk, thread, gloves, besides teacups and plates of Delft ware (*fayence*), knives and forks, tin spoons and plates, a writing-desk, spurs, scales and weights, all closing with two suits of silk, "*couleur de Rose.*" The widow had come from South Carolina to reclaim her husband's things, but, in consideration of the surrender of the slave Moses, she gives up all interest in these articles. Even if Lanham's store had been elsewhere, this list shows what was handled at some Gulf town in Spanish times, and could not have varied much from goods then sold in Mobile.

The commandant had some duties much pleasanter to read of, and it is to be hoped pleasanter to perform, than taking possession of other people's property. An instance is found in the matter of contract for marriage between Monsieur Pierre Trouillet and Demoiselle Isabelle Narbonne, May 18, 1786.

It recites the groom's father and mother as Charles Trouillet and Marguerite Rochon, the bride's as Antoine Narbonne and Marie Joseph Krebs. Friends participated in the arrangement, such as Jean Chastang and Narcisse Brontin, Valentine Dubroca and Louis Dubroca, besides the bride's parents, she being a minor. The instrument provides for a Catholic marriage, to occur as soon as either requests it; that neither is liable for the ante-nuptial debts of the other, but they shall hold in common all property, movable and immovable, according to the custom of Spain, all other customs being renounced. The estate of the bride consisted of a ten-year-old negress named Julie, worth three hundred hard dollars (*piastres gourdes, monnoye sonnante*); while Trouillet brought into the community 8,000 piastres in money, slaves, etc., of which he gave as dower 750 piastres, hard money. In case of death of either without children, the survivor should receive the whole property. All execute before Commandant Favrot.

A contract signed before the notary in 1786 has survived, whereby François David is to work as carpenter for John Joyce at twenty-five piastres a month for three months, and Joyce is also to provide food and washing. The same year we have an apprenticeship of Josuée Faicher to Sieur Thomas Beauvais, a tailor, for six years, approved ("V° B° ") by the commandant, as everything must be. Beauvais promises to teach Josuée that trade, support him, care for him in sickness, and treat him as he did himself; while Josuée swears to conduct himself like a good boy and work out his term. In 1787 is an agreement by which Charles Lucas is advanced by Turnbull & Joyce, merchants, 800 *piastres gourdes* of merchandise, on a credit of ninety days, to use in his business of trade in the "Nation Chis."

Upon the death of any citizen, the commandant and notary sealed up his effects for proper administration. But this procedure has rather a gruesome aspect when we find them on May 7, 1787, hurrying to Jacob Schneider's house for that purpose immediately upon his death that day at five P. M. They made the inventory while the body was lying before them on a bench. There was nothing to seal up, but they opened his trunk and found clothing, razors, and accounts of no value. There were also planes, measures, hatchets, and in fact apparently a fair set of carpenter's tools, besides a cock, two hens, and seven chickens. The poultry three days later were appraised at two piastres, and everything else at sixteen, but Fontanilla paid twenty-three for the whole. This was exactly balanced by the debts and expenses, which included five piastres for a coffin, one to the sacristan for the grave, and four each to judge and notary for sessions (*vacations*) and writings.

One of the most interesting documents which has survived is that giving the proceedings, 1786–87, on the death of Don Juan Pedro Eon, curé and abbé, as Favrot calls him, of the district of Mobile. On hearing the news the commandant, notary, and witnesses went to the house, swore the attendants to there having been nothing disturbed, and then viewed the body on the bed in another room. His trunks and cabinets were sealed with paper strips, to which the commandant affixed his own seal in lack of a royal one, and all was put in charge of Fontanilla. After the funeral the seals were broken, the property inventoried and appraised, and in due course sold to pay debts, as in other cases, although he left sufficient money and paper. The debts were few, one being to his washerwoman. The product of the auction was 153 piastres two escalins. The debts were 74 piastres two escalins, including two piastres to the auctioneer, one to the drummer, and the fees of judge and notary. His coffin cost four piastres and was furnished by Mongoulas, who figures on other such occasions. His net estate was 549

piastres 2½ escalins, which was sent to Governor Miro to remain in the hands of the attorney of unclaimed goods (*procureur des biens vacants*) until heirs appeared. With the money
were also sent a roll of manuscript sermons and eighty-one
books. These last included seventeen volumes of "Confer-
ences Ecclesiastiques," five breviaries, five volumes of "Bour-
daloue's Sermons," sixteen of "Theologie Morale," two of
"Code Ecclesiastique," two of "Prelections Logiques," and
thirty-four books of prayers. This priest was a man of learning, and other effects show him to have been of some refine-
ment also. He had wine, oil, besides empty bottles and
"damejeannes," six knives, three spoons, four forks, six plates
of Rouen ware, four glass goblets, handkerchiefs, besides a
good deal in the way of clothing and bedding. He left tobacco
articles also. He must have been a man of some prominence,
for there were a good many letters from bishops, particularly
from Antoine Joseph des Laurents, bishop of St. Malo. From
orders among his assets, we learn that he was appointed by the
intendant and received a salary of thirty piastres a month,
besides fifty piastres a year for lights, bread and wine for the
church.

The articles belonging to this "chapelle" were carefully
separated, but everything else was auctioned off on December
30 and subsequent days. The officials worked as usual until
noon and from two to five o'clock P. M., but no longer, so that
the proceedings before and at the sale consumed several days.
The priest's clothes and things were bought by a number of
different parishioners. Saussaye bought some of his shirts,
Cassiano several suits; his socks went to Langevin, shoes to
Arnot (at a piastre and a half), razors to Dubroca; and Saussaye paid three piastres for his "parasol." One could hardly
walk the streets for some time without seeing some souvenir of
the late pastor.

Settlement of estates was not necessarily any more prompt
under the Spanish than under the American dispensation.
Upon the death of Sieur Claude Dupont, one Augustin Moreau,
called Belleisle, resident on Pascagoula River, became administrator. There were several distributees, to wit, Marie Anne
Dupont, wife of Mathias Leflaux; Louison Dupont, wife of
Joseph Krebs; Jean Baptiste and Catherine Dupont; and

Marie Jeanne Guillory, widow of Dupont, but then wife of Moreau. This married widow petitioned and obtained from Grimarest an arbitration in 1783, Chastang, Sr., Duret, and Dubroca being selected. In some way they overlooked the debts, and Moreau next year had the governor set aside their award. The same arbitrators were continued, however, and, deducting debts, they ascertained the balance to be 2,347 piastres. Of this, half went to the widow, the rest to the four heirs, all of whom in 1786 sign in satisfaction, renouncing all right of appeal. In connection with this settlement we find Favrot's grant (*homologation*) of Jean Baptiste's request for emancipation, and that Raphael Krebs be made his guardian (*subrogé tuteur*), Jean Baptiste being only twenty-one years old.

Favrot also exercised the right to emancipate slaves on the owner's being paid the price fixed by arbitration. Pierre Trouillet, for some reason (apparently the very good one of paternity), wished Alexis, a young mulatto belonging to the widow Rochon, to be freed, and demanded arbitrators. He appointed one, she another, and the commandant a third. These differed, and Favrot decided between them on 450 piastres. Trouillet paid this to the widow, and the commandant issued the emancipation papers at the fort.

We find Lanzos in November, 1793, taking depositions to return to Pensacola in the matter of a runaway slave, copies being retained at Mobile. The statements were so taken under oath on the petition of Josef Balenzategui, from whose schooner at Mobile a negress valued at $350 had escaped as he was about to take her to Pensacola to deliver Panton for "Tomas Cornis," her owner. The facts brought out by examination of Forbes and Fontanilla, all by question and answer, were that in the preceding spring a trader named Francis, of Little River, (*Pequeña Rivera*) had for $100 (*pesos*) ransomed the woman from the savages, who were about to kill her, as they had her runaway companion (*marron*) for the murder of an Indian. Francis seems to have turned the woman and the matter of her salvage over to Forbes and he to the commandant, who asked Fontanilla to take charge of her; but, as Fontanilla had no accommodation, she was finally lodged in a calaboose (*calavoso*) of the fort until a boat sailed. It happened to be Balenzategui's, and he received her from a corporal, giving a receipt, at first in pencil, but afterwards in ink and due form. That night Balenzategui and the priest, McKenna, took supper at Forbes' house, and the negress came in the room and asked Forbes to buy her. Apparently she did not want to go back to her master. But Forbes declined and told her to leave. She did so, — to good effect, for when Balenzategui after supper went down to the kitchen for her, she had disappeared.

CHAPTER XXXV.

(Commandants, — 1795, Olivier ; 1798, Lanzos ; 1800, Perez ; 1801, Osorno ; 1803, St. Maxent ; 1808, Salazar ; 1809, Perez.)

IT would serve no good purpose to divide our subject into periods corresponding with the rule of the later commandants. They succeeded each other with too great frequency to leave much individual impress on events, and, except Perez and Osorno, none of them are much remembered.

The time from 1795, when Olivier succeeded Lanzos, to 1809, does not present many notable features. Land grants were less numerous, and, when the country had hardened into Spanish formality, there was little change, except that the Indian trade improved considerably.

We have seen how Panton divided with Mather the commerce of West Florida, and now, as his firm comes to Mobile, Mather and Strother disappear, and John Joyce, their successor, turns contractor. As merchants of Mobile, Panton, Leslie & Co. petitioned for a vacant lot on Royal Street running back to the river, bounded north by land of Miguel Eslava, south by vacant land. As granted September 16, 1795, the lot had sixty feet front, and according to Olivier was eligibly situated for commercial purposes. It was the northeast corner of Royal and Government, extending eastwardly to the river.

Panton, Leslie & Co. had not been long in possession before they determined on a great improvement. Royal Street was the front street up to that time, but this was only one of a number of lots extending from the east side of Royal down towards the river. It seems that a shell bank ran along in the river the whole length of the Spanish city, near the shore, and created a shallow lagoon about a hundred feet wide on the land side, which in summer became stagnant and offensive. It also interfered with ready access to water of loading depth. The firm determined to fill up the marsh out to the shell reef, and therefore filed a petition in due form. It was warmly indorsed by Olivier, and on April 25, 1798, granted by Gayoso.

Such filling was quite necessary. Osorno in 1803 made a grant to Gertrude Loysel on the same conditions. The lot she desired was marshy, containing fifty-six feet front by one hundred and thirteen deep, bounded south by the wharf, north by lands of John Forbes (probably meaning the land just mentioned of Panton & Co.), east by the bay, and on the west by the small cabin which served as a dwelling for the sailors of this post. The reason given for the grant was, that filling up .the stagnant place would remove one of the principal causes of fever every summer. Osorno recites that Intendant-general Ramon Lopez de Angulo had previously granted like land to Don Benito Caro to fill for similar reasons, but that grant has not been preserved. In 1804 Espejo also received seventy by one hundred and forty feet south of the wharf for the double purpose of building a house for the manufacture of bread and biscuit, to carry out his contract to supply garrison and public, and to fill the lot and raise grain. He also promised to raise the levee leading to high land. A similar concession is made next to Espejo, extending his lot near Trenier, in the rear of St. Joaquin Street, on condition he fills it; and another to Mary Aygue, at the end of St. Francis Street (near the present Methodist church), bounded north and west by the woods, — both, although away from the river, liable to inundation from the great quantity of water which ran from the woods, and stagnated and injured the public health.[1]

The firm of Panton, Leslie & Co., which began this reclamation, was destined, under that and the later name of John Forbes & Co., to attain to great importance at Mobile and Pensacola. It was composed at first of John Forbes, William Panton, and John Leslie.

Panton was born in Aberdeenshire, Scotland, and, moving to America, he acquired property in South Carolina and Georgia. The American war, however, made him a refugee, and by

---

[1] *Mobile Translated Records*, pp. 305, 306, 308. Ramon de Lopez y Angullo became intendant in 1799 ; 2 Martin's *Louisiana*, p. 172. Many interesting facts have also been gathered from Espejo's papers in the possession of his granddaughter, Mrs. Henry Barnewall, of Mobile.

1785, if not before (Pickett says 1781), he was in business at Pensacola.[1] He made a specialty of the Indian trade, in which the firm was aided by the celebrated chief, Alexander McGillivray, who is said to have been a silent partner. By 1789 Panton, Leslie & Co. are said to have carried at their chief store a stock of $50,000, for they had extensive skin-houses and employed fifteen clerks. Their fleet at one time consisted of fifteen schooners, and they had branch stores at St. John's, St. Mark's, St. Augustine, Mobile, and a trading establishment at Chickasaw Bluff (near modern Memphis) on the Mississippi River. John Forbes was once in their house at New Providence, but in 1793, when he was twenty-four years old, we find him with a home in Mobile, and testifying that he was a member of the firm. In this proceeding he is spoken of as an Englishman of Tensaw (*Ingles de Tinza*). In 1799 Ellicott found him residing in Mobile. On the withdrawal of the interests of Panton and Leslie, John Innerarity and James Innerarity took their places. All were related by blood or marriage. The change of name was in 1804, on the death of Panton, who lived at Pensacola.[2] Forbes was the son of James Forbes and Sarah Gordon, of Scotland, and at least two sisters outlived him in the old country. In the latter part of his life John Forbes was to live at Matanzas, Cuba. He never married, but left two daughters.[3]

There had been constant friction, more especially on the Mississippi, between the western settlers and the Spanish officials. The mouths of the western and southern rivers were all held by Spain, who would let no goods go up or down without heavy duties.

The new American constitution substituted a strong government for the old rope of sand, while on the other hand the French Revolution and Napoleonic wars weakened Spain. These two facts changed the history of America. Instead of Spain's annexing portions of the United States, this country took advantage of Spain's weakness, and, carrying out the plans of John Jay, — who, as envoy in Revolutionary days,

---

[1] 2 Pickett's *Alabama*, pp. 61, 97; Pintado in 2 White's *New Recopilacion*, p. 361 ; Ellicott's *Journal*, p. 211.

[2] Meek's *Southwest*, p. 93.

[3] Forbes' Will, 1 *Mobile Will Book*, p. 153.

had asked Spanish recognition only if navigation of the Mississippi was conceded, — forced the Pinckney treaty of 1795. This assented to the boundary of 31° named by Great Britain in 1783, and, in opening the Mississippi, conceded also the right of deposit or warehousing of merchandise at the mouth of the river.

The Spanish officials still hammered at the old plan of separation, now become treasonable because unnecessary. Wilkinson, at Detroit, was the American commanding general and pronounced the scheme chimerical; but there is every reason to believe that he did not refuse money still.

The Spaniards put off delimiting the boundary of 31° as long as they could, but, when Gayoso was in 1798 actually besieged in his fort by indignant American settlers, he yielded. This boundary became the south line of the Mississippi territory created that year.

The running of the line is mentioned in 1798 as then in progress. Where it would exactly strike no one knew, and for a year or two the Tombigbee settlers were in uncertainty. Lawrence McDonald, for example, was an Indian trader for Panton, Leslie & Co., and Lanzos certifies that McDonald desired to locate in Mobile because he did not wish "to live under the government of the United States of America." Such devotion was appreciated, and he obtained a lot on the north side of "Government" ten by twenty toises. But the lot next north was vacant, and there is nothing whereby to locate this our first refugee.

The Journal of Andrew Ellicott, kept from 1796 to 1800, was published at Philadelphia in 1803, and contains the observations of this American commissioner in running the new boundary. He seems to have begun work near the Mississippi River on April 11, 1798, and worked eastwardly towards Mobile. His movements are not always intelligible to a layman, but we learn that he found the observatory already erected when he arrived at the end of the guide line on the Mobile River. Setting up his instruments there March 18, 1799, he completed a course of observations by April 9. He also sent his assistant Gillespie with a Hadley's sextant up to Fort St. Stephens to take the latitude of that place and make a sketch of the river, which was duly done.

The observations made resulted in fixing the boundary stone on a rise between what are now Cold Creek and Chastang's stations, on the Mobile and Birmingham Railroad. This irregular piece of brown sandstone, about three feet high, is still there, visible from the railroad, and called Ellicott's Stone.

ELLICOTT'S STONE.

It is the basis of all surveying in this part of Alabama. On the north side is, — "U. S. Lat. 31° 1799; " and on the south side, "Dominios de S. M. Carlos IV. Lat. 31° 1799."

The Journal reads:[1] "One serious difficulty presented itself, that was the continuation of the line through the swamp, which is at all times almost impenetrable; but at that season of the year absolutely so: being wholly inundated: — But fortunately we found in the neighborhood of our camp a

[1] Ellicott's *Journal*, p. 198.

small hill, the summit of which was just elevated above the tops of the trees in the swamp. From the top of this hill, we could plainly discover the pine trees on the high land, on the east side. Upon ascertaining this fact, we sent a party through to the other side, (along the water courses, by which the swamp is intersected in various directions), with orders to make a large fire in the night with light-wood; the same was likewise to be done on the hill before mentioned, to obtain nearly the direction from one place to the other. — The atmosphere was too much filled with smoke to discern a flag or other signal, the woods being on fire on both sides of the swamp. — It happened unfortunately that the day before our fires were to be lighted, the fires in the woods had extended over almost the whole of the highlands, on both sides of the swamp; by which so many dead trees were set on fire, that there was no possibility of discriminating between them, and our fires. — It was then agreed that the parties should light up, and extinguish their fires a certain number of times; making stated intervals. — This succeeded so well, that we became certain of not taking a wrong fire in determining the angles. — Contrary to our expectations, a heavy rain fell on the same night, a short time after we had finished the experiment, and extinguished all the fires in the woods. — The storm cleared off with a strong north-west wind, which carried off all the smoke, and enabled us to determine the angles in the day, by erecting signals, which was accomplished on the second day of April."

Ellicott notes that Mobile Bay and River make up the most important waterway between the Mississippi and the Atlantic, because of the inlet they offer for an enemy like the Spaniards to penetrate into the interior.

Running this line lasted some time and cost the Spaniards over $150,000. It narrowed West Florida to a width of only forty to ninety miles, with a length of 450 miles. According to Pintado, himself at this time deputy surveyor of the province, "before the establishment of these limits West Florida was so bare of inhabitants to the south of them that, excepting the part of the Mississippi which appertains to it, and the towns of Mobile and Pensacola, the rest was a complete desert, and, exclusive of the garrison of the two last places, and the posts of St. Mark's of Appalachy and Baton Rouge, there were only counted eight hundred men, in all the extension of the province, capable of bearing arms, and these of all classes and nations, amongst them very few Spaniards; indeed, the number of these was not sixty. The emigration of the evacuated posts procured for West Florida a great number of colonists, which daily increased, to whom lands were granted by the government of Louisiana; but the greater part of these were Anglo-Americans, some Irish and Scotch, a few Germans, and about a dozen of Spaniards, the most of them unmarried." [1]

A change of the method of granting lands was made at the time of this delimitation, and doubtless had some connection with the advance of the American frontier. From 1770 the granting power had vested in the governor of the province; but a royal order given October 22, 1798, in San Lorenzo, changed this and conferred the authority exclusively on the intendant, by whom it was exercised ever afterwards.[2] Intendant Juan Ventura Morales thereupon promulgated a set of regulations on the subject.

December 23, 1800, we first find Joaquin de Osorno, captain of the regiment of Louisiana infantry, acting in the capacity of "Political and Military Commandant," and yet Cayetano Perez sometimes takes acknowledgments of deeds. This was the case August 31, 1801, when Osorno himself bought from Francis Fontanilla the well-known lot, 114 feet front by 126 deep, "bounded on the north by the King's Bakehouse, on the east by a lot belonging to the estate of John Joyce, deceased, on the south fronting on the square of the Fort, and on the west by St. Emanuel Street," with building materials. The price was $200 cash.

Osorno happens to be (in 1801) the first person to whom there was a bill of sale of slaves which is preserved in our Translated Records, and he as commandant in 1803 has the honor of making the first grant of lands on record for the express purpose of cultivating cotton, plantations for which, he says, would contribute greatly to encourage industry in this jurisdiction. It is a concession to Miguel Desiderio Ardaz of twenty arpens front one league from the town, bounded north

---

[1] 2 White's *New Recopilacion*, p. 398 ; 2 Martin's *Louisiana*, p. 221.

[2] 2 White's *New Recopilacion*, p. 339. The regulations are given in an appendix to 3 Gayarré's *History of Louisiana*, p. 632.

by Semandaville, — doubtless Lansemandeville,[1] on the Bay
Shell Road. It is a coincidence that, half a mile lower down
the road from that spot, about 1836, S. H. Garrow made the
first oil obtained from expressing cotton-seed.

By official letter of Juan Ventura Morales dated December
1, 1802, "the sub-delegation at this place" (Mobile) was instructed not to transmit to his tribunal petitions for grants of
land, as the same was closed in consequence of the death of the
assessor-general.[2] But this did not prevent the commandant
from granting provisional titles. The provident Eslava, in
consideration of his great public services, received several in
this way, one tract being that between Favre and De Lusser,
afterwards to be known in front as the Collell Tract. One of
the largest grants was that by Osorno in 1803 of what is called
the Eslava Mill Tract; and the Dubroca, Espejo, and other
concessions by Osorno date from about the same time, and were
due to fear of cession to the United States.[3]

There is no peaceful event in United States history of greater
importance than the purchase of Louisiana from Napoleon,
April 30, 1803, after he had secured its retrocession from
Spain. The United States were to claim vigorously that they
bought to the Perdido, and the Federal courts were to decide
that all Spanish grants after this retrocession of October 1,
1800, at St. Ildefonso, were null and void. It was morally certain that sooner or later Mobile, and Florida, too, must go to
round off the frontier of the great republic, and Eslava was
not the only one who acquired concessions to keep from want
when change of flag would take away his employment. But
Spain ever maintained that Mobile had been in 1763 severed
from Louisiana as much as the Ohio country had been, and then
by the British made a part of West Florida ; that it had been
conquered by Galvez and administered by his successors as part
of her West Florida, and was never ceded with Louisiana to
France. Talleyrand admitted Spain did not intend to cede it,
but his fine hand purposely left it uncertain whether France
had claimed it as retroceded. It was considered of little value,
— the seat, according to Duvallon, only of fishermen. In point

---

[1] *Mobile Translated Records*, p. 300.
[2] *Ibid.*, pp. 294, 295.
[3] See Appendix D.

of fact, Spain calmly held on to Mobile and Baton Rouge. But it did unsettle matters, and this we see reflected in land grants and in the emigration of inhabitants. An unofficial census for 1803 puts the population at 810 only. The king seems to have kept but a launch there, manned by two sailors,[1] who received $10 a month and rations.

The principal effect of the cession was, that New Orleans ceased to have any connection with Mobile, and that Mobilians had as in British times to look to Pensacola as their capital, although it was not half as large as Mobile. There Governor Folch resided, and from there now issued all regulations about land as well as political matters.

Folch and Intendant Morales were bitter enemies, and, when Morales was in effect ejected from New Orleans by Claiborne in 1806, the governor stationed troops at Mobile Point to prevent his getting any nearer Pensacola.[2] The intendant, he said, could put his records in Fort Charlotte. However, Morales did get to the capital, and in August, 1807, we find him describing himself as "Intendant and Superintendent-General, Sub-delegate of West Florida, Judge of Public Lands." Officially the office of the intendancy was at Pensacola from February, 1806.[3]

Delays were not infrequent in grants before and after the cession. Byrnes was in occupancy several years before getting title, and John Trouillet fared worse. In 1787 he had petitioned for a tract of land at Bayou Minet forty (twenty?) by forty arpens, and promptly enough was granted it. The survey, however, did not take place, and after a while Trouillet died. In 1806 his widow revived the claim, and after several decrees the commandant at Mobile was directed to have a survey made and return the result. This was not at first done, but John Forbes, becoming her attorney, the next year pushed the matter through. Collins surveyed the land April 13. Pintado recorded Collins' survey and returned a plat. Morales on August 14, 1807, issued a title to the widow Feliciana from Pensacola for 800 arpens, sealed with his armorial bearings and

[1] Duvallon's *Vue de la Col. Esp. du Mississippi*, p. 65, Paris, 1803 ; 2 Martin's *Louisiana*, pp. 205, 254 ; 9 Howard Rep. (U. S.), p. 127.

[2] 4 Gayarré's *Louisiana*, pp. 69, 70.

[3] 2 White's *New Recopilacion*, p. 368 ; *Mobile Translated Records*, p. 344.

countersigned by Francis Gutierrez de Arroyo, secretary *ad interim* of the intendancy, in whose office, as well as in that of John Francis Arnaud de Courville, the office of the exchequer of the principal minister of finance of West Florida, it is said the grant was duly registered, in folios 68–70 and 94–95 respectively of the books kept for that purpose.[1]

It was seldom such a patent was issued, for it was expensive and the government respected the permits as titles.[2] The Mobile Translated Records after 1798 are made up as a rule, not of true grants, but of petitions and permits to settle on condition of cultivation, with indorsed orders of survey. The theory of the American confirmations later was, not that such title was perfect, but that, where the conditions had been carried out, and so proved before Federal commissioners, the title ought to be confirmed, because the Spanish government should and would on application have furnished such a complete title.

Don Francisco Gutierrez de Arroyo has preserved for us the proceedings of a junta which seems to control the royal finance and land business, too. This, he says, was "held on the 22d of November, 1806, by the order of Don Juan Ventura Morales, provisory honorary intendant of province in this province, with the sub-delegation of this superintendency-general of royal finances annexed, at which were present Doctor Don José Francisco de Heredia, assessor of the said intendancy; Don Juan Francisco Arnaud de Courville, accounting officer and treasurer of these royal treasuries, with the rank of a royal officer, and acting as fiscal of royal finances; Don Manuel Gonzales Armirez, formerly provisory treasurer of the royal treasury of New Orleans, and commissioned to conclude the unfinished business of the retroceded province of Louisiana; and I, the aforesaid provisory secretary of this intendancy of the Junta, with a vote in it; the said intendant presiding."

The action of this august tribunal related to the aggressive Americans. Louisiana was lost, and if they became numerous in West Florida they would certainly overpower the Spaniards even there. A royal order of February 20, 1805, had been issued against their acquiring lands, and the junta was to devise details for carrying that out. This they did by declaring that

[1] *Translated Records,* pp. 344–346.
[2] 2 White's *New Recopilacion,* p. 091.

no gratuitous concession could be made to one of Anglo-American origin, but that sales at the usual price of $2.00 an acre (copied from the American price in Louisiana) could be made to all, regardless of origin, who then were Spanish subjects. This determination included Mobile as well as Baton Rouge and Pensacola.[1]

It was apparently this junta, certainly "the department of finances," which earlier in the year had notified Captain Don Vincente Sebastian Pintado that he had been raised to the office of surveyor-general of West Florida on the withdrawal of Captain Don Carlos Trudeau, to whom he had been deputy since May 1, 1796. The appointment was December 13, 1805, but the royal approval dated from May 9 of next year. His work fixed many titles in West Florida, and both in deeds and elsewhere he sometimes gives us the basis of his surveys. "It is to be observed," he says, "the arpent of Paris, of which use was made in Louisiana and West Florida during the Spanish domination, is a square whose side is of ten perches of Paris, and of course contains 100 square perches; the lineal perch of Paris is of eighteen feet of the same city. The acres are those used by the English in the Floridas, and 512 of these are equal to 605 arpents of Paris."[2] As to fees, we find nine dollars paid on one occasion, but this hardly included the survey.

No doubt the surveyor could identify the "Old Brick Yard abandoned, four arpens front, bounded east by a small ravine formerly used as a washing place, north by the road, and on the other sides by public lands;" but we cannot, unless it be Espejo's, in what was to be the Favre Tract. Similar puzzles abound in the records, and, like the statement of points of the compass, are the despair of an archæologist.[3] We shall have occasion to note several of these brickyards. We see them also up Mobile River, near Bay Minette, and several at Red Bluff, near our Montrose. Forbes & Company seem to have sued Feliciana respecting the legal right to an 150 arpen tract, on the opposite side of the Bay of Mobile, valuable because on it there was a brick and a tile yard, with buildings, and obtained in 1810 a favorable judgment. The merits of the controversy are

[1] 2 White's *New Recopilacion*, pp. 401–403.
[2] *Ibid.*, pp. 338, 347.
[3] *Mobile Translated Records*, p. 261.

not disclosed, but her brother and executor, Eugene Chastang, whose son was a beneficiary under her will, on account of need of money for legacies and to save other more valuable property, finally sold the tract to John Forbes & Co.

Sawmills were, if anything, even more needed than brick-kilns, and there are references which betray their existence at different points.   There had been a French sawmill as far away as Pascagoula, and in 1802 there was one called Durand's, west of the Mandeville Tract.   There are traces of a number of them about Mobile, and a creek twelve miles above the city was named Sawmill Creek.   Folch's first appearance as gov-ernor-general is as encouraging Gerald and Thomas Byrne to erect their proposed sawmill.   While the site is not stated, it was probably on Tensaw River, where the Byrne grant has long been known.

Other local officials there were, although the surveyor and commandant overshadowed every one.   The Indian interpreter was a necessary officer.   For a long time it was Pierre Juzan, but he died, and from Perez' second term it was J. B. Trenier. Artola and Bongarzon are mentioned as custom-house guards. Thomas Price was to receive in 1798 and 1806 rather dispro-portionate recompense for his work as interpreter; and we have already seen that Eslava, royal quartermaster for so long, became an extensive investor at public auctions of lands. Rafael Hidalgo was surgeon of the hospital during much of the Spanish régime, and is often in the records before his death in 1811.   He lived with his wife, Elizabeth Chastang, daugh-ter of Joseph Chastang, in a house they built at the southwest corner of our St. Emanuel and Conti.   It was purchased in 1797 from Chastang, and was to be the subject of litigation in Ameri-can times on account of a deed of Hidalgo to Registe Bernoudy; but the claimants under Bernoudy were barred by time.

The case is interesting as upholding the title of the widow under the Spanish law (2 Partidas, 1101) to inherit from the husband in default of blood kin, and as showing that she might supposably become a rich woman in this way.   For Hidalgo's widow married several times.   About 1813 she married Michael Perrault and lived there with him until 1818 or 1819, when he died, and she then married Victor Gannard.   They, too, lived in the same place for some years, but she died elsewhere in 1824, herself without issue, and Gannard was her devisee.[1]

Antonio Espejo was also an active citizen. He was a son of Bartolome Espejo, of Ronda, in the diocese of Malaga. He lived in the house he built near the wharf, and only visited his ranches on Portage and Salto bayous. His death occurred in 1805 of yellow fever, caught from an Havana vessel, possibly the first death in Spanish times from that dread disease. The Tankersleys and Ingersolls are his descendants.

[1] *Baker* v. *Chastang,* 18 Ala. pp. 418, etc.

CHAPTER XXXVI.

As a traveler walked about Spanish Mobile, he would see little of American energy. At the mouth of great navigable streams, the country trade of the place was with Indians only, and by canoes; at the head of a fine bay, foreign commerce was yet small. The King's Wharf, just south of Government Street, accommodated this traffic, and the house of Panton, Leslie & Co. controlled the bulk of it. Near there, the marshy land was filled up so as to make a quay out to the ledge of oyster-shells which lay about where Water Street now runs; but, north of Dauphin and south of the Fort, lagoon and marsh claimed the river bank. The marshes came down from the Bayou Chateaugué district to near St. Anthony Street; and from about Eslava south also the land was similarly overflowed to the east of the ridge, at or near present St. Emanuel Street, even to the bay at modern Frascati. The little town did not extend as far west as Jackson except at one point, and its principal buildings were on Royal Street, north of the fort. Ellicott, in 1799, thought the situation handsome, some of the houses tolerably good, and, for so small a place, the trade considerable.

South of the fort esplanade were Durette and Don Miguel Eslava's high house, near our Monroe, with his garden in rear, and his negro huts west of where St. Emanuel Street now runs.[1] There was a row of houses east of him across the unnamed street, and on Conception, too, west of the fort, were a few places. Lefleau, for instance, had what is now the Sheffield place on St. Emanuel. Such was the small South District. But the miles of land north and south of the little town were untenanted marshes then, instead of cotton warehouses and lumber yards; and the gently sloping plain to its west, now crowded

[1] Petition of A. Michel before U. S. Senate, January 9, 1840, and exhibits ; Ellicott's *Journal*, p. 201.

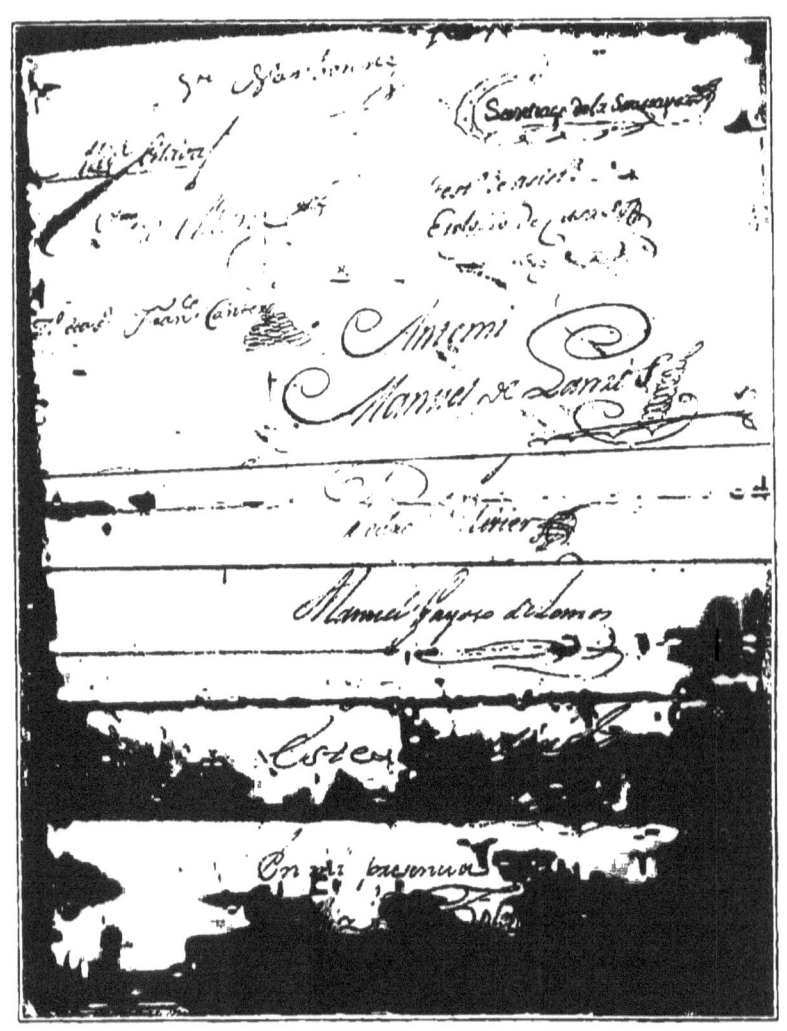

SPANISH AUTOGRAPHS

with humble homes or handsome residences, was then a vast pine forest interspersed with oaks and magnolias.

About the streets walked stolid Spanish officials and the vivacious French inhabitants, together with negro slaves and picturesque Choctaws, while only after the Louisiana purchase of 1803 would be seen a wide-awake Yankee, come to make his fortune.

Any visitor, Yankee or otherwise, would first examine frowning Fort Charlotte, then, as ever before, the principal point of interest. It was kept in good repair, especially after the Louisiana cession. Ellicott found it even in 1799 in a good state of defense. Near the single wharf was Montuse (Mottus) Tavern, hardly a modern Battle House, on land granted Antonio Espejo; for his widow had married Sylvain Mottus, a French refugee. Mottus while a mere boy had gone to Paris in the Terror, but a servant spirited him away to America. He was shipwrecked in Florida, learned to be a cooper, and made his way to Mobile. It is more or less romantic to learn that he met his future wife while acting as appraiser of her deceased husband's effects.

The approach (*plazoleta*) to the wharf adjoining the Mottus place was nearer the south than the north line of Government; and the wharf built by Joyce under contract in 1793 was 380 feet long by twelve wide, with cedar posts and two-inch planks. This famous structure was blown down in 1811 and not rebuilt, except that in 1818 Tankersley was to construct a larger one on the same posts in front of the Espejo lot, at southwest corner of Water and Government streets.[1] West, beyond the elevation of Royal Street, came places facing the esplanade of the brick fort. The palisade had long since disappeared, and the commandant lived northeast Government and St. Emanuel, almost under the Spanish flag floating from the fort. This residence, the old Farmer home, was private property.

Our Government Street extended but little west, probably not beyond the Rochon place at the southeast corner of Conception. It would seem to have received the name from the Government House, which maps of this century show stood a little southeast of the Semmes Monument. It is not unlikely that this was connected with the royal storehouse (*almacen*) erected by Joyce under contract with the crown (*Real Hacienda*) in

---

[1] *Pollard* v. *Greit*, 8 Ala. p. 933. See also original Mobile archives.

1793. The wharf and the warehouse together cost 1280 pesos.

The earliest paper giving the name certainly meant for our Government Street was the application of Elizabeth Forneret in 1788 for grant of a lot ten by twenty-six toises situated on Government Street, opposite the house and lot of Antony Narbonne ("formerly belonging to Mr. Farmar"), which was granted her on March 15.[1] The next mention was in 1803. On April 5 of that year, Miguel Desiderio Eslava — a son of Don Miguel — obtained from Perez a grant ·to 2½ lots of vacant land on Government Street, fronting the fort, extending from St. Emanuel, on which they faced 82 feet, to Royal Street. This land was bounded north by houses of the widow of John Joyce and by Joaquin de Osorno. The St. Emanuel Street frontage, however, was behind the Farmer place, which was not included in the grant.[2]

There were, of course, a number of other streets, all unpaved and narrow, as under the French. Leaving the fort and its esplanade behind, as one walked down Royal Street he would notice that the old Barracks Square had become private property in 1796, — that of Mary J. Krebs, the widow of Antony Narbonne. She sold it in that year, from Conti to the fort front, for $500. It shortly got into the hands of John Joyce, but from 1806 was to be claimed by Armand Duplantier. On the east side of Royal came first the old lot of John Forbes & Co., 140 feet front, adjoining the King's Wharf, and thus taking in part of Government Street. With the canal and privilege of building a private wharf, it was valuable for their foreign trade. Next (the site of the present theatre) came the warehouse of Benito Caro, who also filled out to deep water; and on the corner of Conti in later years Lewis Judson; while, across Conti, Laurendine owned where the Winsor now stands. Thomas Powell was to hold the site of Adam Glass's store, and Judson to come next. For the land east to the water was early taken up, and it, too, had its houses, brick, or frame filled in with brick and clay, all white or yellow washed, and roofed with tile or bark.

The first cross street, our Conti, was then called Govern-

---

[1] _Mobile Translated Records_, p. 89.

[2] _Ibid._, p. 310.

ment, although, from the building of the church on the old De Lusser lots in 1792, it gradually acquired the name of Church Street. It was truly a government street until the barracks became private property. With the removal, before 1793, of the Government House from near the Bakery, the name probably migrated, too, to the more southern avenue. In point of fact, for a few years both were called Government Street.

Proceeding up Royal, we pass the same kind of houses, not all stores by any means. Vines, peach and fig trees abounded elsewhere than on the parsonage land. Many grants of what are now down-town lots were for residences, and made on the condition of building within a year; for the Spaniards wished to build up the waste places and fill the town which so many English had abandoned. From the gabled church to Dauphin Street, and thus including Van Antwerp's, was later the property of James Innerarity, who seems to have acquired it from John Joyce.[1] Innerarity was the managing man for Forbes & Co., and Zadek's corner, too, was owned by that progressive firm.

Dauphin Street had officially another name under the Spaniards. They renamed all the streets but Royal, and mainly for saints. Thus Dauphin was St. John, and even sometimes Conception, as in 1782,[2] although it was probably at first Galvez Street; and there is some reason to think that Conti was once St. Peter.

Spira and Pincus' corner was apparently the residence of Dr. John Chastang, and surrounded by pickets. There is some doubt how far east the pickets extended, and there was to be controversy over how much the Chastang right covered. Next came property confirmed to Pierre Lucien, but which seems to be the property Colomb deeded Fontanilla in 1786. We may remember that a billiard table went with it, and it would appear that this is still one of the appurtenances, for it is probably the site of the Battle House billiard saloon. The Battle House land was the winter home of Simon André, with his daughter Lucy next door. In summer he, his wife Jeanne, and their numerous family stayed up the river. Across on the west side of Royal we find, at Dauphin, Cornelius McCurtin, whose

---

[1] 3 *American State Papers*, p. 398.
[2] *Chastang v. Dill*, 19 Ala. p. 423.

widow and devisee, Euphrosyna Bosage, was to marry McVoy. In her descendants still rests the title to the places next north of Burke's corner. Then came Dubroca, who sold this 100-foot lot in 1808 to Surtill for $1000. The Custom House marks the site of the stores of Forbes & Co., whose property also included St. Francis Street, and even beyond to the - north, for in Spanish times this was no thoroughfare. The southernmost 90 feet was bought October 12, 1801, by Panton, Leslie & Co., of the widow of Augustin Rochon. It extended back 213 feet to St. Charles Street. William Simpson, on behalf of the firm, paid the $800 in drafts on the royal treasury. From here the main business of Panton and Forbes was done.

St. Francis Street east of Royal, like Dauphin and even Conti, was represented only by a lane to the river. In 1811 the free mulattress Mary Jeanne was living with her children in a little house at what is now the northeast corner of St. Francis and Royal. This was next south of another place of Simon André, which crossed our St. Michael. John Forbes & Co. desired the Mary Jeanne place, as it extended 26 toises eastwardly, and was bounded south by the lane going to the river. So they exchanged with her, giving her a place twelve toises front, somewhere on the south side of Church Street, in the rear of the town. There they obligated themselves to build her a house 26 by 18 French feet, "like the house of Peter Lorandine, with a double chimney of bricks," and they paid her $40 cash besides.[1] Thus these merchants got an outlet to the river from their main house. North of Forbes, on the west side of Royal, the residents are not so easy to make out, except that the site of the Southern Express Co. was the residence of Mr. Orbanne (Demouy) by 1808.

St. Michael is a Spanish name, but one of the curiosities of Mobile titles is that it is not in the surviving records applied to that street. It did not extend east of Royal, and west to our St. Joseph it was certainly called St. Jago at first, and later St. Francis; while west of St. Joseph it was in 1811 known as Orbanne Street, from the resident at the corner of Royal. Hugo Krebs came next north of André (or Andry) on Royal (with title confirmed in 1842 to his heirs);[2] and beyond him

---

[1] *Translated Records*, p. 405.   [2] *6 Statutes at Large*, p. 872.

was George Tucker, the English carpenter of Panton, Leslie & Co. In 1804 Innerarity was granted what is now the southeast corner of Royal and St. Louis, bounded north by that unopened street. West of St. Joseph this was in 1811 called Monlouis Street, probably from confusion with the name of the resident on it, but St. Louis also occurs as early as 1803. The site of Princess Theatre was once owned by Simon Andry, who obtained it by a famous exchange with the interpreter Favre. Next south were the Alexandres, who bought from the widow of Narbonne. It would seem that St. Louis, although unopened east of Royal, was dedicated and vested in the public before 1800.[1]

North of St. Louis there were in early times few lots on Royal, — none on the east side, and on the west mainly Raouis (Ruiz?), where the Electric Lighting Company has its plant. About our St. Anthony, Samuel Mims[2] had quite a tract from 1796, and in 1804 he sold to Bready, his brother-in-law, who built a fine house; and where State Street now runs it was that McKenna once moved from the parsonage in order to have more room for his stock and garden. Later come as owners there Innerarity (who bought from Bready), Forbes and Kennedy, even into the marsh lands. The name St. Anthony is in the records first in 1800; and at right angles to this street, on an old plan, is another "Government Street," whose history has been lost. There are unaccountable difficulties and conflicts of title in this neighborhood, especially as to the Sam Mims property.[3]

Parallel with Royal runs the street we call St. Emanuel south of Dauphin, and St. Joseph north of it. As St. Charles it had been always a favorite residence avenue, although in Spanish times, when it was thus renamed, the residents were a singular medley of whites and free blacks. It is first found as St. Joseph in 1808. The break in its course at Dauphin is inexplicable. The English and French maps run it straight north from the fort, while now, and, from Spanish records, evidently in Spanish times, the parallelism ceases at Dauphin. St. Joseph begins its course there about seventy-five feet nearer Royal, and thence proceeds northwardly, getting ever a little farther west. When and why this was we do not know, unless we are to consider it

---

[1] *Kennedy* v. *Jones*, 11 Ala. p. 73.
[2] *Innerarity* v. *Mims*, 1 Ala. pp. 666, etc.
[3] *Mims* v. *Higgins*, 39 Ala. p. 12.

due in some way to the fire at the capture of the city. Certain it is, the Spanish occupation made a greater change in lands and titles than the British or American. Besides new owners, the re-grants cease to regard the French lots, and the size often depends upon the whim of the governor.

On St. Emanuel, in the square north of our Government, we find Durette, Chastang, and others; and, between Conti and Dauphin, Trouillet and Vilars; and William Fisher has a large lot on the east side from Conti northwards.. The southwest corner of Dauphin and St. Emanuel, facing ninety feet on the latter and one hundred and fifty feet on Dauphin, was inclosed in pickets and owned by Anna Surtill, and as Mrs. Littleton Lecatte she held it until American times. Bienville Square was then (except at its southwest corner, where was the Spanish Hospital), and for a half century later, private property. The late Captain Stephen Charpentier was born on it, about opposite the head of St. Emanuel; and Diego Alvarez lived on the Square after coming here from Spain in his vessel Marie Louise. The little, whitewashed Creole houses with trees and shrubbery did not differ from the rest of the town. The northwest corner of St. Charles and Dauphin, twelve by ten toises, was entered, as we would say, by Pedro Lavallet in 1793. Nicholas was next west on Dauphin; Fontanilla was already next north on St. Joseph; Dufeux soon came next to him, and Catherine Durand adjoined her. Fontanilla afterwards obtained the corner and passed it on to Joseph Ortiz. The Athelstan site opposite was owned by McCurtin, who held the more important Royal Street front, and a thirty-nine-foot lot, probably the present Masonic land, sold in 1810 for two hundred dollars. It was described as facing "St. Emanuel Street," and purchased by Rafael Hidalgo, practitioner of the Royal Hospital near by.

The northeast corner of Bienville Square had belonged to an Englishman named Green, but it was granted again by the Spaniards and passed through William Fisher after a long possession to Forbes in 1811. Forbes, it will be remembered, owned from Royal to St. Charles, including the People's Bank and old Bank of Mobile sites, and also owned the bulk of the block bounded by St. Michael on the north and St. Charles on the east. We should probably think of all this large property as used together, — the Royal Street part, perhaps, for stores and skin-houses, the St. Michael Street part for stables and wagon yards.

The site of Temperance Hall has a history as the residence of Julia Vilars, a mulattress of good character, who was granted in 1792 the northeast corner of St. Charles and St. Jago, with the dimensions of 60 by 120 feet, and later even this was enlarged. The same year Martha Triton, a free negress, was granted the lot next north; and next to her was Girard, whose land, extending to St. Louis Street, also came in 1803 to Forbes & Co. The Heustis lot opposite seems to have been from 1800 the home of Thomas Price; and Thomas Powell, an employee of Forbes, recommended by Lanzos as a man of good character, had entered the lot next north, now in St. Louis Street. Don Miguel Eslava was to get the lot south of Price and sell it in 1809 to P. H. Hobart as in "Square 7," — the first number given for a city block. South of the Hobart place was Andrew Bloque, and, on the corner of St. Michael, Pierre Lucien, who sold to Isabelle Baurrien.

In 1810 John Murrell sold Hobart for $75 the corner of St. Joseph and St. Louis, 12 by 20 toises, which he had bought in 1806 of Thomas Powell.[1] But it would seem St. Joseph in 1810 went no farther; for the west boundary of the Gallegos property on Royal Street, and lot inclosed in rear, was "a trail leading to the plantation belonging to the house of Forbes & Co."[2] The buildings made the land of value, and two interests sold for $5500. It was in this transaction that Petronille, whose husband, Morgan Byrne, was absent in a foreign country without knowing when he would return, availed herself of her legal right to convey without him. On another occasion we see the converse of the rule, — the consent of the husband being apparently necessary for the wife to purchase land.[3]

The last important street parallel with the river was Conception, which bore for a while that name and St. Joachim indifferently. Possibly the earliest mention of Conception is in 1792,[4] a grant on what seems to be northwest Conception and Conti, called Government. The widow Trouillet obtained the southeast corner from the authorities, and in 1796 sold for $20

[1] *Translated Records*, p. 386. [2] *Ibid.*, pp. 390, 403.
[3] *Ibid.*, p. 392. [4] *Ibid.*, pp. 115, 120, 133.

to Honoré Colins, a free mulatto, but without referring to its history as the Indian House. South towards our Government were Brontin (afterwards Nicholas) and Dolive on the east, and Girard, Trouillet, and others on the west side.

In 1793 William Mitchell obtains the northeast corner of Conti, extending half way to Dauphin, owned until lately by his heirs; and the lot of Ortiz, bought from Espejo in 1802, filled out the other half. Espejo was paid $1225, for the sale included a house, two kitchens, two brick ovens, and other outhouses.[1] This is the site of Gayfer's store; but also included the Goodman property on the east, sold by Ortiz to Savana eight years later as fronting the Royal Hospital.

Almost as large a lot vis-à-vis the Hospital was the property of Irogoyen, keeper of that institution, and he sold in 1809 to Constanze Higon. Ward's corner was later owned by Trenier; and from there up to St. Francis we find Rosalie and Angelica, free negresses, and Joseph Merero, often named with confusion as to their relative locations. Across the street, next to the Hospital, long lived Bartolemé Laurent; and Auguste Colin, a free mulatto, adjoined him, having the corner on St. Francis, where he seems to have built a home.

Across St. Francis Street, William Fisher in 1796 obtained a grant of a "vacant" lot 120 feet on Conception by 60 feet front, the site of the Bienville Pharmacy; but, except Clara Favre, who was opposite the negro Philip at the northeast corner of St. Michael, we have no other owners on the east side of Conception. On the west side, only late names are noticed, such as Surtill at the corner of St. Francis, and none at all north of St. Michael.

Our Joachim was even in American times to be "New" Street, and so it is not surprising to find on it only Benjamin Dubroca, taking up almost the whole southwest quarter of the block bounded south by St. Michael; and Surtill, occupying 120 feet square in the next block, acquired for $120 from May Aygue. It was of course bounded north and west by the woods. It is doubtful if St. Francis extended west of Conception, as even in 1809 it seems to be spoken of as a street without "passage;"[2] and from about our Government Street a path led southwards from Joachim past a pond to Mandeville, on the Bay.

---

[1] *Translated Records*, p. 287. [2] *Ibid.*, p. 367.

The north and south streets, as we have noticed, seem to have been the principal ones, and on them all lots face as far west as Conception. Even on Conti the only exceptions are the Fisher lands at the corner of St. Emanuel, and the east side of Conception from Conti to Dauphin, whose lots face on Conti and Dauphin respectively.

Dauphin ran up to our Jackson Street, but beyond this there was only the cemetery, and Dauphin was but a path or country road running northwest to reach the Portage of Bayou Chateaugué.

But Dauphin was then, as now, the principal street. The Surtills owned on it from the southwest corner of Joachim almost to Jackson, and opposite were Trenier, Robeshow, and Nicholas. Leon Nicholas fenced in the corner of Jackson from his grant in 1810, and Sylvain Nicholas claimed farther east from the next year.[1] Sangrouber's was Robeshow's, and the Girard House was Pierre Laurendine's, while all the block opposite except Harris' store was the property of Trenier. Trenier was a large owner at the American occupation, but does not occur in the early records.

The more eastern sites on Dauphin have been named in connection with the north and south streets. It must be remembered, too, that not far east of Royal was the river bank, owned by Forbes on the south, and Henry Baudain from his 1798 grant on the north side of Dauphin; so that about McGill's, and even Hammel's, fish were more plentiful than bargains.

Forbes & Co., on November 5, 1811, sold out their many places to William Simpson of New Orleans for $35,000 by the longest document in the Translated Records, as if the principal business of Mobile were going into liquidation. In point of fact, however, it was Innerarity and not Simpson who was to handle the realty of that great house, the origin of so many titles.

No Spanish map of the place has survived, and to that in part, no doubt, is due the varying street names. The regulations of 1798 provided for sale of town lots at Mobile as well as elsewhere, and the occasional mention of estimations or valuations seems to point to this. But from 1801–3 there is little or no evidence of such sales, although there were petitions

---

[1] 3 *American State Papers*, p. 398.

from Mobile and orders of survey and valuation.[1] As late as
1806 we read that the plan of that city had not yet been determined upon.[2]

Under the French, the fee to the soil of the streets was vested
in the public. This was Roman law, and the rule does not
appear to have been modified by the Spaniards when they
assumed dominion over Mobile. English law is otherwise,
but the treaties which have governed the changes of flag have
expressly or impliedly preserved all property rights and the use
of the streets.[3]

[1] 2 White's *New Recopilacion,* p. 372.

[2] *Ibid.,* p. 430.

[3] *Kennedy v. Jones,* 11 Ala. pp. 83–85.

CHAPTER XXXVII

THE Creoles loved the water, and any map giving Spanish concessions will show those oblong white spaces, uncut by the land-office surveys, on the bay and rivers, but with few of them away from the water. This is as true at St. Stephens and Pascagoula as near Mobile. Even Espejo's 1803 ranche at the Cantonment nine miles west of Mobile, near the Great Spring, was on the Bayou del Salto (Cascade).

It would take a volume to discuss the Spanish grants which were confirmed on Mobile River. First above the city there was the St. Louis tract, this side of Chickasabogue; then Dubroca's large claim (afterwards sold to Samuel Acre), besides Duplantier, Hobart, and others on Bayou Sara. Hobart built and operated the mill afterwards owned by Cleveland, and lived there, while Diego Alvarez kept a ferry across Chickasabogue near his extensive grant. Constancia Rochon, widow of John Joyce, in 1798 obtained twenty arpens on Bayou Sara as a ranche, because her place across the bay was unsafe on account of the Indians. Her tract is bounded south by Bayou Tagouacha, a reminder of Bienville's Touacha Indians. Higher, about Twenty-one Mile Bluff, was Dubroca, and there his Creole descendants have ever since remained.

The neighborhood of first Fort Louis was not deserted. In 1792 the widow Rochon obtained the very site, described as land twelve arpens front by forty deep, named the Bluff, "being a piece of land called the Old Fort, distant about nine leagues from this place," situated on Mobile River. A short distance below this, James Innerarity established a cotton plantation, on which to work the negroes of his wife, Eloise Isabelle Trouillet, as she owned a number accustomed to agriculture. He applied for a tract "forty arpens on the river by thirty deep, situated on both sides of a small spring [bottom?]"

commonly known by the name of Fond de Lourse, or otherwise the Old Fort Spring," situated between the plantation belonging to Dubroca and St. Philip and that of Rochon's at the Old Fort on the river." B. Dubroca and Peter Chastang testify that the tract is vacant, and Perez grants it April 6; 1809, the intendancy being closed. Two years later we find a grant to Isabelle Narbonne bounded north by Innerarity's habitation and south by that of St. Philip. This she wanted as a brickyard for her son's slaves.[1]

Dr. John Chastang lived at the bluff named for him, and there was growing up the colored Creole settlement representing his blood. Simon Andry had given the name to his imposing bluff, and about there made tar. His hospitable house rendered a hotel unnecessary. His greatest claim to recollection is, that he is said by his descendants to have brought there from Baton Rouge the ancestor of the innumerable Mobile chinaberry-trees. This is probably true. The tree is not native to this continent, and was brought to America by the French by way of their West Indian Islands. Above were Trenier, Mottus, Durette, Campbell, and other homes or grants, until we reach the St. Stephens region.

Fort Charlotte had not remained the only Spanish post in this part of the country. Fort Tombecbé was still used as Fort Confederation. There Mme. Espejo went on her honeymoon. To conciliate the Indians, and perhaps to guard against American aggression, a new fort also had about 1789 been erected by the government lower down upon the Tombigbee River, which was to give the name to a place familiar in Southern history, — St. Stephens. The earthwork can still be distinctly traced, and Collot represents the fort as a formidable work. Besides the fort there were a number of frame buildings, generally covered with cypress bark. Only the blockhouse, church, and residence of commandant were plastered. In July, 1790, begin certificates from Lieutenant Joseph De Ville Degoutin, commandant of Fort St. Stephens, as to vacancy of tracts applied for on the "Tombagbe." Folch at Mobile is in such cases directed by Miro to put the applicant in possession.

---

[1] *Translated Records*, pp. 395, 116. As to Andry and the Chastangs, much has been learned from their descendants on the river and at Chastang's. Felix Andry, of Mobile, has been of especial assistance.

The garrison in 1791 was one company under Captain Fernando Lisora.

Then for some years we have no record, but by 1795 there is considerable activity in lands about St. Stephens.[1] Eslava's assistant at Mobile, Francis Fontanilla, had moved up there three years before, to become royal storekeeper of that post, and occupied a tract adjoining the fort; but his title was not perfected until 1798. He obtained before that a grant of twenty arpens front about a league from the fort. Hoan Solivan gets ten arpens distant sixteen leagues from the fort, Adam Holinger twenty arpens somewhat nearer, Julian Castro ten, Tobias Rheams twenty, George Brewer twenty, John Baker fifteen, William Powell twenty, Cornelius Rains ten, John Johnston twenty, Daniel Johnston twenty, and Solomon Janson seven. Some of the other settlers were Blackbird, Bant, McGrew, Lorins, McCurtin, Brutin, Moore, and Daniel. A bayou which seems to be a landmark seventeen leagues below the post is called Three Mouths, and easily recognized still as Three Rivers above McIntosh's.

These later grants are for grazing or agriculture, and some of the lands are on one side, some on the other, of the Tombecbé. While many concessions are near the fort, several are as much as eighteen leagues south. The procedure there was the same as at Mobile, — a petition to the governor-general, indorsed favorably by the commandant, — for example, Antonio Palaas, and a grant by Carondelet, directing the surveyor-general of this province, or his duly appointed deputy, to put the petitioner in possession. Most of the applicants state that they have already been in possession from one to ten years, and desire a grant so as to prevent interference by others.

Among the conveyances of this vicinity we find that William Turnbull in 1798 sells to Nathan Blackwell his tract at St. Stephens of six arpens front, acquired by grant from Miro in 1788.[2] In that district, too, was the place Sanflor, our old Sunflower. Dominique Dolive obtained it in 1788, and now (by mark) sells to Young Gaines for $80.[3] Two years later Adam Holinger (by his mark, A. H.) sells John Callier his

---

[1] *Mobile Translated Records*, p. 154 *et seq.*

[2] *Ibid.*, p. 224.

[3] *Ibid.*, p. 237.

forty arpens front, seven miles below Fort St. Stephens, for $400 cash.[1]

The first known sale of land ascertained by the new line to be within the United States was that of C. U. Demouy, for $250, October 23, 1800, to John Brewer, of twenty by forty arpens between lands of said Brewer and Dubroca. Demouy was the ancestor of the Mobile family of that name. Espejo in 1801 acquires from Lieutenant B. Dubroca, as "attorney of the estate of the late John Turnbull & Co.," a forty-arpen tract;[2] but he seems to sell it immediately to Samuel Mims, an inhabitant of Tensaw River, Washington County, for "five hundred silver dollars in Indian corn at the market price, to be paid on the first of January next."[3] Espejo got 500 arpens on the Tombecbé, besides a tract of twenty arpens front across the river, also belonging to John B. Turnbull and John Joyce, deceased.[4] This was at the Niava and Canes places.

Ellicott gives an account of this part of the country as he found it at his visit in 1799.

"The Mobile is a fine large river," he says, "and navigable some distance above the boundary for any vessel that can cross the bar into the bay. One square-rigged vessel has been as high as Fort St. Stephens, in latitude 31° 33′ 44″. . . .

"About six miles north of the boundary, the Tombeckby and Alabama rivers unite, and, after accompanying each other more than three miles, separate; the western branch, from thence down to the bay, is called Mobile. The Alabama retains its name until it joins some of its own waters, which had been separated from it for several miles, and then takes the name of Tensaw, which it retains until it falls into the bay. . . .

"The upland on these rivers is of an inferior quality from their mouths up to the latitude of Fort St. Stephens, and produces little besides pitch-pine and wire-grass, but is said to become better as you ascend the rivers. The lands on those rivers have notwithstanding had a good character for fertility: but this has arisen from not discriminating between the upland, which is generally unfit for cultivation, and the banks of the rivers, which are fertile in the extreme, and to which agricul-

---

[1] *Mobile Translated Records*, p. 251.   [2] *Ibid.*, p. 276.
[3] *Ibid.*, p. 277.   [4] *Ibid.*, p. 280.

ture is almost wholly confined for a number of miles above the
boundary. But those lands are subject to a great inconvenience from the inundations of the river.

"Planting is not attempted in the spring until the waters
have subsided; and it sometimes happens that inundations
follow the first fall of the waters in the spring, and wholly
destroy the previous labors of the planters. This was the case
in May, 1799, after the corn was two feet high. But this inconvenience is by no means so great as it would be in a more
northerly latitude; there still remains summer sufficient to
bring a crop of corn to full maturity."[1]

On the Tensaw were many residents at first, although some
moved to the Tombigbee. McCurtin had in 1787 obtained the
Farmer place, but in 1790 described it as uninhabitable and
moved up to St. Stephens. This Farmer place of 12,800
arpens became, under McCurtin's will, the property of his
widow, and she in 1810, as Mme. Diego McVoy, sold it for $650
to Joshua Kennedy, including Rains' Creek and Farmer's
Bluff.[2]

This Stockton neighborhood is said to have been settled by
Tory refugees. We find Roberts Walsenton, for one, acquiring twenty-four by fifty arpens on the south bank of the Bayou
Defango, where it empties into the Tensaw, in order to continue, after the running of the demarcation, a subject of the
King of Spain, — whom God preserve.[3] Of quite a different
faith should have been Washington Wilkins, if one can judge
from his name, who acquired for a residence and ranche the
land south of Dubroca.

Gerald Byrnes' tract was about three and a half leagues from
the city, on the opposite side of the river, bounded north by the
Apalaches and south by widow Bousage, and having as natural
boundaries the Bayous Willoy (now Byrnes Creek) and Salome.
Cornelius Dunn seems to have in 1793 or 1796 acquired at
least part of Mme. De Lusser's Tensaw tract, it being for a
cow range on Potato Creek. This title was, in the hands of
Root, to prevail over that of De Lusser, represented by Hall.[4]

---

[1] Ellicott's *Journal*, pp. 200, 280.
[2] *Mobile Deed Book* " A," p. 69.
[3] *Translated Records*, p. 339.
[4] *Ibid.*, p. 253 ; *Hall* v. *Root*, 19 Ala. p. 378.

On Tensaw River also was White House, a landmark in the deeds. This had been the seat of the Apalaches, and there, near where that river turns west and the Apalache leaves it for the south, Joseph Chastang had 800 arpens. His use of it went back to 1780, although his grant dates from 1792, and after it passed to Joshua Blakeley of Connecticut it was to have quite an American history. From 1803 Louis Dolive lived on the bay, and his descendants have been numerous about the Village.[1] The Trouillets also lived there.

The lower delta of the Mobile, unlike the part at and above Twenty-one Mile Bluff, had not been granted out to any great extent in French or English times. It was not suitable for habitation and its products were limited. We have seen Colomb obtaining Chucfa Island; and Henry Sossier in 1805 received for cattle-raising the east half of an island extending from the Tensaw to Spanish River, always before, according to old residents, unoccupied. Thomas Powell, an honest, laborious man of large family, obtained the other half of this marsh land about the same time.[2] The land in question, awkwardly described in the Translated Records, is that large double island extending from Spanish River and Grand Bay on the west to Tensaw River on the east, and from Raft River on the north to the Tensaw on the south, divided in two by Middle River, running roughly north and south.

Sossier admits that the land had never been of any use, but pledges himself to ditch and fence and stock it with horses, cattle, and goats, as an experiment. Beef and milk were the two principal things aimed at. How far he succeeded we do not know, but Powell had cotton, rice, and corn growing on his land when he sold to Blakeley in 1808. Sossier sold to him in the same year for $1200, whereas Powell received $1800, having some improvements. The land was cultivated by Blakeley himself from 1810.[3] Blakeley's name has stuck to the large marsh island farther west, directly across the river from Mobile.

---

[1] See Michel's petition before U.S. Senate, January 9, 1840, with Dolive's deposition attached.

[2] *Translated Records*, pp. 330, 335.

[3] 3 *American State Papers*, p. 9 ; *Mobile Records, Deed Book* " A," pp. 41, 45.

Other bayous and islands in the Mobile delta still bear French or Indian names, like the Bateau Bays, Chacaloochee Bay, etc., although the history of these is lost, but there as elsewhere we find little distinctly Spanish. It is indeed remarkable that after a rule of thirty-three years so little survives of direct influence of the Spaniard. The explanation is that under Spain the population remained essentially French, with a sprinkling of British, while only the ruling class was Spanish.

We see the same thing all around the bay, although the first two tracts south of the city are Spanish. These are the Eslava Bay Tract, adjoining the Mandeville, and that of Cornelius McCurtin (afterwards Diego McVoy) still further south, taking up much of the long peninsula between main Dog River and the bay.

This Eslava Bay Tract (which is different from the Mill Tract) rests on papers not now known, but which were to satisfy the United States officials. The McVoy Tract of 4374.09 acres was a claim of Cornelius McCurtin, who seems to have been trying first one part of the district and then another for residence or other purposes. Twenty acres at the mouth of Dog River was in 1798 the property of John Trouillet at a place called Bateau Panché. He wanted it for cattle, of which he had a large stock.

Across that river was where lived Pierre Rochon, of Haldimandie memory, for much of our Hollinger's Island stood in the Rochon name, the origin of its modern titles. The 800 arpens which Powell was to get from Innerarity as the executor of Trouillet's widow, Isabelle Chastang, was probably south of Deer River, and not on the island.

Mary Rochon, widow of Orbanne Demouy, for $400 sold John Murrell 1200 arpens situated "by the junction of Dog River" (Rio del Perro), about three leagues south of Mobile, belonging to her deceased husband, acquired by grant of Carondelet. It was bounded north by Montlimar Creek and lands of Charles Lalande, south by another creek (Cedar in a later deed) and the same estate, west by public lands, and east by Dog River. Four months later Murrell sold the tract to Eliphalet Beebe, and he in 1810 conveyed half of it to Asa Beebe for $300. This is the Beebe tract at the mouth of Hall's Mill Creek.[1]

Farther down the west coast we know Bellefontaine. Charles Mioux had his house and plantation there, part of his unsurveyed tract extending from Pierre Baptiste on the south to Deer River[2] (Rio del Gamo). Upon his death his heirs, who lived at Bay St. Louis, sold it to Mary Anne, a free mulattress, for sixty dollars, or its value in seven head of horned cattle, to be delivered at Pascagoula River on demand. She in turn sold in 1796 to Charles Lalande, a free man of color, for thirty dollars.

Mon Louis Island (between the Bay and Rio del Gallina) was still owned by the Bodins (Baudins), and their man Maximilien Colin (a colored Creole) lived at Jack's Bluff, above the pecan-surrounded home of the Bodins at Miragouane. Henry François had been living on his tract near the north end for many years prior to 1808; and later we find Durands, connections of the Bodins, upon the island also.

Across Mobile Bay a Spanish map shows settlements above the old French Village (Aldea), but none at modern Howard's ; and about Montrose have been found silver coins and antiquities more likely of this than De Soto's time. J. B. Loranding had six or seven arpens, with house and kitchen on it, at Red Bluff, about the site of the British summer camp of Croftown, and Lieutenant Ferriet was to buy it in 1805 for $120.[3] This neighborhood, near Rock Creek, is now the seat of pottery and brick manufacture, and in Spanish times also was the site of kilns. Isabelle Narbonne, the widow Campbell, obtained a tract of twenty arpens front at the Bluffs in order to put her slaves at making brick and tile, and we have already seen the judicial proceedings by which Forbes & Co. in 1811 purchased the Trouillet brickyard there. Durnford had lived near Montrose, but a place at Battle's seems also to perpetuate his name. It is the north boundary in the grant of 1800 to Eugenio Lavalle, of Pensacola, of forty arpens by the usual depth at "Punta Clara," — the first mention of the famous summer

---

[1] *Translated Records,* pp. 373, 378, 381. See *Mobile Deed Book* " A," p. 73.

[2] *Translated Records,* p. 183.

[3] *Ibid.,* p. 334.

resort. In 1815 we find the partition among Baudin heirs of the classic district near by known as "Hog Range."[1]

Fish River (Rio del Pez), where Lavalle had another grant, was better settled. Its east branch under the Spaniards was Rio del Salto, from the waterfall we find on English maps, as under the French it had been Le Saut.

Daniel Jusan acquired by will Daniel Ward's property north of Fish River, and May 2, 1808, we find him selling thirty-five or forty arpens front to Henry Baudin for $200. Next year H. Baudin for $1000 sold N. Weeks this Old Ward Place, from Alligator Creek to the rock fronting the bay.[2] Maps of tracts about Fish River show land to have been in great demand there. West of Weeks Bay was N. Cook, or Durette; south were Baudin, T. Powell, L. Plock, and A. Baudin; and east of the bay, J. Fernandez. Plock and his wife died of exposure, due to being captured by Indians and dragged to Pensacola. Their little daughter Catalina, then nine months old, was dashed against a tree and left by the savages for dead, but was found, and was brought up by Fontanilla on the west side of Mobile Bay. She lived to be Mme. Antonio Espejo.

Up the east fork of Fish River, besides Weeks on the left bank, was on the right the mile-square place of Collins. He could drill his dragoons all on his own heath, near modern Magnolia Springs.

Below on Mobile Bay was Bon Secours, under the Spanish Rio del Buen Socorro. John Ward in 1793 purchased a house and tract of land there, a mile from the mouth of the bay, from John Even. He discovered afterwards that Even had no title, and so he obtained a provisional grant in 1803 from Osorno to eight hundred arpens. Ward represented himself in his petition as the father of a large family.[3]

This neighborhood, too, was well settled. On the north of the Bon Secours River were the claims of the Cooks, N. and J., and La Coste. Augustin La Coste's claim, for 638.40 acres, originates from Perez's permit of December 2, 1803, and was

[1] *Mobile Deed Book* " A," p. 82.
[2] *Translated Records*, p. 353 ; *Deed Book* " A," p. 104.
[3] *Translated Records*, p. 309.

confirmed by the United States in 1840.[1]   On the south were
Johnson, F. Laney (Lamy?), and Buck; while lower, on Bon
Secours Bay itself, was where W. E. Kennedy lived for so long.
He seems in 1809 to have bought from F. Suarez a tract
bounded east by Oyster Bay and west by Lime Kiln Creek,
extending back twenty arpens.[2]

On Mobile Point (Pta. de la Movila) we recall two early
grants, apart from the later claims of Suarez and others.   The
one was to Fr. Simon, for the fishing trade, of a tract on the
bay, from Bon Secours River on the east to Bay Olivier on the
west.   The other was to John Courrège, to carry on the fishing
trade between Mobile and New Orleans.   It included the coast
from Bay Andrew to Mobile Point, and on it this new inhabitant put up the first house.   These grants would be valuable as
giving safe refuges, apart from the oysters which have ever
abounded there.   Pleasant Navy Cove has always been a pilot
settlement, and is famous for nectarines.   There was no fort
on tree-bare Mobile Point, and we do not know that the primi-
tive lighthouse there in English times was kept up under the
Spaniards.   But here was now the usual passage from Seno
Mexicano into the bay, and Spanish maps carefully define the
twelve-foot line within as well as the eighteen-foot channel at
the Point and between adjacent bars.   On the Gulf side, the
mouth of the Lagoon is called Boca Ciega, — Blind Mouth.

In the interior few are the old claims, even on watercourses,
away from Mobile Bay.   On Perdido Bay, only F. Suarez and
J. Suarez occur on the western side, although Spanish coins
have been dug up among many Indian remains; and on the
shore nearer Pensacola the swamps prevented much occupancy.
Pensacola is outside our province, but its neighborhood and
the shores of Escambia Bay and River for miles show grants,
generally of the same twenty by forty arpens as about Mobile
and its waters.

Famous Dauphine Island had fallen into neglect.   We have
already seen how in 1781 it was all granted to Joseph Moro,
and this was in American times confirmed to Augustin Lacoste,
claiming under him.   But across the centre of the island, on
a line with little Dauphine and Pelican islands, ran the claim
of Jean Baptiste Lamy.   His settlement began in 1792, but

[1] 6 *Statutes at Large*, p. 807.   [2] *Mobile Deed Book* "A," p. 63.

was not founded on any grant; and these two are the origin of
the modern titles. There do not seem in Spanish times to have
been many residents; and there is no indication that at this
epoch the old port to the southeast was in use, except that in
1785 the king maintained there a pilot and four sailors at an
expense of $696. Pass Drury would seem to be named from
Thomas Drury, a settler only of 1812 and without a Spanish
grant.[1] The names Isla Delfina, Isla Guillori, Isla Pelicano,
and the like, show that the Spaniards here as elsewhere made no
changes in nomenclature except to translate the French words
into Spanish.

The habitations of Grelot and Bosage may be those of the first
residents of the pleasant Portersville mainland; but they were
followed in later Spanish times by the Baptistes between Bayous
Batterie and Coq d'Inde, and by the occupancy of McGrath,
without a grant, of the land from Bayou Coq d'Inde to Bayou
Common, the real location of Portersville. But, as on Mon
Louis Island, the names of places still recall the French. Point
aux Pins, Bayou La Batré (Batterie), Bayous Coden (Coq
d'Inde), Coquilles, Common (Commun), Fowl (Poule) River,
are French. "Pass Sweet," under Cedar Point, is a ludicrous
Americanization of Passe aux Huitres, — Oyster Pass.

Pass Christian was also within the jurisdiction of Mobile, as
we learn from a deed by Julia de la Brosse, the widow Carrière, November 5, 1799. She does not sign, because blind,
but acknowledges before witnesses. The conveyance deeds to a
negro Charles and family (who had rendered her many services
in her sickness) twenty by forty arpens on the seashore, out of
the tract acquired by her under the English domination from
his "Excellency Aldeman, Governor-General of Pensacola at
that period, the titles of which property were burned at the
office of Mobile when the Spaniards conquered the town."[2]
This is interesting as the only mention of General Haldimand
in the Translated Records, and possibly the only instance of
his granting lands.

Biloxi, nearer Mobile, always continued a settlement, even if
across its bay to the east the memory of Fort Maurepas was lost
in the oaks and pines of that promontory. Piernas early made

---

[1] 3 *American State Papers*, p. 393 ; 2 Martin's *Louisiana*, p. 81.

[2] *Translated Records*, p. 249.

a grant to the widow of Baptiste Christian, who had lived at
Biloxi since her birth; and a little later Mathurin and Careaux
obtained land on Dumanon Point, bounded south by the sea
and east by "the mouth of the Bay of the Old Fort," for cultivation and other uses. James Innerarity in 1809 became the
owner of Round Island, once the property of Francis Krebs.[1]

The new boundary line in ¹798 drove some settlers as far as
Pascagoula. So Adam Hollinger, son-in-law of Pierre Juzan,
who had lived on the Tombecbé,[2] and Gerald Byrnes, a carpenter and farmer too, obtained 800 arpens at Ward's Bluff
for a cattle range, and as much again for cultivation on Bayou
Ward, two and a half miles south of the old French sawmill.[3]
In 1804 he sold the place to Espejo, and he immediately to
Joseph Collins. The next year Isaac Ryan, a carpenter,
brought up among the French, also obtained a grant there of
300 arpens for himself and family. He moved from St. Stephens, he said, because he could not expect the same tranquil-
lity under the Americans as under his Catholic Majesty.[4]

Lanzos could not certify about occupancy of lands at Pascagoula, as he more than once frankly advised Gayoso. But
when Ambroise Gains obtained 500 arpens, this petitioner
produced the indorsement of Charles Ellier, Peter and Francis
Krebs, James Nadeau, and Francis Colin. He had already
been farming there, and as a quiet American he obtained his
grant.[5]

Betsy Wilson, an old inhabitant of Pascagoula, in 1801
obtained twenty by forty arpens front on both sides of that
river, including the first bluff "below the confluence of the
rivers Chicasaha and Estopacha" (Pascagoula), about three or
four miles south of the United States boundary, and she also
had a ferry across Bayou Billieu. Special deputy surveyor
Joseph Collins was duly directed to lay off the bluff tract.
Whether this led to the acquaintance of Collins and Elizabeth
Wilson is not stated, but Collins before 1805 took up his residence at Pascagoula and married her. The ceremony was performed, not by the Mobile priest, but by Mr. White, syndic

---

[1] *Translated Records,* pp. 19, 26, 363.
[2] *Ibid.,* p. 225.
[3] *Ibid.,* pp. 229, 230. See pp. 317, 318.
[4] *Ibid.,* p. 231. [5] *Ibid.,* p. 232.

of the place. They had several children, and one, Sidney, was to settle in the United States Supreme Court that a civil marriage was valid among Spanish colonists, the Council of Trent to the contrary notwithstanding.[1]

Simon Cumbest, William Wilson, and the widow Krebs also obtained lands there, but the last mention of Pascagoula was in the big sale in 1804 by John Lynd to William Simpson of 40,000 arpens on the river for $20,000. This was doubtless for the omnivorous house of Panton.[2]

Such was the country outside of the city.

[1] *Mobile Translated Records*, p. 274 ; 9 How. Rep. (U. S.), p. 174.
[2] *Mobile Translated Records*, pp. 275, 315, 316, 326.

CHAPTER XXXVIII.

CHURCH OF THE IMMACULATE CONCEPTION.

UNDER the Spaniards, Mobile and Pensacola were subject to the same ecclesiastical authority as New Orleans, but, fortunately, escaped the scandalous dissensions which disgraced church government on the Mississippi. Louisiana and Florida under Spain were part of the diocese of Santiago de Cuba, whose bishop was James Joseph de Echeverria.[1] After O'Reilly had subjugated Louisiana, this bishop in 1772 sent the Capuchin Fray Cyril de Barcelona to New Orleans as his vicar, with four Spanish fathers of that order, none of whom came to Mobile. One was the Antonio de Sedella who as parish priest of New Orleans proved so insubordinate to the bishop, and was shipped back to Spain in 1787 by the governor for trying to introduce the Inquisition into this country. The year after Mobile was conquered, Cyril was from Rome appointed Bishop of Tricali and Auxiliar of Santiago de Cuba,[2] but his actual diocese included New Orleans, Mobile, and Pensacola, and on account of these extensive visitations he was allowed $4000 in addition to his regular $3000 salary.

Cyril, both as vicar and as bishop, endeavored to reform the morals of priests and people of Louisiana, but met with secret apathy, if not open hostility. In 1786 he found it necessary to issue a pastoral calling more especially for the better observance of Sunday.[3] To his other difficulties was added that of race antagonism, for it was long before the French of Louisiana became reconciled to Spanish rule.

The change of name of the Mobile parish to "Yglesia de Purissima Concepcion" seems to be due to Don José Espeleta, colonel of the infantry of Navarre, and from March 12, 1780, its records are in Spanish. The Immaculate Conception was

---

[1] Shea's *Archbishop Carroll*, p. 543.
[2] *Ibid.*, p. 547.   [3] *Ibid.*, p. 557.

then a favorite Spanish dogma, and we find it even in the oath of the officials of Louisiana.[1] The new name of the church may have been the origin of that of Conception Street, where the old building was situated.

The number of pastors is surprising, — thirteen until American times; but we read of the burial of at least two at their post. The first entries in the church records are by Fr. Salvador de Esperanza, who describes himself as "religioso mercenario y Parroco," — parish priest of the Mercedarian order. Almost his first duty was to enter Augustin Rochon.

In June, 1781, begins in his stead Fr. Carlos de Veles, of the Capuchin order, who was both pastor of the city and chaplain of the garrison. Carlos prefers the term "campo santo" instead of the "cimenterio" of Salvador. Later priests use the two terms interchangeably. He buried Simon Fabre and Louis Carrier, but on June 5, 1783, Miguel Lamport records the interment of Rev. Padre Carlos himself.

Then comes Fr. Francisco Notario, a Dominican, as cura and capellan, and, in the fall of 1784, Fr. Joseph de Arazena, a Capuchin. He speaks of Mobile sometimes as "Villa," as did the others before him, but also sometimes as "Plaza de la Movila." He had previously been at Iberville, Louisiana.[2]

It is in the time of Arazena that we have the long entry, attested by Dubroca, Chastang Sr., Duret, Brontin, Landry, and others, dated December 25, 1784, which recites that El Sr. Dn. Henrique Grimarest, lieutenant-colonel of the army of his Catholic Majesty, actual "Governador y el Primero" since the Conquest, lost his wife Da. Anna Narbona, December 26, 1783, and that she was buried in the public cemetery of the parish. On this anniversary he builds a brick vault for her remains and as his family tomb, and her obsequies are then duly celebrated. It is remarked incidentally that the church in use was in a ruinous state, and agreed that, if the king or inhabitants should rebuild it elsewhere, Grimarest would similarly change the location of the vault. She as well as he are spoken of in the highest terms.

In 1785 are entries in French by l'Abbé de Levergy (Lescuses, according to Shea)[3] as curé; but next year Pedro Juan

---

[1] Shea's *Archbishop Carroll*, pp. 191, 543.   [2] *Ibid.*, p. 546.
[3] *Ibid.*, p. 192 n.

Eon writes in Spanish again. Eon we know was a man of means, and learning too, but he died soon.

In 1787 is recorded by Lamport the death of Louis Bodin. Most of the entries relate to Spaniards, from Malaga, Sevilla, Galicia, etc., generally soldiers or officials; but in the next year we find an exception in Joseph Calvert, a native of "la provincia de la Virginia, en los Estados Unido," who had been duly received into the church. The well-known Lamport and McKenna were among the Irish priests sent over from the College of Salamanca in 1787 to convert and hold the English in Louisiana and Florida.[1]

From December, 1789, for three years, we have Fr. Manuel Garcia, a Franciscan, as parish cura, who speaks of Mobile as "Ciudad de la Movila," the title which he uses also for the City of Mexico. It became his duty in 1790 to bury his predecessor, Dr. Miguel Lamport, "Clerigo Presbutero y Cura."

In December, 1792, begins Constantine McKenna as "Cura Parroco," and he next year officiated at the funeral of Antonio Narbonne, captain of infantry, and two years later at that of Don Pedro Trouillet. In the time of McKenna came the rebuilding of the church, which was needed even eight years before.

The kings of Spain, under Ferdinand's contract with Popes Alexander VI. and Julius II., in consideration of obtaining for the sovereign all tithes and the right of patronage, became bound to provide for religious instruction in America, and therefore to build churches.

In 1792 the De Lusser heirs for $200 sold two lots, of twelve and a half toises front by twenty-five deep, to the king for the sole use and purpose of erecting thereon a parish church and dwelling-house for the parish priest, but with the privilege of holding or selling the premises at his sovereign pleasure. It was part of the property acquired by Mme. De Lusser, 1757, from Governor Kerlerec.[2]

This land was at the northwest corner of Conti and Royal streets. On the corner lot was duly erected the parsonage, and on the next, facing Royal, the parochial church, destined to survive until 1827. In the public archives Lanzos commemo-

[1] Shea's *Archbishop Carroll*, p. 557.
[2] *Mobile Translated Records*, p. 121.

rates the march of the garrison behind McKenna, as he bore
the cross from the old church to the new foundation, where the
corner-stone was duly laid, January 31, 1793. The whole
work, including parsonage (*casa*) as well as church, was duly
completed by Joyce, the contractor, and on May 22, after
official inspection by carpenters, masons, and blacksmiths commissioned by the commandant, accepted for the crown. It may
be that the erection of this new church was due to the energy of
McKenna and the influence of Bishop Cyril. This bishop
may have lacked in tact, but certainly not in good works and
intentions for the prosperity of his see.

Cyril has been badly treated by history. His efforts for the
reform of the Gulf coast proved almost fruitless, and the king
relieved him of his office in 1793 and directed him to return
to Spain.[1] He went to Havana, however, and was still there
in 1799. The reason alleged for deposing him was, "the
deplorable state of religion and ecclesiastical discipline," and
to correct this the provinces of Louisiana and Florida were
next erected into a diocese, bounded east by the American see
of Baltimore and west by the Mexican sees of Linares and
Durango.[2]

The first bishop was Louis Peñalver y Cardenas, a native of
Havana, a good and experienced man, who arrived at New
Orleans in July, 1795. He found the inhabitants very lax in
their church duties, much of it being due to intermixture of
Protestants and to the democratic and free-thinking tendency
of the French. Peñalver issued regulations on taking charge,
which relate more especially to the conduct of the clergy, and
then set about visiting the different parishes. In 1798 is a
memorandum of a visitation at Mobile, but the entry of "visi-
tado" on the Mobile register is signed, not by the bishop, but
by a "secretario," whose name seems to be Ysidro Quintero.
In this year we know Peñalver was at Pensacola,[3] and there can
be little doubt the entry was made while the clear eyes of his
round, mother-like face were overseeing the affairs of Mobile,
too.

The cession of Louisiana to France in 1800 was not generally
known, but when Peñalver in 1801 was promoted to the see of

[1] Shea's *Archbishop Carroll*, pp. 568, 569.   [2] *Ibid.*, p. 570.
[3] *Ibid.*, p. 579.

Guatemala his place in Louisiana and Florida was not filled. Canon Thomas Hassett and Rev. Patrick Walsh were appointed administrators of the diocese by Peñalver when he left, but Hassett soon died, leaving Walsh to fight it out with the schismatic Sedella in New Orleans.

Mobile escaped that scandal. The bishop of Havana extended his authority over the Florida portion of the diocese, and this lasted until a rearrangement in American times, when Michael Portier became vicar-apostolic of Alabama and Mississippi.[1]

McKenna is probably the best known of the Spanish priests, and his flowing English hand is much more legible than that of his predecessors. He generally speaks of the church as "Iglesia de Nĩa. Sĩa. de la Mobila," which denotes no change of name, for he often has "Nĩa. Sĩa. de la Concepcion" also. In his time came the deaths of Santiago de la Saussaye and Valentin Dubroca, among other well-known names.

From 1800 we have pastor Juan Francisco Vaugeois, whose entries are peculiar in that the "Juan Francisco" is always in the handwriting of the main entry, while the "Vaugeois" is a regular and separate signature, with flourish, in another hand. To him it fell to administer the last rites of his church to Toinette Dufey, Pedro Juzan, Simon de Castro, and Domingo Dolive. At the Castro interment we find witnesses, — almost the only instance under the Spaniards; and they are Antonio Espejo and Rafael Hidalgo. The surgeon's is in a neat, small backhand, while the other is almost undecipherable.

A separate register was kept for negroes, who are generally slaves, although free mulattoes occur, — such as Juan Batista Lusser in 1797. The only difference in the style of entry, and that possibly unintentional, is that for "body" the word in the white register is "cuerpo;" in the colored, "cadaver." The free colored persons held slaves themselves. One or more is mentioned of Julia Vilard, and at least two of Simon Andry. A number of slaves are mentioned of the house of Forbes, — "de la Casa de Dn. Juan Forbes."

This negro register comes down later than the other, and shows two entries in 1807 by Sebastian Pili (or Piti), and others the next year by Dn. (or Dr.) Francisco Lennon, both appar-

---

[1] Shea's *Archbishop Carroll*, pp. 585, 589.

ently acting as pastors *ad interim.* In 1809 began Vicente Genin, who continued until 1823.

The parsonage lot was 65 French feet on Royal by 150 on Conti (then called Church), and the church grounds next north had a front of 85 feet. The parsonage had a house, outbuildings, and fruit trees. It was the regular residence of the ‡acting priest, although we also find McKenna obtaining a grant to a larger place at the north end of Royal (16 by 20 toises), probably above St. Anthony. He said he wanted to have more room for a garden and stock. He only kept the new lot a short time, for he sold it in 1800 for $50 to John Forbes & Co. It was probably too far from the scene of his duties at the church and hospital.[1]

Pastor Vaugeois lived in the old parsonage until 1803, but the authorities allowed it to become so dilapidated, that, fearing it would fall on his head, he moved out in that year, and by direction of the intendant rented a house somewhere in the suburbs for ten dollars a month. The parsonage was leased out to less timid tenants, and in the winter of 1806–7 Dr. William E. Kennedy occupied it at a rental of six dollars a month, he making necessary repairs. Kennedy had taken the oath of allegiance to the Spanish king, and was therefore permitted by Governor-General Folch and Commandant Osorno to settle in Mobile and practice medicine.

Vaugeois, also, found his residence too far from his duties, and on January 27, 1807, while in Pensacola, petitioned Morales to be allowed to purchase the old parsonage at some fair valuation. It seems that a friend of his had promised to make repairs if Vaugeois bought the place.[2]

But other applicants appeared, when St. Maxent, after considering this, reported that the place should be repaired or sold. Two weeks later Thomas Price asked for it, in consideration of having had to sell his own house from not receiving for two years pay as interpreter; and the same day Kennedy asks that it be sold at auction, as he, too, would like to make a bid on it, — rather scouting the idea of a private sale to the priest or any one else.

[1] *Mobile Translated Records,* pp. 235, 267.

[2] *Kennedy* v. *Collins,* printed record for U. S. Sup. Ct. See 10 How. Rep., p. 174.

Morales issued a decree of sale on February 18, 1807, directing the commandant to advertise it by posting bills three times, nine days at a time, and to appoint two mechanics to appraise the house and two citizens to appraise the ground, all, as usual, to act under oath and in the presence of assisting witnesses. Proposals would be received by the commandant pending the advertisement.

St. Maxent appointed as assisting witnesses to notify surveyor, appraisers, etc., Francisco Cañedo and Rafael Suez, for want of a royal notary public in Mobile, and they were duly sworn. Cañedo we often find attesting conveyances in the same capacity. All of the appointees were duly sworn, and acted in their respective capacities. As carpenters we have Antonio Nicolas and Francisco Guiral, and as blacksmiths the even better known Juan Murrell and Thomas Powell. The mason work was to be valued by "the only intelligent man in that department," Marcos Lopez, while B. Dubroca and Rafael Hidalgo were to appraise land and fruit trees. Collins was to plat the property, and Price to act in case any of the "above individuals should not possess the Castilian idiom," he being official interpreter of the French and Spanish languages. On the 24th of March all repaired to the parson's house at 9 A. M. with the witnesses and made valuation, resulting as follows: Ground, $130; carpenter work, $400; blacksmith, $17.04; mason work, $120; total, $667.04, in hard silver, the decimals being rials.

The only bids received were one from Thomas Powell of $700 and one from Pedro Vinsant of $725, which were forwarded to Pensacola with the other original papers, a transcript of 18 pages being filed in the Mobile archives.

Here our record stops; but we know the sale was duly held on June 1, 1807; that Miguel Eslava bid $805, got the property, and was duly put in possession by the intendant.[1]

This northwest corner of Royal and Conti is now a saloon, but previous to the great fires in the first part of this century was occupied by the United States Hotel, a famous inn. In 1827 the Eslava title was contested by the Catholic authorities; but the Alabama Supreme Court concluded, on consideration of the evidence, that, while the land was bought by the King of

---

[1] *Antones* v. *Eslava*, 9 Porter (Ala.) Rep., pp. 527, 532.

Spain from the De Lussers and used for a church parsonage, there was no trust to retain it for that use, and that the Eslava purchase in 1807 was valid.

We have no picture of the adjacent church, unless a rather conventional gabled house with cross on one end, in Dinsmore's map of about 1821, is intended as such. This represents it with its length, not end, on Royal Street, and certainly bears out the unfavorable description by the Saxon duke Bernhard, of Saxe Weimar, who saw it in January, 1826. He describes it as resembling a barn, and having a high altar with vessels of tin and a picture of no value, while on the sides of the room were two small altars.[1] It may have looked far different under the Spaniards, when the whole population was Catholic and it had the weight of official influence.

No more interesting page occurs in the American State Papers than that recounting what is known of the history of the graveyard of 400 by 300 feet at the intersection of Dauphin and Franklin streets.[2] Much of the eloquent reasoning there is pure conjecture; but we learn that from the nineties, at least, the cemetery was located on this, the site of the present Cathedral Square, Catholic Orphan Asylum, bishop's residence, and the property from Dauphin to Conti now or lately owned by the Catholic Church. It was in the pine woods in those days. Spanish funerals, like that of Simon Andry, may have wended their course out Dauphin, but the more natural route would be from the church west along our Conti to the inclosure. The cemetery was in ruins in 1793, but Lanzos then ordered that the "campo santo" be kept in better condition by the citizens and the graves protected from stock.

With the city growth in American times, many of the remains were to be transferred to what has now in its turn become the Old Graveyard, on Bayou Street, south of Government. But graves under Conti Street have even recently been revealed by the digging of a sewer.

[1] 2 *Travels in North America*, pp. 31, etc.
[2] 5 *American State Papers*, p. 131.

CHAPTER XXXIX.

THE INDIAN TRADE.

THE English and Americans recognized the Indian title and extinguished it by treaty; the French and Spanish rather regarded the savages as subjects and made no special purchases of the territory, which they considered already property of the king. As the price paid by the English was always insignificant, the practical result was the same to the Indians; but it cannot be denied that the Latin immigrants, fewer and less aggressive, did not extinguish the native races, although at first more cruel, while the self-assertive Anglo-Saxons have all but wiped them from the earth. Mexico is largely Indian yet; in the United States the aborigines are curiosities.

All these governments recognized the avidity of the Indians for simple wares, firearms, and liquor, and, with each, control was from the first a question of trade. It was so with the Iroquois, swaying between the influences of Albany and Montreal; it was so later in the Ohio Valley; and it was so nearer Mobile with the natives in the southern mountains between the colonies of England and Spain. The early trade was principally by wood-rangers, but from the beginning the respective governments made presents to the chiefs at every conference and kept open table for them at the posts. Under the English and Spanish, there was more system.

On the Spanish side of the line the trade was by individuals, but under government supervision; and after 1789 Panton, Leslie & Co., from their several headquarters, were in effect the agents of Spain in intercourse with the Choctaws, Chickasaws, Creeks, and even Cherokees.[1] The prices were fixed both for buying skins and selling goods, and fixed to meet American competition from Georgia and the Carolinas. Their packhorses carried goods and their traders brought news, and even official communications, from the Ohio region to the Gulf. The

---

[1] 2 White's *New Recopilacion*, pp. 326, 329.

Indian treaty of alliance with Spain in 1792 was largely due to that firm. This trade kept on through war and peace, and even through the disturbed times of William Augustus Bowles, who influenced the Creeks in opposition to McGillivray, but was captured and delivered to the Spaniards by him in 1792. He returned, however, and in 1800 destroyed Panton's house at St. Mark's. Until his final capture in 1804, this American adventurer was to ruin their commerce in every way he could, by sea and land.[1]

The house lost money, particularly after the death of their silent partner McGillivray in 1793 near Mobile, but the governors appreciated the value of their services, and from 1794 induced them to continue the business and look to the king for indemnification. Their "dead capital" by 1800 was estimated at almost $400,000,[2] and included their stocks, salaries, expenses, and claims against the Indians. "The debts due the actual house," wrote a Spanish official of the time, "must amount to one hundred and twenty thousand dollars, rather more than less; in time of peace they would amount, as experience has shown, to one hundred and eighty thousand dollars. The lots, buildings, tools for that trade, amount to forty thousand, more or less. These sums form a dead capital of two hundred and twenty thousand. The debts of the Indians and traders are scarcely ever diminished; and if this happens at some times, at other times they are increased in proportion. To this dead capital must be added the labor of sixty workmen, besides that of the negroes or servants, to prepare a post and pack the skins; to that must be added the value of two vessels, of from two hundred and twenty to two hundred and fifty tons each, for the houses of Pensacola and Mobile, and a brigantine of one hundred and fifty tons for St. Augustine, with three smaller vessels of from fifty to ninety tons, absolutely necessary for the trade and communication between these three said factories; equally are to be charged the goods or merchandise which must always be on hand in the respective store-houses, and those which are navigating, going and coming from Europe, whose value can, without exaggeration, be stated at more than one hundred and fifty thousand dollars, forming a total of

[1] 2 Pickett's *Alabama*, pp. 116, 192.
[2] 2 White's *New Recopilacion*, pp. 326, 333.

three hundred and sixty thousand dollars. To this immense sum must be added other annual inevitable losses, without any other profit or advantage than to conserve the friendship of the Indians, in order not to lose the interest and confidence of the traders, so useful to know from them all the information necessary to the interest of the house, and political views of government, to which it has always contributed in a most complete way. One of these expenses is the cost of the open table (an indispensable circumstance and of absolute necessity) which the house keeps for the Indian chiefs, the traders and factors employed in its trade, hospitably receiving likewise all the other transient Indians. Another very great expense is the presents, which, besides those made by the government, the house is obliged to make to the head men of the distant nations who frequently come to its stores, and which cannot be estimated at less than eighteen thousand dollars."[1] Little of this could have been realized if the great house was forced to discontinue business.

The claim against the Lower Creeks or Seminoles was finally settled by cessions of land at the mouth of the Apalachicola River. The first of these purchases was in 1804, in consideration of the sum of $66,533 of debts, besides admitted robberies; and Forbes & Co. (successors of Panton, Leslie & Co.) were put in possession two years later on petition to Folch, then at Mobile. The second purchase was in 1811 for $19,387.04½, and there was also a third cession of an island, all in the same vicinity. Each was by full council of all chiefs and in the presence of the Spanish officials. The total amount of land was 1,200,000 acres, mostly pine barrens.[2] The claim for indemnity was never abandoned, and was under consideration in Spain at least from 1794. It grew with the years; and a new item set out by Forbes in 1818 related to slaves and goods stolen or otherwise lost during the Anglo-American war of 1812, despite the efforts of the house, through its armed vessels, to recover them. It, too, was finally settled by a similar cession in 1818 by Spain of one and a half million arpens of adjoining lands; for Spain did not, as U. S. agent Seagrove predicted, sacrifice the house which had maintained her hold on the Indians.[3] The

[1] 2 White's *New Recopilacion*, pp. 333, 334.
[2] *Ibid.*, pp. 713, 724, 356, 362.   [3] *Ibid.*, pp. 349, 350, 354, 723.

losses were estimated at about $100,000, and the land was to be in full compensation.

The trade with both Choctaws and Creeks was by trail and river; but the Creeks, going by land, of course went mainly to Pensacola, because nearer. That trail went northeast through Burnt Corn towards Tookabatcha and the heart of the confederacy, who were thus enabled to compare Florida and Carolina prices.

The trade of the eastern Choctaws was with Mobile alone. Fort Tombecbé on the river, rehabilitated as the Spanish Fort Confederation, was again an outpost, and the trading path from Mobile northwestwards to the Choctaw nation was one of the best known things in local geography. It seems near the town to have about followed the line of the present Spring Hill Avenue and Centre Street, and crossed Bayou Chateaugué at Murrell's Ford, sometimes called the Portage. Thence on, in its southern part, it was not far from the later St. Stephens Road, and can be traced still higher at intervals, — as, for instance, at old Washington Court-House. It crossed what was later the north boundary of Mobile County, and continued on northwestwardly into the present Mississippi among the main Choctaw villages. The point where it crossed the 31st degree of latitude, and where it crossed the fifth township north, was in American times to be the starting-place for several counties. The road became in 1809 the west boundary of Baldwin and Washington counties.[1]

The fertile lands on the Tombigbee and lower Alabama rivers, the seat now of vast cotton production, were not thickly settled by the Indians; for the main seats of the Choctaws were in the lower half of our Mississippi, where they lived in northern, southern, and western districts under separate chiefs. Columbus, Meridian, Demopolis, and Selma had no special Indian predecessors, although Pushmataha lived near Meridian. But it would be a mistake to think of the region about the Tombigbee as uninhabited. The district between that and the Alabama River was claimed by both Choctaws and Muscogees; and Choctaw mounds are not infrequent, especially from what is now called the Fork of Greene County in a line up towards Tuskaloosa, where many remains still exist. At Durden's

---

[1] Toulmin's *Laws of Alabama*, pp. 81, 82.

Landing, human bones have been found on the river edge; and beyond Forkland are many mounds, some twenty feet high and a hundred in diameter. Over the Warrior River, near Carthage, has been dug up the skeleton of an Indian seven feet high. Across the river from Bladon was at one time a village, and the records of Washington County show cessions by later chiefs of the lower Tombigbee towns.

The United States early took hold of the Indian problem. To prevent the abuse which had grown out of indiscriminate trading, Congress in 1790 by one act provided for treaties with the tribes, and by another restricted trade to such persons as should be licensed and bonded by the government.[1] Washington as a youth had been much with the Indians, and when President he was from 1791 untiring in his efforts to protect them in their rights and afford them the kind of commerce they needed. On one occasion recalled by Pushmataha he advised them to cultivate the soil, since game would necessarily grow scarcer. Experience showed that individuals could not cope with the great Pensacola-Mobile house, and so, in a message of 1793, he recommended that the government take charge of this trade. He thought the matter so important that the United States should be satisfied if reimbursed their outlay.[2]

This bore fruit in 1796, when Congress authorized the President to establish government trading-posts, and made necessary appropriations for that purpose. March 28, 1797, he made a treaty with the Creeks by which that nation ceded lands for such posts; and shortly afterwards we find Colonel Benjamin Hawkins among the Creeks as government agent, and among the Choctaws John McKee in the time of President Adams.

The first government factory for the Choctaws was a few miles away from Fort Confederation. There the United States agent resided and sold goods to the Indians, largely on the credit of skins to be supplied by them. The name Factory Creek still marks the location. At such posts deerskins and other Indian wares were bought, and supplies, particularly domestic articles and animals, were sold to them on government account. The United States at these factories did directly what Spain at Mobile and Pensacola did indirectly through Panton, Leslie &

[1] 1 *U. S. Statutes at Large*, pp. 136, 137.
[2] 12 *Washington's Works* (Sparks), pp. 20, 30, 40.

Co. and their successors. The cultivated Silas Dinsmore was long the government factor, first on the Chickasahay (near Quitman) and then in Puckshenubbee's district, west of Pearl River. He incurred the enmity of General Jackson for enforcing passports for slaves of travelers,[1] exacted mainly during his attempts to suppress the famous Murrell gang. In 1802 the United States authorities were considering the propriety of establishing a military post for the protection of this Chickasahay factory, but the establishment really did not need it. The Indians transferred to these institutions the respect which they formerly showed the traders. When Dinsmore left the northern Choctaw district, that of Mushulastubbe, he seems to have relied on the influential interpreter John Pitchlyn, resident at the mouth of the Oktibbeha, to control those Choctaws. Dinsmore was enthusiastic at both his stations in improving the condition of the savages. He induced them to make larger truck patches, added cotton to their crops, and introduced poultry, hogs, and horses. The Mayhew missionaries received his warm support. He married a Philadelphia lady, and with Africans operated a large plantation near the agency.

One of the severest blows to the Spaniards was finding St. Stephens on the American side of the boundary line of 31° provided for in the second article of the treaty of October 27, 1795. But when a detachment of American troops marched across from Natchez, the Spaniards promptly surrendered the place, on May 5, 1799, and Lieutenant John McClary of the second infantry received the post for the United States. These troops did not remain long, as they proceeded southwardly to near the actual line, and at Ward's Bluff, among beautiful oaks, built Fort Stoddert in July, named for the acting secretary of war.[2] St. Stephens, however, flourished for many years as a town and as the seat of the U. S. Indian factory established by Joseph Chambers in 1803. Chambers induced George S. Gaines to leave a position in Tennessee and come as his assistant in 1805. Gaines succeeded him next year, and, as the old buildings were in decay, in 1811 built as a warehouse, above the fort, probably the first brick house in what is now Alabama, outside of

---

[1] 1 Parton's *Jackson*, p. 349.

[2] Information from War Department. As to Gaines, see his Reminiscences in *Mobile Register* in June and July, 1872.

Mobile. The old fort was on a bluff above, while the American town grew up just below the ravine. Its commercial importance, predicted by Romans and Ellicott, was due to the fact that it was at the head of sloop navigation; for McGrew's Shoals just above prevented the passage, at the usual stage of water, of everything except canoes. For this reason the government factory at St. Stephens naturally became the centre of American influence among the Choctaws.

Gaines was for a while embarrassed by the duty exacted by the Spaniards at Mobile even on the Federal goods for the savages; but in 1810, although the Indians only permitted packhorses and not the wagon-road desired, he opened a new route. His supplies were sent from Pittsburg down the Ohio and Mississippi, and he had them barged up the Tennessee to Colbert's Ferry and then carried overland to the Tombigbee. Pitchlyn's activity and influence were of the greatest assistance in forwarding the goods down the river to St. Stephens. The next year he found it necessary to have his boat boxed in and armored with beef hides as a protection against Indian bullets; for the time was near when the American Indian policy was to break down, from the savage distrust of the rapid increase of the white settlements.

CHAPTER XL.

VIRGINIANS and other pioneers (all called Virginians by the Indians) crossed those Alleghanies which Iberville designated as barriers, and formed the new States of Kentucky and Tennessee. Georgians, too, were passing through the Creek and Choctaw country and settling about Natchez and on the Tombigbee, while the region of the Tennessee River from 1805 had its immigrants also.

Georgia, like the other colonies, had claimed under her charter to the Mississippi River (as shown on Adair's map of 1775), if not farther, and her Yazoo sales of 1789 and 1795 threatened conflict with the Federal government. They were certainly productive of much fraud. The purchase of her rights, however, by the United States in 1802, for a million and a quarter dollars, removed the trouble. Meantime, on April 7, 1798, the Territory of Mississippi was created, extending from the Chattahoochee to the Mississippi River north of 31° north latitude. At first the north boundary was run parallel from the mouth of the Yazoo, but it was in 1804 changed to the line of Tennessee.

President Adams made Winthrop Sargent of New England, formerly secretary of the Northwest Territory, the first governor; and General Wilkinson promptly built and occupied Fort Adams, near Davion's old mission, on the first bluff north of the demarcation line. The governor, under his extensive powers, then by proclamation divided the Natchez district into counties. On June 4, 1800, he created Washington County, extending from Pearl River to the Chattahoochee, and having a population of 733 whites and 494 slaves, besides 23 free negroes. A representative government had been already established, under which the general assembly met at Natchez on the first Monday in December, 1800. There were nine representatives from the three counties of Adams, Pickering, and Washington, — the last furnishing but one, the others, all on the Mississippi River, four each.

President Jefferson appointed William C. C. Claiborne, of Tennessee, governor, who soon removed the capital from Natchez to the neighboring village of Washington. Claiborne's incumbency was marked by important events, among them the incorporation in 1803 of Natchez, with a mayor's court of extensive and summary jurisdiction, and the Choctaw treaty of the year before at Fort Confederation. This confirmed to the United States the old cession to the British of all land between the Tombigbee and Mobile on the east and the Chickasahay River on the west, south of the Hatchee-Tikibee Bluff on the Tombigbee. Brigadier-General Wilkinson signed for the United States, and Pushmataha and other chiefs for the three divisions of the Choctaw nation.

James Wilkinson was one of the most adroit men of his time. He was of Maryland originally, and eminent in the Revolutionary War; but, if he served under Washington before Boston, he also followed Benedict Arnold in Canada, and, either naturally or by example, was to resemble the traitor more than the patriot. He went to Kentucky in 1784 to represent Philadelphia merchants, and soon was prominent in the movement to make that a State independent of Virginia. In 1787 he followed his tobacco, flour, and bacon down the river to New Orleans, and obtained special trade privileges, and ultimately a pension that made him the leader in the Spanish conspiracy to make Kentucky subject or allied to Spain.

This continued even after he became an officer in the United States army, and when general-in-chief he was strongly suspected of complicity in Burr's plans against both Spain and the Union. His commercial agent at New Orleans, Daniel Clark, seems to have proved the fact in a pamphlet; but a court-martial in 1811 gave him the benefit of a doubt. He was polished and persuasive, and, while he several times turned his coat, he always concealed his tracks. He published memoirs, and managed to stand high in his country's annals, until Gayarré, after his death, unearthed his correspondence with the Spanish officials.

Wilkinson and Claiborne were the commissioners who received for the United States from the French the possession of

Louisiana on December 20, 1803; and when Claiborne became governor of that new province, Robert Williams of North Carolina succeeded him in Mississippi Territory, whose Bigbee district claimed 1500 people.

Under an act of Congress, Washington County was now erected into a judicial district, where the superior court, the germ of our later judicial system, was held on the first Mondays in May and September. Harry Toulmin was appointed by President Jefferson first United States judge of this Tombigbee district. He entered on his duties in 1804 at Wakefield, near McIntosh's Bluff, a place which he named for Goldsmith's vicar.

He was already a man with a history. Born at Taunton, England, in 1766, he was, while a young man, a Unitarian minister with a large congregation. He was republican in sentiment, and, from too free expression of his sentiments in those early days of the French Revolution, found it necessary, in 1791, to emigrate to America. He became president of the Transylvania University at Lexington, then secretary of state of Kentucky, and compiler of a code of laws for that State. As secretary he promulgated the celebrated Resolutions of 1798, strongly suspected to have been written by Madison, and ever after the platform of States' Rights Democrats. It was while secretary of state that he was appointed judge for Mississippi, — "grand juge," as the Creoles always called him.

Harry Toulmin was active in everything, but is chiefly remembered as compiler of the territorial laws in 1806 (as of those of Alabama in 1823), and for his fourteen years' tenure of office as Federal judge. A characteristic letter of his of August 28, 1808, apparently to the Mobile commandant, is preserved in the archives. It seems a Spanish subject named Kilcrease had murdered a Mobile Frenchman on the Tensaw above the line, and then escaped below it. Toulmin writes that if the Spaniards would deliver up the murderer he would see to a proper trial, or, if the commandant would try the man, he would get up the evidence. He closes with this noble and vigorous language: —

"I embrace this opportunity of doing myself the honor to assure you that I feel exceedingly solicitous that no facility should ever be afforded, by a difference of national jurisdictions between settlements so contiguous, to the vicious and abandoned on either side of the line to commit depredations with impunity; and that, as far as it depends upon me, I shall always be ready to coöperate with good men of both governments in the suppression of villainy and licentiousness."

The years 1805 and 1806 marked the acquisition of part of the Tennessee valley from the Chickasaws and Cherokees, the agreement with the former being signed in the Chickasaw country for the United States by James Robertson, of Tennessee, and Silas Dinsmore, of New Hampshire, United States agent in the western Choctaw district. Out of this, Governor Williams in 1808 created the county of Madison, which in two years more was to contain half the population of the Territory. The same commissioners in 1805 acquired a grant from the Choctaws, at the treaty of Mount Dexter, of a strip to connect the Bigbee and Natchez districts, and extending in width from Ellicott's Line to Choctaw Corner, crossing the Bigbee at Fallectabrenna Old Fields, below Tuscahoma. Dinsmore ran the north and east lines, but needed the influence of Young Gaines to get it over the Bigbee Indians.[1]

But these three grants, important as they were, needed highways to make them available. The wagon-road from Natchez to the Cumberland, crossing at Muscle Shoals, came a little earlier; but more important for the Mobile district was the Federal Military Road, cut by the United States in 1805, by permission of the Creeks, from the Ocmulgee in Georgia to Mims' Ferry on the Alabama. The line of this road can still be traced in part, as it was made the eastern boundary of Monroe County. There was also in the same year acquired from the Cherokees the right to a road from Knoxville across the Tombigbee to Natchez. No more important study can be found than that of the early roads; for along them poured the immigration which has claimed the Southwest for the Anglo-Saxon civilization. But this advance was accompanied by alarms.

In consequence of the claim of Spain that the Arroyo Hondo was the east boundary of Texas, General Wilkinson, in

---

[1] The facts in this chapter are derived from many sources, but, besides Monette's *Valley of the Mississippi*, special mention should be made of George S. Gaines' Reminiscences, in the *Mobile Register*, in June and July, 1872.

1806, prepared for war. Besides his march to Natchitoches, he also contemplated the capture of Mobile from Fort Stoddert, whose commandant was to be assisted by 200 Washington militia under Colonel James Caller, while other troops should make a feint in order to hold Pensacola quiet. Captain Peter Philip Schuyler had succeeded Schaumburgh in 1804, and in 1807 was himself succeeded by Captain E. P. Gaines. All were of the second regiment.

But the movement against the Spanish possessions was soon dropped for a greater peril to Spain, and, as it was feared, to the United States alike. An American Iberville was thought to be planning a western empire which should be independent of the Atlantic seaboard. For as long as all west of the Mississippi and south of 31° was Spanish, the grand future in store for the United States could not be imagined, and a Cortez-like invasion of the Southwest seemed more promising.

The brilliant Aaron Burr had become an outcast from New York since his unfortunate duel with Alexander Hamilton, and after expiration of his term as Vice-President he turned to the Southwest to better his fortunes. He bought a Spanish claim on the Sabine, and from there would conquer Mexico. The popularity of the enterprise cannot be doubted, whether we consider Burr's discharge at Lexington in 1806, or the grand jury's action in Mississippi next year. But he delayed too long, and this allowed Jefferson's hostile proclamation to have its effect.

Jefferson was not less inimical than were the friends of Hamilton, and the whole executive branch of the government hounded him. Burr fled when refused release at Washington, near Natchez, and on February 6 Governor Williams offered a reward of $2000. He made his way eastwardly, secreted by friends, and at last sought the house of Colonel Hinson, an admirer of his on the Tombigbee. Inquiring the road at the Wakefield tavern one night, where Colonel Nicholas Perkins and Thomas Malone were playing backgammon, he was recognized by Perkins from the description in the proclamation. Perkins, with Sheriff Brightwell, tracked him to Hinson's, but there he fascinated Mrs. Hinson and the sheriff, too, as he did every one. Hinson was away at the time. Perkins, from Nannahubba Bluff, paddled down to Fort Stoddert, and by sunrise induced Captain Gaines to take the road with a file of mounted soldiers. They met Burr and a companion two miles from Hinson's, and made him prisoner without resistance at 9 A. M. on February 19, 1807.

He was kept in honorable captivity at the fort for over two weeks. He played chess with the wife of the commandant, who was a daughter of Judge Toulmin, and became very friendly with the captain's brother, George S. Gaines, the Indian factor, who gratified his curiosity as to the Choctaw Indians and frontier life.

About March 5 Burr was rowed up the Alabama River to Lake Tensaw Boatyard, where he was committed to a guard of nine men under Colonel Perkins, who conducted him on horseback overland by the trail through the Creeks and other Indians to Georgia, and thence to Richmond.

There he was tried under John Marshall, but finally acquitted. He became a wanderer on the face of the earth, until, in 1836, he was at last laid to rest near his father at Princeton.

The year before Burr's capture Huntsville had begun, and about the same time the St. Stephens settlement commenced, although it was not until 1807 that commissioners under the act of the legislature laid off the latter town on the property of Edward Lewis, reserving for public use the land near Fort St. Stephen. There the land office for the district east of Pearl River was located under the act of 1808. Thomas W. Maury of Virginia was register, and Lemuel Henry receiver. In the summer of 1807 Harry Toulmin, James Caller, and Lemuel Henry completed their duty under another act for opening the first road from Natchez to Fort Stoddert; and in December notice was given in the "Mississippi Messenger" that the ferry was ready across the Alabama and Tombigbee just above Fort St. Stephen. This road had causeways over "boggy guts and branches," and from Natchez to Georgia was marked with three notches on the trees.

David Holmes of Virginia succeeded the unpopular Governor Williams in 1809, and on December 21 of that year there was carved out of the southern part of Washington the county of Baldwin, named for the Georgian signer of the Declaration of Independence. The county seat was McIntosh's Bluff.

The Bigbee population increased rapidly after "the three-chopped way" was finished, and the settlements by 1810 had extended on both sides the river up to Mount Sterling. The lawyers were Nicholas Perkins, L. Henry, R. H. Gilmore, J. P. Kennedy, Samuel Acre, Salle, and Joseph Carson. The population of Washington County was about six thousand, many being recent settlers from the Carolinas, Georgia, and Tennessee. Even three years before, when the settlers were still principally old British colonists, the residents had been active in expressing at Wakefield their indignation at acts of Great Britain which were ultimately to bring on the War of 1812. James Caller, the colonel, representative in the legislature and principal politician, was chairman, and Thomas Malone, long Gaines' assistant at the Trading House, was secretary of the meeting. This patriotic feeling was the more remarkable as they had not only to satisfy the United States customs duties at Fort Stoddert, where D. Darling was long collector after the resignation of Lieutenant Gaines, but on everything imported or exported by the Mobile River, even to another American port, they had to pay the Spanish commandant at Mobile twelve and a half per cent. *ad valorem* in addition. Kentucky flour, which cost in Natchez four dollars a barrel, on the Bigbee sold for sixteen dollars. Even United States supplies for the Indian factories were stopped at Mobile and duty collected by Spain. In fact, the United States government in the fullest sense recognized Mobile as a Spanish port.[1]

The Spanish question was accentuated by the revolt of the Baton Rouge district from Spain in 1810. Governor Holmes took possession of it for the United States, and the Spanish flag disappeared from the Mississippi River. Among the leaders were the Kempers, who had been cruelly treated by the Spaniards. The government was at first that of an independent republic, but the district ultimately became a part of the territory of Orleans, the present Louisiana. Mississippi Territory had to look for extension towards Mobile.

Among those who came over the Creek road to Fort Stoddert, to be ready for that occupation when it occurred, were Miller and Hood, who intended establishing a newspaper at Mobile. They began "The Mobile Centinel" at Fort Stoddert on May 23, 1811, at four dollars a year, and copies of several issues of

---

[1] 3 *American State Papers*, p. 220.

this weekly have survived.   The second number has four pages
of four columns each.   It contains some foreign news of the
Peninsular War, and from the House of Commons, but is filled
principally with articles and news regarding Spanish West
Florida, whose acquisition Poindexter was advocating in Congress, although he had prosecuted Burr in Mississippi for
attempting almost the same thing.[1]   The first newspaper in
Mississippi Territory had been "The Natchez Gazette," founded
by Andrew Marschalk in 1802, but "The Centinel" was the
first within the limits of what was to be Alabama.

[1] For an account of this newspaper, see the *Mobile Register* of July 3,
1893.   Two issues are now in the possession of Thomas M. Owen, Esq.,
of Birmingham, Ala.

CHAPTER XLI.

SPANISH rule below Ellicott's line was mild, and even British, we have seen, remained or came there to live. Of them Cornelius McCurtin was a full-blooded Irishman, but after he had had two successive Creole wives and acquired the Farmer plantation and Mobile real estate, he must have felt himself a good Spaniard. John Forbes we know, and also the brothers Innerarity. James married Louise Trouillet, and in his own or her name acquired lands.

On the other hand, Americans were satisfied that the Union would eventually take possession under the Louisiana purchase, and from this and purposes of business a number, even from New England, gradually became inhabitants, and of necessity Spanish subjects.

Lewis Judson came from Connecticut, and was in time possibly the leading merchant, after the house of Forbes declined. The Hallett family are descendants of his sister. Peter II. Hobart was from Vermont, and married a Creole. In later years he wrote back to the north to explain that this did not mean she was not white. Hobart was the owner of a mill, and lived to be in American times a contractor and the builder of the first court-house. He was in the same epoch to buy our Spring Hill and make it a summer resort. Carolinians we have also. Dr. William E. Kennedy had the misfortune to kill Colonel Maxwell in South Carolina in 1797,[1] and after acquittal removed to Spanish territory. We found him in 1807 a Spanish subject, living in the old parsonage at Mobile. He invested in lands, and after his brother Joshua followed him to this section they became the greatest land-owners of them all. Samuel H. Garrow is said to have been a refugee to Virginia from San Domingo, and, while he was here a few days in Spanish times, he settled in Mobile only in 1813 upon

---

[1] *Kennedy's Exrs.* v. *Kennedy's Heirs,* 2 Ala. Rep. p. 583.

the change of flag.[1] The family are said to have been originally of Toulon. Cyrus Sibley we find on the Tensaw by 1810.

The oath of allegiance of Josiah Blakeley to the Spanish crown still exists in the archives at Mobile, bearing date July 10, 1810. The paper recites that he had already lived four years in the district, and had since 1807 cultivated an island purchased from Don José Collins. He says that he had lived six years in Santiago de Cuba.

We learn much of Blakeley, as well as of the island bought of Hobart, Sossier, and Collins, from his long letter to relatives in Connecticut, recorded at Mobile.[2] Omitting only some family references, not always intelligible now, he writes as follows: —

"MOBILE, 28th Feb., 1812.

"MY DEAR ABBY, — Your very pleasing, interesting [letter of] December 11 came to hand about the middle of February. Could you, my dear niece, know one half the pleasure it afforded me, you would willingly continue your interesting, pleasing correspondence. I love your dear mother very much. She knows I love her; but I have one complaint against her, — that she did not sooner inform me that I had so pretty a niece, who could write so pretty a letter. I thank you for being so particular. Ever was it to me a most consolatory reflection that my dear aged mother was with and under the sole care of your most amiable attentive mamma. . . . The unusual number of years added to the days of my dear mother's life does not lessen the sorrow of bidding her a last adieu. To me she had been an indulgent, kind, affectionate mother. She knew I loved her; with me her beloved memory will be dear and lasting. With your dear mamma and family, and with all weeping friends, do I most affectionately and most sincerely sympathize. . . .

"Mobile, the great object of contention at this moment between the United States and the Spaniards, contains about 90 houses, all of wood and but one story high. At the south end of the town is a beautiful fort, built by the French and called Fort Charlotte. The town is about thirty miles north of the

---

[1] *Kennedy* v. *Collins*, U. S. Sup. Ct. printed record, p. 207.

[2] *Mobile Records*, Misc. Book " E," p. 467.

Gulph of Mexico, at the head of what is called Mobile Bay. This bay is from 10 to 20 miles wide. At the head of this bay, on the west side, stands the now famous town of Mobile. The river Mobile disembogues its waters into the bay by several mouths. From Mobile to the high land on the eastern shore is three leagues, in which are three rich islands, containing about four thousand acres each. Better land for rice and cotton perhaps the world does not afford. These three valuable islands are mine. The unfortunate dispute between the two nations has rendered it impossible for me to either sell or cultivate these lands. Were the Americans here, their value would soon be known. Cattle and hogs do well upon them, and no expense. Upon them I have about 30 head of cattle and hundreds of hogs, the hogs wild. I shoot or catch them with a dog. On one of these islands I have a small house and plantation, called Festino. This year intend growing rice. I have also a large survey of land at the mouth of the river Pascagoula, 50 miles west of this. The Gazettes will from time to time inform you what takes place in this country. I have at my Festino plantation the orange, fig, quince, and peach; all do well. It is here too warm for apples. At Fort Stodert, 50 miles north of this, on the west bank of this Mobile River, is an American garrison of 500 or less troops. A little above Fort Stodert the Alabama from the northeast and the Tombigby from the north form a junction, as you may see from the map. They continue one stream to about a league south of the fort, then again separate, forming the Mobile River on the west and the Tensaw on the east. These channels pass through a swamp or marsh about ten miles wide, very little of which is fit for cultivation. Below this marsh and above Mobile Bay are my islands, free of wood and proper for cultivation. They are one continued meadow farther than the eye can reach. Burn the grass and it is fit for the plough or hoe. Between this and Fort Stodert, on the west side, poor land; but few inhabitants, these French. In Mobile about 20 white families, those French, Spanish, Americans, and English. You can easily calculate my circle of acquaintance in Mobile is small. I am acquainted on both sides the river, for a hundred miles up, with all the best people. My room is directly opposite the Roman Catholic Church, the only one here, and in which I sometimes attend Mass, though no Catholic, I love to see religion attended to; it has a good effect on the conduct and morals of the people. From this for 500 miles north, I do not believe there is a church or clergyman, the people almost savage. Land in general *poor*, and but few inhabitants. Packet boats and other vessels are constantly running between this and Orleans; passage about three days. Orleans is southwest of this. That is a gay, lively place; the young ladies there dance as well and dress with as much taste as any place I was ever in. You know if the French have money they will both dress and dance. But little attention appears to be paid to the improvement of the mind. Yet many of them make lively, pleasant companions. When I came to this place it was supposed the United States would soon be in possession. . . . By this long delay I have been disappointed. At present my property here is almost unproductive. By the Gazette you will be informed of the state of this country. I long once more to visit the land of my nativity. I have not the pleasure of recollecting you, and suppose you do not recollect me. By a steady correspondence we can become better acquainted. My picture, which I hope is with your beloved mother, will inform you how I look; your mamma can inform you how I talk; my letter will how I write. . . . Several Yankees are here. One of the first merchants in this place is from Connecticut, not far from Stratford. His name is Judson, a good man. This market furnishes plenty of good oysters and fish, and during the winter the greatest plenty of wild geese, ducks, etc. Venison is plenty all the year, often for ¼ dollar a quarter. . . .

"My Festino plantation is about three miles from Mobile, where next month, March, I begin planting *Rice*. Rice generally grows about as high as wheat; on my island it grows six feet high. It also produces cotton superior to any other land in this country. But I have not negroes to cultivate it; and as the situation of the country now is, I cannot sell plantations. . . .

"*Respect yourself*, and believe me your sincere friend,
                                                  "J. BLAKELY."

"During this last winter the United States army, which had long been wholly idle in this country, have made a road and bridges from Baton Rouge on the Mississippi to Fort Stodart, also from Fort Stodart to the State of Georgia. I have seen many carriages which came from Savanah to Fort Stodart.

"You may write me, and come all the way by land, and a good road. I inform your dear mamma, soon as the Americans have this country I believe I must beg permission to send for one of her daughters.

"During this last winter we have had one snow two or three inches deep, some of which was on the ground for three days. We have had much cold weather this winter, several times ice half an inch thick; though not so far north as Egypt we have it much colder. I think my islands are as rich as the Delta of the Nile, but they have one advantage: I can water them once in twenty-four hours, which for rice much increases their value. When the waters in the river above are raised forty feet, at my islands they do not rise one inch. They are last in this wild survey."

There has been a question whether Josiah spelled his name "Blakeley," as Alabama later named his town, or "Blakely," as the United States confirmed his island title. On the idea that he, like Shakspere, knew best, we must decide for "Blakeley," despite this paper. For this is but a copy, and several original letters preserved in the Spanish archives have it uniformly with the "e."

Although he had been so long in the Spanish dominions, we find Blakeley shortly before this (August, 1810) declaring in one of these papers that he was unacquainted with the language. This was in a proceeding that corresponds with our garnishment. Thomas Hutchins claimed that Thomas Drury owed him a thousand pesos, and that Blakeley was said to owe Drury something. Thereupon the commandant must have cited Blakeley, for that gentleman answers that he had befriended Drury while sick and among strangers, and then shrewdly states an account for seven gallons best old Madeira at four dollars, and for use of a horse, negro, beef, etc., which more than balances the flour, pork, and beef, which Drury may have turned over to Blakeley's people in Mobile.

Blakeley lived on the Polecat Bay side of his island, above Coffee Bayou. When he bought from Collins in 1807, there was already an unfinished dwelling on it, with a well-ditched plantation growing rice, corn, cotton, domestic grasses, and vegetables.[1]

Other Americans were less patient than Blakeley, and preferred Burr's plan for solving the Spanish problem. The leaders of the Baton Rouge revolt, the Kempers, in 1810 attempted to free Mobile also.

No encouragement was accorded these filibusters. They made their descent at first down the Tensaw, where Dr. Thomas G. Holmes and a few other fiery spirits joined them. Near the site of Blakeley they made speeches and gesticulated towards ancient Mobile, and even sent Cyrus Sibley over to demand its surrender by Folch. But whiskey and dissension ruined the expedition. Part of them crossed over to Sawmill Creek, twelve miles above Mobile, and while fiddling and dancing were betrayed by an old man. Two hundred soldiers were sent up in boats under Parades and captured the party.[2]

Moro Castle at Havana was to hold them prisoners for years to come, and Sibley's mill was operated by his faithful servant in the mean time. Even the United States officials disapproved the expedition, — probably because it was a failure, — and in November, 1811, Colonel Thomas H. Cushing, of the 2d infantry, was stationed with a considerable body of troops in the Orange Grove north of Mobile to protect the city against any other such attempt.[3] Finally the troops marched back to found a new post at Mt. Vernon.

[1] See Appendix D, § 12.
[2] 2 Pickett's *Alabama*, p. 237.
[3] Information furnished by the War Department.

CHAPTER XLII.

SPAIN assisted the United States to establish their independence, but hardly realized what must be the result. Of all countries she had most to suffer from a strong American power, and in the case of our own country the danger to Spain was the greater because of the leavening influence of the new democratic institutions.

There have been three times when our relations to Spain were unfriendly. The first was the period which we have now reached, when the natural expansion of the English colonies was to verify the prediction of Iberville, and they were to clamor for the occupation of those possessions which intervened between the west and the Gulf. The second time was when, in our own century, American principles induced the struggles of all her remaining continental provinces for independence, and sympathy and policy evoked the enunciation of that Monroe doctrine of American freedom from European interference which in our day is of so great importance. The third time was to come in the sympathy of the United States for Cubans in their uprisings, and in the strained relations with Spain which grow therefrom.

Spain had accepted from France the gift of Louisiana with reluctance, but when she had taken possession she held to it with Spanish pertinacity. This was the more true when she recovered the Floridas from the British, and found herself again, as in the sixteenth century, with an unbroken coast line sweeping from Carolina all around the Gulf of Mexico.

The interior of the country concerned her but little after De Soto found that it had no mines, and so her eighteenth century diplomats had not been careful to acquire the country up to the sources of the Gulf rivers. This had mattered little when only savages lived there, and the sea was a Spanish *mare clausum*. But conditions in 1812–13 were vastly different.

In 1812 the United States realized that patience had ceased to be a virtue, and found themselves at war with Great Britain. The British used not only such armies as they could spare from the contest with Napoleon, but by emissaries stirred up the Indians of the west and south.

Spain aided the English indirectly by allowing use of the Gulf ports as points of distribution to the Indians and of rendezvous for British ships. This was not unnatural, as England was helping the Spanish in Europe in their great revolt from Napoleon. But the United States could not permit it, especially as to Mobile, which they had always claimed as their own under the Louisiana purchase. President Madison, under act of Congress in the spring of 1813, directed General Wilkinson, commanding at New Orleans, to take possession of Mobile.

This order was signed by John Armstrong, Secretary of War, and is dated February 16. It was, of course, not received for some weeks, but Wilkinson then lost no time in getting ready. He took with him seven companies of the second and third regiments infantry and one of artillery.

He had had many unexpected delays and cross accidents, he reports from Pass Christian, one of them having nearly brought him to "the unprofessional end of death by drowning instead of shooting." He had expected to find at the Pass three gunboats, which he wished to send to take possession of Mobile Bay and guard the pass to town. But they were gone. One gunboat which he had was grounded, and he had to leave his baggage in it; and another "crazy" one that he would use was for the time out of communication on account of a gale. So he intended waiting for Commodore Shaw to bring two from Bayou St. John. That morning he had dispatched a small vessel with a three-pounder and about twenty men to get into Mobile Bay and prevent all intercourse with Pensacola by sea, at the same time that troops descended from Fort Stoddert, and, by fortifying opposite the town, prevented communication by land.

The plan succeeded admirably. The Spanish troops on Dauphine Island were compelled to retire; vessels were intercepted; and the first intimation which Don Mauricio Zuniga, the governor at Pensacola, had of any hostile intention of the

Americans was on April 12, when the Dauphine Island detachment presented themselves before him. He wrote such a letter of mingled surprise and deferential consideration as only a Spaniard could indite. It was handed Wilkinson by Bernard Prieto at Mobile on the 15th.

The American general landed below Mobile with six hundred men. Colonel Bowyer descended the Tensaw with troops, and, with five brass cannon, took a position opposite the city, while Shaw's gunboats held the bay. Cayetano Perez had sixty men, with sixty-two cannon and munitions, in Fort Charlotte, but no provisions. So unequal the contest!

Wilkinson later wrote the Secretary of War that it was somewhat difficult to give an amicable aspect to the investiture of a military post, but that he made the attempt. Thus he wrote to Perez on April 12 from camp near Mobile: —

"The troops of the United States under my command do not approach you as the enemies of Spain, but by order of the President they come to relieve the garrison which you command from the occupancy of a post within the legitimate limits of those States. I therefore hope, sir, that you may peacefully retire from Fort Charlotte, and from the bounds of the Mississippi Territory [and proceed] east of the Perdido River, with the garrison you command, and the public and private property which may appertain thereto."

The reply of the Spanish commandant was made from the fort the same day, as follows: —

"EXCELLENT SIR, — I have just received by your Aid-de-Camp, Major H. D. Peire, your intimation, and to comply with my duty I cannot do less than protest against it, and propose that, provided you permit me to withdraw from the Fort everything which is in it belonging to his C. M., and that the troops, officers, and those employed by government carry out their equipage and property, and also that the inhabitants be allowed to keep their possessions as they did heretofore, and that you furnish me with transports, I will evacuate it, and the garrison will leave it and go to Pensacola without spilling blood; and leaving the decision respecting the Territory to both nations, not having myself faculty to do it.

"God grant you many years."

The articles as finally settled were as follows: —

"Agreement entered into on this 13th day of April, 1813, between Major-General James Wilkinson, commanding the forces of the United States of America, and Captain Cayetano Perez, commanding the Spanish garrison of Fort Carlota and the post of Mobile.

"Art. 1st.   Captain Perez proposes to evacuate the Fort on the 15th inst.

"Agreed, for the hour of 5 o'clock P. M., but a detachment of the troops of the United States shall take post in the vicinity of the Fort to occupy it in the moment of its evacuation.

"2nd.   The Spanish garrison being destitute of provisions, a supply is requested, together with transports to convey the troops to Pensacola.

"Agreed.   But the Spanish government shall be accountable to the United States for the expense; the vessels to sail as flags of truce, and to be guaranteed by the government of Spain against capture, and also against port charges and pilotage: Major-General Wilkinson engages on the part of the United States to guarantee the safe passage of the Spanish garrison against the vessels of those States and the powers of peace with them.

"3rd.   Captain Perez proposes that the cannon, its attirail and the munitions of war belonging to it, actually in Fort Charlotte, shall be embarked with the troops, or, should this proposition be rejected, an officer shall be appointed by the Spanish commandant to meet an officer of equal rank of the American forces to take an inventory of the Artillery and munitions of war, for which the American officer shall give receipts obligatory on the American government to account for the same to the Spanish government.

"The first proposition being rejected, the alternative is acceded to, and Major-General Wilkinson will see it carried into effect.

"4th.   That, until the Spanish garrison has sailed, the American troops shall not approach the Fort.

"Agreed, under the stipulation of the first article, that precaution being necessary to the safety of the public property.

"5th.   That an officer of Artillery and a quartermaster of the Spanish garrison be permitted to remain, to deliver the artillery and munitions of war appurtenant thereto, and to settle the accounts of the garrison, under a guarantee of safety against the molestation of persons, papers, or property.

"Agreed, until the objects of their respective duties shall be accomplished.

"Mobile, Fort Charlotte, April 13, 1813.

"HENRY D. PEIRE, Major of Louisiana Volunteers, Aid-de-Camp to Major-General Wilkinson, being duly authorized.

"CAYETANO PEREZ."

"Additional Article. The contracting parties agree that Lieutenant Sands of the first regiment of artillery on the part of the United States, and Lieutenant Don Juan Estevez on the part of the Spanish government, shall meet, examine, and form inventories of the artillery and munitions of war which may be left in Fort Charlotte by the Spanish garrison, for which the said Lieutenant Sands shall give duplicate receipts, agreeably to the third Article."

The evacuation took place, under the forms prescribed by Wilkinson in the general order of April 15. "The Spanish garrison," he says, "will evacuate, and the troops of the United States take possession of Fort Charlotte this evening, or to-morrow morning. A detachment consisting of Captain Walsh, Artillerist, and Butler's and Laurence's companies under the command of Major Carson, will enter the place the moment the rear of the Spanish troops have passed the *Glacis*. This detachment is to be formed in front of the Fort, the Artillerist with lighted matches and twenty-four rounds of blank cartridges. The troops will be under arms at four o'clock, and on the discharge of the cannon will march to town and take such position as may be hereafter ordered. On taking possession of the Fort, the standard is to be hoisted and a national salute fired from the batteries, to be followed by a similar salute from the navy, after which the troops will be marched back to camp. A guard of fifty men properly officered is to be mounted into Fort Charlotte, and the call of *all is well* is to be repeated by the sentinels every hour, beginning at the guard-house and passing to the right. The contractor must be prepared immediately to issue fresh provisions to the troops three times a week.

"The General recommends to the commanding officers of battalions and detachments to make the exchange of flour for bread on the best terms for the troops which may be practical."

The American troops had an unexpected accession at Fort Charlotte in the form of a body of Mobile volunteers. Speaking of them with the rest of his "little corps," Wilkinson writes the Secretary of War he believes that, whenever put to test, they will prove themselves worthy the name of Americans, and a match for equal numbers taken from the best troops in the world.

In the same report he says: "As soon as I have looked about me, I shall make the best disposition of my puny force to defend the country and assert our jurisdiction to the Perdido; but, sir, it should be remembered that I am placed in a perilous situation, with the ocean in my front, the Creek nation in my rear, the Choctaws on my right, and the Seminoles on my left. The enclosed will give you my effective strength, and I can expect no succor, but by the abandonment of New Orleans, from any quarter nearer than Tennessee or Georgia: it follows that, should we be attacked in force and with decision by land and water, the country must be lost; for two thousand men and fifteen heavy gunboats would be necessary to resist such an attack successfully. These observations are made from a respect to candor, to justice, and our relative stations, and will, I have no doubt, be received with the spirit in which they are offered; yet you may calculate with confidence on whatever my most active exertions and best judgment can effect with the means I command."

The first of the garrison orders after occupation, which has been preserved, was for April 17, and reads as follows: —

"The guard will, until further orders, consist of one Subaltern, one Sergeant, one Corporal, and twenty-four Privates. In future the vault nearest the flagstaff must be made use of by the soldiers and no other, the door of which must be shut either on going in or coming out. One Sergeant, one Corporal, and thirty Privates will be immediately detailed for fatigue after troops this morning. The Sergeant detailed for this duty will report to the Commanding Officer.

"The Acting Adjutant will cause the water call to beat four or five times per day, at which call eight or ten men of a company can go out for water accompanied by a N. C. Officer.

No soldier is permitted to go into town without a written pass from the commanding officer of his Company (waiters excepted), and not more than five men at one time can go; they must also be accompanied by an N. C.[1] Officer. The men going to town must be in uniform.

"W. Carson, Major Commanding."

On the 20th, General Wilkinson was able to sail for the mouth of the bay to look into establishing a fort. This was actually begun on Mobile Point, and named for the gallant Colonel John Bowyer. The general also marched over to the Perdido and began the construction of a "compact strong work" there to repulse any predatory attack.

Thus Mobile was captured without "the effusion of a drop of blood," as Wilkinson expressed it, and the occupation of the United States extended to the Perdido River, — the boundary which they had always claimed under the Louisiana purchase. The stars and stripes now waved from Fort Stoddert to Mobile, from Fort Charlotte to Fort Bowyer. Mississippi Territory had reached the Gulf.

[1] The capitalization, etc., in this, as in most other documents cited, is that of the original. "C. M." stands for "Catholic Majesty," and "N. C.," of course, for "non-commissioned." As to Fort "Stoddert," it may be remarked that this is the official spelling.

PART VI.

AMERICANIZATION.

1813–1821.

CHAPTER XLIII

THE CREEK WAR.

WITH the capture of Mobile, the United States acquired, on all but the Florida side, what Lord Beaconsfield would have called a "scientific frontier." The Tombigbee residents had not only an outlet to the Gulf, but a new district to settle.

Even before the capture of the city, the governor's proclamation had laid off Mobile County. By act of December 18, 1812, all south of the thirty-first degree, from the Perdido to the ridge between the Mobile and Pascagoula rivers, was to bear that name, and all west to Biloxi was named Jackson County. Mobile was to gain at the expense of Jackson when Mississippi Territory was divided,[1] and was also to grow northwardly, although until only a few years ago its north boundary was the irregular line of the old Federal Road.[2]

The new country had an immediate influx of Americans, while not a few of the Spaniards left for Pensacola, which was to remain under Spain for a few years longer, or went to Cuba, the ever-faithful isle. Cayetano Perez returned to Mobile and lived on the bay near Dog River. One cannot but think, from the language used of him by Manrique next year, that he had found Pensacola an unpleasant abode, for that governor told the Indians in a letter found at the Holy Ground that Mobile had been sold to the Americans by a faithless officer.[3] The early records of Washington County, too, contain the names of not a few Spaniards.

George S. Gaines was at Mobile for a while, but Judge Toulmin preferred his grant and home near Fort Stoddert. Another familiar character to us, Sam Dale, was often at

[1] Toulmin's *Laws of Alabama*, pp. 83, 84.

[2] *Alabama Acts* 1828–29, p. 44.

[3] 2 Monette's *Valley of the Mississippi*, p. 411; *Mobile Deed Book* "A," p. 103.

Mobile, but his regular business was that of guide for the immigrants from Georgia to the Bigbee settlements.

Big Sam, Sam Thlucco, as the Indians called him, was *sans peur et sans reproche*, the Daniel Boone of the Gulf region. Early an orphan, the Virginia boy paid off his father's debts and cared for the large family. He was brought up on the border, and learned to know the wiles of the Indians, but not less to love the generous qualities of his savage foes. Tecumseh he heard at Tookabatcha, and the character of Pushmataha he draws with a loving hand.[1] For Dale, like Cæsar, could write as well as fight, and his autobiography, edited by the son of General Claiborne, has a place of its own in southwestern literature.

There was need of his gun rather than his pen. The Americans were threatened with a greater danger than the Spanish custom-house. The Creek nation, instigated by the British, were in arms, pledged to exterminate the white man from their hunting-grounds. The building of the much used Federal Road in 1811, by consent of some chiefs, had aroused the rest under the very eyes of United States agent Hawkins. The impassioned eloquence of Tecumseh at Creek Tookabatcha in the fall of 1811 or spring of 1812,[2] followed by the intrigues of his emissaries the prophets, raised a war spirit before which the friendly Indians had to flee. The Creeks even conferred with the Choctaws at Pushmataha (in the present Choctaw County, Alabama) in July, 1813, in an endeavor to win them to war with the whites, and Tecumseh had visited them before going to the Creeks.

Occasional murders and outrages alarmed the settlers on the rivers, among them the abduction of Mrs. Crawley, rescued by the brave Tandy Walker from the Creek settlement at the falls of the Black Warrior and brought to St. Stephens. While Fort Stoddert and Mount Vernon were occupied in July, 1813, by regulars under General F. L. Claiborne (brother of the late governor), a line of improvised posts extended across the neck of Clarke County from river to river. Fort Republic was built even in the St. Stephens settlement. A man's house was literally his castle, and many places were

---

[1] Claiborne's *Sam Dale*, pp. 32, 59, 135 n.

[2] Meek's *Southwest*, p. 242 ; Halbert and Ball's *Creek War*, pp. 63, 120.

stockaded and became neighborhood resorts. The Bigbee and Tensaw plantations were deserted. White's Fort, Fort Sinque-field, besides Fort Madison and others in the fork, and Fort Mims by the Tensaw Boatyard, were filled with refugees. Captain Schaumburgh had once at Fort Stoddert to improvise marriage ceremonies for a parsonless people, but this time was over. Dale's occupation as guide to immigrants was gone, and young Jerry Austill now made his perilous night ride as messenger between Fort Madison and Mount Vernon. Pierce's school and the Pierce gin at the Tensaw Boatyard were no longer in operation, and the newer cotton-gin at McIntosh's Bluff had also ceased.

Colonel Caller, of the militia, heard that some Creeks under Peter McQueen had gone to Pensacola for munitions, and he raised a party of one hundred and eighty mounted men to intercept them. This was done at Burnt Corn on July 27, but greed for spoil broke up discipline and the successful attack became a defeat. It was even worse, because it destroyed the white prestige. The capture of Mobile was forgotten in the rout at Burnt Corn, and Indian depredation became more marked.

Wilkinson had been called to the north to command on the Canadian border, and he was succeeded at Mobile and New Orleans by General Flournoy. This commander was misled by the reports of Hawkins at Tookabatcha, — who was perfectly honest, but hardly appreciated the extent of the outbreak, — and ordered Claiborne to confine himself to the protection of Mobile.

It was at noon on the 30th of August, while dancing was going on, and a negro was about to be whipped for giving what was deemed a false alarm of Indians coming, that McQueen and Weatherford and their thousand savages dashed through the open gate of the palisade surrounding the house of Samuel Mims on the Tensaw. Major Beasley redeemed his careless-ness by dying sword in hand, and the noble half-breed Dixon Bailey bravely led on the whites in defense of the women and children. But the odds were too great, and at last fire aided the butchery by the savages. Even Bailey was mortally wounded, and hardly two dozen escaped of the five hundred and fifty men, women, and children in that stockaded acre of ground. God's acre it was, for, when a relief corps came, it was only to find ashes, and mangled and burning dead. Neighboring Fort Pierce was abandoned during that battle and Lieutenant Montgomery led its people to Mobile ; while, among other fugitives from Fort Mims, David Tate and some of his family escaped with the two Pierces on a flatboat down to Fort Stoddert.[1]

The pits that received the victims of Fort Mims are now level with the ground, and only a practiced eye can detect any traces of the rude fort. But that massacre still lives in history, and "Remember Fort Mims!" was the battle-cry that nerved American armies from the west, east, and north to blot the very Creek country from the map. It was the blood of grayheaded Sam Mims crying from the ground, and his spirit leading on, that opened the interior of Alabama to civilization.

George S. Gaines received details the next day, and he sent Edmondson express through the Choctaws and Cherokees to Nashville to ask Andrew Jackson to invade the Creek country with his brigade of mounted volunteers. The general required little urging from Governor Blount to take the field, and sent McKee to "get out" the friendly Choctaws. Gaines met McKee at Pitchlyn's as he was on the same errand. Pushmataha had learned of the massacre through Edmondson, and went with Gaines to Mobile. Claiborne won the heart of the Choctaw chief by giving him a full suit of United States brigadier regimentals, noted as purchased at Mobile for three hundred dollars.[2] At first Flournoy refused the assistance of the Choctaws, nobly tendered at his quarters in Fort Charlotte by that chief in September, 1813, but, realizing his mistake, sent an express and accepted it,[3] just as George S. Gaines had reached St. Stephens with Pushmataha and their dispiriting news. At Flournoy's request Gaines, accompanied by Flood McGrew, attended the council called by Pushmataha near Quitman, and the result was the enlistment of many Choctaws.

A brilliant episode of the bloody war which followed was on

---

[1] 2 Pickett's *Alabama*, p. 284 ; family tradition related by T. T. Tunstall, Tate's grandson ; Halbert and Ball's *Creek War*, p. 157.

[2] Claiborne's *Sam Dale*, p. 133.

[3] 2 Pickett's *Alabama*, p. 290 ; Gaines in Mobile *Register*.

the Alabama River, just above Randon's Creek. On November 12, Sam Dale, Jeremiah Austill, James Smith, and a negro, Cæsar, while on a scouting expedition, deliberately paddled out in a canoe, and engaged in a hand-to-hand conflict with nine Indians. Austill was knocked down and all but killed, but one by one they dispatched the warriors and threw them over into the river.[1]

But this, like McKee's burning of the deserted Creek village at Tuskaloosa, like the lamented death of McGrew in a skirmish, was only an episode. Andrew Jackson, fired by the news of the Fort Mims butchery, on October 13 left Nashville, and with Tennessee volunteers marched for Huntsville and the Creek country. Joined by Cherokees and friendly Creeks, he captured Talleschatche, founded Fort Strother, and on November 9 won the battle of Talladega. Perry's victories on Lake Erie and the death of Tecumseh at the north had their counterpart in Jackson's campaign at the south.

From the east, too, the Georgians under Floyd defeated the Creeks at Autose, but had to retire from lack of provisions. General Claiborne fortunately construed the "defence of Mobile" broadly, and in November, 1813, from the west he also marched into the enemy's territory. Above the site of the Canoe Fight, Fort Claiborne at Weatherford's Bluff was built as a base of supplies, and his square fort can still be traced on the bluff of the Alabama River at Claiborne. His objective point was Econachaca, the Holy Ground, on a bluff of the Alabama in what is now Lowndes County. It had been built by Weatherford as a place of safety, where plunder was secured and white prisoners burned. Impregnable, the prophets said, but Claiborne stormed it on December 23, and drove into the water those savages who were not killed outright, for there was little quarter in this war. Weatherford himself fled, and with characteristic daring leaped his gray horse Arrow over into the river. The town was burned to the ground, after the army reserved some supplies and the plunder had been turned over to Pushmataha.

The term of the Mississippi volunteers being out, the army had soon to disband, and the glory of terminating the war was

---

[1] 2 Pickett's *Alabama*, p. 312; Claiborne's *Sam Dale*, p. 123; Halbert and Ball's *Creek War*, pp. 233, 200.

left for General Jackson and the Tennessee soldiers. The Creek country had been invaded, burned, and devastated from the north, east, and west, and on Jackson's advance the savages were defeated at Emuckfau and in other battles. Finally, on March 27, they were found, twelve hundred in number, concentrated in the Horseshoe Bend of the Tallapoosa River. Jackson attacked the isthmus in front, after Coffee and the Cherokees had crossed the river to cut the foe off from the rear. The Creeks fought as bravely as ever, but hardly two hundred escaped alive. Some saved themselves by such stratagems as that of the wounded Manowa, who staid under water until night, breathing through a cane. The Americans lost comparatively few, among them, however, being the brave Major Lemuel Purnell Montgomery, the first man killed on the breastworks. For him, whom Jackson called "the flower of his army," the county containing the present capital was named. The dead were sunk by Jackson in the river to prevent mutilation by the Indians.[1]

The Americans soon found themselves resting on the site of Bienville's Fort Toulouse. The old French trenches were cleaned out, a stockade and blockhouse built, and the place re-christened Fort Jackson. It was, a few months later, the scene of the surrender of the brave Weatherford, whom the general could hardly protect from the infuriated Americans. The two men lived to be afterwards strong personal friends.

Jackson marched his troops back to Tennessee, but, being promoted to the rank of major-general and to command of the southern army, he was again at Fort Jackson on August 9 to conclude a treaty of peace with the defeated Creeks. By this all their country was surrendered to the United States except the part east of the Coosa River and of a line drawn southeastwardly from Fort Jackson.

The great Creek war, which had threatened the very existence of the Americans on the Mobile and Tombigbee rivers, thus resulted in opening up to them the woods and prairies of the most fertile part of the future State of Alabama. The sites of Forts Tombecbé and Toulouse were no longer isolated,

[1] 2 Monette's *Valley of the Mississippi*, p. 421.

but within territory acquired by the whites, and soon to be well settled.[1]

[1] At least one survivor of Fort Mims, McGirth by name, was on the Mobile wharf to be reunited to the family which he thought killed at Fort Mims, but who, as he learned to his joy, had been rescued by an Indian of the attacking force, whom years before McGirth had adopted and raised with his own children. Pushmataha, the most eloquent man of his day, was to be tried by a Mississippi court and condemned to death for punishing capitally a refractory member of his tribe, but was to live and visit Washington. He died there, burned out with strong drink, it is said, and through *Senator* Jackson's influence there were fired over his grave in the Congressional Cemetery the " big guns " he loved so well. Sam Dale was to dine familiarly with *President* Jackson in the White House, and also feel the hand of civil law in an arrest for debt in Cullum's Hotel at Mobile, from which generous citizens at once released him by paying off the claim. Dale was to be praised and pensioned by the legislature of Alabama and have a county named for him, and his services and supplies paid for by the United States at last. Austill was long in business at Mobile, much loved. Weatherford lived and died at Little River, in Baldwin County, where his descendants still survive, and in Mobile yet are Tunstalls who are proud of their kinship to him.

Fort Jackson is now almost ploughed up, and the same insatiate weapon of peace was gradually demolishing its cemetery, where lay Strother, Machesney, and others ; but on my calling the attention of the War Department to its neglected condition, the remains were transferred to the National Cemetery at Mobile in January, 1897.

See 2 Pickett's *Alabama*, pp. 281, 318 ; Davis' *Recollections of Mississippi*, p. 59 ; Claiborne's *Dale*, p. 135, n. ; Toulmin's *Laws of Alabama*, pp. 607, 608; 6 *U. S. Statutes at Large*, pp. 322, 503.

CHAPTER XLIV.

THE Indian war was over, but the Spaniards still claimed Mobile, dissuading the Indians on that account from burning it,[1] and an English fleet was threatening the coast. Jackson was promoted to the command of the southwest, and in August, 1814, floated down the Alabama.

Jackson apparently took with him the five companies of the 3d regulars, five hundred strong, leaving Colonel P. Pippen at Fort Jackson with Tennessee militia. On the same boat with the commander and his staff went Major Ho. Tatum, of Nashville, summoned by Jackson to act as topographical engineer. To him we are indebted for a full survey of the Alabama River, noting distances, courses, and natural features, the more interesting as it is the first known.[2]

He mentions Coosawda Town as having been on a high bluff to the right as they descended. It had been burned by Colonel Gibson during the war. Taw-wassee Town he identifies on the second day (August 12) as Weatherford's Bluff, lower down on the left, and then on the right, Autauga on a red bluff near an unnamed creek. They proceeded only by day, and thus the observations of Tatum are very full. After noting other bluffs, forests, and windings, on the 13th they passed the Holy Ground, a high bluff forty chains long, on the left, where a prophet had lived before the attack, and next day Durant's extensive place on both sides of the river. On the 15th, the troops landed and took of the corn growing on the right, destroying what they did not need, opposite where Colonel Pearson, of the North Carolina militia, had encamped during the Indian war. Some distance below he describes a

---

[1] 2 Monette's *Valley of the Mississippi*, p. 411, n.

[2] This report is in MS., and is in the possession of Mr. Louis Stein, of Mobile.

high red bluff to the right as the handsomest situation on the
river for a town.   On the next day he mentions only the
usual landmarks, and on the 17th an island, noted as the place
where Colonel Benton, in May or June, had let three or four
hundred Indians escape.   These told him they were on their
way to Fort Claiborne to surrender, but afterwards turned up
in Pensacola under Francis McQueen.

They landed at John Weatherford's ferry on the left, near
Fort Claiborne, at four P. M., and Jackson seems to have staid
at the fort until after ten the next morning.   The ferry was
on the road from Fort St. Stephens to Milledgeville, and,
despite his being brother to the famous William Weatherford,
its owner was a friendly Indian.   Fort Claiborne was on a
bluff called the Alabama Heights, one hundred and fifty feet
in perpendicular.   The fort he describes as a strong stockade,
nearly square, apparently with blockhouses in three corners, so
shaped as to have the effect of bastions in defence.   There was
also a blockhouse at an irregular offset made to avoid including part of a ravine.

After leaving, he mentions Weatherford's improvement on
the left at the ferry, then Jones' on the right; next, but some
distance below, those of the friendly half-breed Peter Randon
on both sides of the river, and on the right, further down,
improvements of the brave Dixon Bailey.   On the 19th, they
passed other improvements, — on the left that of Sizemore, a
white man who married Bailey's sister, then on the right the
plantation of the half-breed Mrs. Dyer, also a small improvement on handsome Choctaw Bluff, and those of the friendly
half-breed Sam Manac on both sides, a mile below Little
River.   Among other plantations he also names one of David
Tait, whom he seems to think only pretended friendship with
the whites during the war so as to cover his own property and
that of his half-brother, William Weatherford.   The Creek
boundary crossed the Alabama at the Cut-off, and there the
observations of Major Tatum ceased, as Jackson determined
now to press forward at night also.   There was the less need
for a survey, he says, as Major-General Gaines had already
reported on the river from there to Mobile.

Tatum was much pleased with the country he saw, and says
the Alabama "can be navigated with large keel-boats with

tolerable ease and expedition from the time the fall rains set
in until about the months of May or June, after which they
become low and are much incommoded, both in ascending and
descending, by a variety of shoals." Of the "Cau-hau-ba"
River, also, he speaks in glowing terms, pictured to him as it
was by officers who had scoured that country, as the "Acadia
of America."

On the Cut-off at Mims' Ferry was Peter Randon's large
and valuable plantation. The ferry-house stood on the left
bank at a small lagoon, and three miles below was the mouth
of a small lake leading up to Pierce's Boatyard, in sight of
Fort Mims.

They encamped fourteen miles above Fort "Stoddard," and
upon his arrival on August 20 Jackson proceeded to Mount
Vernon, where Major Blue commanded part of the 39th regiment. Lieutenant-Colonel Benton had but shortly before
marched the rest to Holmes' Hill, two miles from Fort Mims,
and was building Fort Montgomery to stop the marauding
Indians on the east of the rivers. The next day Jackson proceeded, but had to encamp four miles above Mobile on account
of a gale, and did not reach town until nine A. M. next day.
It would be a pity, however, not to believe the tradition which
makes one of his night stops to have been at the house of the
widow Andry, — for Simon was dead. He declined a bed, for,
"Madame, I am a soldier still," but on reëmbarking next
morning had the misfortune to lose his sword in the river.
There, despite earnest search, it still lies, below Seymour's
Bluff.

Fort Charlotte he found commanded by Colonel Richard
Sparks, of the 2d regiment, with five companies of that regiment and a detachment of artillery under Lieutenant A. L.
Sands. Provisions about that time were good and ammunition abundant, but the fort was in bad order from lack of
means to carry out Lafon's plans for repairs, and a valuable
park of artillery purchased from the French was going to ruin
for lack of plank to shelter it. The soldiers were covered at
their own expense, and claimed back clothing for a year or
more.

The hospital and bake-house were not serviceable, and the
frame barracks within the fort gone beyond repair. The men

were then quartered in town, but the officers seem to have been in tents within the fort.[1]

There were a great many cattle east of the bay, the property of Mobilians, and Indians, more than suspected to be sent out from Pensacola, committed depredations. A place belonging to Dolive, for one, was plundered, and overseer and slaves carried off. Jackson met this by sending out parties of soldiers and Choctaws from Mobile and Fort Montgomery, and when a Baratarian pirate brig, prize to the British brig Sophia, foundered on Dauphine Island, Jackson notified the Spanish governor that he would keep the crew (consisting of prize-master, six British and three Spanish sailors) as hostages. He received about this time an amicable embassy from that governor in the person of a Lieutenant Gilmar, and suffered him to depart ; but events at the mouth of the bay prevented the lieutenant from reaching Pensacola.

With Colonel Sparks and Captain Thomas L. Butler, Jackson looked about him, and in everything had to rely upon his own resources; for Washington had been burned by the British, and the government was migratory in these days.

The general is said to have lived at the southwest corner of Conti and Conception streets, — appropriately opposite the site of the Indian House of former days. The old low, whitewashed building will be remembered as only recently destroyed to make way for pleasant modern residences. Another tradition, however, makes Jackson's headquarters to have been a log cabin where the Battle House billiard-saloon now stands. George S. Gaines had occasion to visit him, and found him on the piazza reading. The town, it is said, had altogether but one hundred and fifty houses. The fort could not hold all of his troops. They are said to have been encamped near our Frascati. He was not idle at Mobile, and his reconnoitring around the town is said to be commemorated by the name of a village over Three Mile Creek. Tradition says that he dined in the woods there, and the tree which shaded him was long pointed out. Certain it is, the place was named Jacksonville in his honor.

---

[1] Report of Assistant Inspector-General Daniel Hughes in War Department files. Much information has also been derived from the Tatum report above mentioned.

The British fleet in the Gulf portended an attack somewhere, and so even more important than Fort Charlotte was the new fort which guarded the entrance to the bay. If their aim was to capture Mobile, the defence must be on Mobile Point.

Fort Bowyer had been begun by Wilkinson, and from there, on September 14, 1813, Bowyer had reported that the British were arming Creeks at Pensacola. Its bricks are said to have been furnished by Major Montgomery from Hollinger's Island, possibly near the old Rochon home. Cannon were mounted in May, 1814, but shortly afterwards the post was dismantled, and Bowyer and his command withdrawn to Mobile.

Why this should have been done in a war with a great naval power is not easy to understand, particularly as the site was healthy, and water and wood abundant. Jackson set about reoccupying it, however, and threw Lieutenant-Colonel Lawrence into it with one hundred and thirty men.

Like Fort Charlotte, it had a glacis which all but concealed it, although here there was no covered way, and in shape it was different. It was near the west end of Mobile Point, and on the sea exposure was round, in fact a semicircular battery, which was connected by curtains with a bastion which faced the land approach. Inside, it was one hundred and eighty feet from the summit of the bastion to the parapet of the battery, whose arc described a chord of two hundred feet. The parapet of the semicircular battery was fifteen feet thick, while the parapet elsewhere above the platform was three feet. The interior front was of pine, but there were no casemates. The fosse was twenty feet wide, but the redoubt was unfortunately commanded by sand mounds two or three hundred yards away.

The artillery consisted of twenty pieces, all but the few twenty-four and twelve pounders being mounted on Spanish carriages of little value. In the bastion were only one ninepounder and three four-pounders.

The first attack was in September, 1814. On the 12th, four large vessels were descried in the offing, and on the next day there were several attempts by the British to throw up intrenchments on the land side, but the cannon of the fort dispersed them. Two days later, however, came the sea attack. The garrison took an oath not to surrender unless in extremity, adopting a motto not unlike the other Lawrence's on the ship — "Don't give up the fort!"

The Hermes, of twenty-eight guns, under Commodore Percy, led the attack at 2 P. M., and by 4.30 she anchored within the bay, and the action became general. A battery was erected by Woodbine about seven hundred yards southeast of the fort, but this was soon silenced, and the battle was between the fort and ships. At 5.30 the flag of the Hermes was cut down, and Lawrence chivalrously ceased firing until it could be replaced. The next brig answered the courtesy by a broadside, and then came a reply from all the fort at once. The flag of the fort also fell, but the guns of the British did not pause. It was quickly secured to a sponge staff, however, and gallantly restored to its place.

As the fleet and the garrison were cannonading each other, the cable of the Hermes was cut, and she drifted directly under the guns of the fort. The Americans seized the opportunity and raked her fore and aft. In such a fire she could not be handled, and finally ran aground a half mile off. Even the brig next her could hardly get out to sea. Finally the commander and crew of the Hermes fired the ship and abandoned her, while the rest of the fleet drew off and sailed towards Pensacola, leaving the burning Hermes to her fate. The illumination was beautiful, and at eleven o'clock that night she blew up, and "with fragments strewed the sea." Jackson heard the report at Mobile, thirty miles away, and was agonized to think it might be the fort itself.

The victory was complete. The loss of the Americans was but four killed and as many wounded; while on the ships there were one hundred and sixty men killed and seventy wounded, besides two killed on land. Jackson rejoiced at the brilliant success, and on September 17 wrote from Mobile a letter of congratulations to Lawrence and his gallant men.[1] He would have been in the fort himself, but for going back to Mobile to send down the reinforcements under Laval, whom the cannonade prevented from landing.

A curious incident of the battle was that it was witnessed by Nolte, a New Orleans cotton speculator, who had two hundred and fifty bales of cotton on boats in the bay awaiting the result.

[1] A. L. Latour's *War in West Florida and Louisiana*, pp. 32–42.

He followed the fleet to Pensacola, sold his cotton at twenty-two cents a pound, bought blankets, and sold them profitably at New Orleans, making about double the cost price each way.[1]

Jackson issued at Mobile, four days later, his two famous proclamations to Louisianians. One of these called on the colored people to arm, and aroused much feeling among the whites on the Mississippi. But as soon as General Coffee arrived on Mobile River with twenty-eight hundred men, Jackson joined him, changed the cavalry into infantry by turning the horses loose on the river bank, and marched in another direction.

As he could not hear from the War Department, Jackson took the responsibility of proceeding from Mobile, in November, with three thousand men to capture Pensacola. His route was by transport across to the Village, where Jackson's Oak is still shown, under which his tent was pitched,[2] and thence overland to his Florida victory. He was soon back at Mobile, however, ready, "by the Eternal," to prevent invasion here or anywhere else. Satisfied that New Orleans would be the point of attack, he marched over to Baton Rouge in December. One of his encampments on the way was in the Espejo grant on Bayou del Salto, between Cottage Hill and Spring Hill, and in consequence both creek and tract have ever since been called "Cantonment." From Baton Rouge he went southwardly, and won his brilliant victory behind cotton-bales below New Orleans on January 8, 1815, — "St. Jackson's Day."

An interested witness of that great battle was Sam Dale, who arrived during its progress, after his remarkable ride of eight days from Hawkins' Creek Agency in Georgia, bearing dispatches from Washington. These were too late to do any good. Jackson said, "They are always too late at Washington." But Dale's time was remarkable, for the express even from Mobile was often fourteen days.

It was Dale who carried east the news of the great victory. For Jackson was so much impressed with his ride from Georgia that he sent him immediately back, and, at Big Sam's own request, on the same tough Georgia pony, Paddy. Even Colonel Sparks could not stop him at the lakes to get the news;

---

[1] Parton's *Jackson*, pp. 600, 604, 608, 611, etc.
[2] Conversations with William R. Yancey, of the Village.

and the third day, past midnight, he roused up Winchester, Jackson's successor at Mobile. Winchester put him off until daylight, then to ten A. M., and then until noon, upon which Dale sent word that if the dispatches were not ready by twelve he would go without them. He got them, however, and at noon was on his way. He had to swim his horse over the swelling Alabama at Randon's Landing, and thus, in freezing weather, he rode on, swimming streams, and bearing to all posts news of the glorious victory over the British. On the fifth day from Mobile he reached McIntosh's army at Fort Decatur, on the Tallapoosa, where a sentinel all but shot him, and the general had to support the half-frozen courier into where a fire and whiskey could thaw him out. But the next morning he left again, and on the third evening out ended his long ride by delivering his dispatch to Governor Early at Milledgeville. There he and Paddy provoked almost as much interest as the news they bore.[1]

Major Lawrence was still in command at Fort Bowyer. No doubt the rejoicing there was tempered with the reflection that the British fleet might next attack that post and try to capture Mobile, in order to hold the Alabama basin and the middle Mississippi behind General Jackson.

Denison Darling was from Fort Stoddert, and Benjamin S. Smoot had been with this, the second regiment, even before the Americans occupied Mobile. Smoot is said to have come to Mobile as a voluntary aide to Jackson, and his miniature shows a beardless youth in a high stock, and blue coat with slashed red facings, a wide purple sash, epaulettes, and white belt supporting a handsome sword. Darling and he about 1813 erected, at a cost of one thousand to fifteen hundred dollars, a store within gunshot of Fort Bowyer. The building was eighteen by thirty-five feet, and a story and a half high. Curtis Lewis was their clerk, and they did a good business. The soldiers traded there, and the officers recognized their orders up to half their pay or more. Captain Reuben Chamberlain says the store was a great convenience. Alas, the fate of war! The store was now to be hastily dismantled and destroyed, by the command of Major Lawrence himself. For

[1] Claiborne's *Dale*, p. 160, etc.

the British were actually coming, and the house of Smoot &
Darling might shelter them in an attack on the fort.[1]

On the 6th of February, the fleet was seen off Dauphine
Island, and early the next day twenty-five vessels anchored,
extending from that island to Fort Bowyer on Mobile Point,
while thirteen were parallel with the coast behind the fort.
On the 8th, not less than five thousand men were landed three
and a half miles from the fort, and they soon communicated
with Keane's division of twenty-five hundred on Dauphine
Island by barges and boats plying incessantly over the bay;
for the British camp extended across the Point.

On the 9th, the siege may be said to have been commenced
by the erection of a trench and battery on a commanding
mound. The garrision were vigilant and fired incessantly, but
sand mounds sheltered the invaders. On the 10th, the British
had a trench on the south side of the Point, and by night
advanced their works to within forty yards of the fort.

Resistance was now futile, and so, when at ten A. M. on the
11th there was a summons to surrender in half an hour, a
parley ensued, and finally it was agreed that the fort be surrendered at noon the next day. The loss to the Americans
had been one killed and ten wounded, including Lawrence
himself; to the British, forty killed.

The articles provided, (1) That the fort should be surrendered
in its existing condition; (2) The garrison should march out
with flags flying and drums beating, and ground arms on the
glacis, the officers, however, to retain their swords; (3) Private property should be respected; and (4) Communication
should be permitted with the officer commanding the seventh
district, and exchange of prisoners effected; (5) The garrison
should remain until noon of the 13th, but there should be a
British guard at the inner gate at three P. M. of the preceding
day, and the new flag hoisted at the same time.

---

[1] See Report of House Committee of Claims, February 4, 1831. Smoot
finally received $1,000. See 6 U. S. Statutes at Large, p. 466. The minia-
ture is in the possession of B. S. Woodcock, of Mobile, a descendant of
Smoot. Mrs. William Calvert, who was rescued as an infant from Fort
Mims, was a daughter, and Mrs. Helen Webster is a granddaughter, of
Darling. Mrs. Curtis Lewis was a granddaughter of Sir Robert Farmer;
she was daughter of De Vauberey, of Dauphine Island.

Winchester had made from Mobile a tardy and unsuccessful attempt to succor the fort. On the 10th and 11th, he sent a detachment across the bay under the command of Major Blue to divert the enemy, with the result that the enemy captured his three small schooners after the troops had landed. The Americans managed in their turn to take a barge with seventeen British seamen, who told them of the surrender of the fort. People in town guessed it from reports of citizens who had gone down to Jack's Bluff on the western shore, and from there, the residence of Maximilien Colin, had seen a boat go ashore to take possession after the firing ceased.

All was confusion at Mobile. On the 15th, Winchester wrote James Monroe, the Secretary of War, of the disaster, and said that he expected the enemy every night; but he was fortunately disappointed, and no further attack was made. Jackson, writing yet later, said he was both astonished and mortified at the defeat; but he was afterwards to do justice to the garrison, and a court-martial on March 25 exonerated Lawrence.[1]

Recently there has been published a history of the famous British Fortieth Regiment, which contains the journal of a lieutenant who was with them at Mobile Bay. He was on Dauphine Island, and gives a very different account of affairs. He says that they landed on the 12th, and that night a corvette attempted to storm the fort, but ran aground and had to be blown up, by illumining the whole bay. The two hundred frightened Indians who had been aboard were captured by the Americans.

---

[1] Latour's *War in West Florida*, etc., pp. 208–212, 215, 219, cl, xxvi, lxxxiii, lxxxvii, xcviii, etc. The garrison surrendered consisted of one field officer, three captains, ten subalterns, two staff officers, sixteen sergeants, sixteen drummers, three hundred and twenty-seven rank and file, twenty women, sixteen children, and three servants not soldiers. The ordnance consisted of one twenty-four-pounder and two nine-pounders outside of the fort, and, within, three thirty-two-pounders, eight twenty-four-pounders, six twelve-pounders, five nine-pounders, besides a small brass piece, an eight-inch mortar, a howitzer, three hundred and fifty-one muskets, five hundred flints, powder, cartridges, etc. The brass mortar was one cast in George II.'s reign, and was the only piece taken away by the British. Admiral Cochrane on the 12th wrote Jackson from H. B. M. ship Tonnant, off Mobile Bay, as to exchange of prisoners.

The Fortieth sailed shortly afterwards for Europe, and at Waterloo were under the personal command of Wellington himself. But even Jove nods, and the lieutenant of the great regiment must have mixed his notes. The burning vessel reminds one of the first attack on Fort Bowyer, and the dates of the official papers discredit the new version; and yet it is confirmed in part by the tradition of the death there of captive Indians from yellow fever.[1]

The second defence was less successful but not less honorable than the first, and there were now to be no further hostilities. The British headquarters on Dauphine Island were at the Shell Banks, and many of their dead were buried on the island. On February 13, Admiral Cochrane from off Mobile Bay sent Jackson the copy of a bulletin, "this moment received from Jamaica," announcing the signing of a treaty of peace at Ghent on December 24, upon which he offers his sincere congratulations. Jackson was suspicious of the report, but it proved to be true.

We remember the French execution in front of the fort after the mutiny at Fort Toulouse, but a noted American execution that followed the conclusion of peace was certainly not near the esplanade.[2] We are told that it was on February 21, 1815, in an open place near Mobile, while the British fleet was still at anchor, but tradition has lost the exact spot. We may fairly conjecture, however, from the location of roads and of Jackson's camp at the time, that it was not far from Frascati.

It came about in this way. In September preceding, a number of Tennessee soldiers abandoned the army in the Creek country, claiming that the three months for which they enlisted had expired. Their commander construed the time differently. The men were court-martialed at Mobile in December, 1814, and six, all brave men, condemned to death. Jackson, after the battle of New Orleans, approved the finding.

The Mobile army of fifteen hundred men under General Winchester marched to the scene of execution, and a large crowd of spectators attended. The six were driven there in a wagon, and after their heads were covered with white caps

[1] It is said that fifty years later, after the capture of Fort Morgan, Federal troops dug up Indian skeletons and ornaments.

[2] 2 Parton's *Jackson*, p. 277.

they were shot down beside their coffins, in due military form, by thirty-six comrades. One victim, named Harris, was a Baptist preacher with a large family. Henry Lewis was the only one not killed outright. He crawled forward, before them all, and climbed on his coffin, where he sat dazed, covered with blood. He was removed from this slaughter-pen by pitying hands and lived several days. Such unnecessary severity threw a pall on the rejoicings over the peace, and was remembered in politics against Jackson long afterwards.

As all captured places held by either nation were, according to treaty, to be surrendered, negotiations were soon in progress looking to the evacuation of Fort Bowyer. On March 17, General Lambert sent word to Mobile by Major Woodruff that he would give it up as soon as the transports could get out of the bay.

There was also animated correspondence and spirited interviews about the surrender of slaves. Lambert contended that the many negroes in his camp on Dauphine Island were refugees, and he could not admit that the agreement for surrender of captured property covered slaves, as England did not recognize property in human beings.

There was much feeling on the subject, but the British commander agreed he would not object, if only persuasion were used by the slaveholders. One Louisianian, Major Lacoste, is said to have gone to Dauphine Island with this view, and, getting his slaves off to one side, he threatened and cajoled and drew such a picture to them of British cruelty, all in plantation French, which the English could not understand, that he got his people away with him without trouble. The major ever afterwards told this story with great gusto.[1]

At last the troops were all embarked, and the ships sailed away for Europe. Dauphine Island had seen her last great gathering of war vessels until the American Civil War.

[1] 4 Gayarré's *Louisiana*, p. 532.

CHAPTER XLV.

WITH the peace, affairs settled down in east Mississippi, and the development began of the vast territory ceded by the Indians. The older towns improved, but the most striking feature of the time was the growth of the interior. The river plantations enriched Mobile, but they also led to the building of inland villages, which have gradually become important cities. From about 1816, we find settlers where Montgomery, Selma, and Tuskaloosa later stood.

The site of Montgomery was an Indian camping-ground and trading-post called Econachattee. Andrew Moore lived there in 1815, and then came Jonathan C. Farley, Andrew Dexter, and J. G. Klinck as the first permanent white residents. Another Moore, Thomas, arrived in 1816 where Selma is, and the place was at first called Moore's Bluff from him. The name Selma was later taken by William R. King from the poetry of Ossian. In the same year Thomas York moved from Blount County to what is now within the corporate limits of Tuskaloosa. The country had started on its development.

The Mississippi half of the territory had grown faster, having the great river as its "promoter," and became a separate State in 1817. The eastern half was organized as the Territory of Alabama, with capital at St. Stephens. Alabama was therefore, geographically, but the river system draining to Mobile, with the Tennessee valley added on the north.

St. Stephens was now in its glory. It was the capital of the Territory, the seat of the Land Office and of a bank, and had many citizens who then or afterwards became prominent. There the first and second legislatures deliberated, when James Titus, of Madison, as the only Alabama member of the divided Mississippi upper chamber, "met" by himself and gravely preserved all parliamentary forms. William Wyatt Bibb, late of Georgia, was governor, and James Magoffin in charge of the United States Land Office. Silas Dinsmore is said to have been collector, and to have lost his office by injudicious wit. The story goes that, when asked by the government authorities at Washington how far the Tombigbee ran up the country, he replied that it did not run up the country at all, but down. The Tombeckbee Bank, some of whose paper of 1818 still exists, had such officers as J. B. Hazard and William Crawford. James G. Lyon was in the merchandise business in the town, selling wood to steamboats and living over his store. Jack F. Ross also settled there, after coming to Mobile at Jackson's instruction to pay off the army. He became treasurer of Alabama, and was relieved by legislative act from loss of the public money burned with his home. He was afterwards sheriff of Mobile, but his son William H. was born in 1819 at St. Stephens.

No map is now known of the town, but even in the Mobile records we find its lots numbered as high as 131, and Lime and High streets mentioned among its thoroughfares.

Had the Mississippi Convention been permitted to have their way, St. Stephens and Mobile, too, would have been placed in that State, for they wished the Tombigbee and Mobile Bay to be the eastern boundary. The project has had even later advocates.

The government of the Mobile district was, of course, military at first, by the general in charge, although we find even in 1813 a number of marriages by Pollard, Mervin, Powell, and Robeshow, justices of the peace of Mobile County, and one by Vicente Genin, the Catholic priest.[1] During the Creek War the territorial legislature of Mississippi, on January 20, 1814, after the battle of the Holy Ground, passed an act for the incorporation of the Mobile citizens.

Under it, on March 11, 1814, a meeting of the inhabitants was held at the house of M. McKinsey, Josiah Blakeley in the chair, and it was resolved to hold the election at the dwelling-house of Wilson Carmon. These residences cannot now be identified, but were no doubt like the few Spanish one-story

---

[1] For marriages, see Appendix. There is some uncertainty whether the justice was named Robeshaw or Robeshow, just as whether another prominent citizen spelled his name Duval or Duvol.

buildings still remaining.   Lewis Judson, James Innerarity, and B. Dubroca were appointed commissioners (inspectors we should now call them), and Innerarity and Samuel Acre, the lawyer, a committee to prepare a few translations of the act into French, to be posted up conspicuously.   These peaceful affairs were contemporaneous with Jackson's march to Horseshoe Bend.   The polls were accordingly open at Carmon's on Monday, March 14, from ten to four o'clock.   Lewis Judson, James Innerarity, B. Dubroca, P. H. Hobart, T. Powell, A. Robeshow, and S. H. Garrow were duly elected commissioners of the town of Mobile, Miguel Eslava treasurer, Michael McKinsey collector, and Dominique Salles assessor, — a mixture of the old and new stocks.   How many property-owners were there to vote we do not know; but three years later, at a similar election, only seventeen voters are mentioned, although we have the names of over a hundred male residents.

The next day the commissioners were sworn into office by Josiah Blakeley, as one of the justices of the quor··· ˒ Mobile County.   Innerarity was elected president, and McKinsey clerk.   On the 16th, a business meeting was held, the first acts being the appointment of a committee on rules on motion of S. H. Garrow, then a resolution establishing the boundaries of the town and of the three wards, and one fixing the tax rate at twelve and a half cents on the hundred dollars. The town limits began at Choctaw Point, then ran due west to where a perpendicular line due north would strike Murrell's Ford over Bayou "Chateaugay" (Three Mile Creek), thence down that creek to the east side of the river, thence south, etc., to the beginning.   These are substantially what the boundaries have now long been; but an act of the legislature of December 1, 1814, made them triangular, running from Choctaw Point to a place two hundred yards above the Portage on Bayou Chotage, thence down the bayou to its mouth, and thence down the river and bay to the place of beginning.[1]   This would seem to take the river out of the town limits, while the ordinance had included it.   The Portage was important as the source of water supply, water being hauled thence for the use of troops and citizens, too.   Even several years later we find the lawful charge for hauling a barrel of water to be fifty

[1] Toulmin's *Laws of Alabama*, p. 781.

cents. The South Ward as established by the commissioners was that part of the town lying south of the fort, as under the Spaniards; and the first American house there was that erected by Joseph P. Kennedy, Eslava's lawyer, at the southwest corner of St. Emanuel and Monroe streets.[1] The Middle Ward extended from the fort to Dauphin Street, and the North embraced all north of Dauphin. Among the rules was one that resolutions adopted should be published by affixing three copies in French in the most public places, showing that and not Spanish to be the predominant language. Non-attendance of commissioners was punished by fine of one dollar, and the commissioners received no compensation, — except the usual honor and abuse. The treasurer had only his stationery; while the collector and assessor were each allowed two and a half per cent. on taxes collected, and the clerk a salary of two hundred dollars per annum. The taxes (exclusive of licenses) seem to have been levied only on land and slaves, and a penalty equal to the tax was added for not making return to the assessor. After demand by the collector at the house, the taxes, when necessary, were sued before justices.

A police commissioner was appointed for each ward to see to enforcement of ordinances, and there were two police constables to make arrests. Fines were declared by the board after hearing the parties, and, unless paid then, sued and collected before a justice. They were divided between the constable and the town.

The early ordinances relate to cows and goats at large, the regulation of balls, to slaves, obstructing and digging in streets, to burning lime, chimneys, licenses, and the like. The discharge of firearms was prohibited, except to kill dogs at large. This dog ordinance was passed on account of hydrophobia at Pascagoula. Their law against drums (like many others still in force) seems aimed at the Spanish custom at auctions. Licenses were legalized by the act of December 1, 1814, and, as laid, the vehicle license applied as well to pleasure as to business conveyances. Licenses on stores where dry goods, groceries, or liquor over a quart were sold, were for the first year five dollars, retail liquor places eight dollars, boarding-houses ten dollars, and billiard-tables twelve dollars. The

---

[1] Michel's petition before U. S. Senate, January 9, 1840.

first injunction suit was over this "grog-shop" tax. The rates were raised the next year, except that billiard-tables were less.

March 28, the board determined on building a frame market-house, fifty by twenty-five feet and nine feet high, closed on the north side. The site, selected on motion of Judson, was that previously occupied for burning lime, at the northeast end of Dauphin Street, adjoining the water. Garrow entered a formal and vigorous protest against the place, on the ground that it was not a proper site, and was against the interest and views of the majority of the inhabitants, but it was adhered to. A clerk of the market was elected by the first board, who should keep a lookout on all weights and standards. Thomas G. Newbold, an arrival in Mobile of 1810, was first market clerk, and late in the fall he was duly provided with wooden and tin measures and iron and lead weights.

On April 4, they established a bread tariff or "assize," and this practice was kept up for a long time. Flour being ten dollars a barrel, the "bit loaf" should weigh twenty-eight ounces, — a bit being the Spanish coin worth twelve and a half cents. The penalty for violation was a fine, and forfeiture to the overseer of the poor of all bread on hand; and a number of convictions are on record.

In April they resolved, on motion of Garrow, that it was expedient to build a wharf. He wished it at the end of Government Street (by the fort esplanade), but the vote on this was a tie. Garrow then left the meeting after forcible remarks, whereupon they made a rule that any one using personalities should be fined ten dollars. However, his plan for the wharf was accepted at the next meeting. The wharf privilege for ten years was to be leased to the highest bidder; this "leassee" should build the wharf as planned by the commissioners, and the town pay him what the structure was worth at the end of the term. He could charge not exceeding certain fixed wharfage, as six and a half cents per bale of cotton and one dollar per day for vessels of ten tons. This sale of wharf privilege (to be advertised in the "Mobile Gazette") did not, any more than the market, materialize during the first year, however.

William Crawford (afterwards United States judge) was elected by the board first counsel for the corporation. He had to appear before some justice to sue for fines (it was before

Blakeley until his death in February next), and also defended injunctions and advised the board on many questions. One was, whether they could stop David Files from putting up a mill below the Portage of Bayou "Chateaugé," "near the watering-place made use of by the inhabitants," for Mottus and his wife undertook to sell the Espejo Tract, including the wash place, to Files and Terrell.[1] The board later asked the legislature for fuller powers over this bayou in order to protect the drinking water, but the act of December 1 prohibited their removing any milldam across the bayou. The city later aided in repair of the bridge there.

The president could not hold a mayor's court (a defect corrected by legislation in 1816), but on resolution of the board he pulled down defective chimneys, removed buildings erected over the street line, and generally represented the police power of the town. A police officer was in August employed at the salary of ten dollars per month, receiving also half the fines levied through his intervention. He was a health officer, too, and compelled the free use of lime in the summer. They believed then in people's burying dead animals and offensive matters on their own premises, although "filth of an inoffensive nature" was to be deposited in the pond west of the fort, earlier used as a "washing place." This was about our Church and Franklin streets, on the road to Mandeville. The police officer was also to see that the inhabitants understood and obeyed the ordinance for cutting down weeds on their lots and out to the middle of the street opposite. They had a "vendue master," of rather indefinite powers, too, like the British.

The board in November, during Jackson's stay in the town, memorialized the legislature for greater powers and larger corporate boundaries. They pointed out that nothing could retard the growth of Mobile, and that the town should have exclusive control of the bay as far south as Dog River, in order to keep the passes open and prevent further injury there from the discharge of ballast; but the only power granted by this legislature not already noticed was that to extend and lay out highways. Congress was also asked for the vacant public lots within the corporate limits. This last request remained unheeded for many years.

[1] *Mobile Deed Book* "A," p. 57.

The first board had to establish the whole machinery of town government. Their ordinances seem original, as most are without reference to French or Spanish precedents, except in that they abolish some old usages. They spent five dollars for a table and sixty-three dollars on a corporation seal, as appears from bills they passed for payment, but little on their own convenience. They even met in the mornings, generally at nine o'clock, and so avoided the expense of lights, and used a room rented for thirty-two dollars a year.

After the declaration of peace the people, in March, 1815, held their second municipal election. Judson (who was the new town president), Hobart, Powell, and Robeshow were reëlected commissioners, and the others were succeeded by William Chenault, Diego McVoy, and Michael Perault. Our first board turned over to them a net balance in the treasury of $69.85½ to begin on.

The second board found it necessary to create the office of street overseer, electing their colleague Diego McBoy, or McVoy, as this Spaniard indifferently spells it. It was during this time, too, that the market-house was built. The plan actually carried out called for a one-story building forty by twenty-five feet, with three rows of five pillars each, gables, and three-foot eaves. The materials were "found by the undertaker," — which ominous word only means contractor. The one in question was Theron Kellogg, and his contract was for three hundred and twenty-five dollars. It was on June 1 that the board went in a body and designated the place where McGill's shoe store now stands as the site on which to raise the market.

Later in the year they paid for the erection of four meat-stalls and one for fish, and about the same time made elaborate market regulations. Fresh meat, fish, and oysters could be sold only there; and fowls, butter, eggs, cheese, dried meat, lard, tallow, corn meal, vegetables, and pulse had to be offered there first. Bread and milk, however, could be carried from house to house. Market hours were from daybreak until ten A. M. Stalls in later years were rented out, but at first there seems to have been a fee of twenty-five to thirty-seven and a half cents charged per animal, depending on the size. We find not only sheep, pigs, and beef, but goats also sold. Later, country butchers were exempt, and dried provisions taken out of the list.

This second board also built the wharf which the first had planned. It was twenty-five feet wide, with wings at the water end, going out to a river depth of nine feet. They leased the privilege at auction, giving the wharf, when built to their satisfaction, over to the builder to collect certain fixed tolls for a period of nine years to reimburse him. This "undertaker" was James Wilson, the business partner of S. H. Garrow. He was to give the next administration much trouble by trying to enter from the government the flooded land adjacent, and indeed his wharf agreement ultimately needed the oversight of the corporation counsel.

A market-house and wharf had now been provided, but a city prison was still wanting. The authorities had to request the commandant of Fort "Sharlot" to loan the city a "calabous" for imprisoning strange negroes. The election of Joseph McCandless as surveyor, and petitioning Congress for the establishment of a marine hospital, complete the more important acts of this administration, which went out of office on March 5, 1816.

Of the new board Innerarity was president, although Judson was also a member. In his time the cow question agitated the public mind as in more recent years, and was settled by allowing each resident to keep five cows instead of two, as in 1814, but next year, however, all restrictions were removed. More important was the construction of Water Street fifty feet wide from Mottus' place to the market, with an outside barrier of three squared timbers at from seven and a half to twelve and a half cents a foot delivered. This great improvement, giving Mobile its first street east of Royal, was accomplished during this and the next year, largely by the coöperation of John Forbes & Co. and Lewis Judson, who voluntarily moved their fences and contributed to payment of the expense in consideration of a quitclaim to lands between the projected street and their fence to the west.

Besides its extra-municipal protest to the postmaster-general about there having been but one mail to Fort "Stoddard" in two months, this board may also be remembered for its establishment of port wardens and their duties, by virtue, doubtless, of the act of December 12, 1816, authorizing appointment of port wardens and pilots under suitable bonds.

In March, 1817, a new board came in, with only McVoy holding over of the old members, and Daniel Duvol was made president. Under them came the first issue of city money, for it was resolved to have struck off five hundred dollars in small-change notes redeemable in specie, Louisiana, Mississippi, or United States Bank notes. The denominations were fifty, twenty-five, and twelve and a half cents, having in the left margins an ox, horse, and eagle respectively. An overseer of the poor dates from this time, and the appointment of bay pilots, — J. B. Lamie, James Roney, N. Cook, and T. W. Dailey. We do not read that any qualified except Roney and Richard Dailey, and these not immediately.

We incidentally learn from the license list in the minutes that there were then twenty-seven merchants with $1,000 stocks, for these are taxed fifteen dollars each ; and fifteen with less, taxed ten dollars each, although three of the last pay as much again for a billiard-table, too.

Possibly the most interesting and important matter then was the extension of streets. To the location of the wharf it was due that Water Street had been finished from Dauphin to Mottus' place south of Government, and now provision was made to extend the barrier south to the old (Spanish) wharf. But building a north and south street was not all. We may remember that in Spanish times there was so little use made of the quay that not only was there but one wharf, but the east and west streets were little used beyond Royal, and some not at all. None were more than lanes at most. Now, how-ever, we find a determined and finally successful effort to open all, and this probably in ignorance of the old French dedica-tion to the water. We see the executors of "André" notified to open the street from Dubroca's to the river; for, as in French or English times, the street names are not given. This street is probably St. Francis, for Andry owned there; and about the same time Innerarity is ordered to open a street from St. Joseph to Royal. This we know must be St. Francis, although, with an almost Spanish interchange of names, it is called St. Charles. In 1819, more vigorous action was taken, the street then being named as St. Francis.

Hardly less important is the beginning of draining in the appropriation of thirty dollars to open a "canal" to drain the pond in the northwest quarter of town. We learn later that this was about Wilson's, at St. Michael and Joachim, a low place still. There was also a smaller drain opened in the district near Church Street, for it emptied into the fort ditch.

After the 1818 election, Garrow was president, and in the settlement of Treasurer Dubroca we find trouble about a counterfeit twenty-dollar note, No. 334 II, of the Nashville Bank. The matter was compromised by the town's standing half the loss and the treasurer the rest.

This administration established a branch of pilots at Dog River Bar, continued street improvement, and contracted for a barrier northwards from the market to Holman's Wharf, near the foot of St. Francis Street. It was early alarmed at finding there were one hundred and sixty-six casks of gunpowder in town. Captain Falk was requested to store them in the fort, and the town limited the amount to be kept by merchants and immediately went about building the first powder-house. Where this was is not stated, but it seems to have been on a half acre of McCandless' land, "in the vicinity of this place," for he claimed and received damages for the ninety pine trees cut without permission. Paupers from vessels being frequent, it was provided that passengers must be officially reported, and bond given where necessary.

Subscriptions were also raised to buy two fire-engines lately brought to town. One we know cost four hundred and thirty dollars. There was a meeting in the president's office under the wide-galleried United States Hotel, northwest corner of Conti and Royal, to organize the first fire company. Suitable houses were afterwards built, one on the Hospital lot. Next year two fire wards were established, divided by Dauphin Street, an engine and company being in each. Each house-owner was required to have handy at least two standard size leather buckets. All of this was in an elaborate ordinance prescribing precautions against fire.

Even before 1818, when the first bank was established, a river steamer had been built, and by that year the port was full of vessels, one being from Liverpool. Seven thousand bales of cotton were handled by the little town of eight hundred inhabitants; and two seasons later it was sixteen thousand bales, with the steamboats Harriet and Cotton Plant plying the rivers and making the growing interior tributary to an extent not dreamed of in the days of Indian trade. The Cotton Plant was, in the spring of 1823, the first steamboat to ascend the upper Bigbee, and on that occasion made her famous trip to Columbus and return in thirteen days.

During Garrow's second term, in 1819, came sinking the public well on Dauphin and Royal, and buying for one hundred and forty dollars a "burying ground" from W. E. Kennedy a half mile southwest of the inhabited part of the town, — what we call the Old Graveyard, in the heart of the present city. It was important just then from a disastrous visitation of yellow fever in the summer of that year, which the commissioners determined to investigate. The cemetery was fenced in 1821 at a cost of four hundred and fifty dollars. A city sexton was put in charge in 1820, who could demand seven dollars for digging graves five feet deep and supplying hearse.

The well on Dauphin and Royal was part of a plan for sinking pumps, which was carried out several years later, but now begins the laying of "sewers," which, with repairs, makes up so much of the early minutes. These were box drains largely, as with the first down Dauphin across the flats to the river. The inhabitants had to make their own sidewalks of earth or gravel. The first book of ordinances also dates from this time, copied by Mr. Willis, covering many subjects, and in a large measure the basis of what still exist.

There was this year a town meeting to increase taxation in order to provide for improvements and the care of the poor, which resulted in a poll-tax of one dollar for the poor fund. With a just appreciation of the future "increase of the town of Mobile," on July 23 a new street one hundred feet wide was provided for, to be ninety feet east of the existing Water Street. The new street was called Water Street, and the old one renamed Market Street. All foundations between Royal and Market were to be brick, or stone; all east of Market, of hewn timber on the sides, — in each case to be, like the wharves, filled up with earth, brick, or other clean material. There is no clear evidence, however, that, beyond temporary use of the name Market Street, any change was made; and next year the city provided for a new street of one hundred feet width, and distant two hundred feet from Water Street. No name was then given to this projected avenue, but it became Commerce Street. The surveyor was ordered to stake it out from Government to St. Francis Street.

But this carries us beyond the time of the town. On December 17, 1819, the place was reincorporated by the new State of Alabama as the Mayor and Aldermen of the City of Mobile.[1]

Across the bay was a nearer rival than St. Stephens. Josiah Blakeley we have seen buying the marsh islands from the Mobile to the Tensaw. He planned a city which should perpetuate his name, and selected as its site the old seat of the Apalaches, where the Bayou Solimé (Salome) empties into the Tensaw. This was the White House plantation, which he had bought from Dr. Joseph Chastang, and after the American occupation he was cautious enough to obtain a release from the Chastang heirs, as he did also from the former owners of his marsh lands.

Accordingly, in May, 1813, he employed James Magoffin, a surveyor from St. Stephens, to lay off a town there, extending a mile and a half back from its front on the Tensaw. He then commenced selling lots. The first sale recorded was in July, of ten to Warren Ross Dodge for one thousand dollars, one having as high a number as 358, and in a later deed 429 is mentioned. We read in this and other deeds that there were at least two "public squares," and that among the street names were Washington, Orleans, Robinson, Franklin, Warren, Greene, Wayne, Clinton, Baldwin, Hancock, Shelby, Clarke, and Blount, besides Plum, Fig, Live Oak, and Ridge alleys. The lots seem to have been 99 by 199 feet. Judson and other Mobilians invested; and the same year Dodge and Garrow bought the neighboring McVoy Mill site of four hundred and eighty acres, with improvements, on Bay Minette.

The town of "Blakeley" was incorporated under an act of January 6, 1814,[2] and Blakeley's plat duly wafered in the Mobile Deed Book "A." This was removed in 1822, however, to grace the Baldwin County records and then disappear.

[1] Toulmin's *Laws of Alabama*, p. 784.
[2] *Ibid.*, p. 796.

Samuel Haines was Blakeley's lawyer, and secured this incorporation, for which, and his general interest in the new town, Blakeley deeded him a number of lots in it.[1]

It is a little singular to think that the founder did not regularly reside there. His papers date from Mobile, where, as member of the county court (a justice of the quorum), he took acknowledgments of many deeds, and, as we have seen, helped organize the town government. He died in 1815 without issue, his affairs, according to his nuncupative will, in some confusion.[2] His own town continued to grow even after his death, and in 1820 we find not only legislation for regulation of the port and harbor of Blakeley, but an elaborate act for government of the corporation. We read two years later that Mobile was quite concerned about a contagious disease in that town.

Blakeley came to be an important place, but finally it, too, yielded to Mobile, and it may be that like St. Stephens some of its houses now face Mobile streets. For its few remaining buildings are in ruins and its site is desolate, while from its oaks and pleasant heights one can see the spires and electric lights of the older city which it once sought to surpass.

The French had settled the country, but it seems strange, after so many changes, to find a new and famous colony by them in 1818 up the Tombigbee, not many miles from the site of old Fort Tombecbé.

After Waterloo many Bonapartists had to seek new homes, and some came to America in 1816. Congress allowed them four townships at two dollars and a half per acre, on a credit of seventeen years, on condition that they would devote forty acres of each section to the vine and olive. They arrived at Mobile in May, 1818, after escaping shipwreck at the mouth of the bay, and Collector Addin Lewis furnished them a barge for the river trip. They settled, on the advice of George S. Gaines, at the place they named Demopolis, but unfortunately not on the ground contracted for. In their honor the new county was named Marengo.

Among their leaders was Lefebvre-Desnouettes, a distinguished general of Marengo, Austerlitz, and Bautzen, who

---

[1] *Mobile Deed Book* "A," p. 93.

[2] *Ibid.*, p. 90.

was remembered in Napoleon's will. In a small cabin, as in a shrine, he kept a bronze of the great emperor and trophies of his victories. Nicholas Raoul, too, was there, commander of the advance guard on the return from Elba, and from necessity ferryman on Big Prairie Creek. Peniers, of the regicide National Assembly, and Rigaud, were other distinguished colonists; and George N. Stewart, who married among them, came out from Philadelphia as secretary of the association. But no olive was planted, the Catawba did not flourish, too much time was given up to gayety, and the unfortunate mislocation of their lands involved them in trouble. In time most of them moved away, although descendants of some still remain. Lallemand sailed to New York; Lefebvre-Desnouettes went down with the packet Albion off the Irish coast; Raoul, after Mexican adventures, returned to be a general in France; and Stewart, Ravesies, Chaudron, and others moved to Mobile, where their grandchildren now live. Demopolis, incorporated in 1821, grew as an American, not a French town.

Huntsville has an American history, but somewhat apart from that of central and south Alabama. It was founded in 1806; was incorporated as a city in 1811, on the model of Natchez; and in 1816 had the first bank. The "Madison Gazette" of 1812 was the second newspaper in the State limits, the "Mobile Centinel" being the first.

Huntsville superseded St. Stephens in 1819 as the temporary capital, and there the convention framed the constitution under which Alabama was admitted into the Union, December 14, 1819. Cahaba was, however, selected as the permanent capital; and the year 1819, which saw the incorporation of Mobile as a city, witnessed also that of Cahaba, Tuskaloosa, and Montgomery, each of which was in turn to be the seat of government of the State.

CHAPTER XLVI.

THERE had been a dispute with the United States ever since the capture, as there had been when the British succeeded the French, about the extent of the public property. Part of the bake-house lot, part of the hospital lot, not to mention grants of the fort esplanade, were in controversy. And it was largely due to absence of official maps.

The French plan of 1760 was not accessible to the town authorities. They knew that there was some official map and felt its want, but could not obtain it. In 1817, we find Innerarity supplied with fifty dollars and authorized to obtain this or a copy from John Lynd, a notary public in New Orleans: but we later learn that the search was unsuccessful, and the money was used for improving the streets. A similar attempt, with similar result, was made in Pensacola; and the town had to develop as best it could without the map. The United States seem to have bought it in 1819 for five hundred dollars from a broker in New Orleans, but, when it became known, too much had been done to be undone. Government Street was by the legislature of 1820 directed to be laid out one hundred feet wide, and became the American basis.

There is an early plan purporting to show Mobile in 1815. A copy is in the City Atlas, and as an annex to Gaillard's city map of 1866. Unfortunately, no one knows where that accurate student obtained it. It shows the town extending as far west as Joachim (or New) Street, with the fort, cemetery, hospital, and bakery, besides roads from St. Michael Street to Kennedy's Spring, from Dauphin to the Portage, and one from near a shot-tower on Joachim past the Ravine Pond to Mandeville. There are but the King's Wharf and Montuse Wharf, the latter by the Montuse Tavern, northeast of the fort. In point of fact, however, the King's Wharf was blown away in

1811 and the Montuse Wharf built on the same pilings. North of the town is a stockade and Round-top House, the house so called from being on a knoll at what is now Royal and St. Anthony. There, about 1821, was an explosion of a cannon on Washington's Birthday, by which James Wilson lost his life; and on pilings there lived afterwards Denison Darling.[1]

Next comes a plan, unofficial in character, made by Williams Mathews in 1818 for the purpose of some contemplated division of lands acquired from time to time by William E. Kennedy and Joshua Kennedy.[2]

The land question was yet to be settled. No community can really flourish without certainty of titles, and everything at first was uncertain in Mobile, because the United States did not recognize Spanish grants after the cession to France in 1800. The vigorous protest of the inhabitants in 1817 against recognition of British grants was unavailing, although they justly said the United States had fully recognized Spanish acts and ownership.[3]

Congress legislated several times on the land question.[4] Commissioner Crawford, under act of Congress of April 25, 1812, and the register and receiver under that of March 3, 1819, were diligent in reporting on the validity of land claims,

[1] Tradition given by Jeremiah Howland, Wilson's grandson, says that this cannon was one of those at St. Michael and Water streets. Mr. William Calvert, who afterwards married Caroline Darling, attended the funeral of her father from the old home.

[2] The Mathews map shows Mobile laid off in squares as far north as St. Anthony (with the Toulmin and Mathews tracts beyond), and as far west as Warren Street, beyond which, from "Dauphine" to Government, run Adams and Pine streets. On Government, from "St. Joakim" to Franklin, James Innerarity owns half the distance north to Conti ; and from Conti to "Dauphine," between Jackson and Franklin, the church property is marked "Public Square." South of Government are Charlotte, Monroe (unnamed Eslava), and Liberty streets, running east and west, and Madison, Washington, Lafayette, and other projected north and south streets, running into Government. No other names occur except "Joshua Kennedy," "Wm. E. Kennedy," and those above given ; and in the north part of town one square each is marked to J. Wilson, S. H. Garrow, and D. E. Robinson, — the first two on the east side of Jackson from St. Michael to St. Anthony, and the last on "New" and "Michael," east of Wilson's. The Kennedy squares are numbered, but not the town as a whole.

[3] 3 *American State Papers*, p. 220.

[4] 2 *U. S. Statutes at Large*, p. 713 ; 3 *Ibid.*, pp. 528, 699.

and their work was confirmed by an act of May 8, 1822. But, at the period we have now reached, much, especially as to town lots, was still unsettled. This is shown nowhere more clearly than in a report of Register Willoughby Barton himself on July 11, 1820, from Jackson Court-house.

"If it were consistent with the nature of his duty," he says, "the Register would endeavor to show the impolicy of holding the claimants of lots in Mobile to strict proof of compliance with the Spanish regulations for the allotment of lands. He will only remark, that it has come within his personal observation that a very large proportion of the granted lots has been built upon, and is inhabited by the grantees and those claiming under them, who are generally the ancient native inhabitants; and the circumstance of the uninterrupted possession they were permitted to hold of them under the Spanish government would seem to entitle them to the favor of Congress in quieting them in their claims. The Register will only further add in relation to this branch of the subject that the lots granted by the French and Spanish authorities, whilst those governments respectively held possession of the country, do not conform in their limits or bounds with the original British map or plan of the town certified by the Spanish surveyor-general Trudeau, and now in the possession of the principal deputy surveyor, Mr. Dinsmore; which fact appeared from the survey recently made by him of the public ground on which Fort Charlotte stands. Should it be determined to adhere rigidly to this or any other plan, great confusion must inevitably ensue in attempting to reconcile the conflicting boundaries, and serious injury result to many, whose principal property consists in their lots and habitations. In relation to actual settlers, it will be sufficient to remark, that they comprise the principal mercantile population of the place; that their improvements are generally the most expensive; and that they cover the most valuable vacant ground in the town." [1]

---

[1] It will be observed that Dinsmore, who prior to the Creek War was the United States Choctaw agent, had returned to surveying. All that the Interior Department files show on this subject is in connection with Surveyor-General Freeman. Thomas Freeman was surveyor of the public lands of the United States south of Tennessee from his appointment in September, 1810, to March 3, 1817, the date of the act which authorized the appointment of

The buildings outside the fort property on the Dinsmore plat are of interest, although the proposed plan, for reasons we shall see, became valueless. On it Judge Edward Hall occupies the northwest corner of Government and Royal; the Government House is near the west end of the west grass-plat of Duncan Place, but at the southeast corner of Government and Royal as projected; while the Post-office and Custom-house are about the northwest corner of Government and St. Emanuel. Montuse Tavern and Wharf are respectively on the west and east sides of Water Street, at about where the south line of Government now runs. Burrow's and Tiddy's are on the two corners of Conti, near Judson's wharf; and the United States Hotel and Catholic church on Conti and Royal. On the west side of Conception then (but now, on account of the bend, east of it) were Stickney's and Tankersley's. Besides Judson's, Montuse's, and the King's or Public Wharf, there is W. Hamilton & Co.'s wharf to the north of the foot of our Monroe Street.

The treaty for the purchase of Louisiana provided that all property, of course including lands and town lots, of the inhabitants, should be respected, and this was done, especially by the acts above noticed as to land claims and other acts of later date. As to Mobile in particular, Congress, by acts of May 8, 1822, and March 3, 1827, donated to residents before the American capture a reasonable quantity of land, and constituted

a surveyor for the northern part of Mississippi Territory, and his jurisdiction as surveyor over the remainder of the Territory continued until the passage of the act of April 20, 1818, entitled "An Act respecting the Survey and Sale of the Public Lands in Alabama Territory." This provided "that the powers and duties of the surveyor for the lands in the northern part of Mississippi Territory shall extend to the whole of the Alabama Territory, and that Territory only." By letter dated May 10, 1818, Mr. Freeman was directed to transmit to the Surveyor-General of Alabama Territory all the maps, contracts, field notes, and other papers appertaining to that Territory.

On May 30, 1819, Mr. Freeman nominated "Silas Dinsmoor, Esq.," late agent of the Choctaw nation, as his principal deputy for the district east of the Island of Orleans, and the indorsement shows the approval of the President. The length of his tenure of the office is unknown. Just before this time, we find Columbus C. Stone also actively surveying in this county, although from his illness George N. Stewart was to finish his plats. Dinsmore surveyed Spring Hill before 1826, and seems to have been living there in 1828.

the register and receiver a tribunal to receive proof. Their reports were full, and were confirmed March 2, 1829. There were later private acts, but by 1829 the great bulk of titles were either settled or put in such condition that they could at least be settled in the courts.[1]

Many of the Mobile titles were actually thus adjudicated, and a number of the relief acts took the same course for construction. A large volume could be compiled from the decisions on Mobile titles by the Supreme Courts of Alabama and the United States, and in fact many of these pages are based on them.

One interesting question was as to ownership of the shore. The act of 1824, which granted the bake-house and hospital lots to the city, also gave to it all public land between high-water mark and the channel of the river from Church to North Boundary streets in front of the city.[2] The second section of the act gave to persons owning west of Water Street the flooded land opposite, when they had made improvements. This was to give rise to lawsuits, of which one of the most famous was Pollard v. Kibbe.

This concerned the title to the property on the north side of Government from Water to Commerce. Forbes & Co., we remember, owned the northeast corner of Royal and Government under Panton, Leslie & Co., who had filled up to about Water Street. Forbes & Co. claimed this eastern lot, too, because they had improved the western one. The question was, on which lot under the act should be the improvement in order to earn the water lot? The United States Supreme Court decided that the water lot itself must have been improved, and thus adversely to Forbes & Co.[3] Pollard's heirs, it is true, had not improved it either; but their claim was under Perez' grant of 1809 to William Pollard of a landing for lumber from his mill, and a special act of 1836 confirming their title.

In this instance Curtis Lewis had antagonized both Forbes and Pollard by taking possession in 1823, and filling the lot for a distance of eighty feet east of Water by about forty

---

[1] 4 *U. S. Statutes at Large*, pp. 239, 358.
[2] *Ibid.*, p. 66.
[3] 14 Peters (U. S.), p. 353.

north of Government, and, although ousted once in the night-time by Innerarity, had regained it.   Kibbe claimed under Forbes, Lewis, and the city, but lost nevertheless.

After Commerce Street was run, a new question was to arise. Pollard *v.* Kibbe had settled the title to the water lots to its west; but who owned the new shore, from Commerce Street eastwardly? [1]   Did the city, under the act of 1824, or was it to be a matter of prescription by individuals against the public?

The Alabama Supreme Court did not hesitate to declare that the act of 1824 was unconstitutional in so far as it attempted to grant the shore to the city, or to any one else.   As Alabama was admitted on an equality with the older States, the United States could not own or grant the river shore, for they did not own it in the original thirteen States.   The United States Supreme Court at first seemed to avoid the question, but finally had to meet it and sustained the Alabama court.   They declared that the common law prevailed in Alabama, and that the Spanish treaty of 1819 as to Florida did not cede Mobile, or pass any sovereign ownership of the shores.   That treaty, they said, only recognized the fact that the United States already owned the district. [2]

[1] *Boulo* v. *N. O. R. R.* 55 Ala. p. 480.

[2] *Pollard* v. *Hagan*, 3 How. (U. S.) p. 212 ; *Mayor* v. *Eslava*, 9 Porter (Ala.), p. 577 ; 16 Peters (U. S.), p. 234.

CHAPTER XLVII.

UP to the present period in our story, Fort Charlotte has been the principal subject of interest. It was so under the French, it was so under the Spaniards, and during the short time it was neglected by the British we saw that Mobile itself was depressed. The fort was the centre of the life of the town, and was its protection, too.

But now it was not so important, although the garrison was maintained. With the establishment of a republican government the centre of civil life was rather the council chamber, and since the conquest by the United States the danger from Indian and foreign attack was greatly lessened. As the town grew up around it, the fort itself, which had so long been a protection, came to be regarded as in the way.

Major George P. Peters, of the artillery, was in command in 1816, and for better oversight of the fort he built a picket fence around it. This interrupted communication with the South Ward. The Board of Commissioners, on motion of Judson, thereupon claimed the free and·undisturbed use of the Common adjoining, as had been the case under former governments, and President Innerarity wrote to the commandant to request removal of the obstruction. Major Peters, on July 19, from Fort Charlotte, declined in the following firm but courteous manner: —

"Your communication of the 17th inst. (in consequence of my absence) did not reach me until this day. I regret much that it contains a requisition which my duty compels me to refuse a compliance with. The fence of which you speak leaves a part of the glacis outside of it, and it is impossible now to pass within it and not travel over some part of the fortification. The winding path, which the citizens were permitted the privilege of passing over during the reign of the

Spanish commandants, never could have been by them considered as a street belonging to the town, because it crosses a part of the glacis of the principal works, and does not correspond with any street of the town. Therefore the permission above alluded to, even in times of peace, never could have grown into an absolute right, nor could that of the grazing cattle on any part of a fortification ever become so. The only excuse for a commanding officer allowing such privileges without [within?] military limits is his possessing absolute authority over the subjects enjoying them, and consequently the power to compel a reparation of damages by the subjects themselves. It is the well-known duty of the commanding officer of a post to protect the public property, and keep in repair the public works intrusted to his care. The object of the fence, therefore, cannot be mistaken, nor the necessity of it denied.

"In fulfilling my duty as an officer of the United States Army, I have ever been cautious of any infringements on the rights of citizens, or debarring them of any convenience which they could consistently enjoy. It is well known that the citizens of this town, far from having lost any privileges by the change of government, have acquired new rights."

So the fence remained until there was a change in the commanding officer. On May 17, 1817, we find the board, apparently on motion of the energetic Garrow, appointing a committee of the president (Duvol), Garrow, and C. S. Stewart to wait on Captain Beale upon his arrival, and request him to open the highway between the north and south ends of this town. They further resolved that, if he refused, the police officer of the town should be authorized to remove said obstruction. Mr. Lemuel Childress was the one lone policeman of the corporation at the time, and it would be interesting to know how he contemplated the responsibility thus thrust upon him of defying the military of the United States. We do not learn that either Captain Beale or Ajax Childress removed the fence and opened the winding path across the eastern glacis, say through the centre of the present market buildings. It is perhaps significant, however, that in a few days we find Childress removed, Timothy McGrath substituted, and elaborate rules declared for the government of the police officer.

About this time we get an official description of the fort.

Brigadier-General Bernard, on December 23, 1817, made a
report to Chief Engineer Swift, U. S. A., on the southern
frontier of the Union, and in the course of it speaks as follows
of Fort Charlotte, the masonry of whose scarf he declares
would be easily breached in a siege.   He says: —

"Fort Charlotte, at Mobile Town, has been constructed at the
beginning of the eighteenth century: of all the forts in Louisiana, this is the only one well and judiciously built; its delinea-
tion and relief are far below that degree of perfection the art
had attained in Europe at that epoch.   However, both were
more than adequate to the purpose for which that fort was
intended.   It has lost its importance (on account of pacification
of the Indians).   It hardly defends the west branch of River
Mobile, and not at all the branches eastward; consequently it
does not defend the opening of the valleys north of Mobile Bay.
However, in the actual state of things, this fort may and ought
to be considered as a depot for the militia of the valleys of
Alabama and Tombigbee, also as a place of arms against Pensacola, and ought to be preserved and kept in repair as long as
the said Port of Pensacola does not belong to the Union."

The dissatisfaction of the municipal authorities and the criti-
cism of the military united for the ruin of Fort Charlotte.
The pen proved mightier than the sword, and on April 20,
1818, Congress passed an act for the sale of Bienville's fort.[1]

This was not actually carried into effect until 1820.   Meanwhile the place continued garrisoned, and routine papers remain
in the War Department relative to returns of property, and
accounts of Captain A. L. Sands of the artillery, and Captain
Willis Foulk of the 8th Infantry.   The fall of 1819 was a
sickly one, and we find medicines and hospital stores sent
Peters and Stebbins, of Mobile, for the attending surgeon.
Pensacola had then just come into possession of the United
States, and hospital stores for that point were also forwarded
through Captain Foulk.

After the conclusion of the treaty by which Florida was
purchased from Spain, the company of artillery at Mobile was,
on March 21, 1821, directed to occupy Pensacola, and the
military stores were also removed there.

---

[1] 3 *U. S. Statutes at Large*, p. 465.   Bernard's report was furnished by
the War Department.

The troops evacuated Fort Charlotte, and everything was prepared for the sale of the land. As provided by the act, Silas Dinsmore, United States deputy surveyor, was directed to plat it into squares, conforming as nearly as practicable to the general city plan. This he did, and the property was divided into nine unequal squares, No. 5 being the fort property. Royal Street was not continued in a straight line, but south of Government it began a little to the east. All streets were to be sixty feet wide, all lots thirty. A street, now Water, was platted through the shallow "Bay" east of the tract. The Fort Charlotte property extended from Water Street to the west of St. Emanuel, in the centre reaching Conception, and stretched more regularly from our Monroe north to Government.

A letter of March 19, 1822, from Dinsmore, regarding his connection with the sale, has survived in the Interior Department. He writes thus to Hon. Josiah Meigs : —

"I am not satisfactorily advised of the names or qualities of my calumniators, but the charge is a supposed criminal interest which it was alleged I had taken in (what is called) the *Willis Speculation!* The whole amount of my sinning is this. Madame Chotard, relict and representative of Henry Willis, applied for a location on the Public Lot in Mobile, including Fort Charlotte, or Fort Condé. On the day of public sale she published a caveat, and, as she did not wish to appear personally in a mixed crowd, requested me to read her caveat aloud, which I did, without comment, and of which no notice was taken by sellers or buyers. It is not in my nature to deny an importunate request delicately urged by a lady; and by such a lady, it became an irresistible command. Nor can I feel conscious that I committed any crime, religious, moral, or political; nor had I any interest, the most remote, in the success or failure of Madame Chotard's claim, nor in any speculation where the interests of the United States were concerned."

There were some individual buyers at this United States sale of October, 1820, but the bulk of the property went to a syndicate, who had raised a fund for the purpose. On the 11th of the month, there met in Armstrong's room in Pope's Hotel a number of gentlemen to consider making "common stock" of all the lots. It would seem that Lewis Judson, John B.

Hogan, Edward Hall, and Addin Lewis were among the movers in this enterprise.

The plan was carried out, and on the 14th a constitution was adopted, providing for trustees, who should have a new survey made, and hold and convey lots from time to time, on credit of a quarter cash and the remaining quarters at intervals of six months. The shares were fixed at one hundred dollars, and an assessment of about thirty per cent. allowed for expenses and improvements. Money collected should be deposited in the Mobile Bank, and there should be semi-annual distribution of the proceeds of sale. It was contemplated, however, that all business should be wound up by January 1, 1824.

The trustees elected were John B. Hogan, Edward Hall, T. W. Armstrong, William Barnett, and Addin Lewis, and of the subscribers of the constitution all but a very few were men then or soon to be prominent citizens of Mobile. Meetings were occasionally held, and the last recorded was in 1822.

The map under which this Lot Company's sales were made was recorded. It was by Thomas Hubbard, city surveyor, and shows the present streets, squares, and lots. This re-arrangement of lots faces them all on Water, Royal, and St. Emanuel; except that west of Royal, all adjacent to Church or Theatre face these two east and west streets. The lot of one hundred and twenty feet on the west side of St. Emanuel by eighty on the north side of Church Street, for a union Protestant church, is shown, and there are lots between Water Street and the river, — a variation from the original survey which was to give trouble. The United States Supreme Court was to declare that the sale of the fort did not embrace anything east of Water Street.[1]

To Hubbard's resurvey we are indebted for better preservation of the plan of the city; but one or more of Dinsmore's lots still exist, and even Hubbard could not prevent the awkward connection of Royal with the old street separating Eslava's house from the colored settlement opposite. We remember the Spaniards never named it, but it was henceforth a narrower Royal Street.

Just as the building of the market had determined the running of Water Street, and was to lead to the reclamation later of

---

[1] *Mobile v. Eslava*, 16 Peters (U. S.), p. 243.

MOBILE IN 1824

Commerce also, so the re-platting of the Fort Charlotte property determined that the streets for several blocks below should run parallel to Government, and not, as in Mathews' fanciful plat of 1818, into Government at an angle from the southeast.

And yet planning streets through the Vauban walls was not altogether the same as opening them, and the new city discussed several plans before the actual demolition was accomplished. Gunpowder was needed to blow down this solid masonry of Mobile brick and oyster-shell lime; and to fill up the new streets the débris was used, instead of the sand which had been industriously hauled before. From time to time in 1821–23, we find amounts expended by the city for pulling down the fort walls that were in the street, and after some hesitation permission seems even to have been granted citizens to use dirt from the old site for filling lots. Water Street was raised with it, and St. Francis and its intersection with Royal were filled up in the same way. Even some of the fort cannon were used to protect street corners, as Royal and Dauphin and St. Michael and Water still testify. One in some way fell over and sank in the ground, to be rediscovered only within the past few years in excavating for a sewer in front of Zadek's. A bomb-proof belonging to Addin Lewis was in 1821 tendered to the city for a prison, and accepted for that purpose. People still alive remember playing as children on the ruins of Fort Charlotte.

This sale of the fort is important for what it ended and for what it began. It was the first of those syndicate land projects which have platted and sold so many Spanish city grants. The Orange Grove auctions, the Favre and Bernoudy divisions, the slow Kennedy sales in the Price Claim, the quicker platting and disposition of the Espejo Tract, all come later, but are a continuation of the process of change from an agricultural to a commercial community begun by the Mobile Lot Company when they bought, platted, and sold Fort Charlotte.

The growth which necessitated the destruction of the fort had already created the first bank, that great Bank of Mobile, so long one of the most famous in the United States. It was chartered November 20, 1818, by the Territory of Alabama, with an authorized capital of five hundred thousand dollars.[1]

---

[1] Toulmin's *Laws of Alabama*, p. 46.

A. W. Gordon was its first cashier. It was significant that the site of this peaceful institution was near that of a fort bastion, on the west side of Royal, north of Church. A projected street through the fort east and west was at first thought of as Charlotte Street, but from 1822 it was known as Church, from the erection of the first Protestant place of worship on the church lot shown on the Lot Company's map. This is the site of the present Christ Church. It was for all Protestant denominations, and was near another bastion, about a block north of where once were Remonville's old Catholic church and cemetery. In 1822, the old hospital on Dauphin was leased out by the city for a theatre; and two years later, the first theatre building of Mobile was erected by N. M. Ludlow, with the assistance of several public-spirited citizens. This was at the northwest corner of Theatre and Royal, on remains of the fort's southeast bastion. Immediately west was then the first county jail, where now stands the pleasant Kirkbride place.

Possibly the first brick house in American Mobile was the extensive building by Henry Stickney on the southwest corner of Water and Church streets, — the old Sailors' Home, torn down only a few years ago. It was near his wharf at the foot of Church Street, and served for residence and business, too. The ground floor was a warehouse; the first floor above had living-rooms, with verandas, and approach from Church Street; and the second floor had bedrooms and wide hall. On the roof was a cupola, containing a telescope which commanded the bay. The present Bethel site was the flower garden.[1]

And not only was the old fort so turned to peaceful uses, but in the esplanade where Beaudrot had been sawn in pieces the county now bought a lot for a court-house; and in the old Officers' Barracks Square, across Government Street, was built the first cotton compress, that of A. F. Stone & Co. Their negroes, in pressing, pulled ropes across Royal until prohibited by the city in 1823. Further down in Government, below Royal, stood from the time of the fort sale the new public markets until after 1837, when the Supreme Court declared

---

[1] Information from Mrs. C. A. Hammond, now of Montgomery, a daughter of Henry Stickney.

them an obstruction;[1] but even the new and handsome municipal buildings and market, erected 1854–55 on the east side of
Royal, stand in part on foundations of Fort Charlotte. The
Goodwin and Haire map of 1824 shows no signs of the fort,
but only the streets and wharves of a modern commercial city.

The fort was demolished. The bustle of the street not less
than the hush of religious service, the zeal of local politics and
the rivalry of business, the bench of justice and the scene of
forensic eloquence, as well as the tears of tragedy and smiles
of comedy, all claimed its site, and have conspired to cause
Bienville's fort to be forgotten. Even as Bienville removed
the Choctaw wigwams in order to build Fort Louis, that fortification now made place for homes and institutions of an
American Mobile.

Truly, "Peace hath her victories no less renowned than war."

Such is the story of Colonial Mobile. Her growth with the
development of the river country of Alabama; her expansion
before the Civil War, with the building of a great railroad,
to be a port of the West, as well as of the Alabama-Bigbee
basin, quite after Iberville's dream; her decline, too, after that
war, until Congress cut the ship channel through the bars at
the mouth of her rivers; and then her present prosperity, —
these are themes of interest, and deserve careful presentation.
But they are beyond the scope of this book.

The civic and material growth, causing the destruction of
Fort Charlotte to make way for a greater Mobile, ended the
colonial period. Mobile had become an incorporated city; its
tributary valleys, a State of the American Union.

Bienville's Mobile and its district had become fully Ameri-
canized. The friendly Choctaws were to leave their seats to
the whites; the free negroes of Spanish times ceased to be
important ; even the gentle creoles gave way to more pushing
Americans. The French and Spanish languages gradually
yielded to the English, their customs to our own. Comparatively few of the old families now survive, and even they are
largely mixed with American blood. The streets extending
out from the original settlement retain French names, but
more numerous new ones commemorate Wilkinson, Jackson,

---

[1] *State* v. *Mayor*, 5 Porter (Ala.), p. 279.

Dearborn, Jefferson, State, Congress, and other American worthies or institutions. The great fires of 1827 and 1839 destroyed the old town, and French and Spanish buildings are now almost unknown. But traditions live, historic spots can still be shown, and imagination loves to wander back and picture the scenes before that change from Latin to American Mobile.

APPENDIX.

APPENDIX.

(From Mobile Church Records.)

Jay sousigné prestre et miss. apost. ateste a tous quil appartiendra que lannee du salut mil sept cents quatre le vint-huit° du mois de 7bre en vertu des lettres de provision et de collation accordee et scollee de Le vingt° de Juillet de lannee derniere, par lesquelles Monseigneur Illustrissime et Reverendissime Eveque de Quebec Erige une Eglise paroissiale dans le lieu dit le fort louis de la louisiane et dont Il donne la Cure et le Soin a m. henri Roulleaux De la Vente miss. apost. Du Diocese de Bayeux, Jay mis led pretre en possession actuelle et corporelle de lad Eglise paroissiale et de tous les droits qui lui apartiennent, apres avoir observé les Ceremonies acoutumees et requises, Scavoir par lentree de Leglise, laspersion de leau benite, le baiser du grand autel, le touché du missel, la visite du tres Sainct Sacrement de lautel et le Son des cloches a laquelle possession Jateste que personne ne sest opposé donné en leglise du fort louis le jour du mois et de lan sud en presence de Jean baptiste de bieville lieuten . . . du Roy et commandant aud fort, pierre Du Qu . . . de boisbriant major, Nicolas de la Sale Ecrivain et faisant faisant fonction de Commissaire de la marine.

> DAVION.
> BIENUILLE.
> BOISBRIANT.
> DELASALLE.

(From Phelypeaux's Map, 1711.)

A. fort Louis, fortiffié suivant la Longueur de Son Coste exterieur d'une pointe de Bastion a L'autre ayant 90 Toises et par cette longueur Lon a donné aux faces des Bastions Vignt trois toises et demie. aux flanc douze toises et demie.

aux Gorges Cinq toises et
aux Courtines quarantes toises.

Le fort est Construit de pieux de Bois de Cédre ayant treize pieds dhauteur dont deux et demies entre en terre, et de quatorzes pouces en quarrées de paisseur, plantées, jointement les uns Contre Les autres. Ces pieux ce terminent par leurs Bout denhaut enpointe Comme des palissades; interieuremant aux Long de ces pieux il règne une espece de Banquette ayant deux pieds de hauteur en talus Sur, un et demie de Largeur. . . .

Il ny a pour tout Logement dans ce fort que La maison du Gouverneur. Le magazin ou Sont les effets du Roy, et un Corp de Garde Succintement; Les officiers les Soldats & les habitans ont tous leurs Logements hors du fort Comme cy est marquez, estant disposez de maniere que les rües ont Six toises de Largeur et toutes paralleles les unes aux autres. Les isles de maison ont Cinquante toises . . . en quarrées hors ceuze de Vis a Vis le fort qui ont Soixante toises de Largeur Sur Cinquante de profondeur, et Les plus proches de La riviere ont Cinquante toises de Largeur Sur Soixante de profondeur. . . .

Les maisons que Lon Batties Sont Construittes de Bois de Cédre et pin Suportées par un fondemens d'une quantité de pieux de Bois qui éxédent de terre d'un pied, qu'on pourroit Nommer pillotis parceque ce terrain se trouve inondées comme vous Le Voÿez marquez dans le Plan dans quelques androits, dans les temps de Pluye; quelques uns ce Sont Servis, pour Suporter leurs maison d'une pierre qui est Comme un Espece de tufle, qui est tres douce et qui Seroit merveilleuze á faire de Beaux Éddifices. Cette pierre ce prand á dix huit Lieux audossus du nouvelle établissement Les Long des Bord de la Riviere de La Mobille. — Les maisons ont 18, 20 á 25 pieds auplus de hauteur, il y en á quelques unes plus Basses Construittes d'un mortié fait avec de la terre et de La Chaud, —

N: cette Chaud est faitte de Coquille d'huistre que lon trouve á Lentré de la Riviere Sur des petittes Îlles qui en porte le nom, &c.

Lon donne á ceuze qui Veute Sétablir dans Cette endroit, de terrain douze toises et de Mie de Largeur, Sur la face d'une rües Sur Vignt Cinq de profondeur; —

Lapierre dont Lon Se Sert pour Supporter les maisons, est Rare et Non commune faute des Voitures qu'il Seroit Necessaires davoir par eaux, Comme des Batteaux plats qu'il ny á pas, ny dont personnes nen veut faire La dépence, ce qui Seroit d'un grand Secours, car ceuze dont les maisons ne Sont Soutenues que de pieux de Bois Sont obligez de Les Changer tous les trois á quatre ans parce qu'il pourisse dans La terre, &c.

B. Maison du Gouverneur.

C. Magazin du Roy.

D. Poudriere ou magazin á Poudre.

E. Corp de Garde.

F. Prizons.

G. Bastion dans le quel on met le pavillon.

H. Bastion dans Le quel est une Cloche nayant point de Chapelle dans le fort.

C. — The Ordinance of 1667.

(From Mobile Church Records.)

Le present registre contenants quatrevignt-dixhuit feuilles a ete paraphé et cotté par premier et dernier par nous conseiller du roy en ses conseils et son procurcur general au conseil superieur de la province de la louisiane pour servir a enregistrer les baptesmes mariages et sepultures de la mobile pour la presente année 1726 et deliveré au reverend pere mathias cure du dit lieu pour sy conformer suivant lordonnance a la nlle orleans Jan. 21, 1726. —

FLEURIAU.

Extrait du titre 20 de lordonnance de 1667.

Seront faits par chacun au deux registres pour ecrire les baptesmes mariages et sepultures en chacune paroisse dont les feuillets seront paraphés et cottées par premier et dernier par le juge royal du lieu ou leglise est sittué lun desquels servira de minutte et demeura as mains du curé ou du vicaire et lautre sera porté au greffier juge royal pour servir de grosse lesquels deux registre seront fournis annuellement aux frais de la fabrique.

Dans larticle des baptesmes sera fait mention du jour de la naissance et seront nommes lenfant le pere et la mere le parain et la maraine et aux mariages les noms et surnoms ages qualites et demeures de ceux qui se marient sils sont enfants de famille en tutelle curatelle ou en puissance dautruy et y assisteront quatre temoins qui declareront sur le registre sils sont parents de quel costé et en quel degré et dans les articles de sepulture sera fait mention du jour du deceds.

Les baptesmes mariages et sepultures seront en un mesme registre selon lordre des jours sans laisser aucun blanc et aussitot quils auront eté fait sils seront ecrits et signé scavoir les baptesmes par le pere sil est present et par les parains et maraines et les actes de mariages par les personnes maries et par quatre de ceux qui y auront assisté les sepultures par deux des plus proches parents ou amis qui auront assiste au convoy et si aucuns deux ne scavent signer ils le declareront et seront de ce interpellés par le curé ou vicaire dont sera fait mention.

Seront tenus les curés ou vicaires six semaines apres chacune année expirée de porter ou denvoyer seurement la grosse et la minutte du registre signe deux et certiflié veritable au greflier juge royal qui laura cotté et paraphé et sera tenu le greflier de le recevoir et y faire mention du jour quil aura apporté et en donnera la decharge apres receu moins que la grosse aura été collationée a la minutte qui demeurera au curé ou vicaire et que le greflier aura bané en lun et en lautre tous les blancs et feuillets qui resteront le tout sans frais Laquelle grosse de registre sera gardée par le greflier pour y avoir recours.

FLEURIAU.

DELALOERE FLAMONT (?)

D. — THE SPANISH CITY GRANTS.

The titles in Mobile outside of the old Spanish town rest on grants mainly Spanish, not a score in number. At the extreme north we have Farmer's Island and Laurent plantation, still marshy for the most part; and nearer are the Orange Grove and Baudin tracts, the seat of the cotton business; while northwest is the Fisher Tract, now given over to negroes. South of the old town came in succession the Favre, Bernoudy, and Choctaw Point tracts, all of them then overflowed, or marshy back to the ridge on which run St. Emanuel and Conception streets, now mainly residence quarters. Immediately west of the fort is the McVoy Tract; while west of the old town is the immense Price Claim (cut across by the De Lusser Tract), the main residence district of the modern city. Cottage Hill and Spring Hill are rather country tracts, but the Espejo, Dubroca, and Murrell claims on Spring Hill Road are fairly parts of Mobile life, although beyond the western corporate limits.

The present city is bounded north by One Mile Creek, or Bayou Marmotte. At its greatest extent the corporation has included the marsh lands to the north of this up to Three Mile Creek, or Bayou Chateaugué; but practically, until the building of the Mobile and Montgomery Railroad, and establishment of sawmills since the American Civil War, this territory was of no great importance. Between these two bayous are two tracts, — an island facing the river, and a marsh west of the island.

1. The former has always gone by the name of The Island, or *Farmer's Island*, and the title dates back to British times. It does not seem to have been coveted under the Spaniards, but the United

States Congress was on March 3, 1839, to confirm the tract to the heirs of the British claimant, Major Robert Farmer.[1]

2. We know more of the western claim, ever called the *Laurent Plantation*. It is even yet principally marsh, traversed now by the Telegraph Road and the Mobile and Ohio Railroad. In Spanish times it could have had little value except for its front on Three Mile Creek and Bayou Marmotte.

Bartholomé Laurent was a land-owner in the city, and obtained a concession to this tract. Laurent had to sign his deeds by mark.[2] In 1803, Panton, Leslie & Co. purchased it of Laurent for $130 cash. It was then described as situated south of Bayou Satulle (Chateaugué?), containing ten arpens front by the usual depth, bounded north by the said bayou, south by uncultivated lands, and east and west by lands belonging to the king.[3] As it adjoined their Orange Grove Tract, and had a front on two streams, these merchants may have been able to use it in the Indian trade.

3. Most of the cotton warehouses of the modern city are in what is called the *Orange Grove Tract*, and thus no name is more familiar, although the exact site of the orangery and the name of the man who planted it have passed into oblivion. The more common name in earlier times was Poplar Grove.

We have already seen that the title dates from British times, being, with the Fisher Tract and Farmer's Island, the only direct survivals of that epoch. The British government in 1767 granted the tract, as having 263 acres, to William Richardson, who conveyed it to Panton, Leslie & Co. This grant is said to have been under a British colonial ordinance of 1765, giving a river front of one third the depth in all river concessions.[4]

In 1796, on the application of John Forbes for Panton, Leslie & Co., Olivier had James de la Saussaie survey this sixty-three English arpens tract, a quarter of a league north of Mobile, as it then was, and put Forbes in possession. William Simpson, before 1802, found the survey to be defective, so represented to Osorno, and prayed that the tract be resurveyed by Joseph Collins, the regular deputy surveyor of the district. Thereupon the following proceedings were had : [5] —

The Deputy Surveyor of this place, Joseph Collins, shall appear before me on to-morrow, the fifth instant, at eight o'clock A. M. of the

---

[1] 6 *U. S. Statutes at Large*, p. 761.

[2] 1 *Mobile Translated Records*, p. 313.

[3] *Ibid.*, p. 313.

[4] *Magee v. Hallett*, 22 Ala. Rep. p. 711.

[5] 1 *Translated Records*, p. 285.

day aforesaid, assisted by two inhabitants the most contiguous to the lands described in the preceding memorial, in order to proceed in my presence, and that of the two witnesses, to the survey of the land aforesaid agreeably to the annexed plat, which is similar to the like one now on file in these archives in the proceedings executed by my predecessor, his Excellency Peter Olivier. and, when completed, let a copy of the same duly authenticated be provided to the petitioner as prayed for.

JOAQUIN DE OSORNO. [Seal.]

I, Joseph Collins, Deputy Surveyor of the town of Mobile and its Dependencies, etc., Do hereby certify, that in obedience to a decree issued by his honor Joaquin de Osorno, Commandant of the Post of Mobile, bearing date Fourth of May one thousand eight hundred and two, I resorted to the tract of land in order to ascertain the boundaries and landmarks recited in the proceedings made and executed by James de la Saussaie, but could not find any, except a cedar post on the south side of the line ; consequently I proceeded to survey the land agreeably to the plat in presence of his honor Joaquin de Osorno, William Simpson, John Trouillet, and James Gold, it resulting from said survey, that the tract of land contains two hundred and eighty superficial arpens, measured by the perches of Paris of eighteen lineal feet, of the same City, according to the usage of this Province, situated in the district of Mobile, distant about a quarter of a league from said Town, containing fourteen arpens in front on the Bay of Mobile, bounded on the north by land of Jeremiah Terry, on the west by land of Mr. Fisher, and on the south by public land, the limits of which, the trees, and other land marks, both natural and artificial, serving as boundaries. In testimony whereof, etc.

John Forbes improved the front, and thought proper to obtain confirmation by the Spanish authorities, and so in 1807 the intendant gave him a concession for 310 arpens and $77\frac{1}{4}$ perches, extending across the marsh, thus including the improvements. This grant was held to run the north and south lines without deflection to the water.[1]

The plan attached to the Spanish concession is of interest in other respects. It shows One Mile Creek as called La Marmata, but the southern prong as named Arroyo Chacta, — Choctaw Creek. About the centre of the tract is a very large " House," apparently fronting a north and south road.

The later Orange Grove litigation is interesting as establishing the principle that riparian owners shall claim reclaimed land perpendicu-

<hr>

[1] *Hagan* v. *Campbell*, 8 Porter (Ala.), pp. 9, 18.

larly to the river bank, regardless of how their land lines strike the shore. The earlier case extended these lines to low water without such deflection, because the Spanish grant so directed, but the rule was different as to accretion and reclamation in front of that grant.[1]

4. On April 26, 1803, Osorno, pending the stoppage of land business at the office of the Intendant-General, granted to Joseph Collins a marshy tract two perches front on Royal, bounded north by lands of Panton, Leslie & Co. (Orange Grove), south by St. Louis Street, now first mentioned by name, and east by Mobile River.[2] This is the origin of the Collins claim to the *Baudin Tract*. The grantee was "captain of dragoons attached to the militia company of Fish River, and special surveyor of this town."

In 1806, W. E. Kennedy undertook to improve the tract by fencing and ditching, and so perfect the title, in consideration of obtaining the northern half. It seems that in 1798, Alexander Baudin had obtained a grant of seven arpens at the same spot, and, by his brother Louis and also J. B. Trenier, made a levee from Royal to the river. Kennedy in 1814 bought up this Baudin claim and secured its confirmation. His executors, after sharp litigation, were finally compelled to carry out the agreement to divide with the heir of Collins,[3] although the Collins title had been rejected by the United States authorities in favor of the Baudin.

5. The *De Lusser Tract* is in no sense a Spanish grant, but in Spanish times Don Miguel Eslava acquired his interest in it. On June 21, 1809, Joseph Chastang, for Hazeur de Lorme, of New Orleans, " heir of Mr. Lusser," sold Eslava the lot, two arpens four toises front by twenty-five in depth, situated on the south of the royal fort of the town, bounded east by the house and lot of the purchaser, south by vacant lands, and west by lot of M. Morsier. This was doubtless the Morsier located north in the earlier deeds, and by a Spanish inquest still extant. The price for this was $100. In point of fact, Chastang did not represent the De Velle branch, and November 22, 1823, a compromise was effected by which that half interest was given up by the Eslavas. The United States confirmed the title by Act of Congress in 1843.[4]

6. On August 13, 1806, *William McVoy* obtained from Intendant-General Morales an order of survey of twenty arpens adjoining Fort Charlotte. He soon sold to Joshua Kennedy, and the tract was culti-

[1] *Magee* v. *Hallett*, 22 Ala. p. 699.
[2] 1 *Mobile Translated Records*, p. 295.
[3] *Hallett* v. *Collins*, 10 How. (U. S.) p. 174 ; *Mobile Deed Book* " A," p. 61.
[4] *Mobile Translated Records*, p. 372 ; 6 *Statutes at Large*, p. 887 ; Senate Committee on Land Claims Report of January 9, 1840.

vated and inhabited by him and a Spaniard in his employ from 1807 to 1820.[1] The use was not such as to conform to the conditions of the sale, and the grant hung fire in American times till confirmed by a special act of Congress, May 5, 1832.[2]

This McVoy tract was shaped like a T, the cross being along our St. Emanuel and Conception, from the Collel line to Government, the upright wedging in between Fort Charlotte and Eslava down to the river. A grant of land so close to the fort as this would naturally be subject to suspicion, especially as, so late as November 22, 1806, the validity of sale of lots near the forts was considered as unsettled.[3]

7. This *Collel Tract* is a small one of three arpens front by six deep on the margin of the river, immediately north of the Favre claim. It was originally granted Don Francisco Collel, September 20, 1806, and surveyed by Collins. The papers were lost or burned in the Pensacola fire of October 24, 1811; and on September 4, 1815, Don José de Soto, colonel, civil and military commandant, intendant *pro tem.*, sub-delegate, etc., at Pensacola, certifies to these facts. This quasi-quitclaim is the existing muniment of title, and shows a purchase by Lieutenant-Colonel Collel, he paying five dollars and one half rial in silver, the value of the twenty-three superficial arpens at two rials each, the royal duty of *media annata*, and the eighteen per cent. for carriage to Spain. In 1823, the south half was to pass by conveyances of Collel's daughter, Anne Marie Cavelier, wife of Du Suau De La Croix, of New Orleans, to Thomas F. Townsley, and gradually the whole tract changed hands. It extended from about Madison to south of Canal Street.[4]

8. Royal Street ran only north of the fort, but curiously enough is connected with the *Favre Tract* to the south, the first in time of these large Spanish grants. On June 11, 1798, Simon Andry exchanged this tract below the city for Favre's lot and a half on Royal, between the lots of Savari Tatan to the north and Barthe Renard to the south. Favre was an interpreter as far back as 1754, as we see from the French baptismal registers, and even now, under the Spaniards, interpreter of the Choctaw nation. Commandant Espeleta had in 1780 directed Grimarest to grant this land to Favre, but in some way it had not been done, although Favre had been ever since in possession.

To effect this exchange, therefore, Favre had now to obtain a grant from Gayoso, the new governor-general, and by a coincidence Andry had to do the same thing for his tract. This concession to Andry is

[1] 3 *American State Papers*, pp. 16, 397; see *Mobile Deed Book* "A," p. 61.
[2] 6 *U. S. Statutes at Large*, p. 485.
[3] 2 White's *New Recopilacion*, p. 403.
[4] *Mobile Deed Book* "G," pp. 142-145, 176, 162, etc.

dated July 10, 1798, when he obtained ten arpens river front (instead of the twenty asked for) by the usual depth of forty, bounded north by a small bayou called Durand, and south by vacant lands. It is recited by Lanzos that old inhabitants testified it had always been vacant property, even before the conquest. Lanzos recommends the grant for the reason that Andry had a sufficient number of slaves to cultivate the land. The usual conditions are imposed, including non-alienation for three years;[1] and yet on June 11 these parties had, before the same commandant, agreed that Andry should at his own expense obtain the grant and pay the official fees for the very purpose of alienation.

9. If we depended entirely on the Mobile records, we should miss a number of grants and conveyances. One instance is what is now called the *Bernoudy Tract*, the vast grant south of the Favre concession.

It seems that on March 3, 1792, José Gaspar Munora obtained from Caroudelet a grant to 600 arpens of land on Mobile River, fifteen arpens front by forty deep. Who Munora was is not known, except that he was of Havana before living in Pensacola. The Spanish regulations concerning such gratuitous concessions required three years' occupancy, and, beyond cultivation and the making of brick thereon by Regis Bernoudy for perhaps four years, including 1809 or 1810, and use by Espejo with Munora's permission, there was no possession by any one in Spanish times. Bernoudy did not get a deed from Munora until March 24, 1813, when he paid $1,130 for the tract. Munora's title seems to have been overlooked towards the end of the Spanish times, for Charles Proffit, on November 28, 1811, obtained some sort of paper from Perez, but never occupied the tract. Joseph McCandless, who acquired from Bready, to whom Proffit sold, actually dispossessed Bernoudy for a time, and was in American times to live there for a while and run a brickyard. A current report was that McCandless obtained his title in consideration of the gift to Perez of a large crop-eared riding-horse which the commandant used.[2]

It would seem that Espejo obtained a government title to this land February 16, 1803. He petitioned for a grant of twenty arpens front on the river by forty deep, in order to make bricks to use in building and repairing ovens in his Majesty's bakery, then in Espejo's charge. He describes the land as a mile and a half below the fort, which is too far, but as being between Fontanilla and Andry, which is correct, for these were the former owners of the tracts south and north respectively.[3] There is no doubt Espejo used the Bernoudy Tract for making

---

[1] *Mobile Translated Records*, p. 213.

[2] 3 *American State Papers*, pp. 400, 401.

[3] *Mobile Translated Records*, p. 303.

brick, and it may be that afterwards, learning of the earlier grant to Munora, he attorned to him and abandoned his own claim. Bernoudy lived until seventy years of age, and since 1830 lies (*ci git*) in a vault in our Old Graveyard.

10. We have seen that the point we now call *Choctaw Point* was so named under the French, and that in British times Mr. Stuart lived on the high land near modern Frascati, overlooking the flooded land extending from the bay to about Canal Street. One Joseph Platin is said to have owned it at the Spanish conquest, but he died without lawful heirs. Thus this tract of fifteen arpens front by forty deep became part of the Spanish royal domain.

The town was too far away, the river shore back to modern St. Emanuel and Conception too marshy, for the point to be very important. Its principal use was for a Blood Hospital, but this was temporary, for Governor Miro did not hesitate, November 9, 1792, to grant it to Francis Fontanilla, assistant storekeeper, for private purposes. Fontanilla sold it with two negro slaves to Commandant Osorno in 1801 for $1200, describing it as a plantation commonly known by the name of Choctaw Point, containing fifteen arpens front by forty arpens in depth, which land is called Blood Hospital, bounded on the west by a small bayou, which is bounded by another tract belonging to John Baptiste Lucer, deceased, and on the east by another tract of land marshy and impassable.[1] This is substantially the description in Miro's grant. It seems this tract was cultivated from 1797 to 1813. A copy of the original survey by Collins in 1802–1803 still survives.

It was not long after this, in 1804, that we find Espejo selling "the place Chato" to William Simpson, partner of the house of Panton, Leslie & Co., for $500. Espejo had purchased from Osorno.

For some reason not now known, it was thought necessary that the grant should be confirmed by Intendant-General Morales on April 17, 1807, to John Forbes & Co., as containing six hundred acres, three days after a survey by V. S. Pintado.

This tract is not even to the present well built up, and its east end is still almost impassable, although the destined seat of railroads and docks. Its north line is just south of our Virginia Street, its east boundary the river at Choctaw Point, its south the bay as far as beyond the toll-gate, and its west line runs somewhat east of Ann Street. In 1811, the property was bounded south by Mrs. Boubell, on the other side of whom was Lansemandeville.

11. This last, the *Mandeville Tract*, is the southernmost of those at any time actually within our city limits. We remember it more especially as the probable location of Bienville's chateau. Under the

[1] *Mobile Translated Records*, p. 283.

English it had belonged to "John McGillebray and his associates in trade," but was now abandoned.

In the year 1796, J. B. Alexandre obtained these twenty arpens front on the bay, at the place called "Lansemanville,"[1]— Mandeville's Bend. It was bounded south by a bayou. When he conveys it to his son Francis in 1802 for $270, he describes it as bounded north by a bluff, south by a small bayou, west by pine lands, and adjoining the sawmill called Durand's. By that description, Francis, on April 23, 1805, sells it for $400 to John Forbes & Co., the source of modern titles. It embraces our Arlington and Fair Grounds.

12. *Blakely Island*, just across the river from Mobile, has been inside the city limits only nominally. Joseph Collins, the surveyor, appears to have been its first owner, having acquired it by permit of Osorno April 26, 1803. No Spanish survey seems to have been made, and so later its acreage was found to be 2280, instead of the estimated 4000. He sold it in 1807 to Josiah Blakeley, of Connecticut, for $1500. In the deed Collins describes it as seven miles long. This Yankee made it a plantation, which he called Festino.[2] It was a matter of *festina lente*, however, for it is even to-day pretty much in the condition in which he left it. The river front is made serviceable by piles and some wharves, but the interior is marshy still. Coffee Bayou, tradition says, was so named from coffee smuggled through it into Mobile by Cyrus Sibley and others in Spanish times. Bull and the other heirs got title from the United States in 1842 only to 1280 acres, and not to the whole island as claimed by Blakeley.[3]

13. *Thomas Price* we know already as Indian interpreter at Mobile, and, on account of valuable services in that capacity during the time of apprehended trouble with the United States, he obtained two grants of land adjoining the town on the west.

First Governor-General Manuel Gayoso De Lemos, on November 18, 1798, granted Price 540 acres, situate in the suburbs of Mobile, bounded on the north by Terisa's lands and those of Mazuria, on the east by the plan of Mobile, — then extending west about to Joachim Street, — and on the south by lands claimed by Simon Andre (Andry) and Favre. As laid off by Pintado and others, this first grant did not reach to either the Favre or Espejo tracts by possibly a half mile, but adjoined the city on the west and Fisher (Mazuria) Tract on the south. Price — or William E. Kennedy for him — found this out, and proceeded to get a grant out to those tracts. Intendant Morales, on September 18,

---

[1] *Mobile Translated Records*, pp. 185, 289.

[2] 3 *American State Papers*, p. 9; *Mobile Deed Book* "A," pp. 41, 45.

[3] Report of House Committee, February 23, 1842; 6 *U. S. Statutes at Large*, p. 836.

1806, made Price a further concession of about 500 acres more. The two grants make up a princely domain, now the principal residence section of Mobile, extending west beyond Ann Street.

On November 24, 1806, Price made Kennedy his attorney to carry through his surveys of land in the vicinity of Mobile, and do what might be necessary to obtain the complete titles. Only two days before the execution of this instrument, Kennedy had bought from Price for $200 all of the second (1806) grant, except ten acres in the northwest corner reserved by Price for himself. Price seems later to have located this reservation near our St. Joseph Street.

It seems that in August, 1807, Price, for $500, also sold Kennedy the tract acquired in 1798 from Gayoso, confirmed by Maxent November 25, 1806, but that this deed of 1807 was in some way lost in the Mobile or Pensacola record office. To cure this, on June 6, 1810, Kennedy for $700 obtained from Price a deed to the whole tract, which is described as "1100 arpens," bounded north by Poplar Grove, claimed by J. Forbes & Co., and by lands claimed by William Fisher, west by "A. Espejho," south by Simon Favre, and east by Franco Collel and William McVoy, and lots on the western part of Mobile occupied by Charles Lelong and Benjamin De Brocar and Mobile River.[1]

The Collel and McVoy tracts are well known, and Dubroca had a lot on the northeast corner of Joachim and St. Michael. The Price Claim came to the river only for a short distance north of St. Louis Street, and, indeed, except so far as it overlapped the Baudin claim, hardly reached the water at all. This was not material, for W. E. Kennedy became the owner of both. In American times there was to be an interesting suit to determine how the Orange Grove and Price grant boundary line ran across the land reclaimed from the river after these concessions, the title to valuable property being thus in dispute.[2]

For some reason, possibly because the deed of 1807 was not executed before the commandant, it was deemed necessary after the American occupation for Kennedy to obtain a further deed to the 540 acres first granted Price, and on that occasion Price reserved two (ten?) acres at the northeast corner.[3] The Price Claim was not patented to Kennedy until 1836, and the whole property was the subject of heavy litigation between the representatives of the two Kennedys.

14. These ten acres, now containing many handsome residences, have a history separate from that of the general Price Claim. Price

---

[1] *Mobile Deed Book* "S," p. 109.

[2] *Hagan* v. *Campbell*, 8 Porter (Ala.), p. 9.

[3] *Mobile Deed Book* "A," p. 8; 3 *American State Papers*, pp. 440, 441; 2 *Alabama Reports*, p. 571, etc.; *Mobile Deed Book* "T," p. 247.

seems to have lived on the reservation, for in 1810 are mentioned as at that point the fields, house, and well made by him. The tract began at the northwest corner of St. Anthony and St. Joseph streets, and was bounded east by St. Joseph Street, north by the Orange Grove line, near our Congress Street, being so platted as to have twenty-one chains on a side. Price agreed to sell the place to *Harry Toulmin* for $250, and this was finally done in 1818 by W. E. Kennedy, as executor of Thomas Price.[1] The west line went about to our Joachim Street.

15. Beginning at Ryland Street, a little west of Ann, and extending out beyond even the old city limits, is the *Espejo Tract*. When granted in 1803–1804, it was a league west of Mobile.[2] It was a concession of land on Three Mile Creek (then *bayu o passage de los portales*), of the usual twenty arpens front by forty deep to the south, which brings it almost to the modern Government Street. The papers are peculiar in apparently reciting only a verbal representation by Espejo.

The grant was February 22, 1803, by Osorno to Antonio Espejo, at a time when the intendant had, on account of the death of the assessor, directed that no petition for lands be sent to his office until a successor had been appointed. The sub-delegate, as in other cases, declares the case urgent, because cultivation of land and increase of population in the vicinity of the town would conduce greatly to public convenience; and makes the concession under seal, on condition that the proper petition shall later be presented with all necessary formalities. He describes Espejo as an old and respectable inhabitant of the town. We have known him as having the bakery contract, and as running a brick-yard, and in another transaction he is described as a carpenter.[3] April 11, next year, Osorno directs Collins to survey this land, so that valuation may be made.

We do not know that Espejo actually resided there himself, although it was inhabited and cultivated 1802–1813. The land proved valuable to his children. He left a widow, afterwards Catalina Mottus (or Montuse), and three children, — Antonio, Jr.; Gertrude, who married Richard Tankersley; and Catharine, who married William I. Ingersoll. The tract was platted into lots and divided between the four persons in interest in 1828,[4] the claim having been duly recognized by the United States upon the favorable report of Commissioner Crawford.[5]

16. Next west of the Espejo Tract was another of similar size, twenty by forty arpens, also fronting Bayou "Chatoga." This was

[1] *Mobile Deed Book* "B," p. 240.
[2] *Mobile Translated Records*, p. 304. [3] *Ibid.*, p. 228.
[4] *Mobile Deed Book* "II," p. 384. [5] *3 American State Papers*, p. 9.

granted *Benjamin Dubroca* by Osorno February 26, 1803, and the land surveyed April 18, 1804. A house was built upon it, and there was some cultivation, but not sufficient, in the eyes of United States Commissioner Crawford, to have merited the issue of a title by the Spanish authorities.[1] Nevertheless, a certificate of confirmation issued under the act of 1819 and a special act of Congress on May 27, 1840, perfected the title,[2] then held by the representatives of William E. Kennedy and by many of his grantees. It covers much of the territory bisected by the present Spring Hill Avenue between the Reservoir and Convent, including the pleasant village of Summerville.

17. Next out towards Spring Hill lies the *Murrell Tract*, now, on account of the street railroad, well occupied by country homes, many of elegance. The extensive grounds of the Convent of the Visitation, as well as the home where Mrs. Augusta Evans Wilson wrote some of her famous novels, are within this Spanish grant. It was granted provisionally by Osorno to John Murrell, an inhabitant of Mobile, May 7, 1804, on his petition for the eight hundred arpens bounded north by the Pass of Suriagne, east by lands of Benjamin Dubroca, south and west by the royal domain. Murrell solicited permission to go immediately in possession, with his stock of cattle and hogs, and to erect a house for his dwelling. As Collins was at the time absent, Charles Proffit, lieutenant of the Spanish militia of the District of Mississippi, was directed to survey the tract, — of course on receiving the customary fees.[3]

18. On June 12, 1800, Cayetano Perez granted Regis Duret a tract of land one mile square. There seems to have been no survey, but it was cultivated and inhabited from 1809 to 1814.[4] This is the origin of the title to *Spring Hill*, a favorite suburb of Mobile in American times. The Hill under the Spaniards was too far away from the little town to attract much attention as a resort. Hobart was in possession as tenant of Duret from 1809. He seems to have aided the heirs in the necessary proof before the United States authorities, and, as purchaser at an administration sale, prevailed over one Richardson, who set up some claim of possession after Duret's death in 1819.[5] Hobart bought from the heirs.

19. Miguel Eslava, the public storekeeper of the town, seems to have been much exercised by the Louisiana Cession. He had some

---

[1] 3 *American State Papers*, p. 17.

[2] 6 *Statutes at Large*, p. 800 ; Reports of Senate Land Claim Committee, January 4, 1839.

[3] *Mobile Translated Records*, p. 319.

[4] 3 *American State Papers*, p. 10.

[5] *Richardson* v. *Hobart*, 1 Stew. Ala. Rep. 501.

Mobile, meaning of word, 8 ; De Soto at, 14–17 ; Iberville selects site, 37 ; reasons, 37 ; foundation, 39 ; named, 43 ; not agricultural, 58 ; trades, 66 ; change of site, 69 ; description of new, 70–74 ; renamed Ft. Condé, 86 ; Indian congress, 105 ; district, 106 ; Charlevoix on, 106 ; Dumont on, 116 ; storm, 1740, 115 ; palisaded, 117 ; Phelypeaux's map, 134 ; real estate under the French, 141 ; British take possession, 177 ; British, according to Roberts, 187 ; British troops removed, 201 ; sickness, 204–212 ; Haldimand on, 205 ; site, 207 ; marshes, 207 ; according to Bartram, 237 ; in Council and Assembly of W. Florida, 244–247 ; names of residents, 246 ; siege by Galvez, 253 ; "villa," "plaza," 261 ; "ciudad," 330 ; treated by U. S. as Spanish, 349 ; described by Blakeley, 352 ; U. S. troops in Orange Grove, 356 ; Perez' capitulation, 360 ; extent, 304 ; appearance, 305 ; no Spanish map, 313 ; square number, 311 ; Spanish expenses at, 272 ; American incorporation, 387 ; first election, 388 ; boundary, 388 ; taxes, 389 ; memorial for greater powers, 391 ; first commissioners, 388, 392 ; second board, 392 ; market, 390, 392 ; wharf, 393 ; surveyor, 393 ; cows, 393 ; town money, 394 ; incorporated as city, 397 ; map of 1760, 400 ; before 1813 recognized by United States as Spanish city, 401 ; United States land donations, 403 ; town *v.* fort, 406, 407 ; Spanish grants, 420–431 (see Maps) ; Durnford's proposed new city, 434.

Mobile Bay, 8, 10, 12, 19 ; Iberville in, 30 ; chart, 228 ; Spanish names, 321.

Mobile County, created, 366.

Mobile Lot Co., 409, 410 ; Hubbard map, 410.

Mobile Point, 30, 324 (see Bowyer, Fort).

Mobile River, 4, 10–13 ; Charlevoix on, 106 ; Ellicott on, 318.

Mobilians, 5, 22, 37, 91 ; images, 41, 91 ; Iberville, 42 ; whipping, 91 ; church registers, 92.

Mohr, Chas., 243 note.

Momberault, 146, 160.

Money under Company, 88 ; Spanish, 88, 145 ; *bons*, 174 ; cattle, 322 ; Mobile, 394.

Mon Louis (Bodin), 139, 154, 264, 322.

Mon Louis Island, 139, 155, 322.

Montgomery, 386, 399.

Montgomery, Fort, 376.

Montigny, 33.

Montreal, 25.

Montrose, 322.

Montuse tavern, 305 ; wharf, 401.

Morales, J. V., intendant, 299.

Morand, 131, 163.

Mornay, De, 127.

Moro, Joseph, granted Dauphine Island, 263.

Moscoso, 15, 17.

Mosquitoes, 85, 167.

Moss, 175, 211.

Mottus, Silvain, 305, 434.

Mount Dexter treaty, 346.

Muscogees, branches, 7 ; traditions, 21 (see Creeks).

Mulattoes at Fort Louis, 65.

Murrell, John, 334, 430.

Murrell Tract, title, 430.

Nana Falaya, 222.

Naniabas, Naniabes, 22 ; relics, 91 ; Island, 226.

Nanipacna, 20.

Nanna Hubba, 226.

Narbonne, Anna, tomb, 329 ; Antoine, 306, 330.

Narvaez expedition, 12.

Natchez, traditions, 21 ; Fort Rosalie, 80, 81.

Naval stores, 281.

Negroes, slaves, 65, 332 ; slave ships, 87 ; Spanish register, 332.

Neride, 87.

New Orleans, founded, 84 ; described by Blakeley, 354.

Newspapers : Mississippi Messenger, 348 ; Centinel, 349 ; Natchez Gazette, 350 ; Mobile Gazette, 390 ; Madison Gazette, 399.

Nolte, 379.

Notario, cura, 329.

Notary, French, 119, 146 ; Spanish, 265 ; none in 1807, 334.

Notre Dame de la Mobile, 132.

Noxubee River, 219.

Noyant, 28, 58.

Nuns, 66.

Ocas Island, 268.

Ochus, 20, 268.

Oglethorpe, 115.

Ohio River, 40, 45, 283.

Okatibbehaw, 217.

Okehays, 183 note ; 221.

"Old fields," 101.

Old Fort, 315.

Olivier, 291.

Ondoyer, 64.

One Mile Creek, 36.

Orange, 84, 107.

Orange Grove, troops, 356 ; Tract, title, 421 ; survey, 422.

Ordinances, 1667, 419 ; American, 389, 395, 396.

Ordonateur, 57.

O'Reilly at New Orleans, 209.

Ortiz, 312, 434.

Oysters, 324, 325.

Pailloux, 69, 71, 73.

Palisade, at Mobile, 117, 135.

Panionacha, 94.

Panmure, Fort, 187, 252.

Panton, Leslie & Co., fill up lot, 291 ; Indian trade, 293, 336 ; capital, 337 ; Indian cessions, 338 ; main store, 308 ; acquire the Laurent Plantation, 421 ; the Orange Grove Tract, 421 ; Choctaw Point, 426.

Panton, Wm., 292.

Parain, 94.
Parker's, 265.
Parsonage, Spanish, 330, 333 ; sale, 334.
Partition, Spanish court proceedings for, 281.
Pascagoula, French, 156 ; Spanish, 326.
Pass, for travel, 283.
Pass Christian, 325.
Patron, 157, 158.
Pauger, surveys river, 86.
Peace, Utrecht, 77 ; Aix-la-Chapelle, 172 ; Paris, 176, 181, 263 ; Ghent, 384.
Pecans, 242, 322.
Pechon, 162.
Peire, H. D., 359.
Pelican, the, 52.
Pelican Island, 19, 40.
Peltries, French, 46, 50, 78.
Peñalver, bishop, 331.
Penicaut, arrival, 33 ; returns to France, 87 (see 67).
Pensacola, cession sought by French, 34 ; Guzman, of, 58 ; aided by Bienville, 61 ; his attack on, 85 ; Galvez' capture, 257 ; capital of W. Florida, 290, 324 ; Jackson captures, 380.
Perdido, ferry, 210, 245 ; bay, 324.
Perez, Cayetano, surrender, 359 ; returns to Mobile, 367 ; horse, 425 ; in American times, 434.
Perier, 108.
Petit, 131.
Petticoat insurrection, 52.
Phelypeaux's map, 134.
Picayune, 284.
Pierre, 132.
Pilots, British, 199 ; Spanish, 325 ; American, 394, 395.
Piñeda discovers Mobile Bay, 10.
Piney woods, 72.
Pintado, V. S., 263, 301.
Pirates, Carthagena, 49 ; Jamaica, 150.
Pitch, 241.
Pitchlyn, John, 341, 342.
Pittman, Lieut., 188 ; survey, 200.
Plocks, 323.
Point Clear, 322.
Police officers, American, 391, 407.
Pollard v. Kibbe, 404.
Pollock, Oliver, 250, 251.
Pontchartrain, 30.
Pontiac, 188, 194.
Poor rate, British, 247.
Poplar Grove, 421.
Population, of Mobile in 1704, 54 ; 1708, 58 ; 1728, 108 ; 1745, 116 ; 1760, 137 ; 1785, 271 ; 1788, 273 ; 1818, 395 ; of French and English colonies, 172.
Portage, 26, 339, 388, 391.
Portersville district, Indian remains, 92 note ; islands, 120 ; Indian legend, 155 ; Spanish, 325.
Potato, 239, 319.
Pottery, 210, 322.
Pousset, 194.
Powder house, 395.
Powell, Thos., 320.
Priber, 160*
Price, Thos., 302, 333 ; house, 311.

Price Claim, title, 427.
Priests, French, 62, 126 ; Spanish, 329.
Privy Council, functions, 247.
Proffit, Charles, 425, 430.
Prosper, 131.
Prostitutes brought to Mobile, 87.
Punishments, Spanish, 281.
Pumps, public, 396.
Pushmataha, 344 ; regimentals, 370 ; offers services, 370 ; trial, 373 note ; at Washington, 373 note ; death, 373 note ; lived near Meridian, 339 ; at Holy Ground, 371.

Quay, 134.
Quebec, seminary of, 33 ; priests at Mobile, 73 ; fall, 173.

Raft, from Tombecbé, 168.
Raoul, 390.
Ravesies, 390.
Records, Spanish, 262 note.
Red Captain, 186.
Red Cliff, 200 ; stockade, 210.
Red Shoe, 109, 116.
Reformed faith, 130.
Registers (see Church), 128, 131, 132 ; negro, 332.
Relics, Indian, 6.
Remonville, memorial, 29 ; brings stores, 77 ; church of, 132.
Renommee, 37, 44, 60, 70.
Requests, court of, 236.
Revolution, American, 242, 244.
Ribero, map, 12.
Rice, 106, 135, 320.
Richardson, claim to Spring Hill, 430.
River bank, title to, 404, 405, 422.
Roads, Indian, 42, 339 ; British, Pensacola to Mobile, 245 ; Muscle Shoals, Military, and Cherokee roads, 346 ; "three chopped way," 348.
Rochemore, intendant, 174.
Rochon, Pierre, (I,) 191 ; contractor, 212 ; and Haldimand, 213, (II.) 228, 232 ; title, 321.
Rochon, A., place, 234.
Rock Creek, 434.
Romans, Bernard, exploration, 215 ; on Tombigbee, 216.
Rosalie, Fort, 80, 108.
Ross, Lieutenant, on Mississippi, 189.
Ross, J. F., 387.
Round Island, 326.
Round Top, 401.
Royal St., named, 76 ; under Spaniards, 296.
Rum, among Indians, 229, 233, 245, 248.
Russian princess, 89, 164.

St. Anthony Street, 309.
St. Charles Street, 309.
St. Cosme, 50, 53.
St. Denis, arrival, 33 ; at Mobile, 55 ; in Mexico, 79 ; lot, 72 ; at Dauphine Island, 85.
St. Emanuel Street, 310.
St. Francis Street, 308 ; opened, 394.
St. Helene, 28, 80.

St. Ildefonso, 298.
St. Joseph Street, 308, 309, 311.
St. Louis Street, 76, 309.
St. Louis Tract, 109, 142.
St. Michael Street, 308.
St. Michel, 43.
St. Stephens, site, 224; fort, 316; Spanish grants, 317; occupied by Americans, 341; laid off, 348; palmy days, 386.
St. Vallier, 63, 126, 127.
Sagean, 34.
Salto, Bayou, 303, 315, 323, 380.
Salvador, 320.
Sands, A. L., 361, 376.
Santabogue, 186.
Sara, Bayou, 315.
Sargent, Winthrop, 343.
Saussaye, J., 265; death, 332.
Sauvole, 32, 35, 38.
Savage House (see Indian House).
Sawing asunder, 89.
Sawmills, 68, 326.
Schaumburgh, Capt., 369.
Schitimachas (Chetimachas), 98.
Sea Warrior, 223.
Sebastien, 132.
Selma, origin, 386.
Seminary of Quebec, 33; vicar-general from, 63.
Serigny, 28, 85, 87.
Seven Years' War, 173.
Seymour's Bluff, 269.
Shell Banks, 71; relics, 92 note; Dauphine Island, 152, 384.
Shipping, American, 395, 396.
Shore, title to, 404, 405, 422.
Sibley, Cyrus, 352, 356.
Sickness at Mobile, 204, 232.
Silver, and Indians, 219.
Sipsey River, 218.
Slavery, Indian, 64; negro, 65; French slave ships, 87; emancipation, 289; Spanish, 282, 332; after Treaty of Ghent, 385; Lacoste's negroes, 385.
Smallpox, 109.
Smith, James, in canoe fight, 371.
Smoot, B. S., 381.
Smuggler, British, 110.
Soldiers, French, 51; pay of British, 249.
Sossier, Henry, 320.
Soto, 14–17.
Sou, 88 note.
Sovager, 136.
Spain, importance in 16th century, 9; and United States, 293, 357.
Spaniards, explorations, 9; forbid French settlement at Biloxi, 33; at Mobile, 58; government of Louisiana, 261, 262; Mobile expenses, 272; policy towards Kentucky, 277; United States and Spain, 293; land grants, 317; names, 321, 325.
Spanish Conspiracy, 277, 294.
Spanish Grants, 298, 420–431 (see their several names).
Sponsors, 94.
Spring Hill, 215, 430.
Star anise, 239.

Steamboats, 395, 396.
Steuernagel, journal, 251.
Stewart, Geo. N., 399.
Stickney, Henry, 403, 412.
Stock, French times, 37, 58; Spanish, 353.
Stockton, 6, 319.
Stoddert (Stoddart), Fort, founded, 341; port of entry, 349; in Blakeley's time, 353; spelling, 363 note.
Stone, scarce, 71.
Storms, 1733, 109; 1740, 115; 1772, 232.
Streets, French names, 74, 313; title, 314; American extensions, 393, 394, 412, 413.
Stuart (or Stewart), John, Indian superintendent, 183, 184, 229.
Stuart (or Stewart), Charles, deputy superintendent, 183 note, 207, 215, 233, 244.
Sunflower, place, 270, 317.
Superior Council, 86, 108.
Surtill, 310, 312, 313.
Surveyors, Spanish, 263, 301; fees, 301; Proffitt, 430; American, 393, 402, 403 note, 410.
Swanson & McGillivray, 238, 242.

Tankersley, 403, 429, 432.
Tanner, the lost, 43.
Taouachas, 96, 374.
Tar, 68, 105, 241, 316.
Tate, D., 370.
Tatum, Maj., surveys Alabama River, 374.
Taxes, Spanish, 262; American, 389.
Taylor, Wm., 182, 198.
Tecumseh, 368, 371.
Temperance Hall, site, 311.
Temperature, 206, 238.
Tensaws (Tanças), at Mobile, 79; slaves, 99; in church registers, 99, 100; De Lusser grant, 142; site, 237; Farmer, 238.
Theatre, 412.
Thomez (Tohomes), 22, 42, 90.
Three Mile Creek, 36, 93, 207, 388.
Three Months, 225, 317.
Titles, Spanish, 265, 274, 300.
Titus, James, 386.
Tobacco, 106.
Tohomes, 22, 42; location, 90.
Tombecbé, Fort, built, 111; description, 165; under the British, 182; abandonment, 199; Romans at, 220.
Tombigbee River, name, 87, 120, 220 note; Romans on, 216.
Tonty, 26, 31; at Biloxi, 33; among Choctaws, 40, 43; life, 48, 49; death, 55.
Tories, 252, 319.
Touachas (Touchas, Taouachas), 96, 315, 374.
Toulmin, Harry, early history, 345; letter, 345.
Toulmin Tract, title, 429.
Toulouse, Fort, founded, 80; history, 158; cannon, 164; appearance, 164; abandoned, 182.

Tournée, Rue de, 134.
Tracts, 298, 420–431.
Trade, French, with Spaniards, 78 ; fur, 78 ; tariff of the Company, 86, 106 ; later French times, 105 ; stations, 106 ; Anglo-Indian, 186, 248 ; exports, 199, 229 ; to London, 246 ; licenses, 248 ; under the Spanish, 271, 281–283, 285 ; Panton, Leslie & Co., 336, 337 ; American Indian agents, 340 ; merchants, 1817, 394 ; American, 395.
Tradesmen, French, 66.
Traditions, Indian, 21.
Trails, Indian, Mobile to Choctaws, 339; Pensacola to Creeks, 339.
Treaty (see Peace, Indians,) of 1795, 294 ; St. Ildefonso, 298 ; Mt. Dexter, 346.
Trenier, J. B., 302, 312.
Trouillet partition, 281.
Trudeau, C. L., 263, 301.
Turnbull & Joyce, 283.
Tuscaroras, 79.
Tuskaloosa and De Soto, 14–16.
Tuskaloosa, village burned by McKee, 371 ; American origin, 386, 399.

Ulloa, arrival at New Orleans, 199; expelled, 202.
Undertaker, Spanish, 287.
U. S. Hotel, 334.
Utrecht, peace of, 77.

Valentin, 132.
Valliguy, 70, 72.
Valuation, Spanish, 334.
Varlet, 126.
Vaudreuil, arrival, 115; Chickasaw expedition, 118; pacifies Choctaws, 117; goes to Canada, 134; surrenders Montreal, 174.
Vaugeois, J. F., 332.
Vaulesar (Volezard) company, 51, 65.
Vauxbercy (Vobiscey), Mme., 238.
Vegetables, 5, 105, 230, 392.
Velasco, 18.
Vestry, under the British, 247.
Vicars-general, 128.
Victorin, 131.
Vilars, Julia, 311.

Village, the, 207, 380.
Vine and olive colony, 398.
Vieux Fort, 38, 315.
Virginia, 330, 343.
Vitry, 128, 131.
Voyageurs, in Mobile, 72.

Waldeckers in British army, 251.
Walker, Tandy, 368.
Ward, 323.
Warden, 130.
Wards, 1814, 380.
Washing place, 391.
Washington, Indian policy, 340.
Washington County, created, 343; judicial district, 345; bar, 349.
Water at Mobile, 206, 208, 388, 391.
Water lily, 239.
Water Street, 393, 396.
Wax-tree, 175, 238.
Weatherford, William, 369, 371, 372, 374.
Weeks, 323.
Wegg, 201, 207, 210, 246, 434.
Wells, American, 396.
Wharves, 138, 304, 305, 393.
White House, 320.
Wilkinson, James, conspirator, 277 ; builds Fort Adams, 343 ; career, 344 ; takes Mobile, 358 ; report, 362 ; sent north, 369.
Willing, James, 250.
Wilson, Elizabeth, 326.
Wilson, James, 393, 395, 401, and note.
Winchester, General, 381, 383, 384.
Wolfenbüttel, 89.
Woodbine, 239.
Woods, Mobile, 3, 30, 39.
Wyman, W. S., 217 note.

Yam, 242.
Yamassees, 95, 97.
Ychuse (see Chusee), 20.
Yellow fever, 55, 56, 396.
York, Fort, 182.
You, M., 79.
Youpon, 7, 239.
Yowanne (Yoani), 166, 216.

Zadek's, 307.